Toyota Cor
Owners
Workshop
Manual

by J H Haynes
Member of the Guild of Motoring Writers
and P G Strasman

Models covered

UK: Corolla E Saloon 1166 cc
   Corolla 30 Saloon*, Coupe*, Estate and Liftback 1166 cc
   Corolla 1600 Liftback 1588 cc

Coverage includes SR versions

USA: Corolla 1200 Sedan 71.2 cu in (1166 cc)
   Corolla 1600 Sedan, Coupe*, Wagon and Liftback* 96.9 cu in (1588 cc)

Coverage includes SR5 and Sport versions

ISBN 0 85696 852 8

All rights reserved. No part of this book may be reproduced or transmitted in
any form or by any means, electronic or mechanical, including photocopying,
recording or by any information storage or retrieval system, without permission
in writing from the copyright holder.

AB

Printed in England *(361 – 8M1)*

Haynes Publishing Group
Sparkford Nr Yeovil
Somerset BA22 7JJ England

Haynes Publications, Inc
861 Lawrence Drive
Newbury Park
California 91320 USA

Acknowledgements

Our thanks are due to the Toyota Motor Sales Company Limited (USA) and Toyota (GB) Limited for their assistance with technical information and the supply of certain illustrations. Castrol Limited supplied lubrication data, and the Champion Sparking Plug Company supplied the illustrations showing the various spark plug conditions. The bodywork repair photographs used in this manual were provided by Lloyds Industries Limited who supply 'Turtle-Wax', 'Dupli-color

Holts', and other Holts range products.

Lastly, thanks are due to all of those people at Sparkford who helped in the production of this manual. Particularly, Brian Horsfall and Les Brazier who carried out the mechanical work and took the photographs respectively; Ted Frenchum who planned the layout of each page and Tim Parker and John Rose for editing the text.

About this manual

Its aim

The aim of this book is to help you get the best value from your car. It can do so in two ways. First it can help you decide what work must be done (even should you choose to get it done by a garage), the routine maintenance and the diagnosis and course of action when random faults occur. It is hoped that you will also use the second and fuller purpose by tackling the work yourself. This can give you the satisfaction of doing the job yourself. On the simpler jobs it may even be quicker than booking the car into a garage and going there twice, to leave and collect it. Perhaps most important, much money can be saved by avoiding the costs a garage must charge to cover their labour and overheads.

Haynes Owner's Workshop Manuals are the *only* manuals, available to the public, which are usually written from practical experience. We buy a second-hand and well used example of the vehicle to be covered by the manual. Then, in our own workshops, the major components of that vehicle are stripped and rebuilt by the author and a mechanic; at the same time all sequences are photographed. By doing this work ourselves, we encounter the same problems as you will and having overcome these problems, we can provide you with practical solutions.

The book has drawings and descriptions to show the function of the various components so that their layout can be understood. Then the tasks are described and photographed in a step by step sequence so that even a novice can cope with complicated work. Such a person is the very one to buy a car needing repair yet be unable to afford garage costs.

The jobs are described assuming only normal spanners are available, and not special tools. But a reasonable outfit of tools will be a worthwhile investment, many special workshop tools produced by the makers merely speed the work, and in these cases guidance is given as to how to do the job without them. On a very few occasions the special tool is essential to prevent damage to components, then their use is described. Though it might be possible to borrow the tool, such work may have to be entrusted to your dealer.

To avoid labour costs a garage will often give a cheaper repair by fitting a reconditioned assembly. The home mechanic can be helped by this book to diagnose the fault and make a repair using only a minor spare part.

The manufacturer's official workshop manuals are written for their trained staff, and so assume special knowledge; detail is left out. This book is written for the owner, and so goes into detail.

Using the manual

The manual is divided into twelve Chapters - each covering a logical sub-division of the vehicle. The individual Chapters are divided into Sections, and the Sections into numbered paragraphs.

Procedures, once described in the text, are not normally repeated. If it is necessary to refer to another Chapter the reference will be given in Chapter number and Section number .

If it is considered necessary to refer to a particular paragraph in another Chapter the reference is given. Cross-references given without use of the word 'Chapter' apply to Sections and/or paragraphs in the same Chapter (eg; 'see Section 8' means also in this Chapter).

There are two types of illustration: (1) Figures which are numbered according to Chapter and sequence of occurrence in that Chapter. (2) Photographs which have a reference number on their caption. All photographs apply to the Chapter in which they occur so that the reference figure pinpoints the pertinent Section and paragraph number.

When the left or right side of the car is mentioned it is as if looking forward from the rear of the car.

Great effort has been made to ensure that this book is complete and up-to-date. However, the vehicle manufacturers continually modify their cars, even in retrospect without giving notice.

Whilst every care is taken to ensure that the information in this manual is correct no liability can be accepted by the authors or publishers for loss, damage or injury caused by any errors in, or omissions from, the information given.

Contents

Use of English

As this book has been written in England, it uses the appropriate English component names, phrases, and spelling. Some of these differ from those used in America. Normally, these cause no difficulty, but to make sure, a glossary is printed below. In ordering spare parts remember the parts list will probably use these words:

Glossary

English	American	English	American
Aerial	Antenna	Interior light	Dome lamp
Accelerator	Gas pedal	Layshaft (of gearbox)	Counter shaft
Alternator	Generator (AC)	Leading shoe (of brake)	Primary shoe
Anti-roll bar	Stabiliser or sway bar	Locks	Latches
Battery	Energizer	Motorway	Freeway, turnpike etc.
Bodywork	Sheet metal	Number plate	Licence plate
Bonnet (engine cover)	Hood	Paraffin	Kerosene
Boot lid	Trunk lid	Petrol	Gasoline
Boot (luggage compartment)	Trunk	Petrol tank	Gas tank
Bottom gear	1st gear	'Pinking'	'Pinging'
Bulkhead	Firewall	Quarter light	Quarter window
Camfollower or tappet	Valve lifter or tappet	Retread	Recap
Carburettor	Carburetor	Reverse	Back-up
Catch	Latch	Rocker cover	Valve cover
Choke/venturi	Barrel	Roof rack	Car-top carrier
Circlip	Snap ring	Saloon	Sedan
Clearance	Lash	Seized	Frozen
Crownwheel	Ring gear (of differential)	Side indicator lights	Side marker lights
Disc (brake)	Rotor/disk	Side light	Parking light
Propeller shaft	Driveshaft	Silencer	Muffler
Drop arm	Pitman arm	Spanner	Wrench
Drop head coupe	Convertible	Sill panel (beneath doors)	Rocker panel
Dynamo	Generator (DC)	Split cotter (for valve spring cap)	Lock (for valve spring retainer)
Earth (electrical)	Ground	Split pin	Cotter pin
Engineer's blue	Prussion blue	Steering arm	Spindle arm
Estate car	Station wagon	Sump	Oil pan
Exhaust manifold	Header	Tab washer	Tang; lock
Fast back (Coupe)	Hard top	Tailgate	Liftgate
Fault finding/diagnosis	Trouble shooting	Tappet	Valve lifter
Float chamber	Float bowl	Thrust bearing	Throw-out bearing
Free-play	Lash	Top gear	High
Freewheel	Coast	Trackrod (of steering)	Tie-rod (or connecting rod)
Gudgeon pin	Piston pin or wrist pin	Trailing shoe (of brake)	Secondary shoe
Gearchange	Shift	Transmission	Whole drive line
Gearbox	Transmission	Tyre	Tire
Halfshaft	Axle-shaft	Van	Panel wagon/van
Handbrake	Parking brake	Vice	Vise
Hood	Soft top	Wheel nut	Lug nut
Hot spot	Heat riser	Windscreen	Windshield
Indicator	Turn signal	Wing/mudguard	Fender
Interior light	Dome lamp		

Miscellaneous points

An "Oil seal" is fitted to components lubricated by grease!

A "Damper" is a "Shock absorber", it damps out bouncing, and absorbs shocks of bump impact. Both names are correct, and both are used haphazardly.

Note that British drum brakes are different from the Bendix type that is common in America, so different descriptive names result. The shoe end furthest from the hydraulic wheel cylinder is on a pivot; interconnection between the shoes as on Bendix brakes is most uncommon. Therefore the phrase "Primary" or "Secondary" shoe does not apply. A shoe is said to be Leading or Trailing. A "Leading" shoe is one on which a point on the drum, as it rotates forward, reaches the shoe at the end worked by the hydraulic cylinder before the anchor end. The opposite is a trailing shoe, and this one has no self servo from the wrapping effect of the rotating drum.

Introduction to the Toyota Corolla

North American Market

The Corolla's new body styling was introduced in early 1975 and various versions have been offered as listed in the title page of this manual. Automatic transmission is optionally available on all models.

In the interest of fuel economy, during 1977 the smaller 71.2 cu in engine was re-introduced but only available in the 2 or 4 door sedan versions.

Owners of these smaller engined vehicles should always refer to the 30 Series (3K-C engine) information where it differs from 1600 material in all Chapters of this manual.

All models in the range covered by this manual are well constructed, easy to maintain and are fully equipped and incorporate the latest developments in safety and emission control devices.

UK Market

Early in 1975, the existing Corolla was superseded by a new body style to be known as the 30 Series. The earlier design of car was not, however, abandoned but was redesignated the 1200E. The 1200E is only sold in two door saloon form with an 1166 cc engine and manual transmission.

The 30 Series range includes all the versions listed on the title page and apart from the 1600 Liftback, the 1166 cc engine is fitted throughout the range. The automatic transmission option is only available on the four door saloon. The SR coupe has twin dual barrel carburettors, five speed gearbox and modified suspension.

Buying spare parts
and vehicle identification numbers

Buying spare parts

Spare parts are available from many sources, for example: Toyota garages, other garages and accessory shops, and motor factors. Our advice regarding spare parts is as follows:

Officially appointed Toyota garages - This is the best source of parts which are peculiar to your car and otherwise not generally available (eg: complete cylinder heads, internal gearbox components, badges, interior trim etc). It is also the only place at which you should buy parts if your car is still under warranty; non-Toyota components may invalidate the warranty. To be sure of obtaining the correct parts it will always be necessary to give the storeman your car's engine and chassis number, and if possible to take the old part along for positive identification. Remember that some parts may be available on a factory exchange basis - any parts returned should always be clean! It obviously makes good sense to go to the specialists on your car for this type of part for they are best equipped to supply you.

Other garages and accessory shops - These are often very good places to buy material and components needed for the maintenance of your car (eg; oil filters, spark plugs, bulbs, fan belts, oils and grease, touch-up paint, filler paste etc). They also sell general accessories, usually have convenient opening hours, charge lower prices and can often be found not far from home.

Motor factors - Good factors will stock all of the more important components which wear out relatively quickly (eg; clutch components, pistons, valves, exhaust systems, brake cylinders/pipes/hoses/seals/shoes and pads etc). Motor factors will often provide new or reconditioned components on a part exchange basis - this can save a considerable amount of money.

Vehicle identification numbers

Modifications are a continuing and unpublicised process in vehicle manufacture quite apart from major model changes. Spare parts manuals and lists are compiled upon a numerical basis, the individual vehicle number being essential to correct identification of the component required.

The vehicle identification number is shown on a plate attached to the rear bulkhead within the engine compartment (photo). Frame KE indicates 3 K Series engine, frame TE indicates 2 T Series engine. This number is also stamped into the sidewall of the engine compartment and on vehicles destined for operation in North America, it is repeated on the upper surface of the instrument panel just inside the windscreen.

The engine number is stamped on a machined surface at the side of the cylinder block (photo).

Vehicle identification plate

Vehicle identification number

Engine number

Toyota Corolla 30

Toyota Corolla 30 Estate

Toyota Corolla 1600 Liftback

View showing the tailgate on the Toyota Corolla 1600 Liftback

General dimensions, weights and capacities

Dimensions and Weights

1200 E

Overall length	155.3 in (3924 mm)
Overall width	59.3 in (1498 mm)
Overall height	54.1 in (1374 mm)
Ground clearance	6.7 in (170 mm)
Wheelbase	91.9 in (2334 mm)
Track	49.4 in (1254 mm)
Kerb weight	1655 lb (750 kg)

Corolla 30

	Saloon	Coupe	Wagon
Overall length	157.3 in (3995 mm)	157.3 in (3995 mm)	159.4 in (4049 mm)
Overall width	61.8 in (1570 mm)	61.8 in (1570 mm)	61.8 in (1570 mm)
Overall height	54.1 in (1374 mm)	53.1 in (1349 mm)	54.7 in (1389 mm)
Ground clearance	6.7 in (170 mm)	6.7 in (170 mm)	6.7 in (170 mm)
Wheelbase	93.3 in (3370 mm)	93.3 in (3370 mm)	93.3 in (3370 mm)
Track:			
front	51.0 in (1295 mm)	51.0 in (1295 mm)	51.0 in (1295 mm)
rear	50.6 in (1285 mm)	50.6 in (1285 mm)	50.6 in (1285 mm)
Kerb weight:			
manual	1840 lb (835 kg)	1915 lb (869 kg)	1930 lb (875 kg)
auto trans.	1885 lb (855 kg)	–	

Corolla (North American market)

Overall length

Sedan, hard top, SR 5	165.2 in (4195 mm)
Wagon	167.7 in (4260 mm)
Lift back	170.1 in (4320 mm)
Sport Coupe	168.3 in (4275 mm)

Overall width

Sedan, Wagon, Hard top deluxe	62.4 in (1585 mm)
Hardtop SR 5	65.0 in (1650 mm)
Liftback and Coupe	63.0 in (1600 mm)

Overall height

Sedan	54.5 in (1385 mm)
	54.1 in (1375 mm) with 3K Series engine
Wagon	54.7 in (1390 mm)
Hard top	53.5 in (1360 mm)
Liftback and Coupe	52.0 in (1320 mm)

Ground clearance

Sedan, Hard top, Liftback Deluxe, Sport Coupe Deluxe	5.7 in (145 mm)
Wagon, Hard top SR 5, Liftback SR 5, Sport Coupe SR 5	6.1 in (155 mm)

Wheelbase 93.3 in (2370 mm)

Track (front)

Sedan, Wagon, Hard top Deluxe, Liftback Deluxe, Sport Coupe Deluxe	51.2 in (1300 mm)
Hardtop SR 5, Liftback SR 5, Sport Coupe SR 5	52.0 in (1320 mm)

Track (rear)

Sedan, Wagon, Hardtop Deluxe, Liftback Deluxe, Sport Coupe Deluxe	50.6 in (1285 mm)
Hardtop SR 5, Liftback SR 5, Sport Coupe SR 5	52.6 in (1335 mm)

Kerb weight *

Sedan	2210 lb (1002 kg) with 3K Series engine 2050 lb (930 kg)
Wagon	2270 lb (1030 kg)
Hard top Deluxe	2215 lb (1005 kg)
Hard top SR 5	2300 lb (1043 kg)
Liftback Deluxe	2250 lb (1021 kg)
Liftback SR 5	2300 lb (1043 kg)
Sport Coupe Deluxe	2215 lb (1005 kg)
Sport Coupe SR 5	2300 lb (1043 kg)

*These are for vehicles with manual transmission. Where automatic transmission is fitted, add approximately 45 lb (20.4 kg). See also individual vehicle sticker.

Capacities

Engine oil (including filter change):

	3K Series	2T Series
	6.2 Imp pints	6.6 Imp pints
	3.7 US qts	3.9 US qts
	3.5 litre	3.7 litre

Cooling system ...   .   13.6 Imp pints (8.1 US qts/7.8 litre)

Fuel tank
1200 E   ...   .   10 Imp gal (12 US gal/45.0 litre)
30 Series and 1600, Saloon and Coupe   ...   .   11 Imp gal (13.2 US gal/50.0 litre)
Wagon   ...   .   10.3 Imp gal (12.4 US gal/47.0 litre)

Manual transmission
K 40 and K 50 gearbox ...   .   1.5 Imp qt (1.8 US qt/1.7 litre)
T 40 and T 50 gearbox ...   .   1.4 Imp qt (1.6 US qt/1.5 litre)

Automatic transmission
Fluid change (A40)   ...   .   2.1 Imp qt (2.5 US qt/2.4 litre)
Refill (with dry torque converter) (A40)   ...   .   5.1 Imp qt (6.1 US qt/5.8 litre)
2-speed Toyoglide   ...   .   4.1 Imp qt (5 US qt/4.7 litre)

Rear axle
6.0 and 6.38 in differential   ...   .   1.8 Imp pt (1.1 US qt/1.0 litre)
5.7 and 6.25 in differential   ...   .   2.2 Imp pt (1.3 US qt/1.2 litre)

Steering gear   ...   .   ½ Imp pt (½ US pt/0.25 litre)

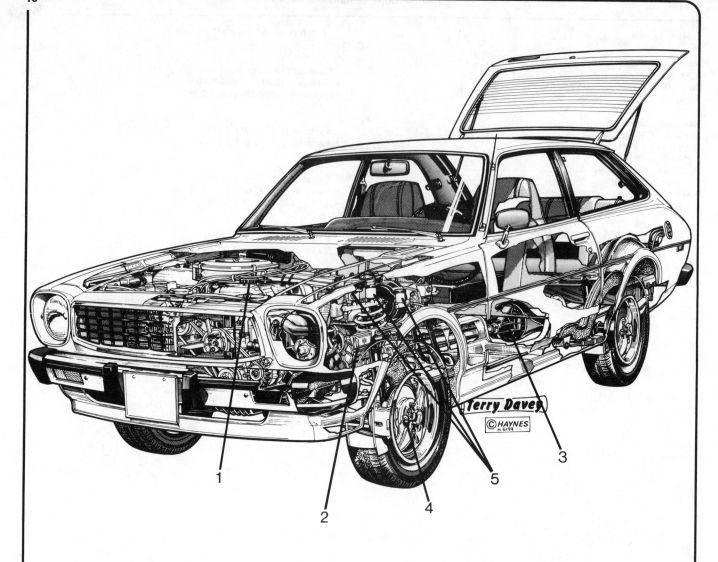

Lubrication chart

Component	Lubricant
Engine (1)	Castrol GTX
Gearbox (2)	
Manual	Castrol Hypoy 90
Automatic	Castrol TQF
Rear axle (3)	Castrol Hypoy B
Wheel bearings (4)	Castrol LM Grease
Clutch and brake systems (5)	Castrol Girling Universal Clutch and Brake Fluid
Steering box	Castrol Hypoy 90
Chassis	Castrol MS3 Grease
Front suspension upper support bearing	Castrol LM Grease

Note: The above recommendations are general; lubrication requirements vary depending upon vehicle specification, operating territory and usage. Consult the operators handbook supplied with the car.

Jacking and towing

Jacking points

1 For emergency roadwheel changing, use the jack supplied with the vehicle tool kit. Always engage the jack with the jacking points located under the side body sills. Fig. A.

2 To remove a roadwheel, apply the handbrake fully and loosen the roadwheel nuts **before** raising the vehicle. Once the vehicle is jacked up, remove the nuts completely and remove the wheel.

3 When carrying out repairs or adjustments jack up the front of the vehicle under the crossmember. Fig. B.

4 Jack up the rear of the vehicle under the differential housing Fig. C.

5 Once the vehicle is raised, support it on axle stands placed under the side sills, the rear spring bracket or the rear axle casing. Figs. D, E and F.

Towing

1 In an emergency your vehicle may be towed or you may tow another vehicle by attaching the tow line to the transportation lash down hooks or by passing the tow line round the rear roadspring shackle.

2 If the vehicle is equipped with A40 type automatic transmission, it should not be towed further than 50 miles (80 km) or in excess of 30 mph (45 km/h) otherwise disconnect and remove the propeller shaft.

Fig. A. Using emergency jack

Fig. C. Raising rear of vehicle under differential

Fig. B. Raising front of vehicle under crossmember

Fig. E. Rear roadspring bracket supported by axle stand

Fig. D. Body sill supported by axle stand

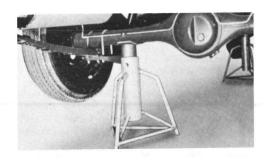

Fig. F. Rear axle casing supported by axle stand

Tools and working facilities

Introduction

A selection of good tools is a fundamental requirement for anyone contemplating the maintenance and repair of a motor vehicle. For the owner who does not possess any, their purchase will prove a considerable expense, offsetting some of the savings made by doing-it-yourself. However, provided that the tools purchased are of good quality, they will last for many years and prove an extremely worthwhile investment.

To help the average owner to decide which tools are needed to carry out the various tasks detailed in this manual, we have compiled three lists of tools under the following headings: Maintenance and minor repair, Repair and overhaul, and Special. The newcomer to practical mechanics should start off with the 'Maintenance and minor repair' tool kit and confine himself to the simpler jobs around the vehicle. Then, as his confidence and experience grows, he can undertake more difficult tasks, buying extra tools as, and when, they are needed. In this way, a 'Maintenance and minor repair' tool kit can be built-up into a 'Repair and overhaul' tool kit over a considerable period of time without any major cash outlays. The experienced do-it-yourself will have a tool kit good enough for most repair and overhaul procedures and will add tools from the 'Special' category when he feels the expense is justified by the amount of use these tools will be put to.

It is obviously not possible to cover the subject of tools fully here. For those who wish to learn more about tools and their use there is a book entitled 'How to Choose and Use Car Tools' available from the publishers of this manual.

Maintenance and minor repair tool kit

The tools given in this list should be considered as a minimum requirement if routine maintenance, servicing and minor repair operations are to be undertaken. We recommend the purchase of combination wrenches (ring one end, open-ended the other); although more expensive than open-ended ones, they do give the advantage of both types of wrench.

Combination wrenches
Adjustable wrench - 9 inch
Engine sump/gearbox/rear axle drain plug key (where applicable)
Spark plug wrench (with rubber insert)
Spark plug gap adjustment tool
Set of feeler gauges
Brake adjuster wrench (where applicable)
Brake bleed nipple wrench
Screwdriver - 4 in. long x ¼ in. dia. (plain)
Screwdriver - 4 in. long x ¼ in. Dia. (crosshead)
Combination pliers - 6 inch
Hacksaw, junior
Tyre pump
Tyre pressure gauge
Grease gun (where applicable)
Oil can
Fine emery cloth (1 sheet)
Wire brush (small)
Funnel (medium size)

Repair and overhaul tool kit

These tools are virtually essential for anyone undertaking any major repairs to a motor vehicle, and are additional to those given in the Basic list. Included in this list is a comprehensive set of sockets. Although these are expensive they will be found invaluable as they are so versatile particularly if various drives are included in the set. We recommend the ½ inch square-drive type, as this can be used with most proprietary torque wrenches. If you cannot afford a socket set, even bought piecemeal, then inexpensive tubular box wrenches are a useful alternative.

The tools in this list will occasionally need to be supplemented by tools from the Special list.

Sockets (or box wrenches)
Reversible ratchet drive (for use with sockets)
Extension piece, 10 inch (for use with sockets)
Universal joint (for use with sockets)
Torque wrenches (for use with sockets)
Self-grip wrench - 8 inch
Ball pein hammer
Soft-faced hammer, plastic or rubber
Screwdriver - 6 in. long x 5/16 in. dia. (plain)
Screwdriver - 2 in. long x 5/16 in. square (plain)
Screwdriver - 1½ in. long x ¼ in. dia. (crosshead)
Screwdriver - 3 in. long x 1/8 in. dia. (electricians)
Pliers - electricians side cutters
Pliers - needle nosed
Pliers - circlip (internal and external)
Cold chisel - ½ inch
Scriber (this can be made by grinding the end of a broken hacksaw blade)
Scraper (this can be made by flattening and sharpening one end of a piece of copper pipe)
Centre punch
Pin punch
Hacksaw
Valve grinding tool
Steel rule/straight edge
Allen keys
Selection of files
Wire brush (large)
Axle stands
Jack (strong scissor or hydraulic type)

Special tools

The tools in this list are those which are not used regularly, are expensive to buy, or which need to be used in accordance with their manufacturers instructions. Unless relatively difficult mechanical jobs are undertaken frequently, it will not be economic to buy many of these tools. Where this is the case, you could consider clubbing together with friends (or an automotive club) to make a joint purchase or borrowing the tools against a deposit from a local garage or tool hire specialist.

The following list contains only those tools and instruments freely available to the public, and not those special tools produced by the vehicle manufacturer specifically for its dealer network. You will find occasional references to these manufacturers special tools in the text of this manual. Generally, an alternative method of doing the job without the vehicle manufacturers special tool is given. However, sometimes, there is no alternative to using them. Where this is the case, and the relevant tool cannot be bought or borrowed you will have to entrust the work to a franchised garage.

Valve spring compressor
Piston ring compressor
Balljoint separator
Universal hub/bearing puller
Impact screwdriver
Micrometer and/or vernier gauge
Carburetor flow balancing device (where applicable)
Dial gauge
Stroboscopic timing light
Dwell angle meter/tachometer
Universal electrical multi-meter

Cylinder compression gauge
Lifting tackle
Trolley jack
Light with extension lead

Buying tools

For practically all tools, a tool factor is the best source since he will have a very comprehensive range compared with the average garage or accessory store. Having said that, accessory stores often offer excellent quality tools at discount prices, so it pays to shop around.

Remember, you do not have to buy the most expensive items on the shelf, but it is always advisable to steer clear of the very cheap tools. There are plenty of good tools around, at reasonable prices, so ask the proprietor or manager of the shop for advice before making a purchase.

Care and maintenance of tools

Having purchased a reasonable tool kit, it is necessary to keep the tools in a clean and serviceable condition. After use, always wipe off any dirt, grease and metal particles using a clean, dry cloth, before putting the tools away. Never leave them lying around after they have been used. A simple tool rack on the garage or workshop wall, for items such as screwdrivers and pliers is a good idea. Store all normal wrenches and sockets in a metal box. Any measuring instruments, gauges, meters, etc., must be carefully stored where they cannot be damaged or become rusty.

Take a little care when the tools are used. Hammer heads inevitably become marked and screwdrivers lose the keen edge on their blades from time-to-time. A little timely attention with emery cloth or a file will soon restore items like this to a good serviceable finish.

Working facilities

Not to be forgotten when discussing tools, is the workshop itself. If anything more than routine maintenance is to be carried out, some form of suitable working area becomes essential.

It is appreciated that many an owner mechanic is forced by circumstances to remove an engine or similar item, without the benefit of a garage or workshop. Having done this, any repairs should always be done under the cover of a roof.
Wherever possible, any dismantling should be done on a clean flat workbench or table at a suitable working height.

Any workbench needs a vice: one with a jaw opening of 4 in (100 mm) is suitable for most jobs. As mentioned previously, some clean dry storage space is also required for tools, as well as the lubricants, cleaning fluids, touch-up paints and so on which soon become necessary.

Another item which may be required, and which has a much more general usage, is an electric drill with a chuck capacity of at least 5/16 in (8 mm). This, together with a good range of twist drills, is virtually essential for fitting accessories such as wing mirrors and backup lights.

Last, but not least, always keep a supply of old newspapers and clean, lint-free rags available, and try to keep any working areas as clean as possible.

Although all nuts and bolts on the vehicles covered by this manual are to Metric specification, the following table of comparative wrench sizes is included for reference purposes.

Wrench jaw gap comparison table

Jaw gap (in)	Wrench size
0.250	¼ in AF
0.275	7 mm AF
0.312	5/16 in. AF
0.315	8 mm AF
0.340	11/32 in AF/1/8 in Whitworth
0.354	9 mm AF
0.375	3/8 in AF
0.393	10 mm AF
0.433	11 mm AF
0.437	7/16 in AF
0.445	3/16 in Whitworth/¼ in BSF
0.472	12 mm AF
0.500	½ in AF
0.512	13 mm AF
0.525	¼ in Whitworth/5/16 in BSF
0.551	14 mm AF
0.562	9/16 in AF
0.590	15 mm AF
0.600	5/16 in Whitworth/3/8 in BSF
0.625	5/8 in AF
0.629	16 mm AF
0.669	17 mm AF
0.687	11/16 in AF
0.708	18 mm AF
0.710	3/8 in Whitworth/7/16 in BSF
0.748	19 mm AF
0.750	¾ in AF
0.812	13/16 in AF
0.820	7/16 in Whitworth/½ in BSF
0.866	22 mm AF
0.875	7/8 in AF
0.920	½ in Whitworth/9/16 in BSF
0.937	15/16 in AF
0.944	24 mm AF
1.000	1 in AF
1.010	9/16 in Whitworth/5/8 in BSF
1.023	26 mm AF
1.062	11/16 in AF/27 mm AF
1.100	5/8 in Whitworth/11/16 in BSF
1.125	1 1/8 in AF
1.181	30 mm AF
1.200	11/16 in Whitworth/¾ in BSF
1.250	1¼ in AF
1.259	32 mm AF
1.300	¾ in Whitworth/7/8 in BSF
1.312	1 5/16 in AF
1.390	13/16 in Whitworth/15/16 in BSF
1.417	36 mm AF
1.437	1 7/16 in AF
1.480	7/8 in Whitworth/1 in BSF
1.500	1½ in AF
1.574	40 mm AF/15/16 in Whitworth
1.614	41 mm AF
1.625	1 5/8 in AF
1.670	1 in Whitworth/1 1/8 in BSF
1.687	1 11/16 in AF
1.811	46 mm AF
1.812	1 13/16 in AF
1.860	1 1/8 in Whitworth/1¼ in BSF
1.875	1 7/8 in AF
1.968	50 mm AF
2.000	2 in AF
2.050	1¼ in Whitworth/1 3/8 in BSF
2.165	55 mm AF
2.362	60 mm AF

Routine maintenance

Maintenance is essential for ensuring safety and desirable for the purpose of getting the best in terms of performance and economy from the car. Over the years the need for periodic lubrication - oiling, greasing and so on - has been drastically reduced if not totally eliminated. This has unfortunately tended to lead some owners to think that because no such action is required the items either no longer exist or will last for ever. This is a serious delusion. It follows therefore that the largest initial element of maintenance is visual examination. This may lead to repairs or renewals.

Every 250 miles (400 km) or weekly

Engine
Check oil level and top up if necessary.
Check coolant level and top up if necessary.
Check battery electrolyte level and top up if necessary.

Brakes and clutch
Check master cylinder reservoir fluid level (photos).

Steering and suspension
Check tyre pressures
Check tyres visually for wear or damage.

Lights, wipers and horns
Check operation of all lights front and rear.
Check operation of windscreen wipers and horns.
Check and top up windscreen washer reservoir fluid.

After first 1,000 miles (1,600 km) - new vehicle

Engine
Check valve clearances.
Check torque of cylinder head bolts.

Check tension of drivebelts.
Check idling speed.
Check dwell angle.
Check ignition timing.
Renew engine oil.

Body and underframe
Check tightness of all nuts and bolts.

Every 6,000 miles (9,600 km)

Engine
Renew engine oil and filter (photo).

Brakes
Check brake pedal and handbrake lever travel.
Check wear of front disc pads.
Inspect condition of all brake hoses and lines.

Transmission
Check gearbox oil level and top up.
Check automatic transmission fluid level and top up.
Check rear axle oil level and top up.

Steering and suspension
Move position of roadwheels to even out tyre wear (front to rear **not** side to side).

Every 12,000 miles (19,000 km)

Engine
Check and adjust valve clearances.
Inspect condition of drivebelts.
Check torque wrench setting of cylinder head bolts.

Brake master cylinder reservoir

Brake master cylinder remotely sited reservoir

Engine sump drain plug

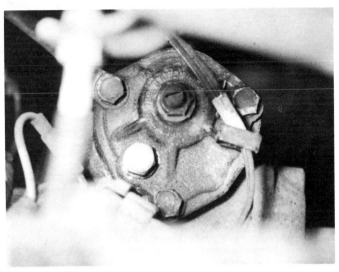

Steering box filler plug

Rear axle drain and filler/level plugs

Gearbox drain and filler/level plugs

Inspect condition of cooling system hoses.
Check condition of exhaust system.
Renew spark plugs.
Renew distributor contact points.
Inspect condition and check operation of all emission control systems and components.
Blow out air filter element and check operation of automatic temperature controlled air cleaner (where fitted).

Brakes
Check rear brake shoe linings for wear.
Check front brake linings for wear (4 wheel drum system).

Steering and suspension
Check all linkages and balljoints for wear.
Check steering box oil level (photo).
Check front wheel alignment (toe-in).
Renew balljoint dust excluders if deteriorated.

Every 24,000 miles (38,000 km)

Engine
Renew drivebelts.
Renew coolant.

Renew fuel filter.
Renew air filter element.
Renew fuel filler cap gasket.
Renew crankcase vent (PCV) valve.

Transmission
Renew rear axle oil (photo).
Renew manual gearbox oil (photo).
Renew automatic transmission fluid.

Steering and suspension
Clean, repack and adjust front wheel bearings.
Lubricate control arm balljoints (remove plug, substitute grease nipple)
Test shock absorbers.

Every 50,000 miles (80,000 km)

Brakes
Renew booster air filter.
Renew all system rubber seals and hydraulic fluid.

Fuel system
Renew carbon canister element (fuel evaporative control).

Chapter 1 Engine

Refer to Chapter 13 for specifications and information applicable to 1979 US models.

Contents

Specifications

Engine type ... Four cylinder in-line, overhead valve

Displacement		
	3K series	71.7 cu in (1166 cc)
	2T series	96.9 cu in (1588 cc)

Bore and stroke		
	3K series	2.95 x 2.60 in (75.0 x 66.0 mm)
	2T series	3.35 x 2.76 in (85.0 x 70.0 mm)

Compression ratios

3K and 3KH	9.0 : 1
3K-B	10.0 : 1
3K-C	8.5 : 1
2T	8.5 : 1
2T-B	9.4 : 1
2T-C	8.5 : 1 (1974 California 9.0 : 1)

Compression pressures

	Specified @ 250 rev/min	Minimum permissible	Difference between cylinders
3K and 3K-H	156 lb/in^2 (11 kg/cm^2)	128 lb/in^2 (9.0 kg/cm^2)	
3K-B	185 lb/in^2 (13.0 kg/cm^2)	142 lb/in^2 (10.0 kg/cm^2)	
3K-C	149 lb/in^2 (10.5 kg/cm^2)	121 lb/in^2 (8.5 kg/cm^2)	less than 14.2 lb/in^2
2T	170 lb/in^2 (12.0 kg/cm^2)	128 lb/in^2 (9.0 kg/cm^2)	(1.0 kg/cm^2)
2T-B	182 lb/in^2 (12.8 kg/cm^2)	142 lb/in^2 (10.0 kg/cm^2)	
2T-C	149 lb/in^2 (10.5 kg/cm^2)	128 lb/in^2 (9.0 kg/cm^2)	
2T-C (California 1974)	171 lb/in^2 (12.0 kg/cm^2)	142 lb/in^2 (10.0 kg/cm^2)	

Cylinder head

	3K series	2T series
Warpage limit	0.004 in (0.1 mm)	0.0020 in (0.05 mm)
Re-grinding limit	0.008 in (0.2 mm)	0.008 in (0.2 mm)
Valve seat surface angle	45°	45°
Contact width	0.047 to 0.063 in (1.2 to 1.6 mm)	0.055 in (1.4 mm)

Refacing angle	1st 30° 2nd 65° 3rd 45°	30° 65° 45°

Cylinder block

Bore diameter (standard)	2.952 to 2.9547 in (75.00 to 75.05 mm)	3.3465 to 3.3484 in (85.00 to 85.05 mm)
Wear limit	0.008 in (0.2 mm)	0.008 in (0.2 mm)
Maximum taper or out of round	Less than 0.0008 in (0.02 mm)	Less than 0.0008 in (0.02 mm)
Difference in bore diameter between cylinders	Less than 0.0020 in (0.05 mm)	Less than 0.0020 in (0.05 mm)
Tappet bore (standard)	0.7874 to 0.7882 in (20.000 to 20.021 mm)	0.8740 to 0.8748 in (22.200 to 22.221 mm)
(oversize) - 0.05	0.7894 to 0.7902 in (20.050 to 20.071 mm)	0.8760 to 0.8768 in (22.250 to 22.271 mm)

Pistons and piston rings

Piston diameter (standard)	2.9512 to 2.9531 in (74.96 to 75.01 mm)	3.3441 to 3.3461 in (84.94 to 84.99 mm)
(oversize)	0.25 - 0.50 - 0.75 - 1.00	0.25 - 0.50 - 0.75 - 1.00
Piston to cylinder clearance	0.0012 to 0.0020 in (0.03 to 0.05 mm)	0.0020 to 0.0024 in (0.05 to 0.07 mm)
Gudgeon pin installing temperature	158 to 176°F (70 to 80°C)	68°F (20°C)
Piston ring end gap		
(top compression)	0.0039 to 0.0110 in (0.10 to 0.28 mm)	0.008 to 0.016 in (0.2 to 0.4 mm)
(second compression)	0.0039 to 0.0110 in (0.10 to 0.28 mm)	0.004 to 0.012 in (0.1 to 0.3 mm)
(oil control)	0.0079 to 0.0354 in (0.2 to 0.9 mm)	
Piston ring groove clearance		
(top compression)	0.0012 to 0.0028 in (0.03 to 0.07 mm)	0.0008 to 0.0024 in (0.020 to 0.060 mm)
(second compression)	0.0008 to 0.0024 in (0.02 to 0.06 mm)	0.0006 to 0.0022 in (0.015 to 0.55 mm)

Connecting rods and big-ends

Big-end running clearance	0.0009 to 0.0039 in (0.024 to 0.10 mm)	0.0009 to 0.0019 in (0.024 to 0.048 mm)
Big-end side clearance	0.0043 to 0.012 in (0.110 to 0.3 mm)	0.0063 to 0.0118 in (0.16 to 0.3 mm)
Big-end bearing undersizes	0.25 - 0.50 - 0.75	0.05 - 0.25 - 0.50 - 0.75

Crankshaft

Endfloat	0.003 to 0.012 in (0.07 to 0.3 mm)	0.003 to 0.012 in (0.07 to 0.3 mm)
Maximum taper (out of round)	0.0004 in (0.01 mm)	0.0004 in (0.01 mm)
Journal diameter (standard)	1.9676 to 1.9685 in (49.976 to 50.000 mm)	2.2825 to 2.2835 in (57.975 to 58.000 mm)
(0.25 U/S)	1.9580 to 1.9584 in (49.733 to 49.743 mm)	0.05 U/S 2.2728 to 2.2732 in ((57.730 to 57.750 mm)
(0.50 U/S)	1.9482 to 1.9485 in (49.483 to 49.493 mm)	0.25 U/S 2.2630 to 2.2634 in (57.480 to 57.500 mm)
(0.75 U/S)	1.9383 to 1.9387 in (49.233 to 49.243 mm)	0.50 U/S 2.2531 to 2.2535 in (57.230 to 57.250 mm)
Journal running clearance	0.0006 to 0.0039 in (0.016 to 0.10 mm)	0.0013 to 0.0022 in (0.032 to 0.056 mm)
Crankpin diameter (standard)	1.6526 to 1.6535 in (41.976 to 42.000 mm)	1.8889 to 1.8898 in (49.976 to 50.000)
(0.25 U/S)	1.6426 to 1.6430 in (41.723 to 41.733 mm)	1.8791 to 1.8799 in (47.730 to 47.750 mm)
(0.50 U/S)	1.6328 to 1.6332 in (41.473 to 41.483 mm)	1.8693 to 1.8901 in (47.480 to 47.500 mm)
(0.75 U/S)	1.6229 to 1.6233 in (41.223 to 41.233 mm)	1.8594 to 1.8602 in (47.230 to 47.250 mm)
Crankpin running clearance	0.0009 to 0.0039 in (0.024 to 0.1 mm)	0.0009 to 0.0019 in (0.024 to 0.048 mm)

Flywheel

Maximum run-out	0.004 in (0.1 mm)	0.004 in (0.1 mm)

Camshaft

Endfloat	0.0028 to 0.012 in (0.07 to 0.3 mm)	0.0028 to 0.012 in (0.07 to 0.3 mm)

Bearing running clearance	0.0010 to 0.004 in (0.025 to 0.1 mm)	0.0010 to 0.004 in (0.025 to 0.1 mm)
Camshaft journal diameter		
No. 1 (front)	1.7011 to 1.7018 in (43.209 to 43.225 mm)	1.8290 to 1.8297 in (46.459 to 46.475 mm)
2	1.6911 to 1.6917 in (42.954 to 42.970 mm)	1.8192 to 1.8199 in (46.209 to 46.225 mm)
3	1.6813 to 1.6819 in (42.704 to 42.720 mm)	1.8094 to 1.8100 in (45.959 to 45.975 mm)
4	1.6716 to 1.6722 in (42.459 to 42.475 mm)	1.7996 to 1.8002 in (45.709 to 45.725 mm)
5	—	1.7897 to 1.7904 in (45.459 to 45.475 mm)
Cam height (intake)	1.438 to 1.4397 in (36.469 to 36.569 mm)	1.5102 to 1.5142 in (38.36 to 38.46 mm)
(exhaust)	1.4318 to 1.4358 in (36.369 to 36.469 mm)	1.5059 to 1.5098 in (38.25 to 38.35 mm)
California 1974 on	—	1.8256 to 1.8295 in (46.37 to 46.47 mm)
Minimum wear height (intake)	1.4240 in (36.17 mm)	—
(exhaust)	1.4201 in (36.07 mm)	—

Valves

Clearance (HOT) (Inlet)	0.008 in (0.20 mm)	0.008 in (0.20 mm)
(exhaust)	0.012 in (0.30 mm)	0.013 in (0.33 mm)
Overall length (inlet)	3.941 in (100.1 mm)	4.29 in (109.0 mm)
(exhaust)	3.941 in (100.1 mm)	4.29 in (109.0 mm)
Valve head contact angle	45º	45º
Stem diameter (inlet)	0.3136 to 0.3140 in (7.965 to 7.975 mm)	0.3138 to 0.3146 in (7.97 to 7.99 mm)
(exhaust)	0.3134 to 0.3140 in (7.960 to 7.975 mm)	0.3138 to 0.3142 in (7.97 to 7.98 mm)
Stem to guide clearance (inlet)	0.0014 to 0.0031 in (0.035 to 0.08 mm)	0.0010 to 0.003 in (0.025 to 0.08 mm)
(exhaust)	0.0014 to 0.0039 in (0.035 to 0.10 mm)	0.0012 to 0.004 in (0.030 to 0.1 mm)
Minimum valve head thickness (inlet)	0.031 in (0.8 mm)	0.020 in (0.5 mm)
(exhaust)	0.035 in (0.9 mm)	0.028 in (0.7 mm)

Valve guides

Projection from cylinder head	0.71 in (18.0 mm)	Snap ring contact
Internal diameter	0.3154 to 0.3161 in (8.01 to 8.03 mm)	0.3154 to 0.3161 in (8.01 to 8.03 mm)
External diameter (standard)	0.5132 to 0.5136 in (13.035 to 13.045 mm)	0.5134 to 0.5138 in (13.04 to 13.05 mm)
(0.05 o/s)	0.5152 to 0.5156 in (13.085 to 13.095 mm)	0.5154 to 0.5157 in (13.09 to 13.10 mm)
Valve guide installation temperature of cylinder head	212 to 266ºF (100 to 130ºC)	176ºF (80ºC)

Valve springs

Free length	1.831 in (46.5 mm)	1.657 in (42.1 mm)
Installed length	1.512 in (38.4 mm)	1.484 in (37.7 mm)

Rocker shaft

Shaft to arm running	0.0008 to 0.0024 in (0.02 to 0.06 mm)	0.0008 to 0.0016 in (0.02 to 0.04 mm)

Tappets (cam followers)

Clearance in block	0.0006 to 0.004 in (0.015 to 0.1 mm)	0.0008 to 0.004 in (0.02 to 0.1 mm)
External diameter (standard)	0.7865 to 0.7874 in (19.978 to 19.999 mm)	0.8732 to 0.8739 in (22.179 to 22.199 mm)
(0.05 o/s)	0.7885 to 0.7893 in (20.028 to 20.049 mm)	0.8752 to 0.8759 in (22.229 to 22.249 mm)

Lubrication system

Oil capacity (including filter change)	3.1 Imp qt 3.7 US qt 3.5 litre	3.3 Imp qt 3.9 US qt 3.7 litre
Oil pump relief valve operating pressure (oil hot)	51 to 63 lb/in^2 (3.6 to 4.4 kg/cm^2)	—

Torque wrench settings

									lb f ft	Nm
3K series engine										
Main bearing cap bolts	...	...	...	...	...	...	...	...	45	62
Big-end cap bolts	...	...	...	...	...	...	...	...	35	48
Camshaft thrust plate bolts	...	...	...	...	...	...	...	...	7	10
Timing chain cover bolts	...	...	...	...	...	...	...	...	7	10
Oil pump securing bolts	...	...	...	...	...	...	...	...	12	16
Crankshaft pulley bolts	...	...	...	...	...	...	...	...	38	53
Cylinder head bolts	...	...	...	...	...	...	...	....	48	66
Camshaft sprocket bolts	...	...	...	...	...	...	...	...	45	62
Rocker support pedestal bolts	...	...	...	...	...	...	...	...	16	22
Manifold bolts	...	...	...	...	...	...	...	...	20	28
Sump drain plug	...	...	...	...	...	...	...	...	30	41
Spark plugs	...	...	...	...	...	...	...	...	15	21
Flywheel bolts	...	...	...	...	...	...	...	...	46	64
Clutch (or torque converter) housing to engine bolts					...	...	...	...	50	69
Torque converter to driveplate bolts	...	...	...	...	...	...	...	...	15	21
Driveplate to crankshaft bolts	...	...	...	...	...	...	...	...	43	59
Clutch cover to flywheel	...	...	...	...	...	...	...	...	16	22
2T series engine										
Main bearing cap bolts	...	...	...	...	...	...	...	...	62	86
Big-end cap bolts	...	...	...	...	...	...	...	...	35	48
Camshaft thrust plate bolts	...	...	...	...	...	...	...	...	10	14
Timing chain cover bolts	...	...	...	...	...	...	...	...	10	14
Oil pump securing bolts	...	...	...	...	...	...	...	...	18	25
Crankshaft pulley bolt	...	...	...	...	...	...	...	...	40	55
Cylinder head bolts	...	...	...	...	...	...	...	...	63	87
Camshaft sprocket bolt	...	...	...	...	...	...	...	...	65	90
Manifold bolts	...	...	...	...	...	...	...	...	10	14
Sump drain plug	...	...	...	...	...	...	...	...	27	37
Spark plugs	...	...	...	...	...	...	...	...	15	21
Flywheel bolts	...	...	...	...	...	...	...	...	46	64
Clutch cover to flywheel	...	...	...	...	...	...	...	...	14	19
Clutch (or torque converter) bell housing to engine				...	...	...	...	48	66
Torque converter to driveplate bolts	...	...	...	...	...	...	...	...	15	21
Driveplate to crankshaft bolts	...	...	...	...	...	...	...	...	43	59

1 General description

1 The engines used in the vehicles covered by this manual may be the 1200 cc 3K series or the 1600 cc 2T series engine (Fig. 1.1 and 1.2).
2 Both units are of four cylinder in-line type having push-rod operated overhead valves.
3 The crankshaft is supported in five main bearings.
4 The oil pump and distributor are driven by a shaft geared to the camshaft.
5 The full-flow type oil filter is of externally mounted cartridge design.
6 The main differences between the two engines are that the 3K series is inclined at an angle and has a single rocker shaft with intake and exhaust manifolds on the same side of the cylinder head while the 2T series engine has separate rocker shafts for the inlet and exhaust valves and the intake and exhaust manifolds are located on opposing sides of the cylinder head, to give a crossflow characteristic to the engine.

2 Operations possible with engine in position and those requiring its removal

1 The majority of major overhaul operations can be carried out without removing the engine from the vehicle.
2 The only exceptions requiring its removal are the following:

   a) *Removal and refitting of the main bearing shells.*
   b) *Removal and refitting of the crankshaft.*
   c) *Attention to the flywheel, crankshaft rear oil seal can be given if the gearbox (or auto. transmission) is first removed.*

3 Methods of engine removal

1 The engine can be removed on its own, or complete with the manual gearbox for later separation.
2 Where the vehicle is equipped with automatic transmission, in view of the weight of the transmission, the engine should always be removed independently as should the transmission (see Chapter 6) if it also requires overhaul or repair.
3 Make sure that adequate lifting gear and if possible a trolley jack, are available before attempting to remove the engine.

4 Engine - removal complete with manual gearbox

1 If the vehicle can be placed over an inspection pit or raised three or four inches on ramps or blocks of wood placed under the roadwheels so much the better, as access to the exhaust mountings and rear engine mounting will be that much easier.
2 Have an assistant available.
3 Open the bonnet to its fullest extent and mark the position of the hinge plates on the underside of the bonnet to facilitate refitting.
4 Disconnect the windscreen washer hose and stay from the underside of the bonnet.
5 Unscrew and remove the bonnet hinge bolts and with the help of an assistant lift the bonnet away and store it somewhere where it will not be scratched.
6 Disconnect the negative lead from the battery.
7 Drain the coolant from the engine cooling system as described in Chapter 2. Retain the coolant for further use if it contains fairly fresh anti-freeze.
8 Drain all the engine oil into a suitable container. Refit the drain plug.
9 Drain the gearbox oil by unscrewing the filler/level plug and then

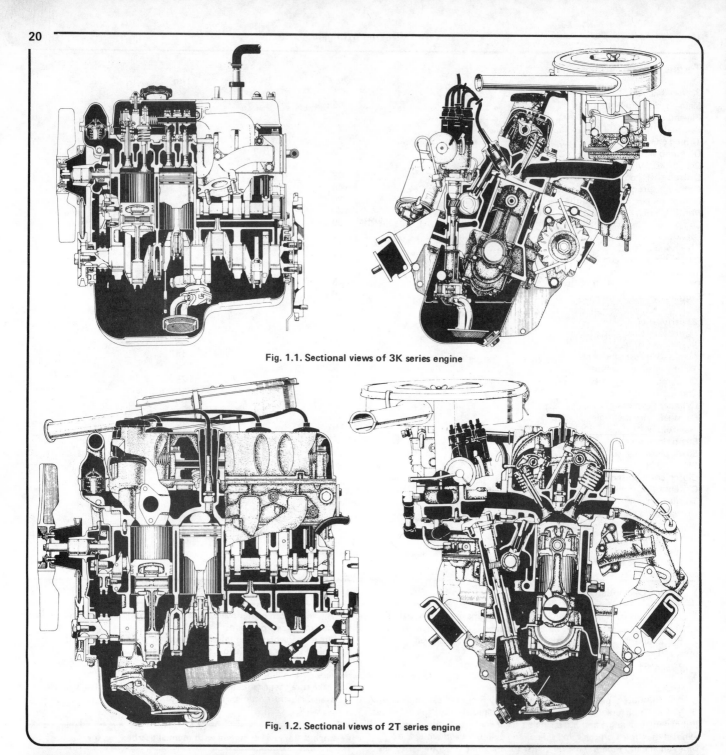

Fig. 1.1. Sectional views of 3K series engine

Fig. 1.2. Sectional views of 2T series engine

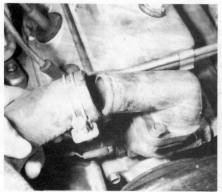

4.10A Disconnecting radiator top hose

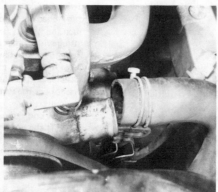

4.10B Disconnecting radiator bottom hose

4.14 Disconnecting heater hoses

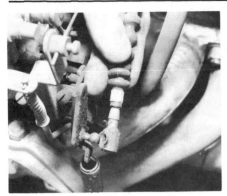

4.15 Disconnecting throttle linkage

4.16 Disconnecting (manual) choke cable

4.18 Water temperature switch

4.19A Engine rear earthing strap

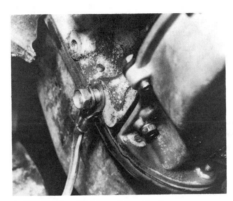

4.19B Engine front earthing strap

4.24 Clutch cable connection (1200 models)

the drain plug. Refit the drain plug and fully tighten it but the filler plug need only be tightened finger tight at this stage.

10 Disconnect and remove the radiator hoses (photos).

11 The radiator should now be unbolted and removed from the engine compartment. If a fan cowl is fitted, this should be unbolted first from the radiator and pushed towards the engine. Once the radiator has been removed, the cowl can be extracted. On late model vehicles equipped with a 3K-C engine, an electrically operated fan is installed. The leads from the fan and the thermostatically controlled radiator switch should be disconnected and the radiator removed complete with fan assembly. If the vehicle is equipped with air conditioning, do not confuse the radiator with the condenser which is mounted just ahead of it. **Refer to paragraph 30.**

12 Remove the air cleaner assembly according to type and by reference to Chapter 3.

13 Disconnect the HT lead from the coil and disconnect the LT lead from the distributor body terminal.

14 Disconnect the heater hoses and their supporting clips and tie them back out of the way (photo).

15 Disconnect the accelerator linkage from the carburettor and on late models with an electrically heated choke, disconnect the leads (photo).

16 Disconnect the choke cable from the carburettor on those models having a manually operated choke type carburettor (photo).

17 Disconnect the fuel inlet hose from the fuel pump and plug the hose. Where a fuel return line is fitted, this should be disconnected at the same time.

18 Disconnect the lead from the water temperature transmitter which is located at the base of the thermostat housing at the front end of the cylinder head (photo).

19 Disconnect the earthing strap which runs between the rear of the cylinder block and the bodyframe. On 3K series engines, a second earthing lead is to be found at the forward right-hand side of the crankcase (photo).

20 Disconnect the leads from the rear of the alternator.

21 Unbolt the exhaust downpipe from the manifold and disconnect the exhaust pipe support bracket on the downpipe.

22 Disconnect all electrical leads and vacuum pipes which are concerned with the emission control system used on the particular vehicle. Identify

and mark the leads and pipes before disconnecting them and remove only those which run from the engine to vacuum switching valves or relays mounted on the sides or rear bulkhead of the engine compartment.

23 Disconnect the electrical leads from the starter motor terminals.

24 Working under the vehicle, disconnect the clutch actuating mechanism. On 1200 models this will necessitate extracting the 'C' ring from the clutch outer cable at the engine compartment rear bulkhead so that the cable can be withdrawn slightly, and disconnected from the clutch release lever. On 1600 models which have a hydraulic clutch actuating mechanism, detach the return spring from the release lever and then unbolt the clutch slave cylinder from the side of the bellhousing and tie it up out of the way. There is no need to disconnect the hydraulic pipe (photo).

25 Disconnect the leads from the reverse lamp switch on the side of the gearbox (photo).

26 Remove the gearshift lever as described in Chapter 6.

27 Remove the propeller shaft as described in Chapter 7.

28 Disconnect the speedometer drive cable from the side of the gearbox. To do this, simply unscrew the knurled ring and withdraw the cable assembly.

29 Unbolt and remove the radiator grille and the cross reinforcement member so that when removing the engine/gearbox, its front end will not have to be raised at such a steep angle.

30 *For vehicles equipped with an air conditioning system,* on no account disconnect any part of the system. The compressor and condenser can be unbolted and moved aside but only as far as their flexible hoses will permit. If insufficient room is provided to allow the engine to be removed, then the refrigerant must be discharged by your dealer or a competent refrigeration engineer.

31 Attach a suitable hoist to slings or chains attached to the engine lifting hooks and just take the weight of the engine.

32 Disconnect the front engine mountings from their brackets on the crossmember by unscrewing the nuts (photo).

33 Place a jack under the gearbox and with its weight supported, unbolt and remove the rear mounting and crossmember.

34 With the engine and gearbox now free and ready for removal, make a final check to see that no wires, cables or controls have been over-looked and are still attached to the engine or gearbox.

35 With the help of an assistant, simultaneously raise the hoist and lower the gearbox jack until the combined assembly can be raised and lifted out of the engine compartment at an inclined angle.

5 Engine - removal, leaving manual gearbox in vehicle

1 Carry out the operations described in paragraphs 1 to 8 and 10 to 23, in the preceding Section.
2 Unbolt and remove the starter motor.
3 Unbolt and remove the bolts which secure the clutch bellhousing to the engine. *Note that two of the bolts pass through reinforcement brackets on 2T series engines.*
4 Refer to paragraphs 29 to 32 and carry out the operations described therein.
5 Place a jack under the gearbox and support its weight.
6 Using the hoist, raise the engine until the rear face of the cylinder head is almost touching the engine compartment bulkhead. Raise the jack to support the gearbox. *Two changes should now have occurred, (i) the engine front mountings should be clear of the crossmember brackets and (ii) the engine sump should be just clear of the cross-member.*
7 Now pull the engine forward to clear the input shaft of the gearbox and lift the engine out of the vehicle.

6 Engine - removal leaving the automatic transmission in vehicle

1 Carry out the operations described in paragraphs 1 to 8 and 10 to 23 in the previous Section 4, but make sure to disconnect (and plug) the transmission fluid cooler hoses from the base of the radiator.
2 Unbolt and remove the starter motor.
3 Working under the vehicle, prise out the two rubber plugs from the semi-circular plate at the lower part of the torque converter housing Fig. 1.3.
4 Some of the bolts which secure the crankshaft driveplate to the torque converter are now visible through these holes. They should be unscrewed but they are accessible one at a time after having brought each one into view by rotating the crankshaft. To rotate the crankshaft,

remove the shield from below the radiator and apply a ring spanner to the crankshaft pulley bolt (Fig. 1.5).
5 Repeat the operations described in paragraph 29 to 32 of Section 4.
2-speed Toyoglide
Removal is similar to that just described but leave the torque converter attached to the engine driveplate and then remove it after the transmission has been withdrawn (see Chapter 6, Part 2, Sec. 32).
6 Using the hoist, raise the engine slightly until the engine front mountings are clear of their crossmember brackets.
7 Place a jack under the base of the automatic transmission using a block of wood as an insulator to prevent damage to the oil pan.
8 Pull the engine forward but have an assistant maintain pressure on the front face of the torque converter to prevent it coming out with the engine and to keep it in positive engagement with the oil pump drive tangs.
9 With the engine free from the transmission, lift it straight up and out of the engine compartment.
10 Make up a small plate, suitably cranked, which can be bolted to one of the torque converter bolt holes to maintain gentle pressure on the front face of the torque converter in order to keep it positioned fully rearward.

7 Engine/manual gearbox - separation

1 Where the engine was removed complete with the gearbox, lower the assembly to the ground and remove the starter motor.
2 Unscrew and remove the bolts which secure the clutch bellhousing to the engine.
3 Support the weight of the gearbox and withdraw it in a straight line from the engine. On no account let the weight of the gearbox hang upon the input shaft while the latter is still engaged in the splines of the clutch driven plate.

8 Engine - dismantling general

A40 type transmission
1 Keen home mechanics who dismantle a lot of engines will

4.25 Gearbox reversing lamp switch

Fig. 1.3. Removing plug from front face of torque converter housing

4.32 Front engine mounting disconnected

Fig. 1.4. Unscrewing a torque converter to driveplate bolt

5.3 Crankcase rear reinforcement bracket (2T series engine)

Fig. 1.5. Removing engine splash shield

probably have a stand on which to put them, but most will make do with a work bench which should be large enough to spread around the inevitable bits and pieces and tools, and strong enough to support the engine weight. If the floor is the only place, try and ensure that the engine rests on a hard wood platform or similar rather than on concrete.

2   Spend some time on cleaning the unit. If you have been wise this will have been done before the engine was removed at a service bay. Good water soluble solvents will help to 'float' off caked dirt/grease under a water jet. Once the exterior is clean dismantling may begin. As parts are removed clean them in petrol/paraffin (do not immerse parts with oilways in paraffin - clean them with a petrol soaked cloth and clean oilways with wire). If an air line is available use it for final cleaning off. Paraffin, which could possibly remain in oilways and would dilute the oil for initial lubrication after reassembly, must be blown out.

3   Always fit new gaskets and seals - but do not throw the old ones away until you have the new one to hand. A pattern is then available if they have to be made specially. Hang them up on a nail.

4   In general it is best to work from the top of the engine downwards. In all cases support the engine firmly so that it does not topple over when you are undoing stubborn nuts and bolts.

5   Always place nuts and bolts back with their components or place of attachment, if possible - it saves much confusion later. Otherwise put them in small, separate pots or jars so that their groups are easily identified.

6   If you have an area where parts can be laid out on sheets of paper, do so - putting the nuts and bolts with them. If you are able to look at all the components in this way it helps to avoid missing something on reassembly.

10.3 Removing the rocker cover (3K series engine)

9   Engine ancillaries - removal

1   If you are stripping the engine completely or preparing to install a reconditioned unit, all the ancillaries must be removed first. If you are going to obtain a reconditioned 'short' motor (block, crankshaft, pistons and connecting rods) then obviously the cylinder head and associated parts will need retention for fitting to the new engine. It is advisable to check just what you will get with a reconditioned unit as changes are made from time to time.

2   The removal of all those items connected with fuel, ignition and charging systems are detailed in the respective Chapters but for clarity they are merely listed here:

  Distributor
  Carburettor (can be removed together with inlet manifold)
  Alternator
  Fuel pump
  Water pump
  Starter motor
  Thermostat
  Exhaust manifold
  Emission control equipment including, air pump, vacuum valves, connecting pipes etc
  The clutch assembly

10.6 Removing rocker assembly (3K series engine)

10   Cylinder head - removal

1   *If the engine is in the vehicle* then the following preparatory work must first be carried out.

  a) *Drain the cooling system.*
  b) *Disconnect all hoses from the cylinder head.*
  c) *Disconnect all electrical leads from the cylinder head and cylinder head ancillary components (emission control, carburettor etc).*
  d) *Disconnect all accelerator and choke controls from the carburettor.*
  e) *Remove the air cleaner.*
  f) *Disconnect the exhaust downpipe from the manifold.*
  g) *Disconnect the fuel inlet pipe from the carburettor, also the distributor vacuum pipe.*

2   Disconnect the breather hose (crankcase ventilation system) which runs between the rocker cover and the air cleaner (now removed).

3   Remove the rocker cover and gasket (photo).

4   On all 3K series engines except the 3K-B, unbolt the intake/exhaust

10.7 Extracting a pushrod (3K series engine)

10.9 Removing cylinder head (3K series engine)

11.1 Removing a tappet (cam follower)

12.2 Compressing a valve spring (2T series engine)

12.3 Removing valve spring and retainer (2T series engine)

12.4 Removing a valve (2T series engine)

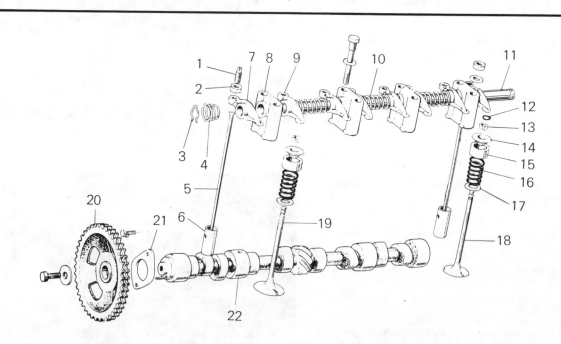

Fig. 1.6. Valve, rocker and camshaft components (3K series engine)

1	Adjuster screw	7	Rocker arm	13	Split collets	18 Valve
2	Locknut	8	Support pedestal	14	Valve spring retainer	19 Valve
3	Clip	9	Rocker arm	15	Spring cover	20 Camshaft sprocket
4	Spring	10	Spring	16	Valve spring	21 Camshaft thrust plate
5	Pushrod	11	Rocker shaft	17	Plate washer	22 Camshaft
6	Tappet (cam follower)	12	Oil seal			

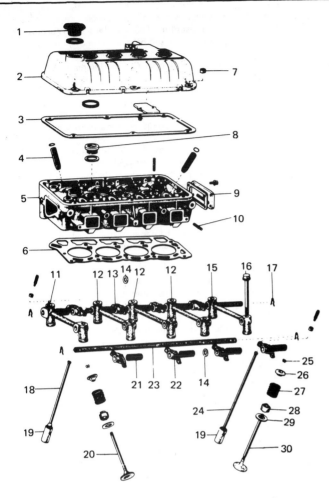

Fig. 1.7. Cylinder head components (2T series engine)

1 Oil filler cap	16 Cylinder head bolt
2 Rocker cover	17 Clip
3 Gasket	18 Pushrod
4 Valve guide	19 Tappet (cam follower)
5 Cylinder head	20 Inlet valve
6 Cylinder head gasket	21 Spring
7 Nut	22 Rocker arm
8 Plug	23 Rocker shaft
9 Cover plate	24 Pushrod
10 Stud	25 Split collets
11 Rocker shaft support pedestal	26 Valve spring retainer
12 Rocker shaft support pedestal	27 Valve spring
13 Rocker arm	28 Valve stem oil seal
14 Oil pipe seal	29 Plate washer
15 Rocker shaft support pedestal	30 Exhaust valve

13.8 Removing the oil pump

manifold assembly and lift it complete with carburettor from the cylinder head. On 3K-B engines, before this can be done, the coolant hoses must be disconnected as this engine has a water heated intake manifold.

5   On 2T series engines, Disconnect the heater pipes which run between the exhaust manifold and the automatic choke on the carburettor. Unbolt and remove the intake manifold complete with carburettor from one side of the cylinder head and then unbolt and remove the exhaust manifold from the opposing side.

6   On the 3K series engine, unbolt and remove the rocker shaft assembly from the cylinder head (photo).

7   Extract the push-rods and keep them in sequence so that they can be refitted to their original locations. A piece of card having holes punched in it and numbered 1 to 8 is a useful device for this (photo).

8   Unscrew and remove the cylinder head bolts. Unscrew the bolts a turn at a time and work in diagonal sequence from the centre two bolts outwards.

9   Lift the head from the cylinder block and remove the gasket. If the cylinder head is stuck, tap it carefully using a hammer and a block of hardwood.(photo).

10 On the 2T series type of engine, the cylinder head bolts also serve to hold the rocker shafts in position. Unscrew the bolts a turn at a time working from the two centre bolts outwards in diagonal sequence.

11 Remove the rocker shaft assembly and then extract the push-rods, keeping them in strict sequence as to position. Make up a suitable card for this purpose marked to ensure that each push-rod is returned to its original location.

12 Lift the cylinder head from the cylinder block and remove the gasket. If it is stuck, tap it carefully with a hammer and a block of hardwood.

11 Tappets (cam followers) - removal

1   Once the cylinder head has been removed, the tappets can be extracted by pushing a finger into each one in turn and drawing them from the cylinder block (photo).

2   Keep the tappets in order so that they can be returned to their original positions. The best way of doing this is to mark each one with a piece of masking tape and number them 1 to 8, starting with 1 nearest the front of the engine. Do not punch or scratch marks on the tappets.

12 Cylinder head - dismantling

1   With the cylinder head removed, it should be dismantled if the valve components are to be inspected and renovated or decarbonising carried out as described in Sections 27 or 30.

2   To remove a valve, a valve spring compressor will be required. Fit the compressor to the valve nearest the front of the cylinder head and compress the valve spring until the split collets which secure the spring retainer can be removed. On 3K series engines an 'O' ring seal must first be extracted (photo).

3   Slowly release the compressor and then remove it. On 3K series engines, extract the spring retainer, the spring shield, valve spring and plate washer. On 2T series engines, extract the spring retainer, the valve spring, the valve stem oil seal and the plate washer (photo).

4   Withdraw the valve from its cylinder head guide (photo).

5   It is essential that all components of this and the other valves are kept together with their valves so that they will all be returned to their original locations. One method of doing this is to have a box with internal divisions numbered 1 to 8, ready before dismantling commences.

6   Repeat the foregoing operations on the remaining seven valves.

13 Sump and oil pump - removal

1   If the engine is out of the vehicle, drain the engine oil (if not already done), unbolt and remove the sump. If it is stuck tight, cut round the upper and lower surfaces of the gasket with a sharp knife. If this operation is carried out carefully, then the gasket can be used again after coating both of its sides with jointing compound.

2   If the engine is still in the vehicle, then dependent upon the vehicle

type and engine, some or all of the following operations must be carried out before the sump can be removed. Inspection will determine the extent to which dismantling must be carried out on your particular vehicle. It is emphasised that removal of the sump without first lifting the engine out of the vehicle is a very difficult and complicated task and no advantage is to be obtained compared with first removing the engine. Where you are still determined, however, to remove the sump from an 'in-situ' engine, proceed in the following way.

3 Unbolt and remove the engine undershield.

4 Unbolt and remove the reinforcement plates which are located at the rear corners of the sump and connect between the clutch or torque converter housing.

5 Unbolt and remove the front suspension stabiliser bar.

6 As the sump will not clear the internally mounted oil pump, the engine front mounting bolts must be released and the engine raised just enough to enable the sump to be unbolted and dropped about two inches (50 mm). Two precautions must be observed during this operation, *(i) jack up under the gearbox or automatic transmission, (ii) only raise the engine the minimum necessary, otherwise the radiator hoses and possibly other leads and controls will be strained.*

7 With the sump dropped as previously explained, the oil pump mounting bolts will now be visible. Insert a spanner through the space between the sump and the crankcase and unscrew the bolts. Lever the oil pump downwards and once the oil pump is released, the sump and oil pump can be removed.

8 Normally, once the sump has been removed, the oil pump is unbolted and withdrawn independently. If it is tight in the crankcase, tap it out gently from the distributor side (photo).

14 Timing gear - removal

1 *If the engine is in the vehicle,* remove the radiator grille, drain the cooling system and remove the radiator. Release and remove the drivebelts from the alternator, water pump, air pump, compressor as applicable, and push the relevant ancillary components aside so that they do not cover the timing cover.

2 Unscrew and remove the crankshaft pulley bolt. To do this, a ring spanner should be used which is of sufficient length to give a good leverage. The problem of preventing the crankshaft from turning while attempting to unscrew the nut should be overcome by jamming the starter ring gear on the flywheel (or driveplate on automatic transmission). Do this with a suitable cold chisel after first having removed the starter motor (photo).

3 With the bolt removed, withdraw the crankshaft pulley. This can usually be done by using two large screwdrivers as levers. If this fails, then a suitable two or three legged puller must be used.

4 Unbolt and remove the water pump from the front face of the timing cover.

5 If the timing cover is being removed from an engine which is still in position in the vehicle, unscrew and remove the bolts which secure the front edge of the sump to the timing cover. If the engine is out of the car then the sump will probably already have been removed, if not remove it.

6 Unscrew and remove all the timing cover securing bolts.
It is advisable to draw the position of the bolt holes on a sheet of paper and then push the bolts through the paper in their original positions as each one is removed. This will facilitate refitting as the lengths of the bolts differ and screwing them into the wrong holes could fracture the casting of the engine.

7 Remove the timing cover and the gasket (photo).

8 Unbolt and remove the chain tensioner (photo).

9 Unscrew and remove the camshaft sprocket bolt. The sprocket can be held still either by placing a block of wood between one of the crankshaft webs and the inside of the crankcase or inserting a rod through one of the holes in the camshaft sprocket and using the rod to lever against the cylinder block (photo).

10 The camshaft sprocket complete with chain should now be pulled away and the chain unlooped from the crankshaft sprocket (photo).

15 Camshaft - removal

1 *If the engine is in the vehicle,* then the radiator grille and radiator must be removed. Disconnect the exhaust downpipe and its retaining bracket and support the transmission on a jack, remove the rear

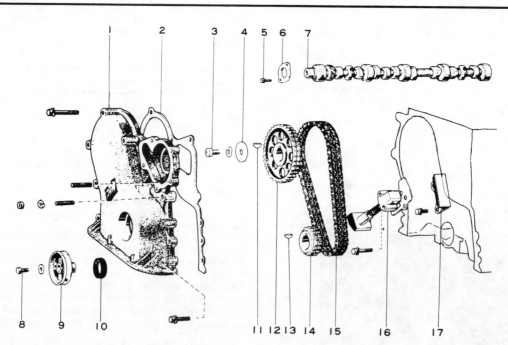

Fig. 1.8. Camshaft and timing components (2T series)

1 Timing cover	5 Thrust plate bolt	9 Pulley	13 Woodruff key
2 Gasket	6 Thrust plate	10 Oil seal	14 Crankshaft sprocket
3 Camshaft sprocket bolt	7 Camshaft	11 Woodruff key	15 Timing chain
4 Washer	8 Crankshaft pulley bolt	12 Camshaft sprocket	16 Chain tensioner
			17 Chain damper

14.3 Removing the crankshaft pulley

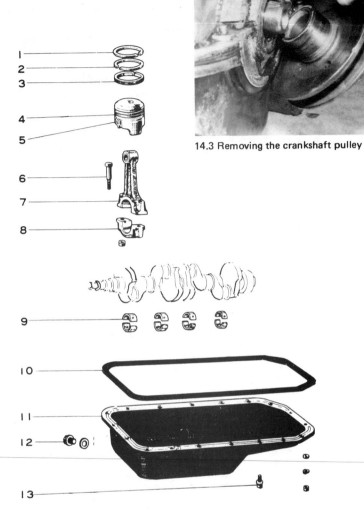

Fig. 1.9. Sump and connecting rod components (2T series)

1	Top compression ring	8	Cap
2	Second compression ring	9	Big-end shell bearings
3	Oil control ring	10	Gasket
4	Piston	11	Sump
5	Gudgeon pin	12	Drain plug
6	Big-end bolt	13	Sump securing bolts
7	Connecting rod		

14.7 Timing cover and gasket removed

14.8 Timing chain and tensioner

14.9 Unscrewing camshaft sprocket bolt

14.10 Removing camshaft sprocket and chain

15.3 Removing camshaft thrust plate

15.4 Removing camshaft

17.2 Removing a connecting rod big-end cap

17.6 Withdrawing a piston/connecting rod assembly from top of cylinder block

18.1 Bending back a flywheel bolt lockplate

mounting crossmember and carefully lower the rear end of the transmission, taking care that none of the engine controls and leads are strained, and that the front universal joint of the propeller shaft is bent at such an acute angle that no further movement is available. The purpose of lowering the rear end of the transmission is to enable the camshaft to be extracted at an inclined angle, otherwise it would be obstructed by the front body panel and reinforcement crossmember. Before lowering the transmission, disconnect the gearshift (or selector) lever and the leads from the reversing light switch.

2   The distributor, cylinder head, sump, oil pump and tappets will all have been removed as described in earlier sections.

3   Unscrew and remove the two bolts which secure the camshaft thrust plate (photo).

4   Remove the thrust plate and withdraw the camshaft, taking great care that the cam lobes do not damage the camshaft bearings as they pass through them (photo).

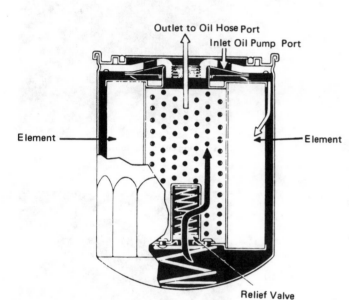

Fig. 1.9A. Sectional view of cartridge type oil filter

Outlet to Oil Hose Port
Inlet Oil Pump Port
Element
Element
Relief Valve

16 Oil filter - removal

1   The disposable type cartridge oil filter should be unscrewed from the engine using a strap or chain wrench. If such a tool is not available, drive a large screwdriver through the filter about 1 in (25 mm) from its outer end and use this to unscrew it (Fig. 1.9A).

2   If the filter is being removed at a regular service interval and the vehicle has just come in from the road, be prepared for some loss of oil as the filter is unscrewed. Also the oil may be very hot.

17 Pistons, connecting rods - removal and dismantling

1   *If the engine is still in the vehicle,* remove the cylinder head and sump as described in previous Sections.

2   Undo and remove the big-end cap retaining nuts using a socket and remove the big-end caps one at a time, taking care to keep them in the right order and the correct way round (photo).

3   Ensure that the shell bearings are also kept with their correct connecting rods and caps unless they are to be renewed. Normally the numbers 1 to 4 are stamped on adjacent sides of the big-end caps and connecting rods, indicating which cap fits on which rod and which way round the cap fits. If no numbers or lines can be found then scratch mating marks across the joint from the rod to the cap with a sharp screwdriver. One line for connecting rod number 1, two for connecting rod number 2 and so on. Alternatively centre punch the adjacent points on the rod and cap but make a note as to which side of the engine your marks face. This will ensure there is no confusion later as it is most important that the caps go back in the position on the connecting rods from which they were removed.

4   If the big-end caps are difficult to remove they may be gently tapped with a soft hammer.

5   To remove the shell bearings press the bearing opposite the groove in both connecting rod and the connecting rod cap, and the bearing shell will slide out easily.

6   Withdraw the pistons and connecting rods upwards and out of the top of the cylinder block. Ensure they are kept in the correct order for replacement in the same bore. Refit the connecting rod caps and bearings to the rods (if the bearings do not require renewal) to minimise the risk of getting the caps and rods muddled (photo).

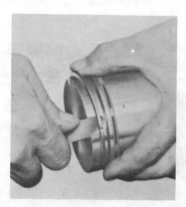

Fig. 1.9B. Using a feeler blade to remove a piston ring

7   On engines which have covered a high mileage, it is possible for a
severe wear ridge to have worn at the top of the cylinder bores. These
ridges should be carefully scraped away to enable the piston rings to
pass out of the tops of the bores.

8   *On 3K series engines,* the piston can be dismantled by extracting one
of the circlips from the ends of the gudgeon pin. Heat the piston in
boiling water and push the gudgeon pin out.

9   *On 2T series engines,* the gudgeon pins are a press fit in the connecting
rod small end and in view of the need for pressing facilities and guide
tools, it is recommended that this work is left to your Toyota dealer.

10 The piston rings may be removed by opening each of them in turn,
just enough to enable them to ride over the lands of the piston body.

In order to prevent the lower rings dropping into an empty groove
higher up the piston as they are removed, it is helpful to use two or
three narrow strips of tin or old feeler blades inserted behind the ring
at equidistant points and then to employ a twisting motion to slide the
ring from the piston (Fig. 1.9B).

**18 Flywheel (or driveplate - auto. transmission) crankshaft and main-
bearings - removal**

1   With the clutch assembly already removed, the bolts which secure
the flywheel (or driveplate) should be unscrewed and removed. On some
models, the flywheel bolts are secured with lockplates and these should
be bent back first (Fig. 1.11) (photo).

2   In order to prevent the flywheel (or driveplate) turning when
attempting to unscrew the securing bolts, either place a block of wood
between one of the webs of the crankshaft and the inside wall of the
crankcase or join the starter ring gear with a cold chisel or something
similar.

3   Remove the flywheel (or driveplate) and then unbolt and remove
the engine rear plate (photos)

4   Unbolt and remove the crankshaft rear oil seal retainer.

5   Undo and remove the ten bolts securing the main bearing caps to the
cylinder block.

Fig. 1.10. Engine lubrication system - 3K series engine

18.3A Removing the flywheel

18.3B Removing the engine rear plate

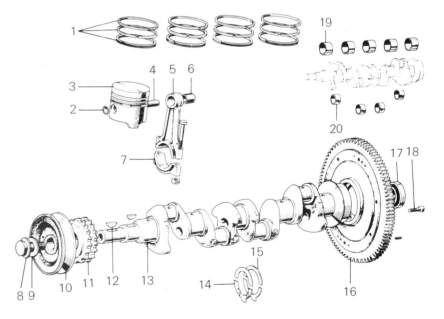

Fig. 1.11. Crankshaft and flywheel components (3K series)

1	Piston rings	11	Crankshaft sprocket
2	Circlip	12	Woodruff key
3	Piston	13	Crankshaft
4	Gudgeon pin	14	Thrust washers
5	Connecting rod	15	Thrust washers
6	Small end bush	16	Flywheel
7	Cap	17	Input shaft (gearbox) bush
8	Crankshaft pulley bolt	18	Bolt
9	Washer	19	Bearing shell
10	Pulley	20	Bearing shell

6   Make sure that the main bearing caps are numbered 1 to 5 on the
fronts faces and also show an arrow towards the front of the engine.
7   Remove the main bearing caps and the bottom half of each bearing
shell, taking care to keep the bearing shells in the right caps (photo).
8   When removing the centre bearing cap, note the bottom semi-circular
halves of the thrust washers, one half lying on either side of the main
bearing. Lay them with the centre bearing along the correct side.
9   Slightly rotate the crankshaft to free the upper halves of the bearing
shells and thrust washers which can be lifted away and placed over the
correct bearing cap when the crankshaft has been lifted out.
10 Remove the crankshaft by lifting it away from the crankcase (photo).
11 Lift away the bearing shells.

19 Lubrication system - description

1   The lubrication system is similar in both types of engine. Oil is
drawn from the sump through a strainer by an oil pump which is
driven by a gear on the camshaft. The pump and strainer assembly is
mounted within the sump Fig. 1.11.
2   Pressurised oil is first passed through the externally mounted full-
flow oil filter and then to the main oil gallery. From there, it passes
through various passages and drilling to all the friction surfaces of the
engine (photo).
3   An oil pressure switch is screwed into the cylinder block which is
connected to the oil pressure warning light on the instrument panel
(photo).
4   On some models, an oil pressure gauge is fitted instead of a warning
light and even an oil temperature gauge and a low oil pressure warning
light (refer to Chapter 10, Section 31).

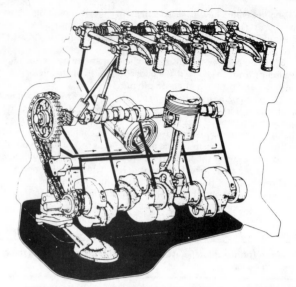

Fig. 1.12. Engine lubrication system - 2T series engine

20 Engine components - examination and renovation general

When the engine has been stripped down and all parts properly
cleaned decisions have to be made as to what needs renewal and the
following Sections tell the examiner what to look for. In any border
line case it is always best to decide in favour of a new part; even if a
part may still be serviceable its life will have been reduced by wear and
the degree of trouble needed to replace it in future must be taken into
consideration. However these things are relative and it depends on
whether a quick 'survival' job is being done or whether the car as a
whole is being regarded as having many thousands of miles of useful
and economical life remaining.

21 Crankshaft, bearings and flywheel - examination and renovation

1   Look at the main bearing journals and the crankpins and if there
are any scratches or score marks then the shaft will need regrinding.
Such conditions will nearly always be accompanied by similar deterioration in the matching bearing shells.
2   Each bearing journal should also be round and can be checked with
a micrometer or caliper gauge around the periphery at several points. If
there is more than 0.0004 in (0.01 mm) of ovality or taper regrinding
is necessary.
3   Your main Toyota dealer or motor engineering specialist will be
able to decide to what extent regrinding is necessary and also supply
the special under-size shell bearings to match whatever may need
grinding off the journals.
4   Before taking the crankshaft for regrinding check also the cylinder
bores and pistons as it may be more convenient to have the engineering
operations performed at the same time by the same engineer.
5   With careful servicing and regular oil and filter changes bearings will
last for a very long time but they can still fail for unforeseen reasons.
With big-end bearings the indications are regular rhythmic loud
knocking from the crankcase, the frequency depending on engine
speed. It is particularly noticeable when the engine is under load. This
symptom is accompanied by a fall in oil pressure although this is not
normally noticeable unless an oil pressure gauge is fitted. Main bearing
failure is usually indicated by serious vibration, particularly at higher
engine revolutions, accompanied by a more significant drop in oil
pressure and a rumbling noise.
6   Bearing shells in good condition have bearing surfaces with a smooth
even, matt silver/grey colour all over. Worn bearings will show patches

18.7 Removing a main bearing cap

18.10 Removing the crankshaft

19.2 Location of oil filter

19.3 Oil pressure sender switch

of a different colour where the bearing metal has worn away and exposed the underlay. Damaged bearings will be pitted or scored. It is nearly always well worthwhile fitting new shells as their cost is relatively low. If the crankshaft is in good condition it is merely a question of obtaining another set of standard size. A reground crankshaft will need new bearing shells as a matter of course.

7 Connecting rods are not normally subject to wear but in extreme cases such as engine seizure they could be distorted. Such conditions may be visually apparent but where doubt exists they should be changed. The bearing caps should also be examined for indications of filing down which may have been attempted in a mistaken idea that bearing slackness could be remedied in this way. If there are such signs then the connecting rods should be renewed.

8 While the flywheel is out of the vehicle, take the opportunity to examine the spigot bearing in the centre of the crankshaft rear flange. If it is worn or noisy when rotated, renew it.

9 The old bearing must be extracted using a suitable puller or alternatively, apply heat to the bearing recess when it is usually possible to lever out the bearing.

10 Drive in the new bearing applying pressure to the outer bearing track only.

11 Examine the flywheel itself. If the clutch surface is scored or grooved, or there are lots of small cracks visible (caused by over-heating) then the flywheel must either be refinished or a new one obtained. Refinishing must be left to your dealer as the overall thickness of the flywheel must not be reduced beyond a specified limit.

12 If the flywheel starter ring gear teeth are worn or chipped, a new ring gear should be fitted. In the case of a driveplate, renew the driveplate complete.

13 Although a starter ring gear can be removed with a cold chisel and a new one fitted after heating it in an oven or oil bath (392°F - 200°C), it is recommended that this work is left to your dealer or specialist engineering works.

22 Cylinder bores - examination and renovation

1 A new cylinder bore is perfectly round and the walls parallel throughout its length. The action of the piston tends to wear the walls at right angles to the gudgeon pin due to side thrust. This wear takes place principally on that section of the cylinder swept by the piston rings.

2 It is possible to get an indication of bore wear by removing the cylinder head with the engine still in the car. With the piston down in the bore first signs of wear can be seen and felt just below the top of the bore where the piston ring reaches, and there will be a noticeable lip. If there is no lip it is fairly reasonable to expect that bore wear is low and any lack of compression or excessive oil consumption is due to worn or broken piston rings or pistons or valves not seating correctly.

3 If it is possible to obtain a bore measuring micrometer, measure the bore in the thrust plane below the lip and again at the bottom of the

cylinder in the same plane. If the difference is more than 0.008 in (0.2 mm), then a rebore is necessary. Similarly a difference of 0.008 in (0.2 mm) or more across the bore diameter is a sign of ovality calling for a rebore.

4 Any bore which is significantly scratched or scored will need reboring. This symptom usually indicates that the piston or rings are damaged in that cylinder. In the event of only one cylinder being in need of reboring it will still be necessary for all four to be bored and fitted with new oversize pistons and rings.

5 Your Toyota dealer or local engineering specialist will be able to rebore and obtain the necessary matched pistons. If the crankshaft is undergoing regrinding it is a good idea to let the same firm renovate and reassemble the crankshaft and pistons to the block. A reputable firm normally gives a guarantee for such work. In cases where engines have been rebored already to their maximum, new cylinder liners are available which may be fitted. In such cases the same reboring processes have to be followed and the services of a specialist engineering firm are required.

23 Pistons, rings and connecting rods - examination and renovation

1 Worn pistons and rings can usually be diagnosed when the symptoms of excessive oil consumption and low compression occur and are sometimes, though not always, associated with worn cylinder bores. Compression testers that fit into the spark plug holes are available and these can indicate where low compression is occurring. Wear usually accelerates the more it is left so when the symptoms occur, early action can possibly save the expense of a rebore.

2 Another symptom of piston wear is piston slap - a knocking noise from the crankcase not to be confused with big-end bearing failure. It can be heard clearly at low engine speed, when there is no load (idling for example) and the engine is cold, and is much less audible when the engine speed increases. Piston wear usually occurs in the skirt or lower end of the piston and is indicated by vertical streaks in the worn area which is always on the thrust side. It can be seen when the skirt thickness is different.

3 Piston ring wear can be checked by first removing the rings from the pistons as described in Section 17. Then place the rings in the cylinder bores from the top, pushing them down about 1.5 in (38.1 mm) with the head of a piston (from which the rings have been removed) so that they rest square in the cylinder. Then measure the gap at the ends of the ring with a feeler gauge. If it exceeds the limits specified at the beginning of this Chapter then they will need renewal.

4 The grooves in which the rings locate in the piston can also become enlarged in use. The clearance between ring and piston, in the groove should not exceed the limits specified at the beginning of this Chapter.

5 However, it is rare that a piston is only worn in the ring grooves and the need to replace them for this fault alone is hardly ever encountered. Whenever the pistons are renewed the weight of the four piston/connecting rod assemblies should be kept within the limit

variation of 8 gms to maintain engine balance.

6   The connecting rod and the gudgeon pin do not normally require renewal. If the pistons are being changed then the new pistons are usually supplied complete with gudgeon pins.

24 Camshaft and bearings - examination and renovation

1   Renewal of the camshaft bearings is normally only required if the camshaft itself is reground in which case undersize bearings will be supplied by the regrinder.
2   The old bearings can be drawn out if the blanking plug is first removed from the rear end of the camshaft and a length of studding with distance pieces and nuts used to withdraw them one by one.
3   Draw new bearings into position in the same way but make quite sure that the oil hole in the bearing is in exact alignment with the hole in the crankcase bearing seat.
4   The camshaft itself may show signs of wear on the bearing journals, cam lobes or the skew gear. The main decision to take is what degree of wear justifies replacement, which is costly. Any signs of scoring or damage to the bearing journals must be rectified and as undersize bearing bushes are available the journals may be reground. If there is excessive wear on the skew gear which can be seen by close inspection of the contact pattern the whole camshaft will have to be renewed.
5   The cam lobes themselves may show signs of ridging or pitting at the high points. If the ridging is light then it may be possible to smooth it out with fine emery. The cam lobes, however, are surface hardened and once this is penetrated wear will be very rapid thereafter. The cams are also offset and tapered to cause the tappets to rotate - thus ensuring that wear is even - so do not mistake this condition for wear.
6   Finally check the camshaft end float. To do this, temporarily refit the thrust plate and sprocket and tighten the securing bolt to the specified torque wrench setting.
7   Using a feeler gauge, measure the clearance between the rear face of the thrust plate and the camshaft front bearing. Where this exceeds 0.012 in (0.3 mm) the camshaft will have to be renewed (Fig. 1.13).

25 Rocker gear - examination and renovation

1   Examine the rocker arms and shafts for wear.
2   If the assembly must be dismantled to renew a component, keep each part in its original sequence for correct refitting.
3   On 2T engines do not mix up the two rocker shafts. The rocker arms and springs can be removed from the shafts after first extracting the spring clips. When reassembling these rocker shafts, note the location of the differing pedestals and the location of the shaft groove to accommodate the cylinder head bolts (Fig. 1.14).

26 Timing sprockets, chain and tensioner - examination and renovation

1   Examine the teeth on both the crankshaft gearwheel and the camshaft gearwheel for wear. Each tooth forms an inverted 'V' with the gearwheel periphery, and if worn the side of each tooth under tension will be slightly concave in shape when compared with the other side of the tooth ie; one side of the inverted 'V' will be concave when compared with the other. If any sign of wear is present the gearwheels must be renewed.
2   Examine the links of the chain for side slackness and renew the chain if any slackness is noticeable when compared with a new chain. It is a sensible precaution to renew the chain at about 30,000 miles (48,000 Km) and at a lesser mileage if the engine is stripped down for major overhaul. The actual rollers on a very badly worn chain may be slightly grooved.
3   The chain tensioner should be checked by applying oil to the plunger and then placing two fingers over the oil passages in the tensioner body. Now pull the plunger and the suction should be strong enough to return the plunger as soon as the hand is removed. If this is not the case, then the tensioner assembly must be renewed.
4   Now measure the thickness of the slipper which rests against the chain. If it is less than 0.492 in (12.5 mm) the plunger must be renewed (Fig. 1.15).
5   Check the chain damper for wear or grooves. If the thickness of the

Fig. 1.13. Checking camshaft end-float

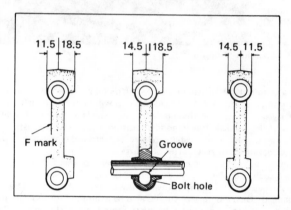

Fig. 1.14. Location and identification of rocker shaft support pillars (2T series engine). F mark is nearest timing cover. Dimensions in millimetres

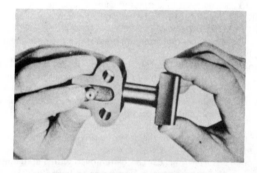

Fig. 1.15. Testing chain tensioner

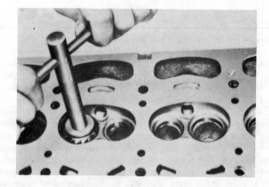

Fig. 1.16. Cutting a valve seat

section which rests against the chain is less than 0.197 in (5.0 mm) it must be renewed.

27 Valves and valve seats - examination and renovation

1 With the valves removed from the cylinder head as described in Section 12, examine the head for signs of cracking, burning away and pitting of the edge where it seats in the port. The seats of the valves in the cylinder head should also be examined for the same signs. Usually it is the valve that deteriorates first but if a bad valve is not rectified the seat will suffer and this is more difficult to repair.
2 If pitting on the valve and seat is very slight the marks can be removed by grinding the seats and valves together with coarse and then fine valve grinding paste.
3 Where bad pitting has occurred to the valve seats it will be necessary either to re-cut the seats or in severe cases, to fit new valve seats. Grinding can be done if pitting on the valve and seat is only very light or if as is usually the case, the valves only are badly burned then a new set of valves can be ground into the seats.
4 Valve grinding is carried out as follows:
Smear a trace of coarse carborundum paste on the seat face and apply a suction grinder tool to the valve head. With a semi-rotary motion, grind the valve head to its seat, lifting the valve occasionally to redistribute the grinding paste. When a dull matt even surface finish is produced on both the valve seat and the valve, wipe off the paste and repeat the process with fine carborundum paste, lifting and turning the valve to redistribute the paste as before. A light spring placed under the valve head will greatly ease this operation. When a smooth unbroken ring of light grey matt finish is produced, on both valve and valve seat faces, the grinding operation is completed.
5 Scrape away all carbon from the valve head and the valve stem. Carefully clean away every trace of grinding compound, taking care to leave none in the ports or in the valve guides. Clean the valves and valve seats with a paraffin soaked rag, with a clean rag and finally, if an air line is available blow the valves, valve guides and valve ports clean.
6 Valve seat cutters can be purchased at most accessory stores with a range of center spigots to fit most valve guides (Fig. 1.16).
7 The cutters should be used in the following sequence (i) 30° cutter, (ii) 65° cutter, (iii) 45° cutter.
8 Aim for a finished seat width of between 0.047 and 0.063 in (1.2 and 1.6 mm).
9 When the seat has been cut, the valve should be lapped with grinding paste as previously described.
10 If new valve seat inserts are needed, then this is definitely a job for your Toyota dealer who will have the necessary equipment for doing the work or will contract the job to a specialist engineering company.

28 Valve guides and springs - examination and renovation

1 Test each valve in its guide for wear. After a considerable mileage the valve guide bore may wear elliptically and can be tested by rocking the valve in the guide.
2 The remedy for wear is to ream the valve guide bores by the

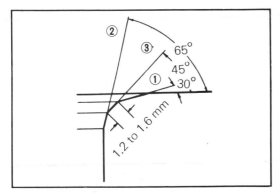
Fig. 1.17. Valve seat cutting diagram

minimum amount to accommodate the smallest oversize valve which may be available at the time. Alternatively a new set of guides will have to be fitted and reamed to a standard size. In both cases this is a job for the local Toyota dealer or engineering works.
3 Compare the face length of the valve springs with that given in the Specifications. If the springs are permanently compressed much below this length, renew them. In any event it is worth renewing the valve springs if they have been in service for 35,000 miles (56,000 km) or more.

29 Pushrods and tappets - examination and renovation

1 The pushrods should be examined visually for straightness, any that are bent should be renewed.
2 The faces of the tappets which bear on the camshaft should show no signs of pitting, scoring or other form of wear. They should also not be a loose fit in their housing. Wear is only normally encountered at very high mileage or in cases of neglected engine lubrication - renew if necessary.

30 Cylinder head - decarbonising and examination

1 When the cylinder head is removed either in the course of an overhaul or inspection of the bores or valve condition when the engine is in the car, it is normal to remove all carbon deposits from the piston crowns and head.
2 This is best done with a cup shaped wire brush and an electric drill and is fairly straightforward when the engine is dismantled and the pistons removed. Sometimes hard spots of carbon are not easily removed except by a scraper. When cleaning the pistons with a scraper take care not to damage the surface of the piston in any way.
3 When the engine is in the car certain precautions must be taken when decarbonising the piston crowns in order to prevent dislodged pieces of carbon falling into the interior of the engine which could cause damage to the cylinder bores, piston and rings - or if allowed into the water passages - damage to the water pump. Turn the piston, therefore so that the piston being worked on is at the top of its stroke and then mask off the adjacent cylinder bore and all surrounding water jacket orifices with paper and adhesive tape. Press grease into the gap all round the piston to keep particles out and then scrape all carbon away by hand, carefully.
4 When completed carefully clean out the grease round the rim of the piston - bringing any carbon particles with it. Repeat the process on the other three piston crowns. It is not recommended that a ring of carbon is left round the edge of the piston on the theory that it will aid oil consumption control. This was valid in the earlier days of long stroke low revving engines but modern engines, fuels and lubricants cause less carbon deposits anyway and any left behind tends merely to cause hot spots.

31 Oil pump - overhaul

1 If the oil pump is worn it is best to purchase an exchange reconditioned unit as a good oil pump is at the very heart of long engine life. Generally speaking an exchange or overhauled pump should be fitted at a major engine reconditioning (Fig. 1.18).
2 If it is wished to check the oil pump for wear undo and remove the three bolts securing the oil pump body to the lower body and pick-up assembly. Separate the two parts.
3 Undo and remove the relief valve plug and withdraw the washer, spring and valve plunger (Fig. 1.19).
4 Check the clearance between the lobes of the inner and outer rotors using feeler gauges. The clearance should not exceed 0.008 in (0.2 mm) (Fig. 1.19). (photo).
5 Replacement rotors are supplied only as a matched pair so that, if the clearance is excessive, a new rotor assembly must be fitted.
6 Lay a straight edge across the face of the pump in order to check the clearance between the faces of the rotors and the bottom of the straight edge. This clearance should not exceed 0.008 in (0.2 mm). If the clearance is excessive the face of the pump body can be carefully lapped on a flat surface.
7 Using feeler gauges measure the clearance between the rotor and

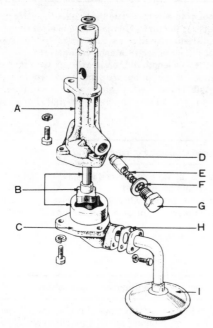

Fig. 1.18. Oil pump (3K series)

A Oil pump body
B Oil pump rotor set
C Oil pump cover
D Relief valve

E Relief valve spring
F Gasket
G Relief valve plug
H Gasket
I Oil strainer

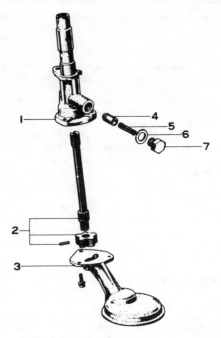

Fig. 1.19. Oil pump (2T series engine)

1 Oil pump body
2 Rotor set
3 Cover assembly
4 Relief valve

5 Spring
6 Gasket
7 Plug

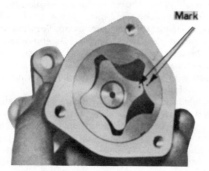

Fig. 1.19A. Oil pump rotor alignment marks

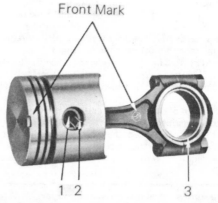

Fig. 1.20. Correct assembly of piston and connecting rod

1 Gudgeon pin   2 Circlip   3 Bearing shell

31.4 Checking oil pump rotor tip clearance

31.7 Checking oil pump outer rotor to body clearance

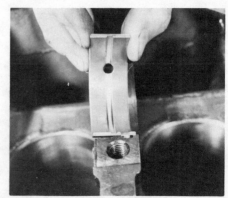

35.1 Installing a main bearing shell to crankcase

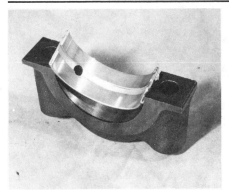

35.4 Installing a main bearing shell to cap

35.6 Installing a thrust washer at centre main bearing

35.7 Installing crankshaft

35.8 Fitting a main bearing cap

35.9 Correctly located crankshaft thrust washer

35.12 Tightening a main bearing cap bolt

the body and this should not exceed 0.008 in (0.2 mm). If wear is evident a new pump will be required (photo).

8   Inspect the relief valve for pitting and the oil passages and sliding surfaces for damage in the form of score marks. Check that the spring is not damaged and finally the pick-up gauze for blockage or tearing.

9   Reassembly of the pump is the reverse sequence to dismantling. Both the drive and driven rotors are provided with punch marks and these must be aligned during reassembly (Fig. 1.19A).

32 Oil seals - renewal

1   At the time of major overhaul, always renew the oil seals as a matter of routine even though they may appear to be satisfactory.

2   The crankshaft front and new oil seals are renewed simply by driving the old ones from the timing cover or rear oil seal retainer and tapping in the new ones, taking care to have the lips of the seals facing the correct way.

3   The timing cover oil seal can be renewed while the engine is still in the vehicle provided that the radiator and crankshaft pulley are removed first.

4   Draw out the old seal using a small claw type puller. Clean the oil seal recess and tap in the new seal using a piece of tubing of suitable diameter.

5   The crankshaft rear oil seal and its retainer are only accessible after removal of either the engine or if the engine is left in the vehicle, then the gearbox must be withdrawn followed by the clutch and flywheel (or driveplate).

33 Crankcase and cylinder block - examination

1   With the engine completely stripped, this is a good time to check for cracks, stripped threads and other faults in the engine castings.

2   Leaking core plugs should be renewed. Old plugs can be extracted by drilling a hole in their centres and either levering them out or tapping a thread in them and then screwing in bolts with a distance

piece to draw them out. If the engine coolant has frozen at some time, the core plugs may have become partially displaced. Always clean the core plug recess and do not use more force than is necessary to ensure a tight fit when installing the new one.

3   If the camshaft bearings have been renewed, remember to install a new blanking plug at the rear end.

4   Finally probe all the oilways and galleries with wire and blow them out with compressed air, if available.

34 Engine reassembly - general

1   Prior to reassembling the engine, make sure that you have all the necessary gaskets ready, also a torque wrench and the correct range of socket and other spanners.

2   Always lubricate each component with fresh engine oil before reassembling or installing it.

35 Crankshaft and main bearings - refitting

Commence work on rebuilding the engine by replacing the crankshaft and main bearings.

1   Fit the five upper halves of the main bearing shells to their location in the crankcase, after wiping the recess clean (photo).

2   Note that on the back of each bearing is a tab which engages in the locating grooves in either the crankcase or the main bearing cap housings.

3   If new bearings are being fitted, carefully clean away all traces of the protective grease with which they are coated.

4   With the five upper bearing shells securely in place, wipe the lower bearing cap housings and fit the five lower bearing shells to their caps ensuring that the right shell goes into the right cap if the old bearings are being refitted (photo).

5   Wipe the recesses either side of the centre main bearing which locate the upper halves of the thrust washers.

6   Smear a little grease onto the thrust washers and slip into position (photo).

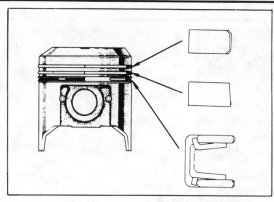

Fig. 1.21. Piston ring fitting diagram

Fig. 1.22. Camshaft sprocket dowel pin aligned with timing mark (3K series engine)

35.13 Checking crankshaft end-float with a feeler blade

36.1 Fitting crankshaft rear oil seal

36.2 Engine rear plate installed

36.3A Fitting flywheel

36.3B Tightening flywheel bolts

37.1 Installing a gudgeon pin (3K series engine only)

37.3 Fitting a gudgeon pin circlip

37.10 Fitting a piston ring compressor

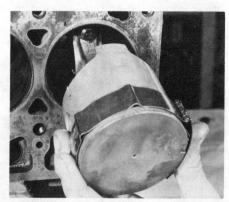

37.11 Inserting piston/connecting rod into cylinder bore

7 Generously lubricate the crankshaft journals and the upper and lower main bearing shells and carefully lower the crankshaft into position. Make sure it is the right way round (photo).
8 Fit the main bearing caps in position ensuring that they locate properly. The mating surfaces must be spotlessly clean or the caps will not seat correctly (photo).
9 When replacing the centre main bearing cap, ensure that the thrust washers, generously lubricated, are fitted with their oil grooves facing outwards and the locating tab of each washer is in the slot in the bearing cap (photo).
10 Replace the main bearing cap bolts and screw them up finger tight.
11 Test the crankshaft for freedom of rotation. Should it be very stiff to turn or possess high spots a most careful inspection must be made, preferably by a skilled mechanic with a micrometer to trace the cause of the trouble. It is very seldom that any trouble of this nature will be experienced when fitting the crankshaft.
12 Tighten the main bearing cap bolts to the specified torque wrench setting (photo).
13 Using a screwdriver between one crankshaft web and main bearing cap, lever the crankshaft forwards and check the endfloat using feeler gauges. This should be between 0.003 and 0.012 in (0.07 and 0.3 mm). If excessive new thrust washers or slightly oversize ones must be fitted (photo).

36 Crankshaft rear oil seal, flywheel (or driveplate) - refitting

1 Place a new gasket on the rear face of the crankcase and then install the crankshaft rear oil seal retainer complete with new oil seal (see Section 32) (photo).
2 Fit the engine rear plate (photo).
3 Install the flywheel, fit the bolts and tighten to the specified torque and bend up the lock plates (if fitted) (photos).
4 On vehicles equipped with automatic transmission, installation of the driveplate is very similar to installing the flywheel.

37 Piston/connecting rods - reassembly and refitting

1 On 3K Series engines, immerse the piston in hot water so that the gudgeon pin can be pushed in or out using finger pressure only.
2 Assemble the piston to the connecting rod so that the notch in the piston crown is on the same side as the 'Front' mark on the connecting rod (Fig. 1.20 - photo).
3 Install one gudgeon pin circlip, push in the gudgeon pin and fit the second circlip making sure that it is well seated in its groove (photo).
2 On 2T Series engines, the gudgeon pins require special equipment for removal and installation and as previously explained, the pistons will have been reassembled to the rods by your dealer.
3 If the same pistons are being used, then they must be mated to the same connecting rod with the same gudgeon pin. If new pistons are being fitted it does not matter which connecting rod is used, but the gudgeon pins are not to be interchanged.
4 If new piston rings have been supplied, it is best to check the compression rings in the piston grooves for side clearance and then insert them into the cylinder bores to check the end gaps. Although the clearances and gaps should be correct, it could be disastrous if the rings are tight when compared with the clearances in the Specifications. Slight easing of the rings in their grooves can be done by rubbing them on emery cloth held on a flat surface. Ring end gaps can be increased by grinding them squarely and carefully.
5 Fit the rings to the pistons over the crown of the piston by reversing the removal operations described in Section 17. The two upper piston rings are compression type while the lower one is an oil control ring.
6 Fit the oil control ring first. This requires a special technique for installation. First fit the bottom rail of the oil control ring to the piston and position it below the bottom groove. Refit the oil control expander into the bottom groove and move the bottom oil control ring rail up into the bottom groove. Fit the top oil control rail into the bottom groove.
7 Fit the second compression ring and then the top compression ring noting that the markings on the rings should face upwards (Fig. 1.21).
8 When all the rings are fitted, stagger their end gaps at equidistant points of a circle to prevent gas blow-by.

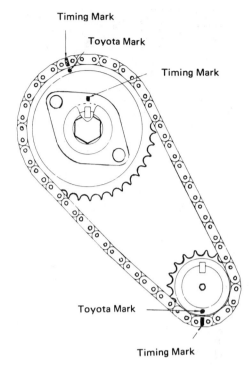

Fig. 1.23. Alignment of timing marks (2T series engine)

9 Wipe the first cylinder bore clean and smear it with clean engine oil.
10 Install a piston ring compressor to the piston rings, first having lubricated the rings liberally. Compress the rings (photo).
11 Lower the big-end of the connecting rod into the bore from above until the piston ring compressor is standing squarely on the top of the cylinder block and the piston crown notch is facing the front (timing cover) end of the engine (photo).
12 Place the wooden handle of a hammer on the crown of the piston and give the head of the hammer a sharp blow to drive the piston assembly into its bore. As this happens, the ring compressor will fly off.
13 Wipe the connecting rod half of the big-end bearing location and the underside of the shell bearing clean, (as for the main bearing shells) and fit the shell bearing in position with its locating tongue engaged with the corresponding groove in the connecting rod. Always fit new shells.
14 Generously lubricate the crankpin journals with engine oil and turn the crankshaft so that the crankpin is in the most advantageous position for the connecting rod to be drawn onto it.
15 Fit the bearing shell to the connecting rod cap in the same way as with the connecting rod itself (photo).
16 Generously lubricate the shell bearing and offer up the connecting rod bearing cap to the connecting rod. Fit the connecting rod retaining nut (photo).
17 Tighten the retaining nuts to the specified torque wrench setting (photo).

38 Camshaft and timing gear - refitting

1 Lubricate the camshaft bearings and install the camshaft taking great care not to damage the bearings with the lobes (photo).
2 Fit the camshaft thrust plate and tighten the two securing bolts to the specified torque.
3 If the engine front plate was removed, now is the time to refit it using a new gasket (photos).
4 Fit the timing chain damper (not the tensioner).
5 If the crankshaft sprocket was removed during overhaul, refit it now with its Woodruff key. Drive the sprocket onto the front end of

Fig. 1.24. Installing chain tensioner

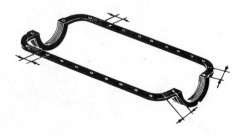

Fig. 1.25. Sump gasket (3K series engine)

the crankshaft with a suitable piece of tubing.

6 Turn the crankshaft (by means of the flywheel or driveplate) in the normal direction of rotation until No. 1 piston is at TDC. The Woodruff key in the crankshaft sprocket should be at the top and perpendicular.

7 *On 3K Series engines,* turn the camshaft until its sprocket mounting dowel pin is in alignment with the timing mark on the camshaft thrust plate (Fig. 1.22).

8 *On 2T Series engines,* turn the camshaft until its sprocket mounting Woodruff key is in alignment with the timing mark on the camshaft thrust plate (Fig. 1.23).

9 Engage the timing chain round the camshaft sprocket so that the 'bright' link on the chain is in alignment with the timing mark on the sprocket (Fig. 1.26).

10 Engage the other loop of the chain round the crankshaft sprocket so that the second 'bright' link is in alignment with the timing mark on the sprocket. Push the camshaft sprocket onto the camshaft mounting flange without moving any of the settings, screw in and tighten the sprocket securing bolt (Fig. 1.27).

11 Refit the chain tensioner (Fig. 1.24).

12 Fit a new timing cover gasket, bolt on the timing cover (complete with new oil seal) and fit the crankshaft pulley (photos).

13 Screw in and tighten the pulley bolt to the specified torque wrench setting. Hold the pulley against rotation by jamming the starter ring gear on the flywheel or by placing a block of wood between a crankshaft web and the inside of the crankcase.

39 Oil pump and sump - refitting

1 Offer up the oil pump complete with strainer to its crankcase location. Install the securing bolts and tighten to the specified torque wrench setting (photo).

2 *On 3K Series engines,* apply jointing compound to the areas shown on the sump gasket (Fig. 1.25).

3 *On 2T Series engines,* the gasket is flat and jointing compound should only be applied to the four corners.

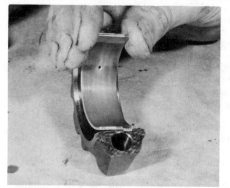

37.15 Fitting shell to big-end bearing cap

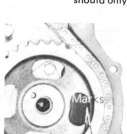

Fig. 1.26. Camshaft sprocket timing mark aligned with chain 'bright' link

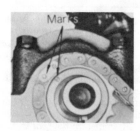

Fig. 1.27. Crankshaft sprocket timing mark aligned with chain 'bright' link

37.16 Fitting big-end cap

37.17 Tightening big-end cap nuts

38.1 Installing camshaft

4 Offer up the sump and bolt it into place (photo).
5 Check that the oil drain plug is tight.
6 If the sump and oil pump were removed with the engine still in position in the vehicle, the oil pump will have to be placed inside the sump and both components offered up together. Once the oil pump is located onto its mounting reach through the gap between the sump and crankcase and screw in the mounting bolts. This is a very difficult operation as explained in Section 13 of this Chapter.

40 Cylinder head - reassembly and refitting

1 Refit the valves to their guides in their original sequence, or if new valves are being fitted, in their 'ground in' sequence. Start by inserting No. 1 valve (nearest the front of the cylinder head).
2 Over the valve stem fit the plate washer, the valve stem oil seal (*2T Series engines only*), the valve spring, the spring cover (*3K Series engines only*) the spring retainer.
3 Compress the valve spring and drop in the split retaining collets.
4 Gently release the compressor making sure that the collets are secure in their valve stem cut outs. On 3K Series engines, install a new 'O' ring seal to the end of the valve stem.
5 Repeat the procedure on the remaining seven valves.
6 At this stage it is recommended that the tappets (cam followers) are fitted in their original positions.
7 After checking that both the cylinder block and head mating faces are perfectly clean, generously lubricate each cylinder bore with engine oil.
8 Always use a new cylinder head gasket. The old gasket will be compressed and incapable of giving a good seal as well as probably being damaged during removal.
9 Never smear gear or gasket cement either side of the gasket for pressure leaks may blow through it.
10 The cylinder head gasket is usually marked 'Front' and should be fitted in position according to the markings. Ensure that all holes line up.
11 Carefully lower the cylinder head onto the block so that it is correctly located on its dowels.
12 *On 3K Series engines,* insert all the cylinder head bolts finger tight and then tighten them to the specified torque in the sequence shown (Fig. 1.28).
13 *On 2T Series engines,* as the cylinder head bolts also retain the rocker shaft support pedestals, the following procedure must be followed.
14 Install the pushrods into their original positions.
15 Locate the rocker shaft assembly onto the cylinder head so that the 'F' mark on the end support pedestal is nearest the front (timing cover end) of the engine. The rocker arm adjuster screws should be fully unscrewed and the ends of the pushrods not trapped under the rocker

38.3A Engine front plate gasket installed

38.3B Fitting engine front plate

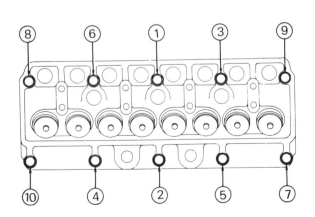
Fig. 1.28. Cylinder head bolt tightening sequence (3K series engine)

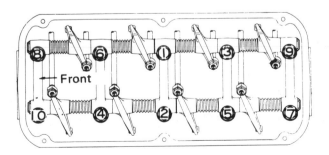
Fig. 1.29. Cylinder head bolt tightening sequence (2T series engine)

38.12A Timing cover gasket installed

38.12B Fitting the crankshaft pulley

39.1 Installing the oil pump

39.4 Refitting the sump

40.14 Installing pushrods (2T series engine)

40.15 Refitting rocker shaft assembly (2T series engine)

40.16 Tightening cylinder head bolts (2T series engine)

41.1 Installing pushrods (3K series engine)

41.3 Refitting rocker shaft assembly (3K series engine)

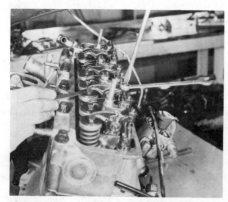
42.5 Checking a valve clearance (3K series engine)

43.6 Checking a valve clearance (2T series engine)

45.3 Fitting the oil filter cartridge

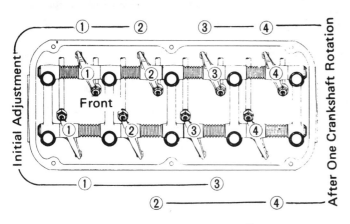

Fig. 1.30. Valve clearance adjustment diagram

arms as the rocker assembly is lowered (photo).
16 Screw in the cylinder head bolts finger tight and then fully tighten them to the specified torque wrench setting and in the sequence shown (Fig. 1.29 photo).
17 Engage the pushrods under the rocker arms and tighten the adjuster screws finger tight. The crankshaft will have to be rotated in order to be able to engage all the pushrods under the rocker arms.

41 Rocker shaft assembly (3K Series engines) - refitting

1 Install the pushrods into their original locations (photo).
2 Release all the rocker arm adjuster screws and unscrew them as far as possible.
3 Install the rocker shaft assembly, engaging the pushrods with the rocker arms (photo).
4 Insert the rocker support pedestal bolts and tighten them evenly a turn at a time to the specified torque wrench setting working from the centre bolts towards the ends.

42 Valve clearances (3K Series engine) - adjustment

1 The valve clearances should normally be adjusted with the engine at operating temperature. During engine reassembly, adjust them temporarily COLD. The importance of correct rocker arm valve stem clearances cannot be overstressed as they vitally affect the performance.
2 If the clearances are set too wide, the efficiency of the engine is reduced as the valves open late and close earlier than was intended. If the clearances are set too close there is a danger that the stem and pushrods upon expansion when hot will not allow the valves to close properly which will cause burning of the valve head and possible warping.
3 If the engine is in the car, to get at the rockers, it is merely necessary to remove the top cover. Once the cable support bracket and hose bracket have been detached undo and remove the two securing nuts and sealing washers then lift off the top cover and gasket.
4 It is important that the clearance is set when the tappet of the valve being adjusted is on the heel of the cam (ie; opposite the peak). This can be done by carrying out the adjustments in the following order, which also avoids turning the crankshaft more than necessary:

Valve fully open	Check and adjust
Valve number 8 Ex	Valve number 1 Ex
Valve number 6 In	Valve number 3 In
Valve number 4 Ex	Valve number 5 Ex
Valve number 7 In	Valve number 2 In
Valve number 1 Ex	Valve number 8 Ex
Valve number 3 In	Valve number 6 In
Valve number 5 Ex	Valve number 4 Ex
Valve number 2 In	Valve number 7 In

Valves are numbered from the front of the engine - inlet 2 - 3 - 6 - 7 exhaust 1 - 4 - 5 - 8.
5 The correct valve clearances are given in the 'Specifications' Section at the beginning of this Chapter. Clearance is obtained by slackening the hexagonal locknut with a spanner while holding the adjusting screw against rotation with a screwdriver. Then, still pressing down with the screwdriver, insert a feeler gauge of the required thickness between the valve stem and head of the rocker arm and adjust the adjusting screw until the feeler gauge will just move in and out without nipping. Then still holding the adjusting screw in the correct position, tighten the locknut (photo).

43 Valve clearances (2T Series engine) - adjustment

1 The valve clearances should normally be adjusted with the engine at operating temperature. During engine reassembly, they will have to be adjusted temporarily COLD and re-checked later.
2 If the engine is in the vehicle, first remove the air cleaner and the rocker cover.
3 Turn the crankshaft until No. 1 piston is at TDC on its compression stroke. Turn the crankshaft by applying a ring spanner to the pulley nut. TDC can be determined by reference to the ignition timing marks (see Chapter 4). Also check that both No. 1 cylinder valves are closed.
4 If you are at all doubtful about the position of No. 1 piston, remove the spark plug and as you turn the crankshaft place a finger over the plug hole and feel the compression being generated. As soon as this is felt, refer to the ignition timing marks.
5 Now check and adjust the valve clearances 1 and 2 on the INLET side and 1 and 3 on the EXHAUST side (Fig. 1.30).
6 The appropriate feeler blade should be a stiff sliding fit between the end of the valve stem and the rocker arm. If it is not, release the adjuster screw locknut and turn the adjuster screw in or out as necessary to achieve the gaps specified in the Specifications. Re-tighten the locknut (photo).
7 Now turn the crankshaft through one complete turn (360°) and check and adjust valve clearances 3 and 4 on the INLET side and 2 and 4 on the EXHAUST..

44 Engine ancillaries - refitting

1 Detailed fitting instructions for the ancillary components are given in the Chapters indicated but the following sequence should be followed.
Distributor (Chapter 4).
Carburettor and inlet manifold (Chapter 3).
Alternator (Chapter 10).
Fuel pump (Chapter 3).
Water pump (Chapter 2).
Starter motor (Chapter 10).
Thermostat (Chapter 2).
Exhaust manifold (Chapter 3).
Clutch assembly (Chapter 5).
Emission control equipment (Chapter 3).

45 Engine/transmission - refitting

1 The operations are reversals of removal and reference should be made to the appropriate Section at the front of this Chapter.
2 When reconnecting the engine and manual gearbox, make sure that the clutch driven plate has been centralised as described in Chapter 6.
3 Once the engine (and transmission) have been installed and there is no longer any danger of damaging it, fit a new oil filter cartridge. Smear the rubber sealing ring of the filter with grease and screw it on using hand pressure only. On no account use any sort of wrench or tool to tighten it. The engine, transmission and cooling system should now be filled (photo).
4 Remember to connect the battery and then double check for loose connections, hoses and controls and make sure that all tools have been removed from the engine compartment. It is only too easy to forget that ring spanner which is still attached to the crankshaft pulley bolt and was used to turn the crankshaft during valve adjustment!

46 Engine - initial start up after overhaul or major repair

1   Make sure that the battery is fully charged and that all lubricants, coolant and fuel are replenished.
2   If the fuel system has been dismantled, it will require several revolutions of the engine on the starter motor to pump petrol to the carburettor.
3   As soon as the engine fires and runs, keep it going at a fast tickover only (no faster) and bring it up to normal working temperature.
4   As the engine warms up, there will be odd smells and some smoke from parts getting hot and burning off oil deposits. Look for water or oil leaks which will be obvious if serious. Check also the clamp connection of the exhaust pipe to the manifold as these do not always 'find' their exact gas tight position until the warmth and vibration have acted on them, and it is almost certain that they will need tightening further. This should be done of course with the engine stationary.

5   When the engine running temperature has been reached, adjust the idling speed as described in Chapter 3.
6   Stop the engine and wait a few minutes to see if any lubricant or coolant leaks.
7   Road test the car to check that the timing is correct and giving the necessary smoothness and power. Do not race the engine. If new bearings and or pistons and rings have been fitted, it should be treated as a new engine and run in at reduced revolutions for 500 miles (800 km).
8   At the end of the first 1,000 miles (1,600 km) renew the engine oil and filter if a number of new components were installed at time of overhaul, also check the torque of the cylinder head bolts. To do this, unscrew each bolt (one at a time) in the specified sequence one quarter of a turn and then retighten it to torque. Follow with the next bolt in sequence and so on.
9   Finally check and adjust if necessary, the valve clearances.

47 Fault diagnosis - engine

Symptom	Reason/s
Engine fails to turn over when starter operated	Discharged or defective battery.
	Dirty or loose battery leads.
	Defective starter solenoid or switch.
	Engine earth strap disconnected.
	Jammed starter motor drive pinion.
	Defective starter motor.
Engine turns over but will not start	Ignition damp or wet.
	Ignition leads to spark plugs loose.
	Shorted or disconnected low tension leads.
	Dirty, incorrectly set or pitted contact breaker points.
	Faulty condenser.
	Defective ignition switch.
	Ignition LT leads connected wrong way round.
	Faulty coil
	Contact breaker point spring earthed or broken.
	No petrol in petrol tank.
	Vapour lock in fuel line (in hot conditions or at high altitude).
	Blocked float chamber needle valve.
	Fuel pump filter blocked.
	Choked or blocked carburettor jets.
	Faulty fuel pump.
	Too much choke allowing too rich a mixture to wet plugs.
	Float damaged or leaking or needle not seating.
	Float lever incorrectly adjusted.
Engine stalls and will not start	Ignition failure - sudden (see Chapter 4).
	Ignition failure - misfiring precludes total stoppage (see Chapter 4).
	Ignition failure - in severe rain or after traversing water splash.
	No petrol in petrol tank.
	Petrol tank breather choked.
	Sudden obstruction in carburettor.
	Water in fuel system.
Engine misfires or idles unevenly	Ignition leads loose.
	Battery leads loose on terminals.
	Battery earth strap loose on body attachment point.
	Engine earth lead loose.
	Low tension leads to SW and CB terminals on coil loose.
	Low tension lead from CB terminal side to distributor loose.
	Dirty or incorrectly gapped spark plugs.
	Dirty, incorrectly set or pitted contact breaker points.
	Tracking across distributor cap.
	Ignition too retarded.
	Faulty coil.
	Mixture too weak.
	Air leak in carburettor.
	Air leak at inlet manifold to cylinder head, or inlet manifold to carburettor.
	Incorrect valve clearances

Symptom	Reason/s
	Burnt out exhaust valves. Sticking or leaking valves. Worn or broken valve springs. Worn valve guides or stems. Worn pistons and piston rings.
Lack of power and poor compression	Burnt out exhaust valves. Sticking or leaking valves. Worn valve guides and stems. Weak or broken valve springs. Blown cylinder head gasket (accompanied by increase in noise) Worn pistons and piston rings. Worn or scored cylinder bores. Ignition timing wrongly set. Too advanced or retarded. Contact breaker points incorrectly gapped. Incorrect valve clearances. Incorrectly set spark plugs. Carburettor too rich or too weak. Dirty contact breaker points. Fuel filters blocked causing fuel starvation. Distributor automatic balance weights or vacuum advance and retard mechanisms not functioning correctly. Faulty fuel pump giving fuel starvation.
Excessive oil consumption	Badly worn, perished or missing valve stem oil seals. Excessively worn valve stems and valve guides. Worn piston rings. Worn pistons and cylinder bores. Excessive piston ring gap allowing blow-by. Piston oil return holes blocked.
Oil being lost due to leaks	Leaking oil filter gasket. Leaking rocker cover gasket. Leaking timing case gasket. Leaking sump gasket. Loose sump plug.
Unusual noises from engine	Worn valve gear (noisy tapping from rocker box).

Chapter 2 Cooling system

Refer to Chapter 13 for specifications and information applicable to 1979 US models.

Contents

Specifications

System type	Pressurised, pump assisted with thermostat. Later models have reservoir tank and electric cooling fan (3K Series engine)
Thermostat	
Type	Wax
Opening temperature:	
Standard	177 to 182°F (80.5 to 83.5°C)
Cold climates	188 to 193°F (86.5 to 89.5°C)
Fully open at	203°F (95°C)
Radiator type	Corrugated fin
Radiator pressure cap opening pressure	12.8 lb/in^2 (0.9 kg/cm^2)
Drivebelt deflection	½ in (12.0 mm)
Coolant capacity	6.8 Imp. qts (8.1 US qts/7.8 litre)

Torque wrench settings	lb/ft	Nm
Thermostat housing cover bolts	20	28
Water pump bolts	24	33

1 General description

1 The engine cooling water is circulated by a thermo syphon, water pump assisted system, and the coolant is pressurised. This is both to prevent the loss of water down the overflow pipe with the radiator cap in position and to prevent premature boiling in adverse conditions. (Fig. 2.1).

2 The radiator cap is, in effect, a safety valve designed to open at a pressure slightly above atmospheric pressure, which means that the coolant can reach a temperature above 212°F (100°C) before the pressure generated opens the valve. It then boils: steam escaping down the overflow pipe. When the temperature (therefore the pressure), decreases, the valve reseats until the temperature builds up again. (Fig. 2.3).

3 This means that the engine can operate at its most efficient temperature, which is around the normal boiling point of water, without the water boiling away.

4 In addition there is a vacuum valve in the cap which permits air to enter the system as it cools down thereby preventing collapse of the radiator or hoses.

5 It is, therefore, important to check that the radiator cap fitted is of the correct specification (the release pressure is stamped on the top) and in good condition, and that the spring behind the sealing washer

has not weakened. Some garages have a device in which radiator caps can be tested. Check that the rubber sealing washer is in good condition, without signs of distortion or perishing.

6 The system functions in the following manner: Cold water in the bottom of the radiator circulates up the lower radiator hose to the water pump where it is pushed around the water passages in the cylinder block, helping to keep the cylinder bores and pistons cool.

7 The water then travels up the cylinder head and circulates round the combustion space and valve seats absorbing more heat, and then when the engine is at its correct operating temperature water flows past the open thermostat into the upper radiator hose and so into the header tank.

8 The water travels down through the radiator where it is cooled by the passage of cold air through the radiator core, which is created by both the fan and the motion of the car. The water, now much cooler, reaches the bottom of the radiator, where upon the cycle is repeated.

9 When the engine is cold the thermostat (a valve which opens and closes according to the temperature of the water) maintains the circulation of the same water in the engine excluding that in the radiator.

10 Only when the correct minimum operating temperature has been reached does the thermostat begin to open, allowing water to return to the radiator.

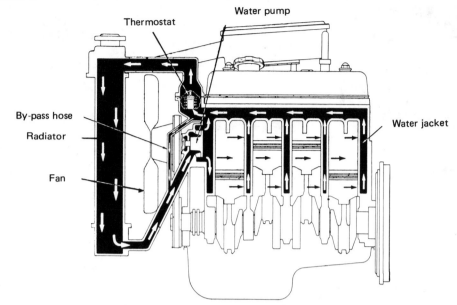

Fig. 2.1. Coolant flow diagram

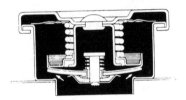

Vacuum Valve Operation

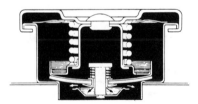

Pressure Regulating Valve Operation

Fig. 2.2. Diagram showing two functions of radiator cap

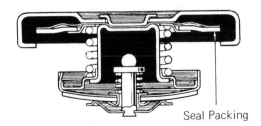

Seal Packing

Fig. 2.3. Radiator cap used in systems with expansion tank

11 The cooling system comprises the radiator, top and bottom hoses, heater hoses, the impeller water pump mounted on the front of the engine (it carries the fan blades and is driven by the fan belt), the thermostat and the drain plugs.
12 On many models, an expansion tank is fitted within the engine compartment into which the radiator overflow pipe fits. The tank is maintained half full with coolant and the radiator overflow pipe exhausts into it when the system is hot, and draws coolant from it as the system cools down. The arrangement prevents loss of coolant through the overflow pipe and in consequence, the system should require no regular topping up.
13 Late models equipped with a 3K Series engine have an electrically driven radiator cooling fan.
14 2T Series engines have a water heated inlet manifold.

2 Cooling system - draining

With the car on level ground drain the system as follows:
1 If the engine is cold, remove the filler cap from the radiator by turning it anticlockwise. If the engine is hot, then turn the filler cap very slightly until the pressure in the system has had time to disperse. Use a rag over the cap to protect your hand from escaping steam. If, with the engine very hot, the cap is released suddenly, the drop in pressure can cause the water to boil. With the pressure released the cap can be removed.
2 If antifreeze is in the cooling system drain it into a clean bowl for re-use. A wide bowl will be necessary to catch all the coolant.
3 Open the radiator and cylinder block drain plugs/taps. When the water has finished running probe the plug holes or taps with a piece of short wire to dislodge any particles of rust or sediment which may be causing a blockage and preventing all the coolant draining out (photo).

3 Cooling system - flushing

1 With time the cooling system will gradually lose its efficiency as the radiator becomes choked with rust scale, deposits from the water and other sediment. To clean the system out, first drain it - leaving the drains open. Then remove the radiator cap and leave a hose running in the radiator cap orifice for ten to fifteen minutes.
2 In very bad cases the radiator should be reverse flushed. This can be done with the radiator in position. A hose must be arranged to feed water into the lower radiator outlet pipe. Water, under pressure, is then forced up through the radiator and out of the header tank filler orifice.

2.3 Typical cylinder block drain plug

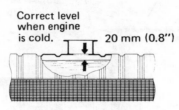

Fig. 2.4. Coolant level in radiator without expansion tank

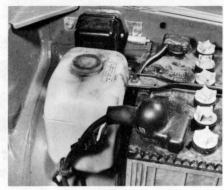

5.5 Expansion tank showing proximity of fusible link from battery

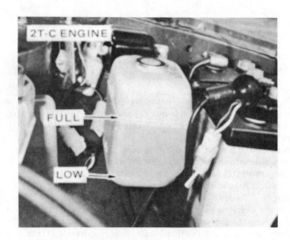

Fig. 2.5. Typical cooling system expansion tank

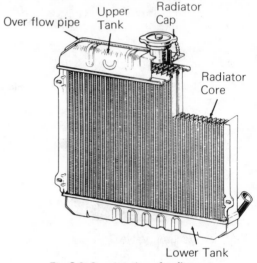

Fig. 2.6. Construction of radiator

3   The hose is removed and placed in the filler orifice and the radiator washed out in the usual manner.

4   Cooling system (without expansion tank) - filling

1   Close the radiator and cylinder block drain taps.
2   Move the heater control to HOT and then fill the system through the radiator filler neck, slowly, with anti-freeze mixture.
3   The coolant level should be about 0.75 in (19.0 mm) below the bottom of the filler neck (Fig. 2.4).
4   Refit the radiator cap and run the engine at a fast idle for a few minutes. Remove the cap and add more coolant if the level has dropped.
5   Refit the cap and switch off the engine.

5   Cooling system (with expansion tank) - filling

1   Refit and tighten the radiator and cylinder block drain plugs.
2   Move the heater control lever to HOT.
3   Remove the radiator cap and pour anti-freeze mixture slowly into the radiator until it is full to the brim.
4   Start the engine and let it run at a fast idle. The coolant level in the radiator will drop; make this up by adding more coolant until the level no longer falls.
5   Switch off the engine, refit the radiator cap and then fill the expansion tank to the level mark half way up its side (Fig. 2.5/photo).

6   Radiator - removal, servicing and refitting

1   Refer to Section 2 and drain the cooling system.
2   Slacken the clip which holds the top water hose to the radiator and carefully pull off the hose.
3   Slacken the clip which holds the bottom water hose to the radiator bottom tank and carefully pull off the hose.
4   On models fitted with the automatic transmission wipe the area around the oil cooler pipe unions and then detach these pipes from the radiator. Plug the end to prevent dirt entering the pipes.
5   If a fan shroud is fitted this should be detached from the radiator and placed over the fan.
6   Undo and remove the radiator securing bolts and lift the radiator upwards and away from the front of the car. The shroud (if fitted) may next be lifted away (photos).
7   *On 3K Series engines* having an electrically-operated cooling fan, detach the electrical leads from the fan motor and the thermostatic switch in the radiator. The radiator is removed complete with fan which is unbolted afterwards together with its supporting frame.
8   Clean out the inside of the radiator by flushing as described in Section 3. When the radiator is out of the car it is well worthwhile to invert it for reverse flushing. Clean the exterior of the radiator by hosing down the matrix with a strong water jet to clean away embedded dirt and debris, which will impede the air flow. When an oil cooler is fitted (automatic transmission) make sure no water is allowed to enter.
9   If it is thought that the radiator is partially blocked, a good proprietary chemical product should be used to clean it.
10 If the radiator is leaking, a temporary repair may be made by plugging with a fibreglass type filler or by using a leak sealing product in the coolant. Permanent repairs should be left to your dealer or a radiator repair specialist. Localised heat has to be used to repair a radiator, obviously experience is necessary otherwise the problem could be made worse (Fig. 2.6).
11 Inspect the radiator hoses for cracks, internal or external perishing and damage caused by the securing clips. Renew the hoses as necessary. Examine the radiator hose securing clips and renew them if they are

rusted or distorted.

12 Refitting the radiator is the reverse sequence to removal. If automatic transmission is fitted check and top-up its fluid level.

7 Thermostat - removal, testing and refitting

1 To remove the thermostat, partially drain the cooling system as described in Section 2. The removal of 4 pints (2.27 litres) is usually enough (Fig. 2.7).

2 Slacken the radiator top hose at the thermostat housing elbow and carefully draw it off the elbow (photo).

3 Unscrew the two bolts and spring washers securing the thermostat housing elbow, (photo) and lift the housing and gasket away. If it has stuck because a sealing compound has been previously used, tap with a soft faced hammer to break the seal.

4 Lift out the thermostat and observe if it is stuck open. If this is the case discard it.

5 Suspend it by a piece of string together with a thermometer in a saucepan of cold water. Neither the thermostat nor the thermometer should touch the sides or bottom of the saucepan or a false reading could be obtained.

6 Heat the water, stirring it gently with the thermometer to ensure temperature uniformity, and note when the thermostat begins to open. Note the temperature and this should be comparable with the figure given in the 'Specifications' Section at the beginning of this Chapter.

7 Continue heating the water until the thermostat is fully open. Now let it cool down naturally and check that it closes fully. If the thermostat does not fully open or close then it must be discarded and a new one obtained.

8 Refitting the thermostat is the reverse of the removal procedure. Always clean the mating faces thoroughly and use a new flange gasket.

8 Water pump - removal and refitting

1 Refer to Section 2 and drain the cooling system.
2 Refer to Section 6 and remove the radiator.
3 Refer to Section 12 and remove the fan belt.
4 Slacken the bottom hose clip and carefully detach the radiator top hose from the water pump.
5 Slacken the water bypass hose clip and carefully detach the bypass hose from the water pump. Disconnect the heater hose from the water pump.
6 Undo and remove the four bolts securing the fan and hub assembly from the water pump spindle flange and lift away the fan assembly.
7 Undo and remove the bolts securing the water pump body to the

6.6a Removing radiator

6.6b Removing radiator shroud

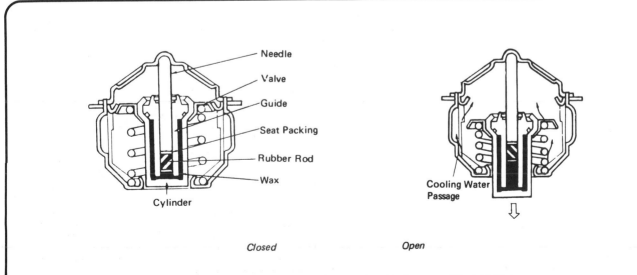
Fig. 2.7. Diagram of thermostat showing closed and open positions of valve

48

7.2 Disconnecting radiator top hose

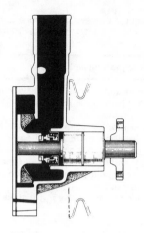

Fig. 2.8. Cut-away view of water pump

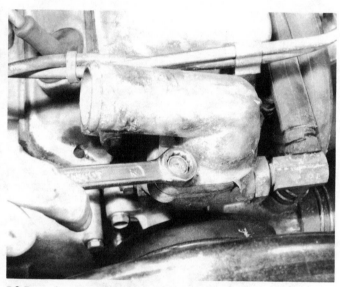

7.3 Removing thermostat housing cover bolts

Bearing

Pump Body

Fig. 2.9. Correctly installed bearing/spindle assembly in water pump body

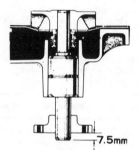

7.5mm

Fig. 2.10. Correctly installed pulley mounting flange on water pump spindle

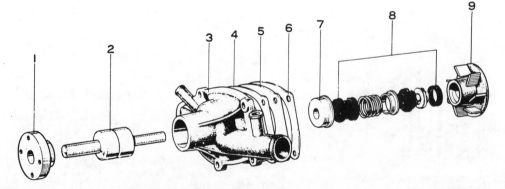

Fig. 2.11. Exploded view of water pump

1 Pulley mounting flange
2 Bearing/spindle assembly
3 Body
4 Gasket
5 Cover plate
6 Gasket
7 Seal cover
8 Seal assembly
9 Impeller

cylinder block. Lift away the water pump and recover the old gasket.
8   Refitting the water pump is the reverse sequence to removal, but the following additional points should be noted:

   a) Make sure the mating faces of the pump body and cylinder block are clean. Always use a new gasket.
   b) Refer to Section 12 and adjust the fan belt tension. If the belt is too tight undue strain will be placed on the water pump and alternator bearings. If the belt is too loose, it will slip and wear rapidly as well as giving rise to possible engine overheating and low alternator output.

9 Water pump - overhaul

1   When the water pump becomes noisy in operation or develops a leak, it is recommended that a new or factory reconditioned unit is obtained. This is usually a sound economic proposition compared with the purchase of spare parts for the original pump.
2   Where the spare parts are available, however, and it is preferred to overhaul the original unit, first clean away all external dirt.
3   With a suitable puller draw off the pulley mounting flange. (Fig. 2.11).
4   Again using the puller, draw off the impeller.
5   Remove the cover plate and the gaskets.
6   Extract the pump seal assembly.
7   Heat the pump body in boiling water and press the bearing/spindle assembly from the body. Discard the bearing/spindle once removed.
8   Heat the pump body again and press in the new bearing/spindle assembly. Use a tubular distance piece to do this which should be located on the shoulders of the bearing. Do not apply pressure to the end of the spindle. The shoulders of the bearing should be fitted flush with the end face of the pump body (Fig. 2.9).
9   Fit the seal assembly.
10 Fit the gasket and seal to the impeller.
11 Locate the cover plate and gasket and press the impeller to the water pump spindle so that the spindle end face is flush with the impeller. This will give an impeller to body clearance of 0.020 in (0.5 mm).
12 Support the end of the spindle and press the pulley mounting flange onto the spindle until the spindle projects 0.3 in (7.5 mm) (Fig. 2.10).

10 Anti-freeze solution

1   Apart from climatic considerations, anti-freeze mixture should always be used in the engine cooling system to help combat rust and corrosion.
2   Standard solutions should be renewed every year while 'long life' products usually give protection for periods of two years. Renew the coolant just before the winter season commences.
3   Before refilling the cooling system with anti-freeze solution it is best to drain and flush the system as described in Sections 2 and 3 of this Chapter.
4   Because anti-freeze has a greater searching effect than water make sure that all hoses and joints are in good condition.

5   Ideally, a 50% solution of anti-freeze with 50% soft water should be used but where financial considerations dictate weaker mixtures, the table gives the protection to be expected from smaller percentages.

%	complete protection	
25	− 11°C	12.2°F
30	− 14°C	6.8°F
35	− 19°C	− 2.2°F
40	− 23°C	− 9.4°F
45	− 29°C	− 20.2°F
50	− 35°C	− 31.0°F

Mix the equal quantity of anti-freeze with 4 pints (2.27 litres) of water and pour into the cooling system. Top-up with water and check the level as described in Sections 4 or 5.

11 Electric radiator fan (3K Series - late models)

1   This type of fan was introduced in order to improve fuel consumption and to reduce noise (Fig. 2.12).
2   The system incorporates the fan/motor assembly, a relay and a thermostatically operated switch together with the necessary circuitry.
3   The fan thermostat is pre-set to turn the fan on and off at pre-set temperature levels. This prevents over cool running when the ram effect of the cooling air provided by the forward motion of the vehicle is adequate.
4   **Take great care to keep away from the fan blades when working on an engine which is idling as the fan could cut in at any time due to the rise in coolant temperature level.**
5   If the fan fails to operate, first check the fuse in the main fuse block and then switch on the ignition and listen for a distinct 'click' from the relay which is located under the instrument panel (Fig. 2.14).
6   If these tests prove satisfactory, again turn on the ignition switch (engine cold) and disconnect the lead from the thermoswitch on the

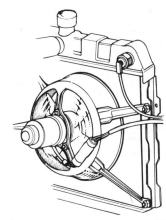

Fig. 2.12. Electrically-operated radiator fan (3K series engine)

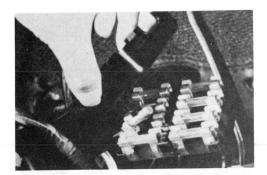

Fig. 2.13. Checking electrically-operated fan fuse

Fig. 2.14. Location of radiator fan relay

13.6 Location of water temperature sender switch

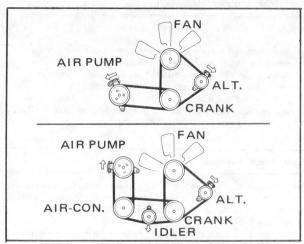

Fig. 2.15. Alternative drivebelt arrangements

radiator header tank. As soon as the lead is disconnected, the fan should turn. It should stop when the lead is reconnected.

7 Now check high temperature operation by letting the engine run until the coolant temperature reaches about 203°F (95°C) when the fan should cut in.

8 If these tests prove satisfactory then there must be a fault in the fan motor itself.

9 Renewal of the thermoswitch will of course necessitate partial draining of the cooling system.

12 Drivebelts - adjustment and renewal

1 The number of drivebelts fitted and their arrangement will depend upon the equipment fitted (water pump, emission control air pump, alternator, air conditioning compressor) (Fig. 2.15).

2 All belts should have a deflection at the centre point of their longest run of 0.5 in (12.0 mm).

3 Adjustment is carried out by slackening the mounting and adjustment link bolts of the driven component and pushing it in towards or pulling it away from the engine. The exception to this is that the air conditioner compressor has an idler pulley and the pulley should be moved to alter the belt tension.

4 If a drivebelt requires renewal because of wear, cuts, fraying or breakage, always release the mountings of the driven components and push it in towards the engine as far as possible so that the belt can be slipped over the pulley rims with the least strain.

5 With multiple belt arrangements, if a rear belt requires renewal then the ones nearer the front will of course have to be removed first.

6 With a new belt check the tension 250 miles (400 Km) after fitting.

7 Periodic checking of the belt tension is necessary and there is no hard and fast rule as to the most suitable interval, because a fan belt

does not necessarily stretch or wear at a predetermined rate. Assuming most owners check their own oil and water levels regularly it is suggested as a good habit to check the fan belt tension every time the bonnet is opened.

13 Water temperature gauge and sender - testing

1 Should a fault occur in the water temperature indicated reading, first check that the cooling system is correctly filled and then check the security of all connecting leads.

2 Reach up behind the temperature gauge (or withdraw the panel - see Chapter 10) and pull off the lead from the back of the gauge. Earth its terminal having a 12v, 3.4W bulb in the lead.

3 Turn the ignition on when the bulb should light up. After a few seconds, the bulb should start to flash and the gauge needle deflect.

4 If this test proves satisfactory, then check the sender unit by measuring the resistance between the sender unit terminal and earth using a circuit tester. The results should be in accordance with the following table:

Temperature	Resistance
122° F (50°C)	154 ohms
176°F (80°C)	25 ohms
212°F (100°C)	27.5 ohms
248°F (120°C)	16 ohms

5 Renewal of the gauge can be carried out after withdrawing the instrument panel (see Chapter 10).

6 Renewal of the sender unit can be carried out after unscrewing it from its thermostat housing location. The cooling system will of course have to be drained first (photo).

14 Fault diagnosis - cooling system

Symptom	Reason/s
Heat generated in cylinder not being successfully disposed of by radiator	Insufficient water in cooling system. Fan belt slipping (accompanied by a shrieking noise on rapid engine acceleration) Radiator core blocked or radiator grill restricted. Bottom water hose collapsed, impeding flow. Thermostat not opening properly Ignition advance and retard incorrectly set (accompanied by loss of power and perhaps, misfiring). Carburettor incorrectly adjusted (mixture too weak). Exhaust system partially blocked. Oil level in sump too low. Blown cylinder head gasket (water/steam being forced down the radiator overflow pipe under pressure). Engine not yet run-in. Brakes binding.
Too much heat being dispersed by radiator	Thermostat jammed open. Incorrect grade of thermostat fitted allowing premature opening of valve. Thermostat missing.
Leaks in system	Loose clips on water hoses. Top or bottom water hoses perished and leaking. Radiator core leaking. Thermostat gasket leaking. Pressure cap spring worn or seal ineffective. Blown cylinder head gasket (pressure in system forcing water/steam down overflow pipe). Cylinder wall or head cracked.

Chapter 3 Carburation, fuel and emission control systems

Refer to Chapter 13 for specifications and information applicable to 1979 US models.

Contents

Specifications

System type ... ... Rear mounted fuel tank, mechanical fuel pump and single or twin down draught carburettors depending upon vehicle model

Fuel tank capacity
1200E models ... ... 10 Imp. gal. 12 US gal. 45 litre
30 Series and 1600 models
   Hardtop, Liftback, Saloon and Coupe ... ... 11 Imp. gal. 13.2 Us gal. 50 litre
   Wagon ... ... 10.3 Imp. gal. 12.4 US gal. 47 litre

Fuel pump
Delivery capacity ... ... In excess of 900 cc per minute
Discharge pressure ... ... 2.8 to 4.3 lb/in^2 (0.2 to 0.3 kg/cm^2)

Carburettor
(3K series engine)

(All jet sizes in mm)	3K	3K-H	3K-B	3K-C
Primary main jet	1.04	1.05	0.83	1.00
Secondary main jet	1.44	1.41	1.26	1.41
Primary slow jet	0.47	0.45	0.44	0.47
Power jet	0.68	0.90	0.55	0.80
Pump jet	0.40	0.40	0.40	0.50
Accelerator pump stroke	0.24 in (6.0 mm)	0.138 in (3.5 mm)	0.138 and 0.177 in (3.5 and 4.5 mm)	0.1910 in (4.85 mm)
Idle speed (rev/min)				
Manual transmission	600	600	650	750
Automatic transmission	700	700	not fitted	not fitted
Maximum vacuum at idle				
Manual transmission	16.9 in Hg (430 mm Hg)	16.9 in Hg (430 mm Hg)	16.9 in Hg (430 mm Hg)	not applicable
Automatic transmission	15.7 in Hg (400 mm Hg)	15.7 in Hg (400 mm Hg)	not fitted	not fitted
Throttle positioner setting speed (rev/min)	—	—	—	1500

(2T series engine)

	2T	2T-B	2T-C (up to 1974)	2T-C (1975 on)
(All jet sizes in mm)				
Primary main jet	1.06	0.80	1.07	1.07 man. trans. 1.04 auto. trans. 1.10 man. trans. California
Secondary main jet	1.62	1.32	1.62	1.68
Primary slow jet	0.50	0.47	0.50	0.50 0.525 California
Secondary slow jet	0.70	0.55	0.70	0.70
Power jet	0.60	0.47	0.60	0.60 0.55 California
Pump jet	0.50	0.50	0.50	—
Accelerator pump stroke	0.20 in (5.0 mm)	0.12 in (3.0 mm)	0.20 (5.0 mm)	0.20 in (5.0 mm)
Idle speed (rev/min)				
Manual transmission	700 to 850	700 to 850	750 850 California	850
Automatic transmission	850 to 1000	not fitted	800 850 California	850
Fast idle speed (rev/min)	2500 to 2700	2400 to 2600	2600 to 2800	2800 to 3200 2500 to 2900 California
Throttle positioner setting speed (rev/min)				
Manual transmission	—	—	—	1400 to 1600
Automatic transmission	—	—	—	1300 to 1500
Maximum vacuum at idle				
Manual transmission	17.0 in Hg (430 mm Hg)	17.0 in Hg (430 mm Hg)	17.0 in Hg 430 mm Hg) 15.7 in Hg (400 mm Hg) California	in excess of 15.7 in Hg (400 mm Hg)
Automatic transmission	14.2 in Hg (360 mm Hg)	14.2 in Hg (360 mm Hg)	15.7 in Hg (400 mm Hg)	

1 General description

1 All models are fitted with a rear mounted fuel tank, and mechanically operated fuel pump.

2 All engines except 'B' suffix versions have a single dual barrel carburettor. 'B' version engines are fitted with two carburettors, also of dual barrel down draught type.

3 An in-line fuel filter is fitted within the engine compartment.

4 The air cleaner type and the complexity of the emission control system depends upon the operating territory for which the vehicle is destined.

5 The type of cold start device fitted may be a manual choke, an exhaust gas-heated or electrically-heated automatic choke depending upon the date of production and operating territory for which the vehicle is destined.

6 Some engines have a coolant heated intake manifold (see Section 24).

2 Air cleaner element - renewal

1 One of three different types of air cleaner may be encountered. The standard type has a slide on the air cleaner casing to vary the air intake source (cold or hot) according to season or climate conditions. The later standard air cleaner has a similar variable valve on the end of the cold air intake spout. Latest type (2T-C engines) air cleaners have an automatic air temperature control valve mounted on the air intake spout and no manual seasonal changes in the air intake source are therefore required (Fig. 3.1).

2 Access to the air cleaner element is obtained in the same way for all types. Unscrew and remove the wing nut and release the toggle clips and remove the lid. Extract the element (photo).

3 If the element is only discoloured in one spot move its position round to present a new surface to the air intake flow.

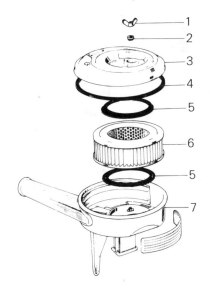

Fig. 3.1. Exploded view of standard type air cleaner

1 *Wing nut*   5 *Sealing ring*
2 *Sealing ring*   6 *Filter element*
3 *Lid*   7 *Casing*
4 *Gasket*

2.2 Removing air cleaner lid

2.8 Hose clipped to rear of air cleaner casing

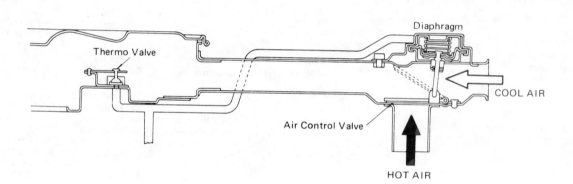

Fig. 3.2. Diagram of air temperature controlled air cleaner

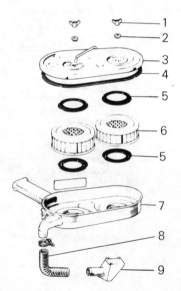

Fig. 3.3. Exploded view of standard type air cleaner fitted to twin
carburettor installations

1   Wing nuts   6   Filter element
2   Sealing washers   7   Casing
3   Lid   8   Hose
4   Gasket   9   Air intake
5   Sealing rings

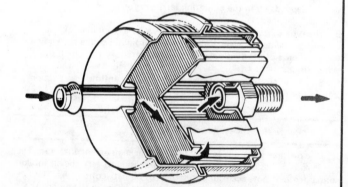

Fig. 3.4. Cut-away view of in-line fuel filter

4   If the element is dirty all round and oil stained or it has been in use for the specified mileage, extract it and discard it.

5   Wipe out the air cleaner casing and fit a new element, making sure that the rubber sealing rings are in good condition and are in position.

6   Refit the lid, wing nut and toggle clips.

7   On twin carburettor units, the procedure is similar except that two wing nuts are used and, of course, two new elements will be required (Fig. 3.3).

8   If the air cleaner is being removed completely from the engine, after unscrewing the securing bolts, do not pull the body away from the engine without having released the flexible pipes which are clipped to its underside (photo).

9   To verify that an automatic temperature control type air cleaner is functioning correctly, hold a mirror at the end of the air intake spout with the engine cold and running, check that the valve plate is closed against cold air. Allow the engine to warm up and again check to see that it is open to cold air.

3   Fuel filter - renewal

1   A disposable type fuel filter is fitted in the line to the fuel pump (Fig. 3.4).

2   At the specified intervals, disconnect the fuel lines from the filter and discard the filter.

3   Fit the new filter making sure that the directional arrow on the outside of the unit is pointing in the direction of fuel flow to the pump.

4   Later types of filter are mounted in a clip at the side of the engine compartment and have inlet and outlet nozzles placed at right-angles so that there can be no confusion as to which way to connect them.

4   Fuel pump - general description

1   The mechanically operated fuel pump is actuated through a spring loaded rocker arm. One end of the split rocker arm bears against an eccentric on the camshaft and the other end operates the diaphragm. pullrod (Fig. 3.5).

2   As the engine camshaft rotates the eccentric moves the pivoted rocker arm outwards which in turn pulls the diaphragm pullrod and diaphragm drum against the pressure of the diaphragm spring.

3   This creates sufficient vacuum in the pump chamber and non-return inlet valve.

4   The rocker arm is held in constant contact with the eccentric by an anti-rattle spring, and as the engine camshaft continues to rotate, the eccentric allows the rocker arm to move inwards. The diaphragm spring is thus free to push the diaphragm upwards forcing the fuel in the pump chamber out to the carburettor through the non-return outlet valve.

5   When the float chamber in the carburettor is full the float chamber needle valve will close so preventing further flow from the fuel pump.

6   The pressure in the delivery line will hold the diaphragm downwards. against the pressure of the diaphragm spring, and it will remain in this position until the needle in the float chamber opens to admit more fuel.

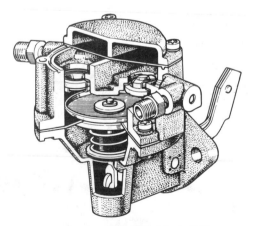

Fig. 3.5. Cut-away view of fuel pump

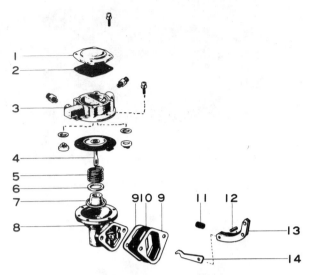

Fig. 3.6. Exploded view of fuel pump

1	Cover	8	Lower body
2	Gasket	9	Gaskets
3	Upper body	10	Insulator
4	Diaphragm	11	Spring
5	Spring	12	Pivot pin
6	Oil seal retainer	13	Rocker arm
7	Oil seal	14	Link

5   Fuel pump - testing in vehicle

1   Where lack of fuel is evident at the carburettor, (level visible through float chamber sight glass) first check that there is fuel in the tank and that the in-line filter is not choked through not being renewed at the specified mileage.

2   Disconnect the fuel inlet pipe from the carburettor and place its open end in a container.

3   Disconnect the HT lead from the coil to prevent the engine firing and turn the ignition switch to 'start'. Let the starter motor turn the engine over for several revolutions when regular spurts of fuel should be seen being ejected from the open end of the fuel pipe.

4   If no fuel is observed then the pump must be faulty, there is a break in the fuel line or tank union is allowing air instead of fuel to be drawn in.

6   Fuel pump - removal, overhaul and refitting

1   Disconnect the flexible inlet hose and outlet pipe from the fuel pump. Tape over the ends to stop dirt entering.

2   Undo and remove the nuts and spring washers or bolts securing the fuel pump to the engine. Lift away the fuel pump. Recover the gasket.

3   Before dismantling, clean the exterior of the pump and wipe dry with a clean non-fluffy rag.

Undo and remove the screws securing the top cover to the upper body. Lift away the screws, spring washer, top cover and gasket (Fig. 3.6).

Make a mark across the upper and lower bodies so that they may be refitted in their original positions.

4   Undo and remove the screws and spring washers securing the two body halves together.

5   Carefully lift off the upper body. It is possible for the diaphragm to stick to the mating flanges. If this is the case free with a sharp knife.

6   Using a parallel pin punch carefully tap out the rocker arm pin Fig. 3.7.

7   Lift out the rocker arm and recover the spring.

8   Depress the centre of the diaphragm and detach the rocker arm link. Lift away the rocker arm link (Fig. 3.8).

9   Carefully lift the diaphragm and spring up and away from the lower body.

10 The valves should not normally require renewal but in extreme cases

Fig. 3.7. Driving out fuel pump rocker arm pin

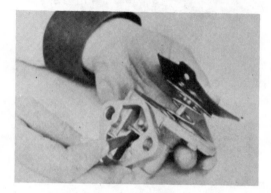

Fig. 3.8. Removing rocker arm link

this may be done. Carefully remove the peening and lift out the valves. Note which way round they are fitted.

11 To remove the oil seal from the lower body, note which way round it is fitted and then prise out the seal and retainer using a screwdriver.

12 Carefully examine the diaphragm for signs of splitting, cracking or deterioration. Obtain a new one if suspect.

13 Obtain a new oil seal ready for reassembly.

14 Inspect the pump bodies for signs of cracks or stripped threads. Also inspect the rocker arm, link and pin for wear. Obtain new parts as necessary.

15 Clean the recesses for the two valves and refit the valves making sure they are the correct way round. Use a sharp centre punch to peen the edges of the casting.

16 Carefully refit the oil seal and retainer.

17 Replace the diaphragm spring and insert the diaphragm pull rod through the oil seal.

18 Insert and hook the end of the rocker arm link onto the end of the pullrod.

19 Replace the rocker arm into the lower body and locate the spring.

20 Insert the rocker arm pin, lining up the hole with a small screwdriver. Peen over the pin hole edges with a sharp centre punch to retain the pin in position.

21 Fit the upper body to the lower body and line up the previously made marks. Where retaining screws are used these should next be refitted.

22 Refit the cover and gasket to the upper body and secure with the screws and spring washers.

23 The fuel pump is now ready for refitting to the engine, which is a reversal of removal.

7 Fuel return cut-off valve (2T-C engine)

1 On late models with a 2T-C engine, a fuel cut-off valve is used in conjunction with the fuel pump.

2 The purpose of this device is to control the amount of fuel returned to the tank from the pump in accordance with the prevailing engine load.

3 To test the valve for correct functioning, disconnect the pipe from the return nozzle on the valve and then connect a spare piece of tubing

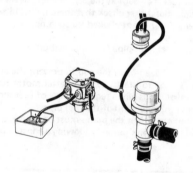

Fig. 3.9. Fuel return cut-off valve arrangement and fuel flow test

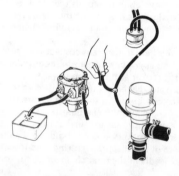

Fig. 3.10. Fuel return cut-off valve arrangement and vacuum test

8.3 Fuel tank drain plug and suspension strap (Lift-back)

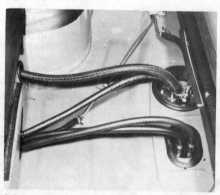

8.8 Fuel tank breather hoses (Lift-back)

8.10 Fuel tank sender unit cover plate (Lift-back)

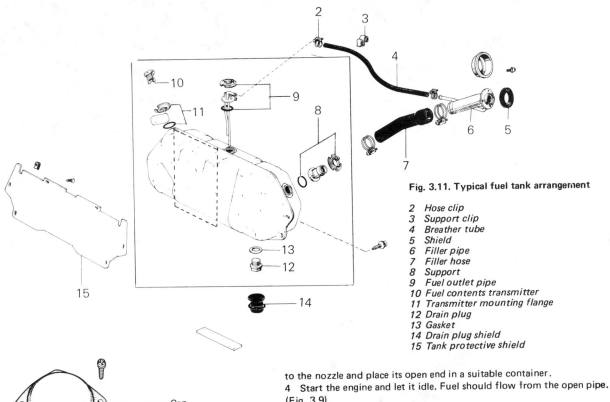

Fig. 3.11. Typical fuel tank arrangement

2   Hose clip
3   Support clip
4   Breather tube
5   Shield
6   Filler pipe
7   Filler hose
8   Support
9   Fuel outlet pipe
10 Fuel contents transmitter
11 Transmitter mounting flange
12 Drain plug
13 Gasket
14 Drain plug shield
15 Tank protective shield

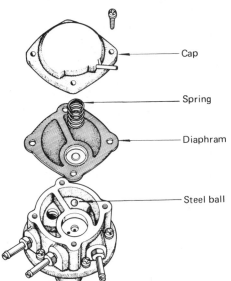

Fig. 3.12. Components of fuel cut-off valve

- Cap
- Spring
- Diaphram
- Steel ball

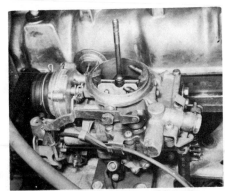

11.1 Typical carburettor used on 2T series engine

to the nozzle and place its open end in a suitable container.
4   Start the engine and let it idle. Fuel should flow from the open pipe.
(Fig. 3.9).
5   Now pinch the vacuum pipe which runs to the valve. The fuel flow
should stop (Fig. 3.10).
6   Any fault in the valve can usually be traced to the diaphragm. Dismantle the valve by extracting the cover screws. Do not lose the steel
ball which lies in the centre recess within the pump. (Fig. 3.12).

8   Fuel tank - removal, renovation and refitting

1   The rear mounted fuel tank may be suspended under the rear of the
car (Liftback), fitted at the side of the luggage boot (Saloon) or located
under the luggage area floor (Estate Wagon). (Fig. 3.11).
2   If a leak is detected in a fuel tank, a temporary repair may be made
with fibreglass or similar material but never attempt to weld or solder a
leak. Renew the tank complete or the take it for professional
repair.
3   To remove a fuel tank, drain or syphon out the fuel (photo).
4   Remove the panel or shield which covers the tank.
5   Disconnect the fuel filler pipe.
6   Disconnect the fuel outlet pipe.
7   Disconnect the leads to the fuel level sender unit.
8   Disconnect all breather or fuel evaporative system hoses (see Section
27) according to type (photo).
9   Disconnect the tank mounting straps or withdraw the mounting
bolts and lift the tank from the vehicle.
10 The fuel contents sender unit can be unscrewed using a suitable pin
wrench (photo).
11 Water and sediment often collect at the base of the tank, this can
be removed using two or three changes of clean paraffin with a final
rinse of fuel. Shake the tank and tip out the flushing solvent but having
removed the sender unit.
12 Refitting is a reversal of removal but always use a new sealing gasket
for the sender unit.

9   Fuel contents gauge and sender unit - testing

1   Should a fault develop in the fuel gauge reading, first check the
security of the electrical leads to the gauge and to the sender unit in the
fuel tank.

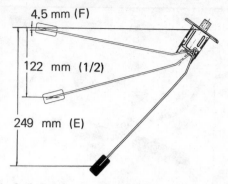

Fig. 3.13. Fuel tank transmitter float arm positions

Fig. 3.14. Carburettor adjusting screws (3K series engine except - 3K-B and 3K-C)

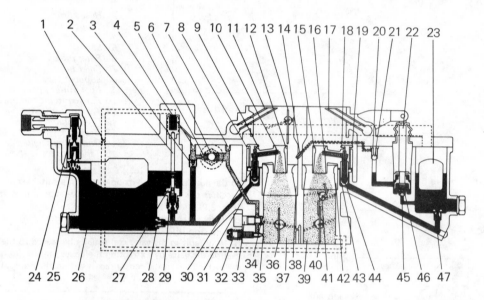

Fig. 3.15. Sectional view of carburettor (3K series engine type)

1 Restrictor	13 Choke valve plate	25 Needle valve	37 Primary bore
2 Power piston	14 Pump jet	26 Float	38 Primary large venturi
3 Slow jet	15 Secondary small venturi	27 Power valve	39 Secondary bore
4 Primary air bleed	16 Secondary main nozzle	28 Primary main jet	40 Secondary throttle valve plate
5 Economiser jet	17 Air vent tube	29 Power jet	41 High speed valve
6 Solenoid valve (3K-C engine only)	18 Main air bleed	30 Main air bleed tube	42 Secondary large venturi
7 Primary air bleed	19 Secondary vapour bleed	31 Tube	43 Tube
8 Primay vapour bleed	20 Pump discharge weight	32 Idle mixture adjuster screw	44 Main air bleed tube
9 Main air bleed	21 Pump discharge steel ball	33 Plug	45 Inlet ball
10 Primary main nozzle	22 Pump plunger	34 Slow port	46 Ball retainer
11 Air vent tube	23 Float	35 Idle port	47 Secondary main jet
12 Primary small venturi	24 Fuel inlet needle valve seat	36 Primary throttle valve	

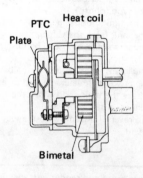

Choke cross-section

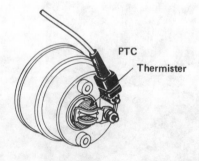

PTC thermistor

Fig. 3.16. Electrically heated type automatic choke

2 Disconnect the lead which runs from the fuel gauge to the sender unit, from the back of the fuel gauge.

3 From this terminal on the gauge run a lead to a good earth incorporating a 3.4W bulb in the lead. Turn the ignition switch on when the test bulb should light and then start to flash after a few seconds. The gauge needle should also deflect. If this test proves satisfactory then the gauge is in good condition and the sender unit is probably at fault.

4 To check the sender unit, remove it from the fuel tank as described in the preceding Section.

5 Using a circuit tester, measure the resistance between the terminal on the sender unit and earth. Move the float arm smoothly and compare the readings obtained with those shown in the following table. (Fig. 3.13).

Float position	Resistance
FULL	3 ± 2.1 ohms
½ FULL	32.5 ± 4.8 ohms
EMPTY	110 ± 7.7 ohms

6 The fuel level warning light is actuated by a level switch mounted on the sender unit. When just over 1 Imp. gal. (5.0 litre) of fuel remains in the tank the light comes on as a reminder to re-fuel.

10 Accelerator linkage - removal, refitting and adjustment

1 Generally, 1200 models are fitted with an accelerator cable while 30 series and 1600 models have rod and balljoint linkage.

2 To remove either type, disconnect the ends of the cable or rods from the lever on the carburettor and from the accelerator pedal.

3 Release the cable grommets and support bracket.

4 With rod systems, unbolt the trunnions which support the iron rods.

5 Refitting is a reversal of removal then adjust the cable outer conduit or the effective length of the control rods so that when the accelerator pedal is depressed to within 0.5 in (12.7 mm) of the floor, the throttle valve plate in the carburettor is fully open.

6 On vehicles equipped with automatic transmission, disconnect the downshift cable from the carburettor until the accelerator linkage has been set and then connect and adjust the downshift cable as described in Part 2 of Chapter 6.

11 Carburettors - description

1 The carburettor fitted to all models is of dual barrel down draught type. According to engine type and operating territory, the differences between the units used includes the type of choke, which may be manual or automatic (exhaust gas or electrically heated) and the various modifications dictated by the complexity of the emission control system fitted. (Fig. 3.15) (photo).

2 On 'B' suffix engines twin carburettors are used but the overhaul and adjustment procedures are the same as for single units unless described otherwise.

3 The carburettor design gives correct and efficient performance under all operating conditions so giving a good engine performance whilst maintaining an acceptable fuel economy. It is similar to two single barrel carburettors but built into one body.

4 The primary system incorporates a double type venturi whilst the secondary system is provided with a triple type venturi. Each system comprises an air horn, main nozzle and throttle valve. One set forms the primary circuit whilst the other set forms the secondary circuit. The primary circuit comprises the low speed, high speed, power valve, accelerating and choke systems and is able to supply the correct air/fuel ratio for normal operation.

5 When the throttle valve is fully open as for fast motoring or acceleration, or a fully laden car, the secondary system also operates to supply an additional air/fuel mixture together with the primary circuit. The throttle valves of both the primary and secondary circuits are operated by a linkage which is interlocked so enabling both the throttle valves to open fully simultaneously. The high speed valve is located in the secondary circuit together with the power valve and enables the performance range to be extremely smooth.

12 Idle speed (3K series engines except 3K-B and 3K-C) - adjustment

1 Bring the engine to normal operating temperature.

2 Turn the idle mixture screw fully in (do not force it home) and then unscrew it 3 turns. (Fig. 3.14).

3 Connect a vacuum gauge to the inlet manifold in place of the screw plug.

4 Connect a tachometer to the engine in accordance with the manufacturer's instructions.

5 Start the engine and turn the throttle speed screw until the idling speed is as specified for the type of transmission.

6 Now turn the idling mixture screw in or out until the highest vacuum is indicated on the gauge.

7 Readjust both screws until the highest vacuum is obtained at the specified idling speed.

8 Now screw in the idle mixture screw until the idling speed and vacuum reading both just start to drop. Switch off the engine.

9 Disconnect the vacuum gauge, refit the plug, disconnect the tachometer.

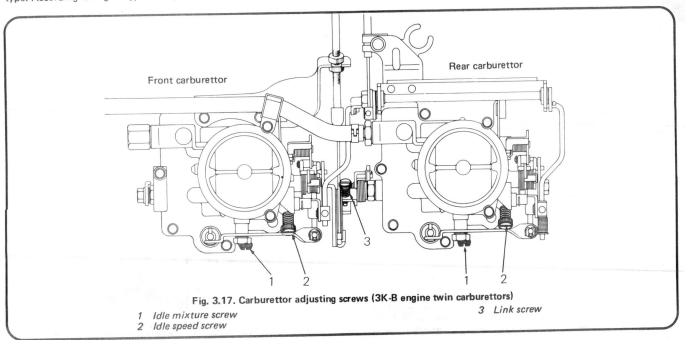

Fig. 3.17. Carburettor adjusting screws (3K-B engine twin carburettors)

1 Idle mixture screw
2 Idle speed screw
3 Link screw

13 Idle speed (3K-B engine) - adjustment

1   To adjust this twin carburettor installation, first bring the engine to normal operating temperature.
2   Connect a vacuum gauge to the inlet manifold and a tachometer to the engine (if not already so equipped) in accordance with the manufacturers instructions.
3   Separate the two carburettors by loosening the link adjusting screw (3). Remove the air cleaner. (Fig. 3.17).
4   Using a carburettor balancer (flow meter) turn each throttle speed screw until the air intake flow is equal when the balancer is used on first one carburettor and then the other and at the same time the idling speed is as specified.
5   Now turn each of the idle mixture screws until the maximum vacuum reading is obtainable on the gauge.
6   If as a result of the last adjustment, the engine idling speed has altered, repeat all the adjustments again to bring it to specified level.
7   Now turn each idle mixture screw in to the point where any further movement of the screw would cause the speed and vacuum to drop.
8   Reconnect the carburettors by tightening the link screw (3) until it just makes contact with the lever on No. 1 carburettor.
9   Switch off the ignition, remove the tachometer and vacuum gauge and refit the air cleaner.

14 Idle speed (3K-C engine) - adjustment

1   Bring the engine to normal operating temperature. Do not remove the air cleaner.
2   Turn the throttle speed screw until the idle speed is 750 rev/min.
3   Turn the idle mixture screw in a clockwise direction to the point where the engine becomes very rough and immediately before it stalls. (Fig. 3.18).
4   Now turn the idle mixture screw in an anti-clockwise direction two complete turns.
5   Turn the throttle speed screw to regain the specified idle speed.
6   Repeat the foregoing adjustments.
7   Switch off the engine.

15 Idle speed (2T series engines except 2T-B and 2T-C) - adjustment

1   The procedure is as described in Section 12 for the 3K series engine. Refer to Specifications for idling speeds.

16 Idle speed (2T-B engine) - adjustment

1   The procedure is similar to that described in Section 13 for the 3K-B engine twin carburettor unit except that before adjustment is carried out, do not remove the air cleaner and make sure that the crankcase ventilation hose (PCV) is connected. Refer to the Specifications for idling speeds.

17 Idle speed (2T-C engine) - adjustment

1   Before commencing adjustment check the following:

    a) Engine is at normal operating temperature
    b) Choke valve plate fully open.
    c) All electrical equipment is switched off.
    d) All vacuum hoses are connected.
    e) Ignition timing correctly set.
    f) Transmission is neutral or 'N'.
    g) Air cleaner installed.

2   Start the engine and turn the idle speed screw until the engine is running at specified level.
3   Now turn the idle mixture screw until the position is obtained where the engine speed is at its highest.
4   Turn the idle speed screw until the engine is running at 830 rev/min.
5   Repeat the last two operations until no further increase can be obtained with movement of the idle mixture screw over 830 rev/min.

Fig. 3.18. Carburettor adjusting screws (3K-C engine)

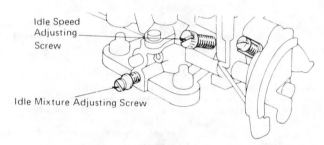

Fig. 3.19. Carburettor adjusting screw (2T-C engine)

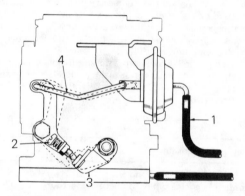

Fig. 3.20. Throttle positioner (3K-C engine)

1   Vacuum hose   3   Lever
2   Adjuster screw   4   Link rod

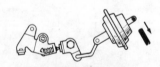

Fig. 3.21. Throttle positioner (2T-C engine)

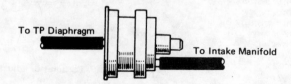

Fig. 3.22. Throttle positioner filter

6   Now slowly turn the idle mixture screw in a clockwise direction until the idling speed drops to 750 rev/min. This is known as the 'lean drop' method (Fig. 3.19).
7   Switch off the engine.

18 Exhaust emission level - checking

1   The operations described in the previous sections for adjustment of the idling speed should always be verified with a CO meter attached to the exhaust pipe to monitor the CO concentration in the emitted gas.
2   This requirement applies particularly to 'C' suffix engines and vehicles operating in North America. Before measuring the CO level, increase the engine speed to 2000 rev/min and hold it there for between ½ and 1 minute, then measure within three minutes of returning to idle.
3   Refer to the individual vehicle sticker for specified permissible CO concentration level which is usually between 3 and 4%.
4   On many later vehicles, the carburettor adjustment screws are fitted

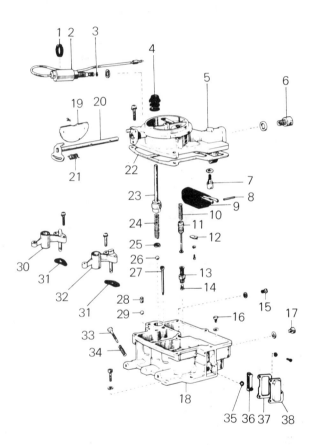

Fig. 3.23. Carburettor body and air horn components (3K series engine)

1 Support (3K-C only)	20 Choke valve spindle
2 Solenoid fuel cut-off valve (3K-C only)	21 Relief spring
	22 Gasket
3 'O' ring (3K-C only)	23 Pump plunger
4 Flexible boot	24 Damping spring
5 Air horn	25 Choke ball retainer
6 Union	26 Steel ball
7 Fuel inlet needle valve	27 Slow jet
8 Float pivot pin	28 Pump discharge weight
9 Float	29 Steel ball
10 Power piston spring	30 Primary small venturi
11 Power piston	31 Gasket
12 Power piston stop	32 Secondary small venturi
13 Power valve	33 Throttle speed adjuster screw
14 Power jet	34 Spring
15 Primay main jet	35 'O' ring
16 Secondary main jet	36 Thermostatic valve
17 Main passage plug	37 Gasket
18 Body	38 Cover
19 Choke valve plate	

with limiter caps. Under normal circumstances, adjustment should be able to be carried out within the travel of the screws permitted by these caps. Where this is not so or if the carburettor has been extensively overhauled then the limiter caps should be broken off. After adjustment, new caps should be fitted to the screws so that the cap stops are at the centre point of travel.

19 Throttle positioner - description and adjustment

1   This device is fitted to the carburettor on 3K-C and 2T-C engines and it is designed to hold the throttle valve plate slightly open during deceleration when the accelerator is released. Without this, the throttle valve plate would close to the idle position and in consequence compression pressure would drop, the mixture becoming rich and would then not burn completely so causing increased emission of noxious fumes.
2   On 3K-C engines, to adjust the throttle positioner, first run the engine to normal operating temperature and then check the idle speed is as specified (Fig. 3.20).
3   Disconnect the vacuum hose from the diaphragm unit of the throttle positioner.
4   Rev up the engine and release the accelerator pedal sharply. The throttle positioner screw should now be holding the throttle valve open by pressing against the throttle lever of the carburettor.
5   This 'above idling' speed must be checked visually on the vehicle tachometer or a separate instrument attached to it temporarily. The speed should be approximately 1500 rev/min.
6   If the engine speed with throttle positioner in action is outside the specified range, turn the adjuster screw and re-check.
7   On 2T-C engines, the checking and adjustment procedure is similar except that the 'speeds with the throttle positioner in action should conform to the following and the different arrangement of the throttle positioner adjuster screw should be noted.

Manual transmission	1400 to 1600 rev/min
Automatic transmission	1300 to 1500 rev/min

8   On completion of adjustment, reconnect the vacuum hose when the engine speed will decrease to normal idling. Switch off the engine.
9   On some models, a vacuum control valve filter is fitted in the throttle positioner system. The filter should be removed, cleaned with compressed air and then refitted (Fig. 3.22).

20 Carburettor - removal and refitting

1   Remove the air cleaner.
2   Disconnect the throttle linkage from the carburettor.
3   Disconnect either (i) the manual choke cable or (ii) the pipes which convey the exhaust gas to the automatic choke housing or (iii) the electrical leads to the electrically heated automatic choke.
4   Disconnect the fuel inlet and return pipes from the carburettor.
5   Disconnect the distributor vacuum pipe from the carburettor.
6   Unscrew and remove the carburettor mounting bolts and washers and lift the unit from the inlet manifold.
7   Remove the gasket and clean the mating flanges.
8   Refitting is a reversal of removal but always use a new flange gasket.
9   On twin carburettor units, the procedure is similar except that if one carburettor is being removed at a time then the connecting link between the two units must be disconnected.

21 Carburettor - overhaul

1   The carburettor should not be dismantled unnecessarily. Infact, removal of the air horn in order to clean out the float chamber is usually sufficient and this can be done without removing the unit from the manifold (Fig. 3.23).
2   If considerable wear has occurred, it is often more economical to purchase a new or rebuilt unit rather than to obtain individual spare parts as even then, the bushes and bearing surfaces within the carburettor body may be worn and this wear cannot be rectified.
3   Complete dismantling instructions are given in this Section, but only carry out those operations which are needed to give access to a particular

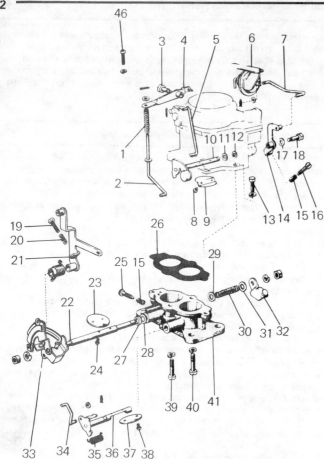

Fig. 3.24. Throttle valve housing components (3K series engine)

1	Pump arm spring	21	Fast idle adjusting lever
2	Link	22	Primary throttle spindle
3	Accelerator pump arm pivot screw	23	Primary throttle valve plate
4	Pump lever	24	Valve plate screw
5	Fast idle connector	25	Idle mixture screw
6	Throttle positioner (3K-C only)	26	Gasket
7	Link rod (3K-C only)	27	Collar
8	Valve plate screw	28	Shim
9	Valve plate	29	Shim
10	Valve spindle	30	Spring
11	Shim	31	Shim
12	Retaining clip	32	Throttle lever
13	Screw	33	Primary throttle arm
14	Stop lever (3K-C only)	34	Link
15	Idle screw spring (3K-C)	35	Secondary throttle return spring
16	Idle speed screw (3K-C)	36	Secondary throttle spindle
17	Shim (3K-C)	37	Secondary throttle valve plate
18	Pivot screw (3K-C)	38	Valve plate screw
19	Fast idle screw	39	Set screw
20	Fast idle spring	40	Set screw
		41	Flange/throttle housing

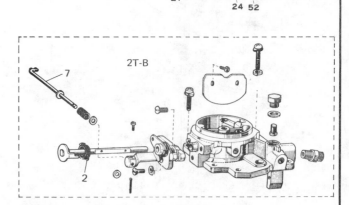

2T-B

Fig. 3.25. Air horn and body components (2T series engine)

1	Fast idle cam	30	Choke valve plate
2	Choke valve plate spindle	31	Flexible boot
3	Choke piston link	32	Plug
4	Vacuum piston	33	Fuel inlet filter
5	Fast idle cam follower	34	Filter
6	Auto choke housing cover	35	Plug
7	Link	36	Unions
8	Thermostatic valve cover	37	Fuel inlet needle valve seat gasket
9	Secondary small venturi	38	Needle valve
10	Gasket	39	Float
11	Primary small venturi	40	Float pivot pin
12	Gasket	41	Power piston spring
13	Auto choke housing	42	Power piston
14	Flexible boot	43	Pump plunger
15	Sliding rod	44	Power valve
16	Gasket	45	Power jet
17	Thermostatic valve	46	Pump damping spring
18	Slow jet	47	Check ball retainer
19	'O' ring	48	Ball
20	Clip	49	Air horn gasket
21	Carburettor body	50	Sight glass frame
22	Main jet gasket	51	Plug
23	Secondary main jet	52	Gasket
24	Primary main jet	53	Gasket
25	Ball	54	Sight glass (fuel level)
26	Pump discharge weight	55	Gasket
27	Stop	56	Auto choke coil housing plate
28	Gasket		
29	Air horn		

Fig. 3.26. Removing accelerator pump lever pivot bolt (1) from lever (2) and disconnecting link (3) from 3K series carburettor

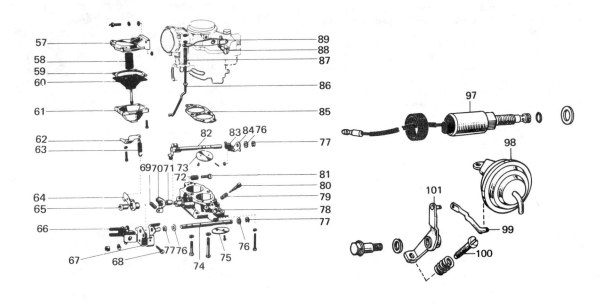

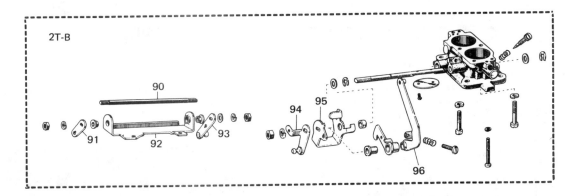

Fig. 3.27. Flange/throttle housing components (2T series engine carburettor

57 Diaphragm housing cover	82 Secondary throttle spindle
58 Diaphragm spring	83 Diaphragm relief spring
59 Gasket	84 Diaphragm lever
60 Diaphragm	85 Gasket
61 Diaphragm housing	86 Pump connecting link
62 Return spring anchor	87 Accelerator pump spring
63 Return spring	88 Accelerator pump arm pivot
64 Secondary kick lever	bolt
65 Sleeve	89 Pump lever arm
66 Primary throttle lever	90 Choke connector spindle
67 Primary throttle spindle arm	91 Lever
68 Bolt	92 Bracket
69 Spring	93 Lever
70 Fast idle lever	94 Primary throttle lever
71 Collar	95 Primary throttle arm
72 Spring	96 Fast idle lever
73 Secondary throttle valve plate	97 Solenoid valve
74 Primary throttle spindle	98 Throttle positioner diaphragm
75 Primary throttle valve	(2T-C engine)
76 Throttle spindle shim	99 Connecting link (2T-C engine)
77 Ring retainer	100 Throttle positioner adjusting
78 Flange/throttle housing	screw (2T-C engine)
79 Spring	101 Throttle positioner link lever
80 Idle mixture adjusting screw	(2T-C engine)
81 Idle speed adjusting screw	

worn component or to correct a fault.

4 There are detail differences between the carburettors used on the different engines but these will be apparent from the exploded drawings.

5 If complete dismantling is being carried out, always purchase a repair kit in advance. This will contain all the necessary gaskets and other renewable items required.

6 Remove the carburettor from the inlet manifold as previously described and clean away all external dirt.

7 Unscrew and remove the accelerator pump arm pivot bolt, detach the arm and connecting link (Fig. 3.26).

8 Remove the fast idle connector.

9 Remove the throttle positioner link rod ('C' suffix engines only). (Fig. 3.28).

10 Extract the securing screw and remove the air horn and gasket.

11 If the air horn is to be dismantled, push out the float pivot pin, remove the float and fuel inlet needle valve components (Fig. 3.29).

12 Remove the power piston, spring and boot assembly from the air horn (Fig. 3.30).

13 If an automatic choke is fitted, remove the housing, gasket and housing plate. Do not dismantle beyond this unless essential, in which case the peened choke valve plate screws will have to be filed flat before the choke valve and spindle can be removed (Fig. 3.31).

14 Turn the carburettor body upside down and remove the pump discharge weight and steel ball (Fig. 3.32).

15 Unscrew and remove the solenoid fuel cut-off valve ('C' suffix engines only) (Fig. 3.33).

16 Extract the securing screws and separate the carburettor body from the flange.

17 To dismantle the body, extract the primary venturi screws and the venturi followed by the secondary venturi (Fig. 3.34).

18 Remove the thermostatic valve.
19 Use a pair of tweezers to extract the check ball retainer from the bottom of the pump bore. Turn the body upside down and let the steel ball drops out (Fig. 3.35).
20 Remove the plugs, jets, fuel level sight-glass and other components as necessary. It is a good idea to check the jet markings against those listed in the Specifications in case a previous owner has substituted any for ones of incorrect calibration (Figs. 3.36 and 3.37).
21 On carburettors fitted to 2T series engines, remove the diaphragm from the carburettor body and dismantle it by extracting the cover screws (Fig. 3.38).
22 Do not dismantle the throttle valve plates or spindles from the flange unless absolutely essential as the valve plate securing screws are peened and they must be filed off to extract them.
23 With the carburettor dismantled, clean all components in fuel and examine for wear. Clean out jets with air from a tyre pump, never probe them with wire for their calibration will be ruined.
24 Reassembly is a reversal of dismantling but as work proceeds, carry out the checks and adjustments given in Section 22 or 23 according to carburettor type.
25 When an overhauled carburettor is refitted to the engine, always check and adjust the idling speed and throttle positioner setting as described in earlier Sections of this Chapter.

22 Carburettor (3K series engine) - adjustment during reassembly

Float level

1 Turn the air horn upside down so that the float hangs by its own weight and depresses the fuel inlet valve (Fig. 3.39).
2 Measure the distance between the nearest point on the float and the surface of the air horn. This should be 0.26 in (6.5 mm). Adjust if necessary by bending float tag A (Fig. 3.40).
3 Now gently raise the float with the finger and measure the distance between the face of the fuel inlet needle valve and the tag B on the float. This should be 0.035 in (0.9 mm (Fig. 3.41).

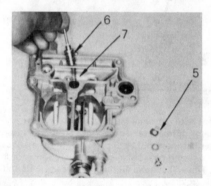

Fig. 3.30. Removing power piston components (3K series engine carburettor

5   Stop   7   Piston spring
6   Power piston

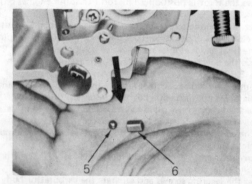

Fig. 3.32. Removing accelerator pump discharge weight (6) and ball (5) from body of 3K series engine carburettor

Fig. 3.28. Throttle positioner stop link (4) on 3K series engine carburettor

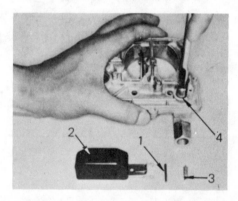

Fig. 3.29. Float components (3K series engine carburettor)

1   Pivot pin   3   Fuel inlet needle valve
2   Float   4   Needle valve seat

Fig. 3.31. Choke valve plate attachment (2T engine carburettor)

1   Set screw   3   Vacuum piston link
2   Choke valve spindle   4   Auto choke housing

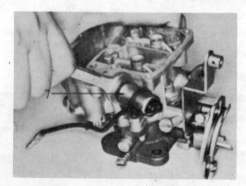

Fig. 3.33. Removing solenoid fuel cut off valve (3K-C engine carburettor)

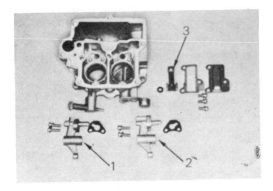

Fig. 3.34. Removal of primary small venturi (1) secondary small venturi (2) and thermostatic valve (3) from 3K series engine carburettor

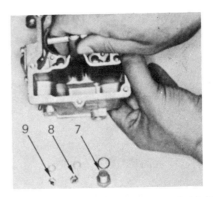

Fig. 3.35. Removing check ball retainer (4) and ball (5) from carburettor body

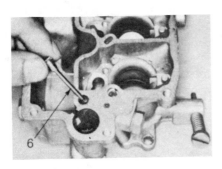

Fig. 3.36. Removing slow jet (6)

Fig. 3.37. Removing power valve, plug (7) primary main jet (8) and secondary main jet (9)

Fig. 3.38. Removal of throttle diaphragm (2T series engine)

1 Cover
2 Housing
3 Diaphragm
4 Spring
5 Gasket

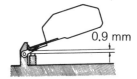

23.1 Carburettor fuel level sight glass (2T series engine)

Fig. 3.39. Checking float setting with air horn inverted (3K series engine carburettor)

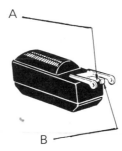

Fig. 3.40. Float adjustment tags

Fig. 3.41. Checking float raised setting (3K series engine carburettor)

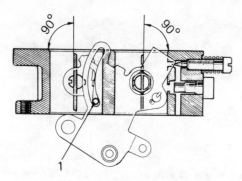

Fig. 3.42. Secondary throttle valve plate opening diagram (3K series engine carburettor)

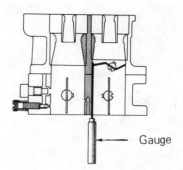

Fig. 3.43. Checking high speed valve plate opening (3K series engine carburettor)

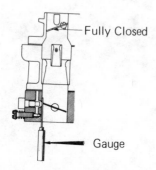

Fig. 3.44. Checking fast idle setting of throttle valve plate (3K series engine carburettor)

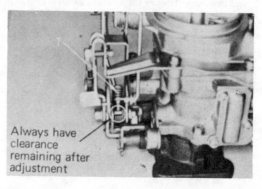

Fig. 3.45. Fast idle screw (1) (3K series engine carburettor except 3K-B)

Secondary throttle valve plate opening

4   Open the primary throttle valve plate fully with the fingers. Check that the secondary throttle valve plate is fully open.
5   If this is not so, bend the throttle shaft link as necessary (Fig. 3.42).

High speed valve clearance

6   Open the high speed valve fully and check the clearance between the edge of the valve plate and the bore (Fig. 3.43).
7   The clearance should be between 0.008 and 0.016 in (0.2 and 0.4 mm) Use a twist drill of suitable diameter to check this.
8   If adjustment is required, loosen the valve screws and move the valve plate as necessary.

Fast idle setting

9   Pull the fast idle lever until the choke valve plate is completely closed. Check the clearance between the edge of the primary throttle valve plate and the carburettor bore. This should be: (Fig. 3.44)
All 3K series engines except 3K-B 0.051 in (1.3 mm), 3K-B 0.020 in (0.5 mm).
Use a twist drill of suitable diameter to check this.
10 Carry out adjustment where necessary by turning the fast idle screw except on 3K-B engines when the alignment mark on the fast idle lever must be opposite the centre of the roller before turning the adjuster screw. If the mark is not in alignment, bend the fast idle connecting rod. (Figs. 3.45 and 3.46).

23 Carburettor (2T series engine) - adjustment during reassembly

Float level

1   The setting of the float is as described in the preceding Section except that the dimensions are as follows: (photo).

Air horn inverted   0.138 in (3.5 mm)
Air horn normal attitude   0.047 in (1.2 mm)

Secondary throttle valve plate opening and kick-up

2   Open the primary throttle valve plate fully and check the secondary throttle valve plate is also fully open (parallel to carburettor bore)

(Fig. 3.47).
3   If necessary, correct by bending the throttle levers.
4   Now check and adjust the kick up, if necessary, by bending the secondary throttle lever to obtain an 0.008 in (0.2 mm) clearance between the secondary throttle valve plate and the bore when the primary throttle valve plate is open at an angle of 62⁰ to the bore. A piece of card cut to the correct angle can be used as a gauge for this job (Fig. 3.48).

Fast idle setting

5   On 2T series engines except 2T-B, fully close the choke valve plate with the fingers and then measure the clearance between the edge of the throttle valve plate and the bore using a twist drill of suitable diameter as a gauge. The clearance should be for all except 2T-C, 0.031 in (0.8 mm) and for 2T-C 0.043 in (1.1 mm). Adjust by turning the fast idle screw (Fig. 3.49).
6   On carburettors fitted to 2T-B engines fully close the throttle valve and then fully open the choke valve plate. Push the lever in the direction arrowed and then turn the screw so that there is a clearance at its end of 0.15 in (3.5 mm) (Fig. 3.50).

Choke unloader

7   On all 2T series engine carburettors except 2T-B, open the primary throttle valve fully and check that the choke valve plate is at an angle of 47⁰ to the bore. If necessary, bend the fast idle cam follower or lip on the choke shaft to achieve this setting (Fig. 3.51).

Accelerator pump

8   The accelerator pump stroke should be in accordance with the following: (Fig. 3.52).

Except 2T-B	0.20 in (5.0 mm)
2T-B	0.12 in (3.0 mm)

9   Adjust if necessary by bending the neck of the connecting rod (A).

Automatic choke

10 The automatic choke is designed to close the choke valve plate fully

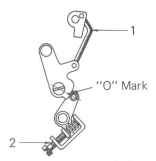

Fig. 3.46. Fast idle screw and alignment
marks (3K-B engine)

1   Connecting link
2   Adjuster screw

T   0.9 mm
2T   0.8 mm
2T-C   1.1 mm

Fig. 3.49. Fast idle adjustment diagram
(2T series engine carburettor except
2T-B)

1   Adjuster screw

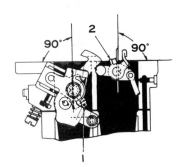

Fig. 3.47. Secondary throttle valve plate
opening and kick-up setting diagram (2T
series engine)

1   First throttle valve
2   Second throttle valve

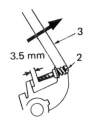

3.5 mm

Fig. 3.50. Fast idle adjustment diagram
(2T-B engine carburettor)

2   Adjuster screw
3   Lever

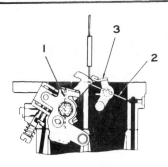

Fig. 3.48. Kick-up adjustment points (2T
series engine carburettor)

1   First throttle valve
2   Second throttle valve
3   Second throttle lever

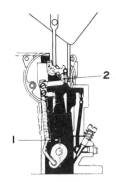

Fig. 3.51. Choke unloader setting diagram
(2T series engine carburettor)

1   Primary throttle valve plate
2   Tag on choke spindle

at an ambient temperature of 77°F (25°C) through the medium of its
temperature sensitive bi-metal spring coil. Fig. 3.53.
11 For normal operating conditions, set the centre line on the thermostat coil housing cover in alignment with the centre of the scale. In
extremes of climate, the cover can be turned clockwise to weaken the
cold start mixture or anti-clockwise to enrichen it.
12 It should be remembered that movement through one gradation on
the scale is equivalent to a 9°F (5°C) temperature change.

24 Manifolds and exhaust systems

1   On 3K series engines the inlet and exhaust manifolds are located on
the left-hand side of the engine (Fig. 3.54).
2   On 3K-B engines only, the inlet manifold is of coolant heated type
(Fig. 3.55).
3   On 2T series engines the intake manifold is located on the right-hand
side of the engine while the exhaust manifold is mounted on the opposite
side to give a crossflow characteristic to the engine (Fig. 3.56).
4   The intake manifold is coolant heated on all 2T series engines.
5   The layout of the exhaust system is similar on all models although
the individual components may vary in detail design (Fig. 3.60).
6   The system is supported on flexible mountings and incorporates one
main silencer and an expansion box.
7   Examination of the exhaust pipe and silencers at regular intervals
is worthwhile as small defects may be repairable when, if left, they will
almost certainly require renewal of one of the sections of the system.
Also, any leaks, apart from the noise factor, may cause poisonous
exhaust gases to get inside the car which can be unpleasant, to
say the least, even in mild concentrations. Prolonged inhalation could
cause sickness and giddiness.
8   As the sleeve connections and clamps are usually very difficult to
separate it is quicker and easier in the long run to remove the complete
system from the car when renewing a section. It can be expensive if
another section is damaged when trying to separate a bad section from
it.
9   To remove the system, jack-up the car at front and rear and then

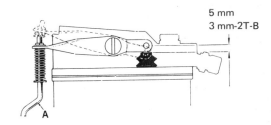

5 mm
3 mm-2T-B

A

Fig. 3.52. Accelerator pump stroke setting diagram (2T series engine
carburettor)

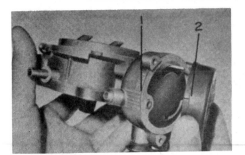

Fig. 3.53. Automatic choke adjustment marks

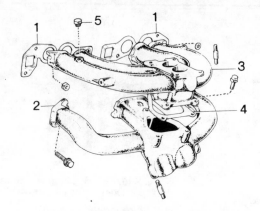

Fig. 3.54. Manifolds (3K series engine carburettor except 3K-B)

1 Gasket
2 Exhaust manifold
3 Intake manifold

4 Gasket
5 Plug

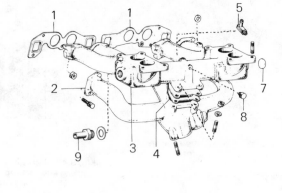

Fig. 3.55. Manifolds (3K-B engine)

1 Gasket
2 Exhaust manifold
3 Intake manifold
4 Gasket
5 Coolant union

7 Plug
8 Plug
9 Heater hose union

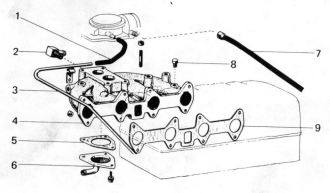

Fig. 3.56. Intake manifold (2T series engine except 2T-B)

1 Exhaust gas inlet pipe to automatic choke
2 Coolant union
3 Exhaust gas inlet pipe for automatic choke
4 Intake manifold

5 Gasket
6 Coolant outlet union
7 Exhaust gas outlet from automatic choke
8 Plug
9 Gasket

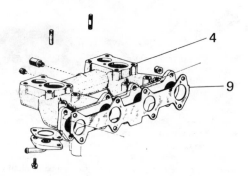

Fig. 3.57. Intake manifold (2T-B engine)

4 Manifold   9 Gasket

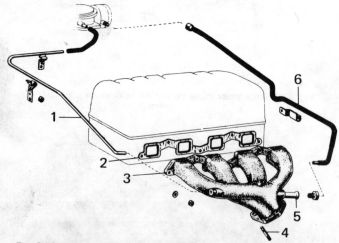

Fig. 3.58. Exhaust manifold (2T series engine except 2T-B)

1 Exhaust gas inlet pipe to automatic choke
2 Gasket
3 Exhaust manifold
4 Stud

5 Exhaust gas outlet nozzle to automatic choke
6 Exhaust gas return line from automatic choke

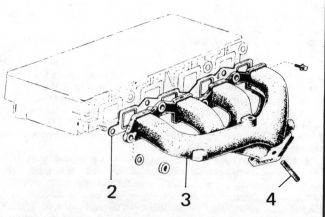

Fig. 3.59. Exhaust manifold (2T-B engine)

2 Gasket
3 Manifold   4 Stud

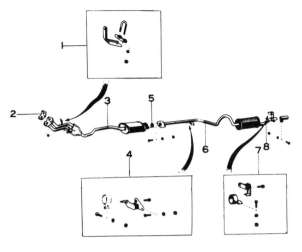

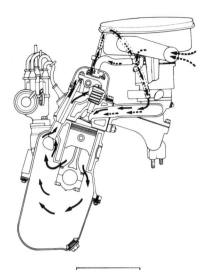

Fig. 3.60. Typical exhaust system

1	Support bracket	5	Gasket
2	Gasket	6	Centre section
3	Front section	7	Support bracket
4	Support bracket	8	Tail pipe section

At Idling

Fig. 3.61. Positive Crankcase Ventilation System (3K series engine)

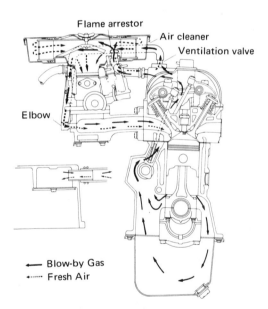

← Blow-by Gas
←···· Fresh Air

Fig. 3.62. Positive Crankcase Ventilation System (2T series engine)

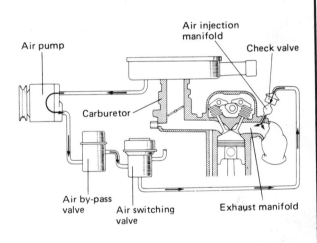

Fig. 3.63. Layout of Air Injection System

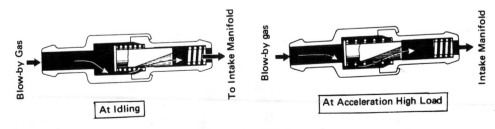

Fig. 3.64. Crankcase ventilation valve diagram

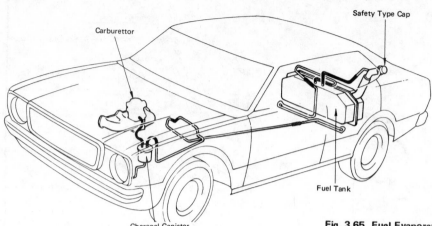

Fig. 3.65. Fuel Evaporative Emission Control System (Saloon and Hardtop)

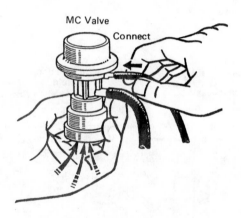

Fig. 3.66. Checking Mixture Control Valve

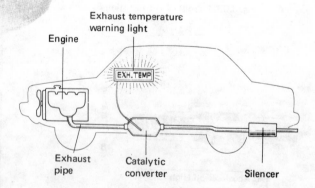

Fig. 3.67. Catalytic Converter System

disconnect the front downpipe from the exhaust manifold.
10 Disconnect all the flexible mountings and withdraw the complete system from below and to the rear of the vehicle.
11 Cut away the bad sections, taking care not to damage the good sections which are to be retained.
12 File off any burrs at the ends of the new sections of pipe and smear them with grease. Slip the clamps over the pipes and connect the sockets but do not tighten the clamps at this stage.
13 Push the complete system under the vehicle and jack it up so that the front pipe can be bolted to the manifold and the rear tail pipe mounting connected.
14 Now turn the silencer sections to obtain their correct attitudes so that they will not touch or knock against any adjacent parts when the system is deflected to one side or the other.
15 Tighten all clamps and flexible mountings.

25 Emission control - general description

1   To prevent pollution of the atmosphere, a number of (fume) emission control systems are fitted to all vehicles. Their complexity depends upon the operating territory but as a general rule, vehicles with the larger capacity engine and destined for North America have the most comprehensive and sophisticated systems.
2   All vehicles have a Positive Crankcase Ventilation (PCV) System.
3   Many models have a Fuel Evaporative Emission Control System.
4   Some vehicles have one or more of the following in order to reduce the emission of noxious gases from the exhaust system.

Throttle Positioner (TP) see Section 19, this Chapter.
Spark Control (SC) System, see Section 28.
Air Injection (AI) System, see Section 29.
Mixture Control (MC) System, see Section 30.
Catalytic Converter - California only, see Section 31.
Transmission Controlled Spark (TCS) system, see Section 32.
Exhaust Gas Recirculation (EGR) system, see Section 33.
Choke Opener system, see Section 34.
Choke Breaker (CB) system, see Section 35.
Choke Return system, see Section 36.
Auxiliary Acceleration Pump (AAP) system, see Section 37.
Deceleration Fuel Cut system, see Section 38.
High Altitude Compensation (HAC) system, see Section 39.
Double vacuum advance distributor, see Section 40.

5   It must be emphasised that correct tuning and adjustment of the fuel and ignition systems are extremely important for the maintenance of low levels of fume emission from the exhaust.

26 Positive Crankcase Ventilation (PCV) System - description and maintenance

1   The system is designed to draw blow-by gas from the crankcase and rocker chamber into the air cleaner where it is led into the intake

manifold and is then burned during the normal combustion cycle. (Fig. 3.61).

2   A ventilation valve is incorporated in the connecting hoses.

3   Periodically inspect the hoses for security of connections and for splits or deterioration.

4   Check the operation of the valve by having the engine running at idling speed and then pinch the valve connecting hose several times and listen for the valve seating. If this can be heard, the valve is operating satisfactorily. If it cannot be heard seating, renew the valve. Renewal should be carried out in any event at the specified intervals (Fig. 3.64).

27 Fuel Evaporative Emission Control Systems - description and maintenance

1   The system is designed to reduce the emission of fuel vapour to the atmosphere by directing the vapour from the fuel tank through a non-return valve into an absorbent charcoal-filled canister (Figs. 3.65 and 3.68).

2   Some layouts have a fuel/vapour separator and all models are fitted with a special filler cap which although normally sealed, does include a valve to admit air when partial vacuum conditions are created within the system or fuel tank.

3   At certain road speeds, a vacuum switching valve is actuated and the vapour stored in the canister is then drawn into the intake manifold where it is burned as a controlled fuel/air mixture within the engine combustion chambers.

4   Check the system hoses at the specified intervals (see Routine Maintenance) also the condition of the filler cap seal.

5   Renew the non-return valve as specified.

6   Renew the charcoal canister every 50,000 miles (80,000 km).

28 Spark Control (SC) System - description and maintenance

1   This arrangement delays the distributor vacuum advance of the ignition timing for a predetermined period in order to reduce the formation of noxious gases which would normally be produced by shortening the combustion time as the ignition is advanced.

2   Maintenance consists of periodically inspecting the condition of the connecting hoses.

29 Air Injection (AI) System - description and maintenance

1   This system injects air, generated by a belt-driven air pump, close to the exhaust ports where it mixes with the hot exhaust gases to promote burning of unburned hydrocarbons and carbon monoxide (Fig. 3.63).

2   Where a catalytic converter is installed (see Section 31) the air injected is also used as the source for the oxidising reaction.

3   At the specified intervals, check and adjust if necessary, the tension of the air pump drivebelt.

4   Inspect the hose connections and the condition of the hoses, renewing any which have deteriorated.

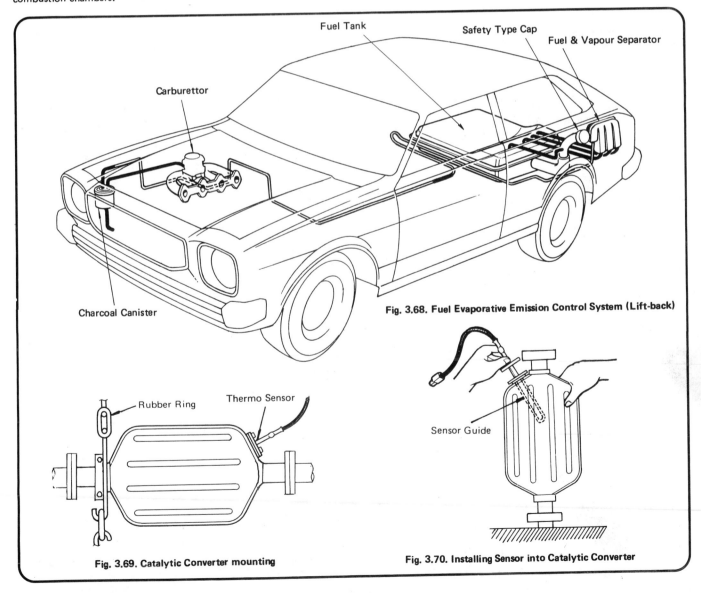

Fig. 3.68. Fuel Evaporative Emission Control System (Lift-back)

Fig. 3.69. Catalytic Converter mounting

Fig. 3.70. Installing Sensor into Catalytic Converter

30 Mixture Control (MC) System - description and maintenance

1   This device is fitted to 3K-C engines and to 2T-C engines with manual transmission only.
2   Its purpose is to permit fresh air to enter the intake manifold at time of sudden deceleration in order to improve combusion and reduce the emission of hydrocarbons.
3   Maintenance consists of checking the hoses and connections.
4   In the event of a suspected fault, start the engine, disconnect the vacuum sensing hose from the valve and block the hose. Now place the hand over the air intake of the valve, no vacuum should be felt.
5   Reconnect the hose and as it is connected, vacuum should be felt momentarily, together with rough idle condition.
6   If the valve does not operate as described, renew it as a sealed unit.

31 Catalytic Converter - description and maintenance

1   This device (fitted to California vehicles only) is an integral part of the exhaust system and comprises a steel casing holding an alumina carrier coated with a catalyst metal such as platinum or palladium (Fig. 3.67).
2   As the exhaust gases pass through the catalytic converter, the HC and CO content of the gas is oxidized and converted into water and carbon dioxide.
3   Excessive quantities of unburned gases passing through the catalytic converter will cause its temperature to rise excessively and this condition is monitored and a warning light comes on to warn the driver to trace the cause.
4   Grossly incorrectly adjusted carburettor or faulty ignition could be the cause, or, in fact, the descent of an exceptionally long gradient. With the latter, resuming normal roadspeeds with the throttle partly open will rectify the aituation.
5   Apart from occasional checking of the catalytic converter flange bolts, the suspension rings and the sensor lead, no routine maintenance is required (Fig. 3.69).
6   If the exhaust system is being dismantled, only withdraw the sensor with the converter in the upright position otherwise, the catalyst will be spilled (Fig. 3.70).
7   New converters are supplied complete with a sensor guide tube to facilitate fitting the sensor to it.

32 Transmission Controlled Spark (TCS) system - description and maintenance

1   This system is only fitted to vehicles operating in California and controls the vacuum ignition timing in accordance with the coolant temperature and vehicle speed. Thermo-switches are fitted to the engine inlet manifold and radiator to monitor the engine coolant temperature, and a speed sensor attached to the transmission monitors the speed of the vehicle.
2   A computor and valve are used to cut out the vacuum advance at the distributor during certain combinations of vehicle speed and engine temperature, and this reduces the formation of noxious gases.
3   Maintenance consists of periodically checking the hoses for signs of deterioration.

33 Exhaust Gas Recirculation (EGR) system - description and maintenance

1   This system was introduced on 1977 models and is designed to re-introduce small amounts of exhaust gas into the combustion cycle to reduce the generation of oxides of nitrogen (NOx) by the reduction of combustion temperatures. The amount of gas re-introduced is governed by engine vacuum and temperature.
2   The EGR valve is connected to the inlet and exhaust manifold; the

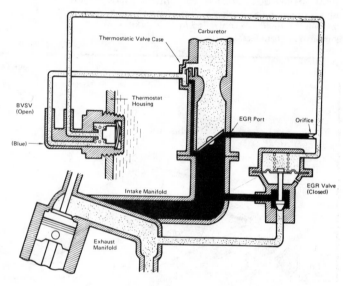

Fig. 3.71. Exhaust Gas Recirculation System (3K-C engine)

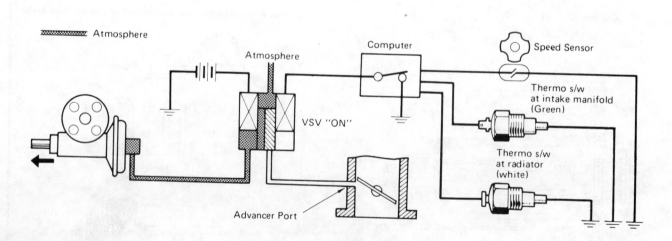

Fig. 3.72. Transmission Controlled Spark System (ON condition shown)

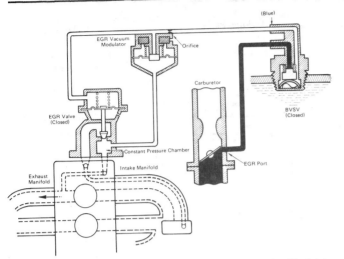

Fig. 3.73. Exhaust Gas Recirculation System incorporating Modulator (2T-C engine)

internal spring-tensioned diaphragm is operated by inlet manifold vacuum and is controlled by a thermal valve (BVSV).

3 When the engine coolant temperature is below 50°C (122°F), the thermal valve is open and atmospheric pressure from the inlet manifold allows the EGR valve to be closed, thus restricting any exhaust gas recirculation.

4 When the engine coolant temperature exceeds 50°C (122°F), the thermal valve closes and prevents atmospheric pressure reaching the EGR valve. Vacuum from the inlet manifold opens the EGR valve and exhaust gas is thus recirculated.

5 On vehicles operating in California or at high altitude, a vacuum modulator is included in the EGR system which effectively increases the amount of gas recirculated when the engine is under high load. The vacuum modulator is controlled by the amount of exhaust pressure present in a constant pressure chamber.

6 Maintenance of the EGR system consists of cleaning the EGR port orifice when it becomes restricted and, on vehicles operating in California and at high altitudes, periodically cleaning the filter in the vacuum modulator. Should any component fail to function correctly it must be renewed in accordance with local regulations.

34 Choke Opener system - description and maintenance

1 This system reduces unnecessary emission of noxious gases when the automatic choke is in operation by forcibly holding the choke valve open.

2 On 1976 and 1977 models the choke valve is opened by a diaphragm which is operated by inlet manifold vacuum through a

thermal valve. When the engine coolant temperature exceeds 60°C (140°F), the thermal valve opens and allows vacuum to open the choke valve. When the engine coolant temperature falls below 35°C (95°F), the thermal valve shuts and the automatic choke operates normally.

3 1975 models employ a similar system but, instead of the thermal valve, a thermo-switch, speed sensor, computor and valve are fitted.

4 Maintenance of the choke opener system consists of periodically checking the vacuum hoses for deterioration and also checking that the electrical wires are securely fitted to their terminals.

35 Choke Breaker (CB) system - description and maintenance

1 This system operates in an identical manner to the choke opener system in that it holds the choke valve open. It is only fitted to 1977 models.

2 When the engine is started and idles with the throttle valve closed, vacuum from the engine side of the throttle valve operates a diaphragm which in turn opens the choke valve.

3 When the throttle valve is opened the vacuum to the diaphragm is reduced and the choke valve closes to enrich the fuel/air mixture.

4 Maintenance is confined to checking the hoses for deterioration.

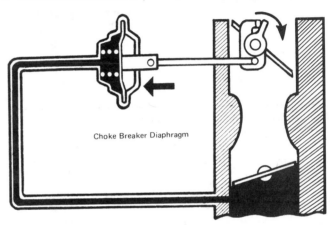

Fig. 3.74. Choke breaker System

36 Choke Return system - description

1 This system is only fitted to 3K-C engines with manual choke control, and prevents the catalytic converter from overheating if the choke control is left out for excessive periods.

2 When the engine coolant temperature exceeds 40°C (104°F), a thermal switch de-energises the choke control holding coil and the control cable returns to the OFF position by means of a return spring.

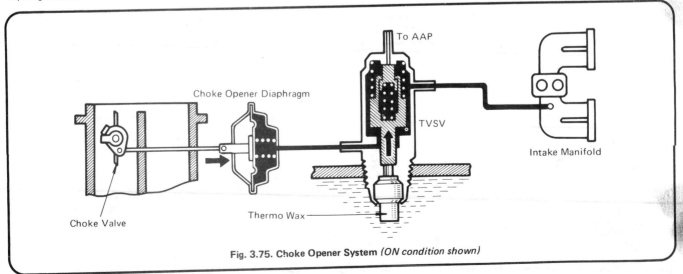

Fig. 3.75. Choke Opener System *(ON condition shown)*

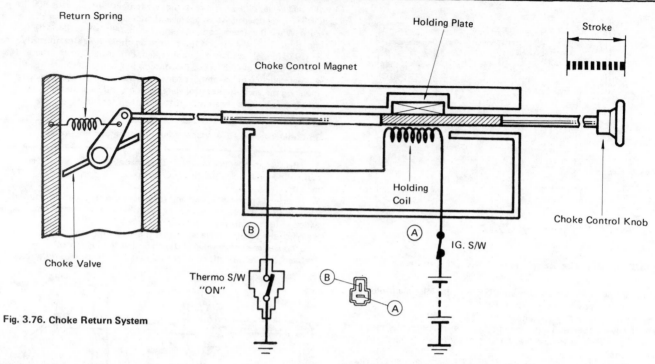

Fig. 3.76. Choke Return System

37 Auxiliary Acceleration Pump (AAP) system - description and maintenance

1 This system supplements the main accelerating pump when the engine coolant is cold and thus the quantity of fuel required for acceleration is increased.
2 A thermal valve is employed to connect the intake manifold depression to a diaphragm on the acceleration chamber and, when the throttle valve is closed, the high vacuum acts on the diaphragm to draw fuel into the chamber.
3 When the throttle valve is opened for acceleration, the inlet manifold depression drops and spring pressure acts on the diaphragm to inject additional fuel into the carburettor venturi.
4 The system only operates when the engine is cold and maintenance is confined to checking the hoses for deterioration.

38 Deceleration Fuel Cut system - description and maintenance

1 This system is only fitted to 3K-C engines and effectively controls the idle circuit of the carburettor.
2 When the engine speed is lower than 2100 rpm, or the carburettor vacuum below 13 in Hg, a solenoid valve is energised and the idle

circuit is opened.
3 In addition to providing the normal idle function, the system reduces overheating and afterburn in the exhaust system during periods of protracted deceleration.
4 Maintenance consists of checking the security and condition of the vacuum hoses and electrical wiring.

39 High Altitude Compensation (HAC) system - description

1 This system supplies additional air to the carburettor when the vehicle is being operated at high altitudes. The ignition timing is also advanced in order to improve engine control.

40 Double vacuum advance distributor - description

1 When the engine is cold, this system provides additional ignition advance to the distributor by means of a secondary diaphragm and a thermal switch.
2 Under normal operating conditions when the engine has reached its normal temperature, the thermal valve closes and the secondary diaphragm is rendered inoperative.
3 The system reduces the emission of noxious gases when the engine is cold.

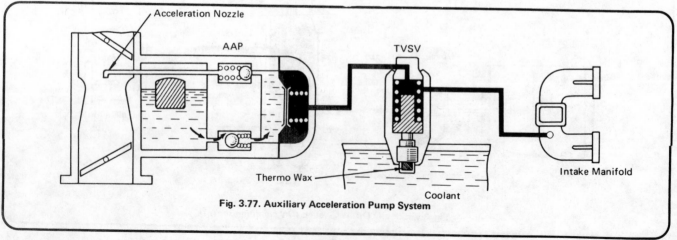

Fig. 3.77. Auxiliary Acceleration Pump System

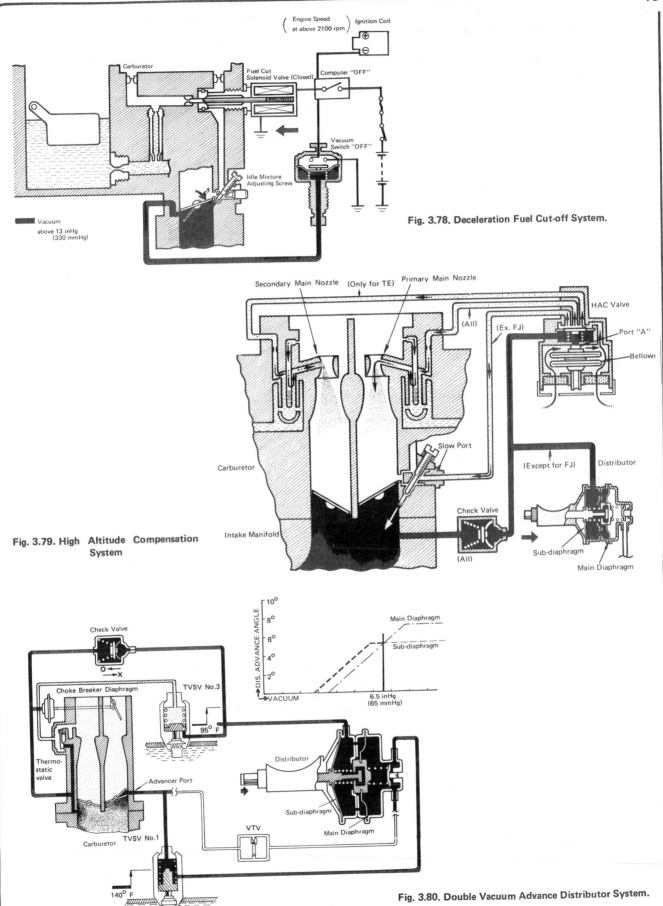

Fig. 3.78. Deceleration Fuel Cut-off System.

Fig. 3.79. High Altitude Compensation System

Fig. 3.80. Double Vacuum Advance Distributor System.

41 Fault diagnosis — carburation, fuel and emission control systems

Fuel system and carburation

Symptom	Cause
Excessive fuel consumption	Air cleaner choked.
	Leakage from pump, carburettor or fuel line or fuel tank.
	Float chamber flooding.
	Distributor capacitor faulty.
	Distributor weights or vacuum capsule faulty.
	Mixture too rich.
	Contact breaker gap too wide.
	Incorrect valve clearances.
	Incorrect spark plug gaps.
	Tyres under inflated.
	Dragging brakes.
Fuel starvation or mixture weakness	Clogged fuel line filter.
	Float chamber needle valve clogged.
	Faulty fuel pump valves.
	Fuel pump diaphragm split.
	Fuel pipe unions loose.
	Fuel pump cover leaking.
	Inlet manifold gasket or carburettor flange gasket leaking.
	Incorrect adjustment of carburettor.

Emission control system

System or circuit	Symptom	Cause
Positive Crankcase Ventilation System	Oil fume seepage from engine	Stuck or clogged PCV valve.
		Split or collapsed hoses.
Fuel Evaporative Emission Control System	Fuel odour	Choked canister.
		Stuck filler cap valve.
	Vapour will not be drawn into manifold	Collapsed or split hoses.
		Vacuum switching valve defective.
	Rough running engine	Defective check valve.
Spark Control System	No movement of vernier adjuster (octane selector) under any engine speed conditions	Split vacuum hoses.
		Split vacuum diaphragm.
		Seized advance leakage or mechanism.
Air Injection System	Fume emission from exhaust pipe	Slack or broken air pump drivebelt.
		Split or broken hoses.
		Defective air pump.
		Clogged air cleaner element.
Throttle Positioner System	Fumes emitted on deceleration	Incorrectly adjusted positioner screw.
Mixture Control System	Fumes emitted on deceleration	Split or disconnected hoses.
		Choked air intake mesh on valve.
		Faulty control valve.
Catalytic Converter	Excessive heat build up	Rich mixture.
		Engine out of tune.
		Fault in other emission control systems.
		Excessive deceleration of gradient (will rectify on acceleration).

Note: The efficiency of the fume emission control system is also dependent upon the correct setting and adjustment of all other engine components. These include the ignition, cooling and lubrication systems, the valve clearances and the condition generally of the engine. Refer to the appropriate Sections and Chapters of this manual for servicing procedures.

Chapter 4 Ignition system

Refer to Chapter 13 for specifications and information applicable to 1979 US models.

Contents

Specifications

System type	Battery, coil, distributor
Firing order	1 - 3 - 4 - 2

Distributor

Contacts points gap	0.016 to 0.020 in (0.4 to 0.5 mm)
Dwell angle	50 to 54°
Rotational direction	Clockwise

Ignition timing *(3K Series engine)* static setting

3K manual gearbox	8° BTDC @ 600 rev/min	Auto. transmission 8° BTDC at
3K-H manual gearbox	8° BTDC @ 600 rev/min	700 rev/min
3K-B manual gearbox	10° BTDC @ 650 rev/min	No option for auto.
3K-C manual gearbox	5° BTDC @ 750 rev/min	transmission

Centrifugal advance (3K and 3K-H engine)

500 rev/min	Advance begins
1750 rev/min	12°
300 rev/min	14°

Vacuum advance (3K and 3K-H engine)

4.33 in Hg (110 mm Hg)	Advance begins
7.87 in Hg (200 mm Hg)	6°
10.24 in Hg (260 mm Hg)	9°

Centrifugal advance (3K-B engine)

450 rev/min	Advance begins
900 rev/min	6°
1900 rev/min	12°

Vacuum advance (3K-B engine)

3.54 in Hg (90 mm Hg)	Advance begins
7.87 in Hg (200 mm Hg)	3°
11.81 in Hg (300 mm Hg)	5°

Centrifugal advance (3K-C engine)

650 rev/min	Advance begins
2100 rev/min	14°

Vacuum advance (3K-C engine)

4.33 in Hg (110 mm Hg)	Advance begins
7.87 in Hg (200 mm Hg)	6°
10.24 in Hg (260 mm Hg)	9°

Ignition timing *(2T Series engine)* static setting

2T manual gearbox	10° BTDC @ 800 rev/min	Auto. trans. 10° BTDC @ 950 rev/min
2T-B manual gearbox	12° BTDC @ 800 rev/min	No auto. trans. option

2T-C manual gearbox ... ...   5° BTDC @ 750 rev/min   Auto. trans. 5° BTDC @ 800 rev/min
California - all transmissions ... ...   10° BTDC @ 850 rev/min

Centrifugal advance (2T engine)
500 rev/min ... ...   Advance begins
1200 rev/min ... ...   9°
2700 rev/min ... ...   13°

Vacuum advance (2T engine)
3.5 in Hg (90 mm Hg) ... ...   Advance begins
4.7 in Hg (120 mm Hg) ... ...   3°
11.8 in Hg (300 mm Hg) ... ...   9°

Centrifugal advance (2T-B engine)
500 rev/min ... ...   Advance begins
1000 rev/min ... ...   6°
1800 rev/min ... ...   9°

Vacuum advance (2T-B engine)
3.3 in Hg (83 mm Hg) ... ...   Advance begins
4.7 in Hg (120 mm Hg) ... ...   2° 30'
10.2 in Hg (260 mm Hg) ... ...   9°

Centrifugal advance (2T-C engine with manual transmission)
500 rev/min ... ...   Advance begins
1000 rev/min ... ...   8° 30'
2300 rev/min ... ...   16° 30'

Centrifugal advance (2T-C engine with automatic transmission)
500 rev/min ... ...   Advance begins
1500 rev/min ... ...   11°
2300 rev/min ... ...   16° 30'

Vacuum advance (2T-C engine with manual transmission)
3.15 in Hg (80 mm Hg) ... ...   Advance begins
4.06 in Hg (103 mm Hg) ... ...   3°
5.51 in Hg (140 mm Hg) ... ...   7°

Condenser capacity ... ...   0.20 to 0.24

Coil
Primary coil resistance ... ...   3.3 ohms
Secondary coil resistance ... ...   8500 ohms

Spark plugs
Type ... ...   Nippondenso W16EP or NGK BP5ES-L
Gap ... ...   0.028 to 0.032 in (0.7 to 0.8 mm)

Torque wrench settings   lb/ft   Nm
Spark plugs   15   21
Distributor clamp plate bolt   18   25

1 General description

1   In order that the engine can run correctly it is necessary for an electric spark to ignite the fuel/air mixture in the combustion chamber at exactly the right moment in relation to engine speed and load. The ignition system is based on feeding low tension voltage from the battery to the coil where it is converted into high tension voltage. The high tension voltage is powerful enough to jump the spark plug gap in the cylinders many times a second under high compression, providing that the system is in good condition and that all adjustments are correct. The ignition system is divided into two circuits: low tension and high tension.

2   The low tension circuit (sometimes known as the primary) consists of the battery, the lead to the ignition switch, the lead from the ignition switch to the low tension on primary coil windings, and the lead from the low tension coil windings to the contact breaker points and condenser in the distributor.

3   The high tension circuit consists of the high tension or secondary coil windings, the heavy ignition lead from the centre of the coil windings, the heavy ignition lead from the centre of the coil to the centre of the distributor cap, the rotor arm, and the spark plug leads and the spark plugs.

4   The system functions in the following manner: Low tension voltage is changed in the coil into high tension voltage by the opening and closing of the contact breaker points in the low tension circuit. High tension voltage is then fed, via the carbon brush in the centre of the distributor cap, to the rotor arm of the distributor cap, and each time it comes in line with one of the four metal segments in the cap, which are connected to the spark plug leads, the opening and closing of the contact breaker points causes the high tension voltage to build up, jump the gap from the rotor arm to the appropriate metal segment and so, via the spark plug lead, to the spark plug, where it finally jumps the spark plug gap before going to earth.

5   The ignition is advanced and retarded automatically, to ensure the spark occurs at just the right instant for the particular load at the prevailing engine speed.

6   The ignition advance is controlled both mechanically and by a vacuum operated system. The mechanical governor comprises two weights, which move out from the distributor shaft as the engine speed rises due to centrifugal force. As they move outwards they rotate the cam relative to the distributor shaft, and so advance the spark. The weights are held in position by two light springs and it is the tension of these springs which is largely responsible for correct spark advancement.

7   The vacuum control consists of a diaphragm, one side of which is connected, via a small bore tube, to the carburettor, and the other side to the contact breaker plate. Depression in the inlet manifold and carburettor, which varies with engine speed and throttle opening, causes the diaphragm to move, so moving the contact breaker plate, and advancing or retarding the spark. A fine degree of control is achieved by a spring in the vacuum assembly.

8   The resistor short circuiting cable shown in the diagram is only fitted to vehicles equipped with automatic transmission (Fig. 4.1).

9   On vehicles destined for the North American market the ignition system is semi-transistorised. The action of the distributor contact breaker points causes the igniter transistors to switch the coil primary circuit on and off.

10 The system improves the serviceable life of the contact breaker points and assists engine starting by improving low speed secondary voltage.

11 Some 1588 cc engines manufactured in 1975 for the North American market are fitted with a distributor equipped with dual contact breaker points. The system advances the ignition timing when the engine is cold in order to provide more efficient combustion and improved torque.

12 The main contact point is switched into the ignition circuit by means of a thermo-switch and a relay when the coolant temperature exceeds 20°C (95°F); when the coolant temperature is below this figure the thermo-switch closes and energises the relay which leaves the sub-point only in the ignition circuit.

2 Contact breaker points - adjustment

1   To adjust the contact breaker points to the correct gap first release the two clips securing the distributor cap to the distributor body, and lift away the cap. Clean the cap inside, and out, with a dry cloth. It is unlikely that the four segments will be badly burned or scored, but if they are the cap will have to be renewed. On some distributors, a moisture proof cover is fitted which must be released before the distributor cap can be removed (photo).

2   Inspect the contact located in the centre of the cap and make sure it is serviceable.

3   Lift off the rotor arm and dust proof cover (photo). Gently prise the contact breaker points open and examine the condition of their

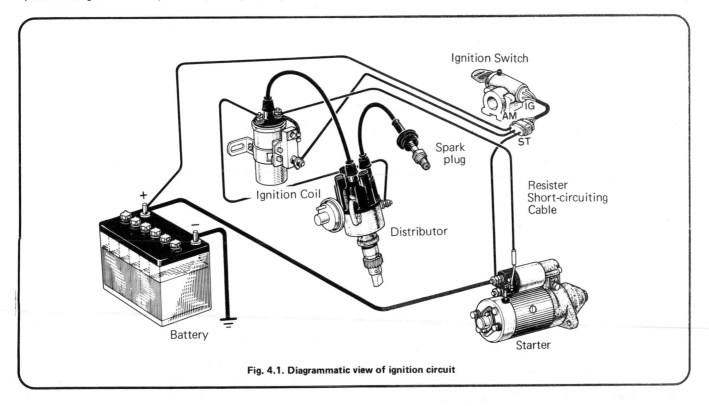

Fig. 4.1. Diagrammatic view of ignition circuit

2.1 Distributor moisture-proof jacket

2.3A Removing rotor arm and dustproof cover

2.3B View of distributor contact breaker assembly

2.6 Checking contact breaker points gap

4.7A Engine to bulkhead earth bonding strap

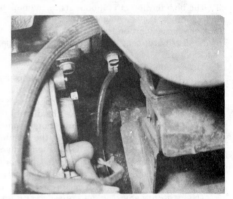

4.7B Engine front earth bonding strap

faces. If they are rough, pitted or dirty it will be necessary to remove them for refacing or for a replacement set to be fitted (photo).

4 Presuming that the points are satisfactory, or that they have been cleaned and refitted, measure the gap between the points by turning the engine over until the heel of the breaker arm is on the highest point of the cam.

5 A 0.016 - 0.020 in (0.4 - 0.5 mm) feeler gauge should now just fit between the points.

6 If the gap varies from this amount, slacken the lockscrew and adjust the contact gap by resetting the moving contact position. When the gap is correct, tighten the securing screw and check the gap again (photo).

7 Refit the dust cover and rotor and replace the distributor cap. Clip the spring blade retainers into position.

8 This adjustment must be regarded as an initial setting and the dwell angle must now be checked as described in the following Section.

9 On vehicles fitted with a dual point contact breaker system, the main points may be adjusted as described in the previous paragraphs. The sub-points can also be adjusted in the same manner to a gap of 0.018 in (0.45 mm) although, if available, the use of a stroboscopic timing light and dwellmeter is recommended.

10 To check the sub-points with a timing light and dwellmeter, first remove the connector from the thermo-switch terminal, and use a split cotter pin or similar object to earth the supply wire to the engine. With the dwellmeter connected, the dwell angle should be 52° (see Section 3); adjust the points gap if necessary (see Section 3.4). With the sub-points adjusted correctly, the ignition timing advance at idling should be between 19° and 25° btdc.

11 Refit the thermo-switch lead when the adjustment is completed.

3 Dwell angle - checking

1 On modern engines, setting the distributor contact breaker gap with feeler blades must only be considered an initial step to get the engine running. For optimum engine performance, the dwell angle must always be checked as soon as possible.

2 The dwell angle is the number of degrees through which the distri-

butor cam turns between the closure and opening of the contact breaker points. It can only be checked using a dwell meter.

3 Connect the dwell meter in accordance with the makers instructions (usually between the negative LT terminal on the coil and a good earth) and with the engine running at the specified idling speed, check the dwell angle on the meter.

4 If the dwell angle is larger than that specified, switch off the engine and increase the points gap, if it is too much, decrease the gap. Recheck the dwell angle.

4 Contact breaker points - renewal

1 If the contact breaker points are burned, pitted or badly worn they must be removed and renewed.

2 With the distributor cap removed lift off the rotor arm by pulling it straight up from the spindle. Also remove the dust cover.

3 Detach the contact breaker points lead from the LT terminal on the side of the distributor body. Release the terminal nuts to do this.

4 Extract the two securing screws which hold the contact breaker arm to the distributor baseplate. Note that an earth lead is retained by one of these screws.

5 Lift the contact breaker set from the distributor.

6 If the contact points are only lightly pitted or burred they can be cleaned up using fine abrasive paper and used again. Severe burning or pitting will mean renewal of the contact breaker assembly.

7 Consistent severe burning or pitting of the points may mean that the condenser is faulty (see next Section) or that one of the engine earth bonds is loose or that one of the distributor baseplate or earth lead screws requires tightening (photos).

8 Refitting is a reversal of removal, set the points gap and check the dwell angle as described in Section 2 and 3.

5 Condenser - removal, testing and refitting

1 The purpose of the condenser, (sometimes known as a capacitor) is to ensure that when the contact breaker points open there is no spark-

7.4 Distributor clamp plate

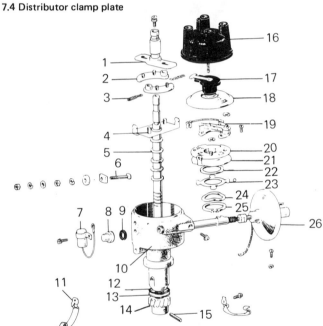

Fig. 4.2. Exploded view of distributor (3K engine)

1 Cam assembly	14 Driven gear
2 Counterweight	15 Pin
3 Spring	16 Distributor cap
4 Distributor shaft	17 Rotor arm
5 Washer	18 Dustproof cover
6 Low tension terminal	19 Contact breaker assembly
7 Condenser	20 Contact breaker baseplate
8 Vernier adjuster cap	(movable)
9 Seal	21 Fixed baseplate
10 Distributor body	22 Washer
11 Cap clip	23 Spring
12 'O' ring	24 Wave washer
13 Washer	25 Circlip
	26 Vacuum diaphragm assembly

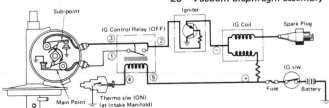

Fig; 4.3. Diagram of the duel point distributor curcuit (cold engine condition)

ing across them which would waste voltage and cuase wear.

2 The condenser is fitted in parallel with the contact breaker points. If it develops a short circuit, it will cause ignition failure as the points will be prevented from interrupting the low tension circuit.

3 If the engine becomes very difficult to start or begins to misfire after several miles running and the contact breaker points show signs of excessive burning, then the condition of the condenser must be suspect. A further test can be made by separating the points by hand with the ignition switched on. If this is accompanied by a flash it is indicative that the condenser has failed.

4 Without special test equipment the only sure way to diagnose condenser trouble is to replace a suspected unit with a new one and note if there is any improvement.

5 To remove a condenser from the distributor take off the distributor cap to give better access.

6 Detach the condenser lead from the terminal block.

7 Undo and remove the screw and washer securing the condenser to the distributor body. Lift away the condenser and lead.

8 Refitting the condenser is the reverse sequence to removal.

6 Distributor - lubrication

1 It is important that the distributor cam is lubricated with petroleum jelly and the contact breaker arm, centrifugal weights and cam spindle lubricated with engine oil at the specified mileage.

2 Apply a thin smear of petroleum jelly to the high points of the cam, any excess that finds its way onto the contact breaker points could cause burning and misfiring.

3 To gain access to the cam spindle, lift away the rotor arm and place no more than two drops of engine oil onto the spindle screw. This will run down the spindle when the engine is hot and lubricate the bearings.

4 To lubricate the automatic timing control allow a few drops of oil to pass through the hole in the contact breaker baseplate through which the four sided cam emerges. Apply not more than one drop of oil to the moving contact pivot post and remove any excess.

5 Refit the rotor arm and distributor cap.

7 Distributor - removal

1 Disconnect the LT lead from the terminal on the side of the distributor body.

2 Disconnect the vacuum pipe from the distributor diaphragm capsule.

3 Prise off the spring clips which hold the distributor cap in position and move the cap to one side. There is no need to disconnect the HT leads from spark plugs or cap.

4 Unscrew and remove the bolt which holds the distributor clamp to the cylinder block and then withdraw the distributor from the engine (photo).

8 Distributor - overhaul

1 There are detail differences between the distributors used on the two engine types but the dismantling operations for both are similar (Figs. 4.2 and 4.4).

2 The distributor is driven from a gear on the engine camshaft but its location varies slightly between the two engine series type.

3 With the distributor on the bench, release the two spring clips retaining the cap and lift away the cap.

4 Pull the rotor arm off the distributor cam spindle.

5 Lift away the dust proof cover.

6 Refer to Section 4 and remove the contact breaker points.

7 Unscrew the terminal post through bolt securing nut and disconnect the condenser lead.

8 Undo and remove the screw securing the condenser to the distributor body. Lift the condenser and lead away from the distributor body.

9 Unscrew the vacuum unit vernier adjuster (octane selector) and draw the assembly from the distributor body (Fig. 4.6).

10 Undo and remove the two screws securing the distributor cap spring clips to the distributor body. Lift away the two clips noting that the earth wire is retained by one of the clips securing screws.

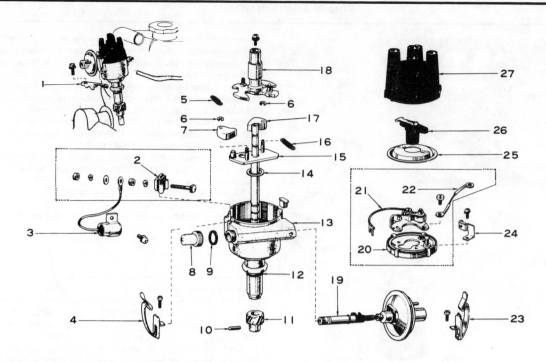

Fig. 4.4. Exploded view of distributor (2T series engine)

1	Distributor clamp plate	8	Vernier adjuster cap	15	Distributor shaft	22 Earth lead
2	Low tension terminal	9	Seal	16	Counterweight spring	23 Cap clip
3	Condenser	10	Pin	17	Counterweight	24 Damper
4	Cap clip	11	Driven gear	18	Cam	25 Dustproof cover
5	Counterweight spring	12	'O' ring	19	Vacuum diaphragm	26 Rotor arm
6	Circlip	13	Distributor body	20	Baseplate	27 Cap
7	Counterweight	14	Washer	21	Contact breaker assembly	

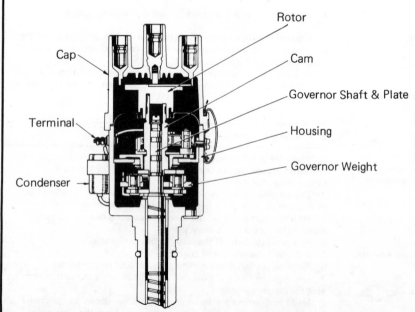

Fig. 4.5. Sectional view of 3K series engine type distributor

Fig. 4.6. Removing vacuum diaphragm unit from distributor

Fig. 4.7. Removing distributor baseplate

Measuring plug gap. A feeler gauge of the correct size (see ignition system specifications) should have a slight 'drag' when slid between the electrodes. Adjust gap if necessary

Adjusting plug gap. The plug gap is adjusted by bending the earth electrode inwards, or outwards, as necessary until the correct clearance is obtained. Note the use of the correct tool

Normal. Grey-brown deposits, lightly coated core nose. Gap increasing by around 0.001 in (0.025 mm) per 1000 miles (1600 km). Plugs ideally suited to engine, and engine in good condition

Carbon fouling. Dry, black, sooty deposits. Will cause weak spark and eventually misfire. Fault: over-rich fuel mixture. Check: carburettor mixture settings, float level and jet sizes; choke operation and cleanliness of air filter. Plugs can be re-used after cleaning

Oil fouling. Wet, oily deposits. Will cause weak spark and eventually misfire. Fault: worn bores/piston rings or valve guides; sometimes occurs (temporarily) during running-in period. Plugs can be re-used after thorough cleaning

Overheating. Electrodes have glazed appearance, core nose very white – few deposits. Fault: plug overheating. Check: plug value, ignition timing, fuel octane rating (too low) and fuel mixture (too weak). Discard plugs and cure fault immediately

Electrode damage. Electrodes burned away; core nose has burned, glazed appearance. Fault: pre-ignition. Check: as for 'Overheating' but may be more severe. Discard plugs and remedy fault before piston or valve damage occurs

Split core nose (may appear initially as a crack). Damage is self-evident, but cracks will only show after cleaning. Fault: pre-ignition or wrong gap-setting technique. Check: ignition timing, cooling system, fuel octane rating (too low) and fuel mixture (too weak). Discard plugs, rectify fault immediately

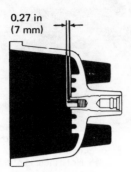

Fig. 4.8. Correct projection of carbon brush in distributor cap

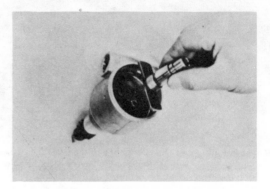

Fig. 4.9. Removing distributor cam

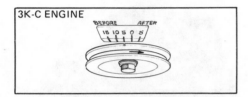

Fig. 4.10. Static ignition setting on 3K-C engine

11 The contact breaker plate assembly may now be lifted from the distributor body. To assist refitting note which way round it is fitted. (Fig. 4.7).

12 Undo and remove the screw located at the top of the cam spindle and lift away the cam (Fig. 4.7).

13 Using a pair of pliers carefully disconnect and lift away the two centrifugal weight springs (Fig. 4.9).

14 Carefully remove the circlips and lift away the centrifugal weights.

15 Using a suitable diameter parallel pin punch carefully tap out the pin securing the spiral gear to the spindle. It may be found that the pin ends are peened over. If so it will be necessary to file flat before attempting to drift out the pin. The gear may now be removed from the spindle (Fig. 4.12).

16 The spindle may now be drawn upwards from the distributor body. Take care to recover the washer(s) fitted between the centrifugal weight plate and distributor body (Fig. 4.13).

17 Wash all parts and wipe dry with a clean non-fluffy rag. Check the contact breaker points for wear. Inspect the distributor cap for signs of tracking (Indicated by a thin black line between the segments). Also look at the segments for signs of excessive corrosion. Renew the cap if necessary.

18 If the metal portion of the rotor arm is badly burned or loose renew the arm. If only slightly burned, clean the end with a fine abrasive paper.

19 Check that the contact in the centre of the distributor cap is in good order (Fig. 4.8).

20 Examine the centrifugal weights and pivots for wear and the advance springs for slackness. These can be best checked by comparing with new parts. If they are slack they must be renewed.

21 Check the points assembly for fit on the breaker plate, and the cam follower for wear.

22 Examine the fit of the spindle in the distributor body. If there is excessive side movement it will be necessary to obtain a new distributor body and spindle.

23 Check the resistance of the breaker plate sliding part. Ideally it should have a resistance of 2.2 lbs (1 kg). If it appears to be tight lubricate with a little engine oil.

24 Check the fit between the cam and spindle. If it is slack new parts will be necessary.

25 To reassemble, first, refit the centrifugal weights to the place and retain with the circlips.

26 Lubricate the outer surface of the spindle and slide the cam over the spindle and hook the springs onto the posts.

27 Fit the steel washer onto the shaft and lubricate with a little engine oil. Slide the shaft into the body and locate the spiral gear. Line up the pin holes and insert the pin.

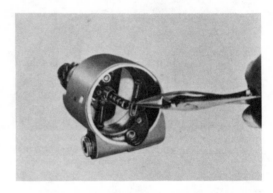

Fig. 4.11. Disconnecting a distributor counterweight spring

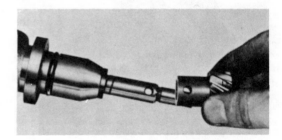

Fig. 4.12. Removing distributor driven gear

Fig. 4.13. Withdrawing distributor shaft

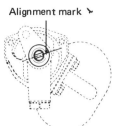

Alignment mark ↘

Fig. 4.14. Oil pump driveshaft alignment prior to installation of distributor

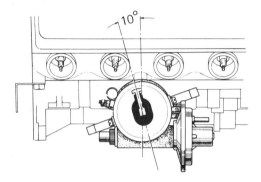

Fig. 4.15. Distributor (3K series engine) ready for installation

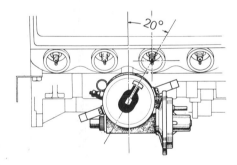

Fig. 4.16. Distributor (3K series engine) correctly installed

28 Using feeler gauges measure the shaft thrust clearance which should be 0.0006 - 0.020 in (0.15 - 0.50 mm). If adjustment is necessary select a steel washer of suitable thickness. These are available in a range of thicknesses: 0.098, 0.106 and 0.114 in (2.5, 2.7 and 2.9 mm).
29 Peen over the ends of the spiral gear retaining pin.
30 Refit the breaker plate assembly to the distributor body and locate the two distributor cap spring clips. Secure the clips with the screws and washers. Do not forget the earth wire is secured by the screw on the terminal side.
31 Note that the four breaker plate clips must be in position in the distributor body. Also the cap spring without the cap position locator must be on the terminal side of the distributor body.
32 Refit the terminal insulator and through bolt. Position the condenser cable terminal onto the through bolt and retain with the nut. Do not tighten the nut fully at this stage.
33 Fit the contact breaker points onto the breaker plate and secure with the two screws and washers. Do not forget the earth wire to be attached to the arm side securing screw.
34 Insert the vacuum advance unit to the housing, engaging it with the breaker plate and screw on the vernier adjuster (octane selector) until it is set at the standard position.
35 Secure the condenser to the side of the distributor body with the screw and washer.
36 Refer to Section 2 and adjust the contact breaker points. Connect the wire to the terminal block and tighten the nut.
37 Lubricate the distributor as described in Section 6 and then replace the dustproof cover, rotor arm and distributor cap. The distributor is now ready for refitting.

9 Distributor (3K Series engine) - refitting

1 Turn the crankshaft by applying a spanner to the pulley bolt until No. 1 piston is rising on its compression stroke. This can be ascertained by removing No. 1 spark plug and placing a finger over the plug hole to feel the compression being generated.
2 Continue turning until the notch on the crankshaft pulley is opposite the specified static (BTDC) timing mark on the timing cover scale. *This is not TDC setting* (Fig. 4.10).
3 Using a thin screwdriver, turn the end of the oil pump shaft so that the groove is in alignment with the mark on the oil pump body.

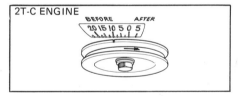

Fig. 4.17. Static ignition setting on 2T-C engine

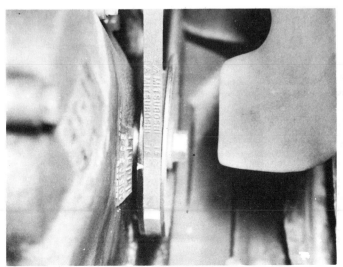

10.1 2T series engine timing marks with drivebelt in position

12.1 Coil showing externally mounted resistor fitted on some types

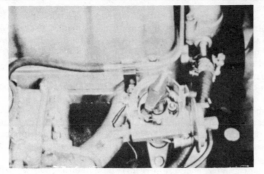

Fig. 4.18. Distributor (2T series engine) correctly installed

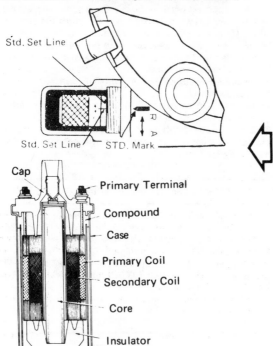

Fig. 4.20. Cut-away view of ignition coil

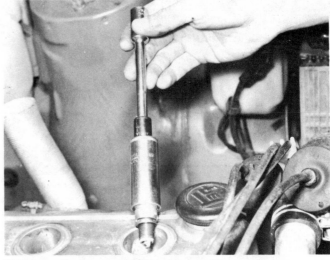

13.13 Removing a spark plug (2T series engine)

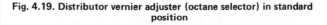

Fig. 4.19. Distributor vernier adjuster (octane selector) in standard position

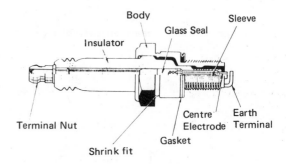

Fig. 4.21. Cut-away view of spark plug

4   Hold the distributor over its hole in the cylinder block so that the vacuum diaphragm unit is towards the front of the engine and parallel to the engine centre line.

5   Set the rotor arm as shown and push the distributor into its recess.

6   As the distributor gear meshes with the one on the camshaft, the rotor arm will turn in a clockwise direction through approximately 30°. The rotor arm will now be pointing at No. 1 spark plug segment in the distributor cap (when fitted).

7   Turn the distributor body gently until the points are just about to open and tighten the clamp bolt. The vernier adjuster (octane selector) should be in the standard position.

8   Fit the distributor cap and HT leads.

9   Reconnect the LT head and vacuum pipe.

10 Check the ignition timing as described in Section 11.

10 Distributor (2T Series engine) - refitting

1   The procedure is very similar to that described in the preceding Section, but note the forward location of the distributor and the different scale on the engine timing cover. (Figs. 4.17 and 4.18/photo).

11 Ignition timing

1   Setting of the static (BTDC) advance angle should only be regarded as an initial setting. A stroboscope should then be used to check and adjust the timing more precisely.

2   Check that the dwell angle is correct, the vernier adjuster (octane selector) is in the standard position and that the contact breaker points are just about to open when the notch on the crankshaft pulley is opposite the specified static timing mark on the engine timing cover scale.

3   Run the engine to normal operating temperature and check that the idling speed is as specified.

4   Pull off the vacuum pipe from the distributor diaphragm and plug the pipe.

5   Connect a stroboscope in accordance with the manufacturer's instructions (usually between No. 1 spark plug and the end of No. 1 spark plug lead).

6   Point the stroboscope at the timing cover scale when the notch in the crankshaft pulley and the appropriate (BTDC) mark on the scale will appear stationary. Any difficulty in observing these marks clearly can be overcome by painting them with quick drying white paint.

7   If the timing is correct, the notch should appear to be in alignment with the specified BTDC mark on the scale. If it is out of alignment by a small amount, correct by turning the vernier adjuster (octane selector). If the misalignment is considerable then loosen the distributor clamp bolt and turn the distributor body one way or the other. Retighten the clamp bolt when adjustment is correct. Gross errors in ignition timing will be due to incorrect installation of the distributor. Refer to Section 9 or 10.

8   While the stroboscope is connected, it is useful to check the efficiency of the centrifugal and vacuum advance mechanisms of the distributor.

9   With the vacuum pipe still disconnected and plugged, speed up the engine. The timing marks which were in alignment at idling will move

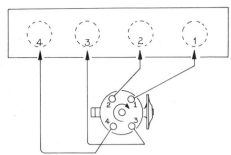

Fig. 4.22. HT lead connecting diagram

apart, proving that the centrifugal advance mechanism is operating.
10 Now reconnect the vacuum pipe to the distributor and again speed
up the engine. The timing marks will move apart a much greater
distance for the same relative engine speed. This proves that both the
centrifugal and vacuum advance mechanisms of the distributor are
functioning.

12 Coil polarity and testing

1 High tension current should be negative at the spark plug terminals.
If the HT current is positive at the spark plug terminals then the LT
leads to the coil primary terminals have been incorrectly connected. A
wrong connection can cause as much as 60% loss of spark efficiency and
can cause rough idling and misfiring at speed (Fig. 4.20/photos).
2 With a negative earth electrical system, the LT lead from the distributor connects with the negative (primary) terminal on the coil.
3 The simplest way to test a coil is by substitution. If an ohmmeter
is available use it to carry out the following checks but first apply a
12 volt current to the coil to bring it to normal operating temperature.
4 Check the primary resistance between the coil (+) and (—) terminals
which should be between 3.3 and 4.3 ohms.
5 Check the secondary resistance (secondary to primary terminals)
this should be between 7500 and 10000 ohms.
6 Insulation breakdown can only be satisfactorily tested using a
megohmmeter between the coil casing and the primary terminals. The
resistance should be in excess of 50 megohms.

13 Spark plugs and HT leads

Refer to page 83 for plug condition photographs.

14 Fault diagnosis - ignition system

1 The correct functioning of the spark plugs is vital for the correct
running and efficiency of the engine. The plugs fitted as standard are
listed in the Specifications page.
2 At specified intervals, the plugs should be removed, examined,
cleaned and, if worn excessively, renewed. The condition of the spark
plug will also tell much about the overall condition of the engine.
3 If the insulator nose of the spark plug is clean and white, with no
deposits, this is indicative of a weak mixture, or too hot a plug.
4 If the top and insulator nose is covered with hard black looking
deposits, then this is indicative that the mixture is too rich. Should the
plug be black and oily, then it is likely that the engine is fairly worn,
as well as the mixture being too rich.
5 If the insulator nose is covered with light tan to greyish brown
deposits, then the mixture is correct and it is likely that the engine is
in good condition.
6 If there are any traces of long brown tapering stains on the outside
of the white portion of the plug, then the plug will have to be
renewed, as this shows that there is a faulty joint between the plug
body and the insulator, and compression is being allowed to leak away.
7 Plugs should be cleaned by a sand blasting machine, which will free
them from carbon more thoroughly than cleaning by hand. The
machine will also test the condition of the plugs under compression.
Any plug that fails to spark at the recommended pressure should be
renewed.
8 The spark plug gap is of considerable importance, as, if it is too
large or too small the size of the spark and its efficiency will be
seriously impaired. The spark plug gap should be set to between 0.028
and 0.032 in (0.7 and 0.8 mm) for the best results.
9 To set it, measure the gap with a feeler gauge, and then bend open,
or close the outer plug electrode until the correct gap is achieved. The
centre electrode should never be bent as this may crack the insulation
and cause plug failure.
10 The HT leads to the coil and spark plugs are of internal resistance,
carbon core type. They are used in the interest of eliminating interference caused by the ignition system. They are much more easily
damaged than copper cored cable and they should be pulled from the
spark plug terminals by gripping the metal end fitting at the end of the
cable. Occasionally wipe the external surfaces of the leads free from oil
and dirt using a fuel moistened cloth.
11 Always check the connection of the HT leads to the spark plugs is
in correct firing order sequence 1 - 3 - 4 - 2 (Fig. 4.22).
12 On 2T Series engines, pull the rubber plugs out of the rocker cover
to detach the leads from the spark plugs. *Grip the rubber plugs not the
leads.*
13 Note the insulating tubes and the fact that the spark plugs are so
deeply recessed that they require the use of a box spanner or long
socket (photo).

Symptom	Reason/s
Engine turns over normally on starter but will not fire	Damp HT leads or moisture inside distributor cap. Faulty condenser. Oil on contact breaker points. Disconnected lead at distributor, ignition switch or coil.
Engine runs but misfires	Faulty spark plug. Faulty HT lead. Contact breaker gap too close, too wide or pitted points. Crack in rotor arm. Crack in distributor cap. Faulty coil. Faulty distributor condenser.
Engine overheats or lacks power	Seized centrifugal advance weights or cam on shaft. Perforated vacuum pipe from vacuum diaphragm unit. Incorrectly timed ignition.
Engine 'pinks' (pre-detonation) under load	Ignition timing too advanced. Centrifugal advance mechanism stuck in advance position. Broken centrifugal advance spring. Octane rating of fuel too low.

Chapter 5 Clutch and actuating mechanism

Refer to Chapter 13 for specifications and information applicable to 1979 US models.

Contents

Specifications

Type ... ...

Single dry plate, diaphragm spring with cable actuation on 1200E and 30 Series models and hydraulic actuation on 1600 models.

Pedal free movement (1200E and 30 Series models)	0.8 to 1.4 in (20.0 to 35.0 mm)
Pedal height (1200E and 30 Series models)	5.5 to 5.9 in (140.0 to 150.0 mm)
Pedal free movement (1600 models)	1.0 to 1.8 in (25.0 to 45.0 mm)
Pedal height (1600 models)	6.4 to 6.8 in (160.0 to 170.0 mm)
Clutch driven plate diameter	7.09 in (180.0 mm)
Minimum lining depth above rivet head	0.012 in (0.3 mm)
Maximum driven plate run-out	0.020 in (0.5 mm)

Torque wrench settings

	lb/ft	Nm
Clutch bellhousing to engine bolts (K40, K50 gearbox)	45	62
Clutch bellhousing to engine bolts (T40, T50 gearbox)	50	
Clutch cover bolts to flywheel	16	69
Clutch pedal pivot bolt (1200E and 30 Series models)	50	69
Clutch pedal pivot bolt (1600 models)	30	41
Clutch release fork support bolt (1200E and 30 Series models)	20	28
Clutch master cylinder mounting bolt	20	28

1 General description

1 The models covered by this manual are fitted with a diaphragm spring clutch operated mechanically on models 1200E and 30 Series models and hydraulically on 1600 models.

2 The clutch comprises a steel cover which is bolted and dowelled to the rear face of the flywheel and contains the pressure plate and clutch disc (driven plate).

3 The pressure plate and diaphragm spring are attached to the clutch assembly cover.

4 The clutch disc is free to slide along the splined gearbox input shaft and is held in position between the flywheel and pressure plate by the pressure of the diaphragm spring.

5 Friction lining material is riveted to the clutch disc which has a cushioned hub to absorb transmission shocks and to help ensure a smooth take off.

6 The mechanically operated clutch system utilises a pendant pedal which is attached to a heavy duty cable. The other end of the cable is attached to the clutch release arm.

7 With the hydraulically operated clutch system the pendant clutch pedal is connected to the clutch master cylinder and hydraulic fluid reservoir by a short pushrod. The master cylinder and fluid reservoir are mounted on the engine side of the bulkhead in front of the driver.

8 Depressing the clutch pedal moves the piston in the master cylinder forwards so forcing hydraulic fluid through to the slave cylinder.

9 The piston in the slave cylinder moves rearwards on the entry of the fluid and actuates the clutch release arm, via a short pushrod. The opposite end of the release arm is forked and carries the release bearing assembly.

10 As the pivoted clutch release arm moves rearwards it pushes the release bearing forwards to bear against the diaphragm spring and pushes forwards so moving the pressure plate backwards and disengaging the pressure plate from the clutch disc.

11 When the clutch pedal is released the pressure plate is forced into contact with the high friction bearings on the clutch disc and at the same time pushes the clutch disc a fraction of an inch forwards on its splines so engaging the clutch disc with the flywheel. The clutch disc is now firmly sandwiched between the pressure plate and the flywheel so the drive is taken up.

2 Clutch adjustment (cable actuation)

1 Measure the distance between the upper surface of the clutch pedal pad and the surface of the floor carpet. This should be between 5.5 and 5.9 in (140.0 and 150.0 mm).

2 If adjustment is required, release the locknut on the stop bolt and adjust the effective length of the stop bolt as necessary.

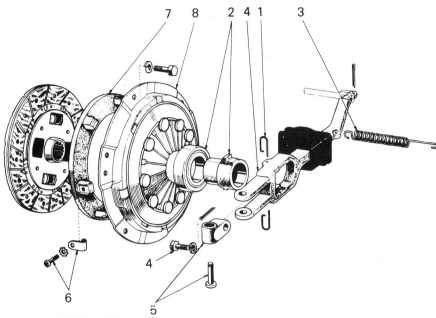

Fig. 5.1. Clutch assembly (1200E and 30 series)

1 Release bearing clips
2 Bearing/hub
3 Return spring
4 Release lever/fork
5 Release fork support

6 Pressure plate retracting
   springs and screws
7 Pressure plate
8 Clutch cover and
   spring

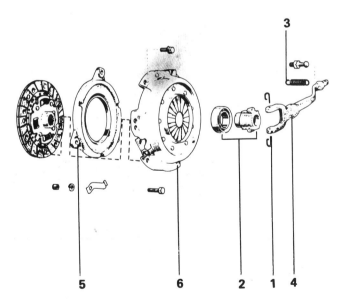

Fig. 5.2. Clutch assembly (1600 models)

1 Release lever and bearing hub
   clips
2 Release bearing and hub
3 Return spring

4 Release lever/fork
5 Pressure plate
6 Clutch cover and
   diaphragm spring

3 Working within the engine compartment, grip the clutch outer cable conduit and pull it until a resistance is felt. A total of 5 or 6 grooves and ridges should now be able to be counted between the 'E' clip and the end face of the conduit support.

4 If necessary, move the position of the 'E' clip to achieve this.

5 Let the clutch cable resume its normal position and then depress the clutch pedal several times and measure the free movement at the pedal pad. The free movement is the distance through which the pedal can be depressed with the fingers until firm resistance is met with. The free movement should be between 0.8 and 1.4 in (20.0 and 35.0 mm).

3 Clutch adjustment (hydraulic actuation)

1 Refer to paragraphs 1 and 2 of the preceding Section and check and adjust the clutch pedal height noting however that the distance of the pedal from the floor carpet is between 6.4 and 6.8 in (160.0 and 170.0 mm).

2 With the pedal correctly set, check that there is just the slightest amount of clearance between the pedal pushrod and the master cylinder piston. The best way to judge this is to depress the pedal very gently using one finger. If necessary, release the locknut on the pedal pushrod and turn the rod to achieve the specified clearance which is between 0.02 and 0.20 in (0.5 and 5.0 mm).

3 Working under the vehicle, release the locknut on the slave cylinder pushrod and turn the rod until there is a free movement at the end of the release lever of between 0.08 and 0.12 in (0.5 and 5.0 mm).

4 Once this is set there should be a free movement at the pedal pad of between 1.0 and 1.8 in (25.0 and 45.0 mm).

5 As it is very difficult to measure the free movement at the end of the release lever, it is more practical to adjust the slave cylinder push-rod until the pedal free movement is within the range specified.

4 Clutch hydraulic system - bleeding

1 Gather together a clean glass jar, a length of rubber/plastic tubing which fits tightly over the bleed nipple on the slave cylinder, and a tin of hydraulic brake fluid. You will also need the help of an assistant.

2 Check that the master cylinder reservoir is full. If it is not, fill it and also fill the bottom two inches of the jar with hydraulic fluid.

3 Remove the rubber dust cap from the bleed nipple on the slave cylinder, and with a suitable spanner open the bleed nipple approximately three-quarters of a turn.

4 Place one end of the tube over the nipple and insert the other end in the jar so that the tube orifice is below the level of the fluid.

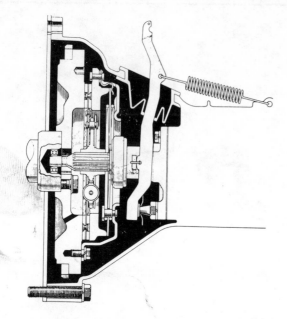

Fig. 5.3. Cut-away view of clutch (1200E and 30 series)

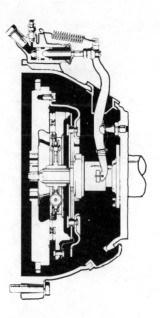

Fig. 5.4. Cut-away view of clutch (1600 models)

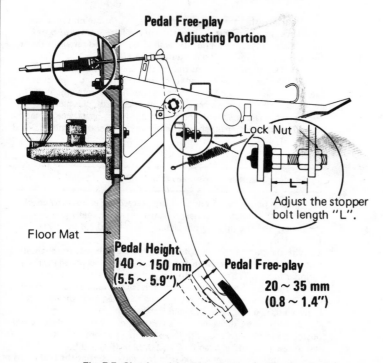

Pedal Free-play Adjusting Portion

Lock Nut

Adjust the stopper bolt length "L".

Floor Mat

Pedal Height 140 ~ 150 mm (5.5 ~ 5.9")

Pedal Free-play 20 ~ 35 mm (0.8 ~ 1.4")

Fig. 5.5. Clutch pedal setting diagram (cable actuation)

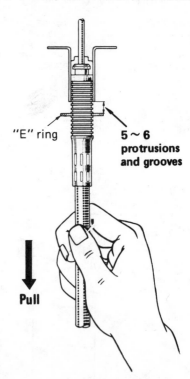

"E" ring

5 ~ 6 protrusions and grooves

Pull

Fig. 5.6. Setting clutch pedal free play by adjusting cable

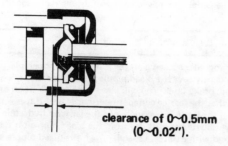

clearance of 0~0.5mm (0~0.02").

Fig. 5.7. Pushrod to master cylinder piston clearance

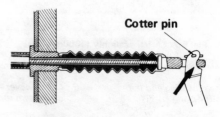

Cotter pin

Fig. 5.8. Clutch cable attachment to release lever

5 The assistant should now depress the pedal and hold it down at the end of its stroke. Allow the pedal to return to its normal position.
6 Continue this series of operations until clean hydraulic fluid without any traces of air bubbles emerges from the end of the tubing. Be sure that the reservoir is checked frequently to ensure that the hydraulic fluid does not drop too far, thus letting air into the system.
7 When no more air bubbles appear tighten the bleed nipple during a downstroke.
8 Replace the rubber dust cap over the bleed nipple.

5 Clutch cable - renewal

1 Remove the 'E' ring from the top end of the clutch release outer cable.
2 Remove the split pin and then disconnect the lower end of the inner cable from the clutch release fork.
3 Detach the release cable from the transmission case.
4 Disconnect the top end of the release cable from the clutch pedal and withdraw the release cable assembly.
5 Inspect the hooks at both ends of the inner cable for signs of wear or damage. If evident a new cable assembly will be required.
6 Inspect the outer cable, 'O' ring and rubber boot for damage.
7 Refitting the clutch release cable is the reverse sequence to removal but the following additional points should be noted:

   a) Lubricate the ends of the inner cable with a little grease.
   b) Adjust the clutch pedal free movement (Section 2).

6 Clutch pedal - removal and refitting

1 On 1200E and 30 Series models, disconnect the clutch cable from the pedal as described in the preceding Section.
2 Unscrew the nut from the pedal pivot bolt and extract the bolt and bushes.
3 Renew bushes and components as necessary. Apply grease to the pivot when installing and tighten the pivot bolt nut to specified torque.
4 On 1600 models, the clutch and brake pedals operate on a common pivot shaft.
5 To remove either pedal, disconnect the pedal return springs and the pushrod clevis forks from the pedal arms.
6 Unscrew the nut from the pivot shaft, withdraw the pivot shaft and remove the pedals, bushes and washers.
7 Renew any worn components and bushes and grease them before reassembly.
8 Tighten the pivot shaft nut to specified torque.

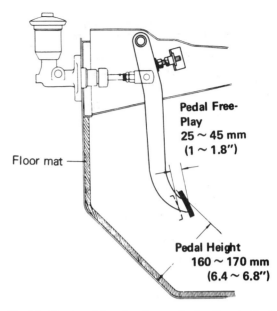

Pedal Free-Play
25 ~ 45 mm
(1 ~ 1.8")

Floor mat

Pedal Height
160 ~ 170 mm
(6.4 ~ 6.8")

Fig. 5.9. Clutch pedal setting diagram (hydraulic actuation)

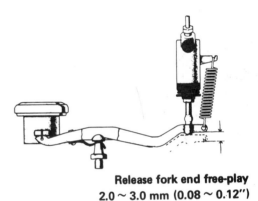

Release fork end free-play
2.0 ~ 3.0 mm (0.08 ~ 0.12")

Fig. 5.10. Clutch slave cylinder pushrod adjustment diagram

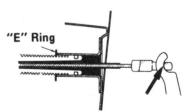

"E" Ring

Fig. 5.12. Clutch cable attachment to clutch pedal

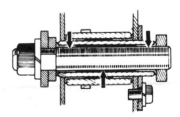

Fig. 5.13. Clutch pedal pivot (cable actuated clutch)
Arrows indicate grease application areas

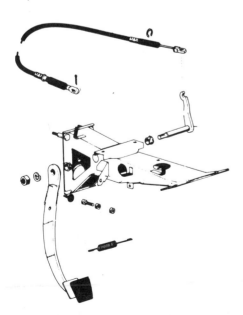

Fig. 5.11. Clutch pedal components (cable actuated type)

7 Clutch master cylinder - removal and refitting

1   Drain the fluid from the clutch master cylinder reservoir by
attaching a rubber or plastic tube to the slave cylinder bleed nipple.
Undo the nipple by approximately three-quarters of a turn and then
pump the fluid out into a suitable container by operating the clutch
pedal repeatedly until the fluid reservoir is empty.
2   Place a rag under the master cylinder to catch any hydraulic fluid
that may be spilt. Unscrew the union nut from the end of the metal
pipe where it enters the clutch master cylinder and gently pull the
pipe clear.
3   Withdraw the split pin that retains the pushrod yoke to the pedal
clevis pin and remove the clevis pin.
4   Undo and remove the two nuts and spring washers that secure the
master cylinder to the bulkhead. Lift away the master cylinder taking
care not to allow hydraulic fluid to come into contact with the paintwork as it acts as a solvent.
5   Refitting the master cylinder is the reverse sequence to removal.
Bleed the system as described in Section 4 and finally adjust the pushrod clearance as described in Section 3.

8 Clutch master cylinder - overhaul

1   Peel back the flexible boot from the end of the master cylinder to
expose the circlip. Extract the circlip so that the pushrod and piston
stop plate can be withdrawn.
2   Remove the piston/seal assembly by either tapping the end of the
master cylinder on a block of hardwood or by applying air pressure at
the fluid outlet port.
3   The assembly is separated by lifting the spring retainer leaf over
the shouldered end of the plunger. The seal should then be eased off
and discarded. Note which way round the seal is fitted.
4   Depress the piston retaining spring allowing the valve stem to slide
through the keyhole in the retainer thus releasing the tension in the
spring.

5   Detach the inlet valve case taking care of the spring dished washer
which will be found under the valve head.
6   Remove the valve seal from the valve shank.
7   Examine the bore of the cylinder carefully for any signs of scores
or ridges and, if this is found to be smooth all over, new seals can be
fitted. If there is any doubt of the condition of the bore then a new
cylinder must be fitted complete.
8   If examination of the seals shows them to be apparently oversize
or swollen, or very loose on the piston suspect oil contamination in
the system. Ordinary lubricating oil will swell these rubber seals, and
if one is found to be swollen it is reasonable to assume that all seals
in the clutch hydraulic system will need attention. Fit them using the
fingers only to manipulate them into position.
9   Thoroughly clean all parts in either fresh hydraulic fluid or
Methylated Spirit. Ensure that the bypass parts are clean.
10 All components should be assembled wetted with clean brake
fluid. Fit a new valve seat the correct way round so that the flat side
is seating on the valve head.
11 Place the spring dished washer with the dome against the underside
of the valve head. Hold it in position with the valve case ensuring that
the legs face towards the valve seal.
12 Replace the plunger return spring centrally on the spacer, insert
the retainer into the spring and depress until the valve stem engages
in the keyhole of the retainer.
13 Ensure that the spring is central on the spacer before fitting a new
piston seal onto the piston with the flat face against the face of the
piston.
14 Insert the reduced end of the piston into the retainer until the leaf
engages under the shoulder of the plunger, and press home the leaf.
15 Check that the master cylinder bore is clean and smear with clean
hydraulic fluid. With the piston suitably wetted with hydraulic fluid,
carefully insert the assembly into the bore - valve end first. Ease the
lips of the piston seal carefully into the bore.
16 Replace the pushrod and refit the snap ring into the groove in the
cylinder bore. Smear the sealing areas of the dust cover with a little
rubber grease and pack the cover with the rubber grease so as to act
as a dust trap. Fit the cover to the master cylinder body. The master
cylinder is now ready for refitting to the car.

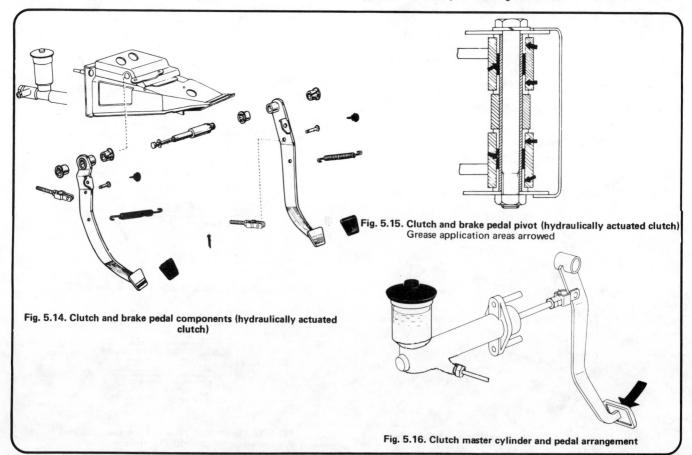

Fig. 5.14. Clutch and brake pedal components (hydraulically actuated
clutch)

Fig. 5.15. Clutch and brake pedal pivot (hydraulically actuated clutch)
Grease application areas arrowed

Fig. 5.16. Clutch master cylinder and pedal arrangement

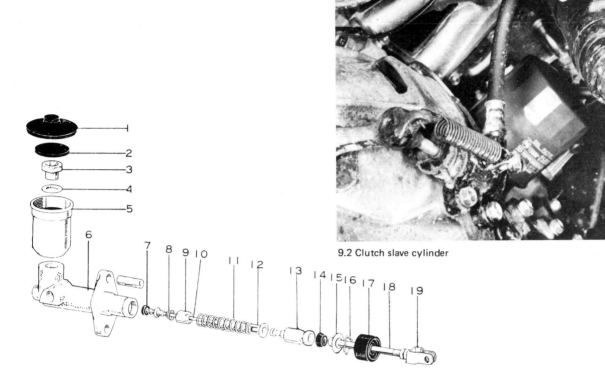

9.2 Clutch slave cylinder

Fig. 5.17. Exploded view of clutch master cylinder

1 Reservoir filler cap
2 Reservoir float
3 Bolt
4 Washer
5 Master cylinder reservoir
6 Master cylinder body
7 Inlet valve
8 Conical spring
9 Inlet valve case
10 Inlet valve connecting rod
11 Compression spring
12 Spring retainer
13 Piston
14 Cylinder cup
15 Piston stop plate
16 Snap ring (circlip)
17 Rubber dust cover
18 Pushrod
19 Pushrod clevis

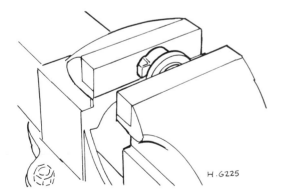

Fig. 5.18. Pressing a new clutch release bearing onto hub

9 Clutch slave cylinder - removal and refitting

1 Wipe the top of the clutch master cylinder, unscrew the cap and place a piece of polythene sheet over the top to create a partial vacuum and to stop hydraulic fluid syphoning out when the slave cylinder is removed. Refit the cap.
2 Wipe the area around the union on the slave cylinder and unscrew the union. Tape the end of the pipe to stop dirt entering (photo).
3 Detach the return spring between release arm and cylinder body.
4 Slacken the locknut, unscrew the pushrod and lift away from between the release arm and cylinder body.
5 Undo and remove the two cylinder securing bolts and lift away from the side of the clutch housing.
6 Refitting the clutch slave cylinder is the reverse sequence to removal. It will be necessary to bleed the hydraulic system as described in Section 4 and then adjust the pushrod clearance as described in Section 3.

10 Clutch slave cylinder - overhaul

1 Clean the exterior of the slave cylinder using a dry non-fluffy rag.
2 Carefully ease back the dust cover from the end of the slave cylinder and lift away.
3 The piston and seal assembly should now be shaken out. If a low pressure air jet is available, the piston and seal may be ejected using this method. Place a rag over the open end so that when the piston is ejected it does not fly out onto the floor.
4 Remove the piston seal and discard it. Do not use a metal screwdriver as this could scratch the piston. Note which way round the seal is fitted.
5 Inspect the inside of the cylinder for score marks caused by

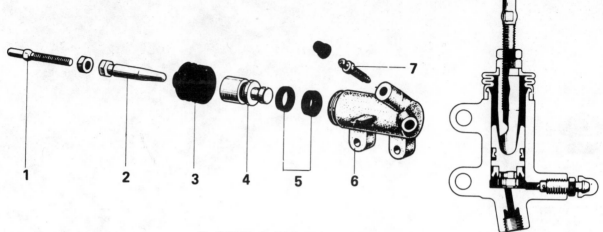

Fig. 5.19. Exploded view of the clutch slave cylinder

1 Pushrod assembly
2 Pushrod assembly

3 Flexible boot
4 Piston

5 Seals
6 Body

7 Bleed screw

11.3 Removing a clutch cover bolt

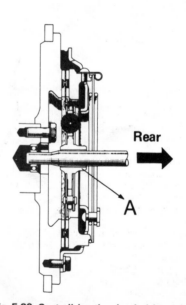

Fig. 5.20. Centralising the clutch driven plate

A   Greater projecting side furthest from flywheel

11.4 Withdrawing clutch driven plate

12.2A Extracting clutch release bearing carrier clip

12.2B Withdrawing clutch release bearing and carrier

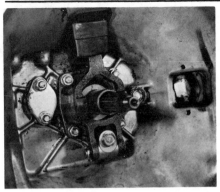

12.5 Clutch release bearing assembly
(1200E and 30 series)

13.1 Refitting clutch cover

13.5 Clutch cover installed showing centralised
driven plate

impurities in the hydraulic fluid. If there are any found, the cylinder
and piston will require renewal.

6   If the cylinder is sound, thoroughly clean it out with clean
hydraulic fluid.

7   The old rubber seal will probably be swollen and visibly worn.
Smear the new rubber seal with fresh hydraulic fluid and refit it to the
stem of the piston ensuring that the smaller periphery, or back of the
seal is against the piston. Use the fingers only to manipulate the seals
into position.

8   Wet the piston and seal in fresh hydraulic fluid and insert the
piston and seal into the bore of the cylinder. Gently ease the edge of
the seal into the bore so that it does not roll over.

9   Smear the sealing areas of the dust cover with rubber grease and
pack the cover with rubber grease to act as a dust trap. Fit the cover
to the slave cylinder body. The slave cylinder is now ready for refitting
to the car.

11 Clutch - removal and inspection

1   Remove the gearbox as described in Chapter 6.

2   With a centre punch, mark the relative position of the clutch cover
and flywheel to ensure correct refitting if the original parts are to be
reused.

3   Remove the clutch assembly by unscrewing the six bolts holding the
cover to the rear face of the flywheel. Unscrew the bolts diagonally half
a turn at a time to prevent distortion of the cover flange, also to
prevent an accident caused by the cover flange binding on the dowels
and suddenly flying off (photo).

4   With the bolts removed, lift the assembly off the locating dowels.
The driven plate or clutch disc will fall out at this stage, as it is not
attached to either the clutch cover assembly or flywheel. Carefully
note which way round the driven plate is fitted (greater projecting
side away from flywheel) (photo).

5   It is important that no oil or grease gets on the clutch disc friction
linings, or the pressure plate and flywheel faces. It is advisable to
handle the parts with clean hands and to wipe down the pressure plate
and flywheel faces with a clean dry rag before inspection or refitting
commences.

6   In the normal course of events clutch dismantling and reassembly
is the term for simply fitting a new clutch pressure plate and friction
disc. Under no circumstances should the pressure plate assembly be
dismantled. If a fault develops in the assembly an exchange replacement must be fitted.

7   If a new clutch disc is being fitted it is false economy not to renew
the release bearing at the same time. This will preclude having to
replace it at a later time when wear on the clutch linings is very slight,
see Section 12.

8   Examine the clutch disc friction linings for wear or loose rivets and
the disc for rim distortion, cracks and worn splines.
   Renew the driven plate complete, do not attempt to reline this
component yourself.
   Check the machined faces of the flywheel and the pressure plate.
If either is badly grooved it should be machined until smooth, or
replaced with a new item. If the pressure plate is cracked or split it
must be renewed.

Examine the hub splines for wear and make sure that the centre
hub is not loose.

12 Clutch release bearing - removal and refitting

1   To gain access it is necessary to remove the gearbox as described in
Chapter 6.

2   Detach the spring clips from the release bearing carrier and release
fork. Draw the release bearing carrier from the flat bearing retainer
(photos).

3   Check the bearing for signs of overheating, wear or roughness, and,
if evident, the old bearing should be drawn off the carrier using a
universal two or three leg puller. Note which way round the bearing is
fitted.

4   Using a bench vice and suitable packing, press a new bearing onto
the carrier (Fig. 5.19).

5   Apply some high melting point grease to the contact surfaces of
the release lever and pivot assembly, and bearing carrier. Pack some
grease into the inner recess of the bearing carrier (photo).

6   Refitting the bearing and carrier is the reverse sequence to removal.

13 Clutch - centralising and refitting

1   To refit the clutch plate, place the clutch disc against the flywheel
with the larger end of the hub away from the flywheel. On no account
should the clutch disc be replaced the wrong way round as it will be
found impossible to operate the clutch (photo).

2   Replace the clutch cover assembly loosely on the dowels. Replace
the six bolts and tighten them finger tight so that the clutch disc is
gripped but can still be moved, sideways but stiffly.

3   The clutch disc must now be centralised so that when the engine
and gearbox are mated, the gearbox input shaft splines will pass
through the splines in the centre of the hub.

4   Centralisation can be carried out quite easily by inserting a round
bar or long screwdriver through the hole in the centre of the clutch,
so that the end of the bar rests in the small hole in the crankshaft containing the input shaft bearing bush. Moving the bar sideways or up
and down will move the clutch disc in whichever direction is necessary
to achieve centralisation.

5   Centralisation is easily judged by removing the bar or screwdriver
and viewing the driveplate hub in relation to the hole in the centre of
the diaphragm spring. When the hub is exactly in the centre of the
release bearing hole, all is correct. Alternatively, if an old input shaft
can be borrowed this will eliminate all the guesswork as it will fit the
bearing and centre of the clutch hub exactly, obviating the need for
visual alignment (photo).

6   Tighten the clutch bolts firmly in a diagonal sequence to ensure
that the cover plate is pulled down evenly and without distortion of
the flange.

7   Check that the bolts are tightened to specified torque wrench
setting.

8   Install the gearbox (see Chapter 6).

9   Adjust the clutch free movement.

14 Fault diagnosis - clutch

Sympton	Reason/s
Judder when taking up drive	Loose engine or gearbox mountings. Driven plate linings worn or contaminated with oil. Worn splines in driven plate hub or on input shaft of gearbox. Worn flywheel centre spigot bearing.
Clutch spin (failure to disengage completely so that gears cannot be meshed)	Incorrect clutch pedal free movement. Air in clutch hydraulic system. Damaged or misaligned pressure plate assembly.
Clutch slip (increase in engine speed does not result in vehicle speed increasing - particularly on uphill gradients)	Incorrect pedal free movement. Driven plate friction linings worn out or oil contaminated.
Noise evident on depressing clutch pedal	Faulty or worn release bearing. Insufficient pedal free movement. Weak or broken pedal or release lever return spring.
Noise evident as clutch pedal released	Distorted driven plate. Weak driven plate torsion shock absorbers in hub. Insufficient pedal free movement. Weak or broken pedal or release lever return spring. Distorted or worn input shaft. Release bearing loose on retainer hub.

Chapter 6 Gearbox Part 1

Contents

Specifications - Part 1 - Manual gearbox

Application

Type K40 gearbox ... ...   Vehicles fitted with 3K series (71.1 cu in - 1166 cc) engine, except Liftback

Type K50 gearbox ... ...   Liftback with 3K series engine and option on certain other 1200 models

Type T40 gearbox ... ...   Vehicles fitted with 2T series (96.9 cu in - 1588 cc) engine

Type T50 gearbox ... ...   Standard equipment on 1600 SR-5 and Liftback models and option on all other 2T series engine models, except base 2 door version

Type K40 and T40 gearboxes are of four forward speed type with reverse. Synchromesh on all forward speeds

Type K50 and T50 gearboxes have five forward speeds and reverse. Synchromesh on all forward speeds. Fifth speed is really an overdrive top gear

Ratios											K40	K50	T40	T50
1st	...	...	...	...	...	...	...	...	...	...	3.684 : 1	3.789 : 1	3.587 : 1	3.587 : 1
2nd	...	...	...	...	...	...	...	...	...	...	2.050 : 1	2.220 : 1	2.022 : 1	2.022 : 1
3rd	...	...	...	...	...	...	...	...	...	...	1.383 : 1	1.435 : 1	1.384 : 1	1.384 : 1
4th	...	...	...	...	...	...	...	...	...	...	1.000 : 1	1.000 : 1	1.000 : 1	1.000 : 1
5th	...	...	...	...	...	...	...	...	...	...	—	0.865 : 1	—	0.861 : 1
Reverse	...	...	...	...	...	...	...	...	...	...	4.316 : 1	4.316 : 1	3.484 : 1	3.484 : 1

Oil capacities

K40 and K50 type gearbox ... ...   1.5 Imp. qt, 1.8 US qt, 1.7 litre
T40 and T50 type gearbox ... ...   1.4 Imp. qt, 1.6 US qt, 1.5 litre

Tolerances (K40 and K50 gearboxes)

Countershaft endfloat ... ...   0.0020 to 0.0098 in (0.05 to 0.25 mm)
Mainshaft gear endfloat
    1st gear ... ...   0.0071 to 0.0110 in (0.18 to 0.28 mm)
    2nd gear ... ...   0.0039 to 0.0078 in (0.10 to 0.25 mm)
    3rd gear ... ...   0.0020 to 0.0059 in (0.05 to 0.15 mm)
    5th gear ... ...   0.0079 to 0.0118 in (0.20 to 0.30 mm)
Maximum endfloat all gears ... ...   0.012 in (0.3 mm)
1st, 2nd, 3rd gear running clearance on mainshaft ... ...   0.0020 to 0.0039 in (0.05 to 0.10 mm)

Shift fork to synchro sleeve groove clearance (maximum) ...   .   0.0032 in (0.8 mm)
Synchro ring clearance when pressed onto cone of gear (maximum)   ...   0.032 in (0.8 mm)

Circlip thicknesses
Input shaft bearing to shaft circlip   ...   .   0.0925 to 0.0945 in (2.35 to 2.40 mm)
                                                                                      0.0965 to 0.0984 in (2.45 to 2.50 mm)
Mainshaft front synchro hub to shaft circlip   ...   .   0.0807 to 0.0827 in (2.05 to 2.10 mm)
                                                                                      0.0827 to 0.0845 in (2.10 to 2.15 mm)
                                                                                      0.0845 to 0.0866 in (2.15 to 2.20 mm)
                                                                                      0.0866 to 0.0886 in (2.20 to 2.25 mm)
                                                                                      0.0886 to 0.0906 in (2.25 to 2.30 mm)
                                                                                      0.0906 to 0.0925 in (2.30 to 2.35 mm)
                                                                                      0.0925 to 0.0945 in (2.35 to 2.40 mm)
                                                                                      0.0945 to 0.0965 in (2.40 to 2.45 mm)
Mainshaft rear bearing (K50) circlip   ...   .   0.0807 to 0.0827 in (2.05 to 2.10 mm)
                                                                                      0.0827 to 0.0846 in (2.10 to 2.15 mm)
                                                                                      0.0846 to 0.0866 in (2.15 to 2.20 mm)
                                                                                      0.0866 to 0.0886 in (2.20 to 2.25 mm)
                                                                                      0.0886 to 0.0906 in (2.25 to 2.30 mm)
                                                                                      0.0906 to 0.0925 in (2.30 to 2.35 mm)
                                                                                      0.0925 to 0.0945 in (2.35 to 2.40 mm)
                                                                                      0.0945 to 0.0965 in (2.40 to 2.45 mm)
                                                                                      0.0965 to 0.0984 in (2.45 to 2.50 mm)
                                                                                      0.0984 to 0.1004 in (2.50 to 2.55 mm)
Countershaft rear (K50) circlip   ...   .   0.0886 to 0.0925 in (2.25 to 2.35 mm)
                                                                                      0.0925 to 0.0965 in (2.35 to 2.45 mm)
                                                                                      0.0965 to 0.1004 in (2.45 to 2.55 mm)
Fifth gear (K50) circlip thickness   ...   .   0.0807 to 0.0827 in (2.05 to 2.10 mm)
                                                                                      0.0827 to 0.0846 in (2.10 to 2.15 mm)
                                                                                      0.0846 to 0.0866 in (2.15 to 2.20 mm)
                                                                                      0.0866 to 0.0886 in (2.20 to 2.25 mm)
                                                                                      0.0886 to 0.0906 in (2.25 to 2.30 mm)
                                                                                      0.0906 to 0.0925 in (2.30 to 2.35 mm)
                                                                                      0.0925 to 0.0945 in (2.35 to 2.40 mm)
                                                                                      0.0945 to 0.0965 in (2.40 to 2.45 mm)
                                                                                      0.0965 to 0.0984 in (2.45 to 2.50 mm)
                                                                                      0.0984 to 0.1004 in (2.50 to 2.55 mm)
                                                                                      0.1004 to 0.1024 in (2.55 to 2.60 mm)
                                                                                      0.1024 to 0.1043 in (2.60 to 2.65 mm)
                                                                                      0.1043 to 0.1063 in (2.65 to 2.70 mm)
                                                                                      0.1063 to 0.1083 in (2.70 to 2.75 mm)
                                                                                      0.1083 to 0.1102 in (2.75 to 2.80 mm)

Thrust washers and spacers
Mainshaft 3rd gear to synchro hub spacer thickness   ...   .   0.1693 to 0.1713 in (4.30 to 4.35 mm)
                                                                                      0.1713 to 0.1732 in (4.35 to 4.40 mm)
                                                                                      0.1732 to 0.1753 in (4.40 to 4.45 mm)
Front bearing retainer gasket thickness   ...   .   0.020 in (0.5 mm)
                                                                                      0.012 in (0.3 mm)
Countergear thrust washer thickness (K40)   ...   .   0.0512 to 0.0532 in (1.30 to 1.35 mm)
                                                                                      0.0551 to 0.0561 in (1.40 to 1.45 mm)
                                                                                      0.0591 to 0.0610 in (1.50 to 1.55 mm)
                                                                                      0.0630 to 0.0650 in (1.60 to 1.65 mm)
Countergear thrust washer thickness (K50)   ...   .   0.0673 to 0.0713 in (1.71 to 1.81 mm)
                                                                                      0.0720 to 0.0760 in (1.83 to 1.93 mm)
                                                                                      0.0768 to 0.0807 in (1.95 to 2.05 mm)

Tolerances (T40 and T50 gearboxes)
Reverse idler gear endfloat
   Standard   ...   .   0.0020 to 0.0197 in (0.05 to 0.50 mm)
   Maximum   ...   .   0.04 in (1.0 mm)
Mainshaft gear endfloat
   1st   ...   .   0.0059 to 0.0108 in (0.15 to 0.275 mm)
   2nd   ...   .   0.0059 to 0.0098 in (0.15 to 0.25 mm)
   3rd   ...   .   0.0059 to 0.0118 in (0.15 to 0.30 mm)
   Reverse   ...   .   0.0079 to 0.0127 in (0.20 to 0.325 mm)
   5th   ...   .   0.0059 to 0.0108 in (0.15 to 0.275 mm)
Maximum 1st, 2nd, 5th gears ...   .   0.020 in (0.5 mm)
Maximum 3rd, reverse gears   ...   .   0.024 in (0.6 mm)
Shift fork to synchro sleeve groove clearance   ...   .   0.039 in (1.0 mm)
Synchro ring to gear clearance when ring pressed against cone of gear   ...   0.04 to 0.08 in (1.0 to 2.0 mm)
   Maximum   ...   .   0.032 in (0.8 mm)
Input shaft bearing to shaft circlip thickness   ...   .   0.0925 to 0.0945 in (2.35 to 2.40 mm)
                                                                                      0.0945 to 0.0965 in (2.40 to 2.45 mm)
                                                                                      0.0965 to 0.0984 in (2.45 to 2.50 mm)
                                                                                      0.0984 to 0.1004 in (2.50 to 2.55 mm)
                                                                                      0.1004 to 0.1417 in (2.55 to 2.60 mm)

Countergear circlip thickness

T40 gearbox ...	...	...	...	...	...	...	...	...	0.0709 to 0.0728 in (1.80 to 1.85 mm)
									0.0748 to 0.0768 in (1.90 to 1.95 mm)
T50 gearbox ...	...	...	...	...	...	...	...	...	0.0787 in (2.0 mm)
									0.0709 in (1.8 mm)
									0.0630 in (1.6 mm)
Mainshaft front synchro hub to shaft circlip thickness			...	...	...		0.0768 to 0.0787 in (1.95 to 2.00 mm)
									0.0787 to 0.0807 in (2.00 to 2.05 mm)
									0.0807 to 0.0827 in (2.05 to 2.10 mm)
									0.0827 to 0.0847 in (2.10 to 2.15 mm)
									0.0847 to 0.0866 in (2.15 to 2.20 mm)

Torque wrench settings

	lb/ft	Nm
K40 and K50 type gearboxes		
Clutch bellhousing to engine bolts	45	62
Extension housing to gearbox bolts	30	41
Mainshaft nut	70	97
Front bearing retainer bolts	12	16
Countershaft cover bolts	12	16
Reverse idler shaft lock bolt	13	18
Gearshift lever retainer bolts	12	16
Drain plug	30	41
Reverse lamp switch	35	48
T40 and T50 type gearboxes		
Clutch bellhousing to engine bolts	50	69
Extension housing to gearbox	30	41
Clutch bellhousing to gear casing	30	41
Mainshaft nut	50	69
Countergear end bolt	30	41
Gear casing cover bolts	12	16
Reverse idler gear lock bolt	12	16
Gear case half section bolts	16	22
Reverse lamp switch	35	48
Extension housing to gearbox bolts	30	41
Gearshift lever retainer bolts	12	16

1 General description

1   The manual gearbox may be one of two types of four speed unit (see Specifications), or one of two five speed assemblies (Figs. 6.1 and 6.2).

2   The two types of four speed gearbox may be identified by the difference in their casings. The gearbox fitted in conjunction with the smaller (1200cc) engine has a one piece casing, while that fitted in conjunction with the 1600cc engine has a casing which is split longitudinally.

3   The five speed gearbox is essentially the same unit as the four speed one fitted in conjunction with the 1600cc engine, but with the addition of a fifth (overdrive) gear.

4   All forward gears have synchromesh.

5   The gearshift is by means of a floor-mounted lever.

2 Gearbox - removal and installation

1   If the engine is being removed at the same time, refer to Chapter 1 for removal procedure.

2   If the gearbox is to be removed on its own, carry out the following operations.

3   If an inspection pit is not available, run the rear roadwheels up on ramps or jack-up the rear of the vehicle and secure on axle stands so that there is a clearance below the gearbox at least equal to the diameter of the clutch bellhousing to enable the gearbox to be removed from below, and to the rear of, the vehicle.

4   Disconnect the lead from the battery negative terminal.

5   If a centre console is fitted inside the vehicle, extract its securing screws and remove it.

6   Peel back the floor carpet to give access to the base of the gearshift

2.6 Removing interior carpet

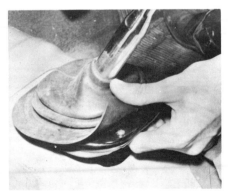

2.7 Removing gearshift lever boot (T series gearbox)

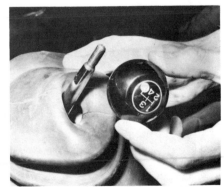

2.8 Removing flexible boot and knob (T series gearbox)

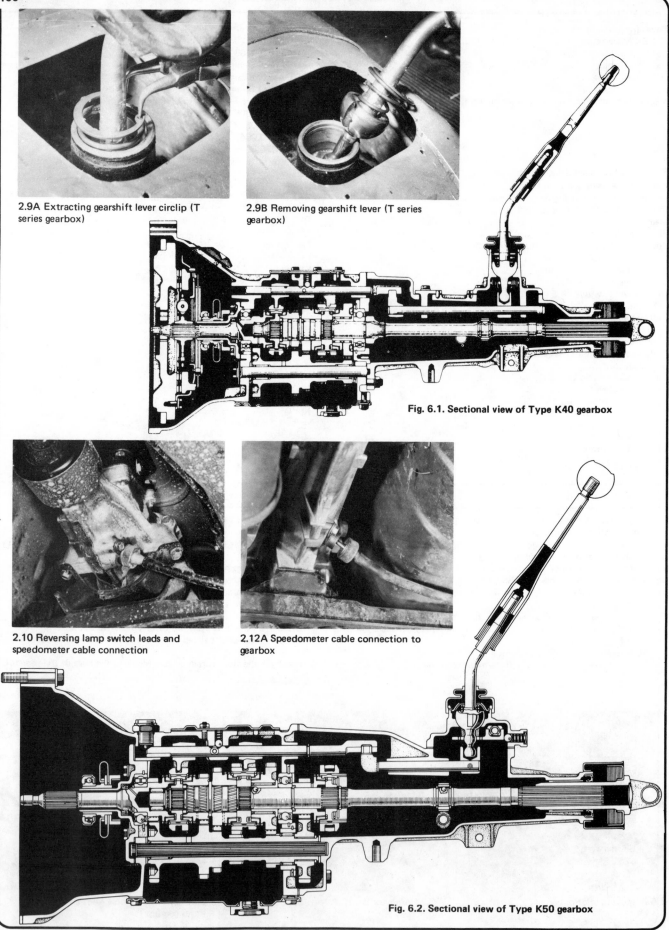

2.9A Extracting gearshift lever circlip (T series gearbox)

2.9B Removing gearshift lever (T series gearbox)

Fig. 6.1. Sectional view of Type K40 gearbox

2.10 Reversing lamp switch leads and speedometer cable connection

2.12A Speedometer cable connection to gearbox

Fig. 6.2. Sectional view of Type K50 gearbox

lever (photo).

7   *On K series gearboxes,* the gearshift control lever is held in its retainer by means of a circlip. This is accessible for removal either by peeling off the rubber dust excluder or by using a pair of narrow nosed pliers through the small hole in the neck of the gearshift lever retainer.

On T series gearboxes, extract the screws from the flexible boot which covers the base of the gearshift lever (photo).

8   Unscrew the knob from the gearshift lever and slide off the flexible boot (photo).

9   Extract the circlip which secures the gearshift lever and then withdraw the lever and conical spring (photos).

10 Disconnect the leads from the reversing lamp switch on the gearbox (photo).

11 Remove the propeller shaft as described in Chapter 7.

12 Disconnect the speedometer cable from the gearbox by unscrewing the knurled ring. Take care not to lose the felt seals (photos).

13 Disconnect the exhaust downpipe from the manifold and disconnect the exhaust pipe support bracket from the gearbox.

14 Disconnect the earth bonding strap at the rear of the engine cylinder block.

15 Remove the air cleaner.

16 *On vehicles with hydraulic clutch actuation,* unbolt the clutch slave cylinder from the clutch bellhousing and tie it up out of the way. There is no need to disconnect the hydraulic system.

17 *On vehicles with a cable-operated clutch mechanism,* extract the 'C' washer from the clutch cable at the engine compartment rear bulkhead and then disconnect the cable from the clutch release lever.

18 Remove the starter motor.

19 Drain the cooling system and disconnect the radiator upper hose.

20 Place a jack under the engine sump using a block of wood as an insulator and support the weight of the engine.

21 Unbolt the rear mounting crossmember from the bodyframe (photo).

22 Unbolt the crossmember from the gearbox extension housing and remove it (photo).

23 Lower the engine support jack enough to give access to the upper bolts which secure the clutch bellhousing to the engine. Remove the remaining bolts (photo).

24 Support the gearbox on a trolley jack and then lower both jacks together until the gearbox can be withdrawn rearwards and removed from below the vehicle. If the vehicle is over an inspection pit then the help of two assistants should be obtained to withdraw the gearbox. On no account let the weight of the gearbox hang upon the input shaft while the latter is still engaged in the splines of the clutch driven plate (photo).

25 Installation is a reversal of removal but if the clutch mechanism has been disturbed, make sure that the clutch driven plate has been centralised as described in Chapter 5.

26 If the gearbox has been dismantled and reassembled, make sure that it is refilled with the correct grade and quantity of lubricant.

3   Gearbox (Type K40) - dismantling into major assemblies

1   Drain the lubricant and clean the outside of the unit with paraffin

2.12B Speedometer cable felt bush

2.21 Gearbox rear mounting crossmember bolt to body

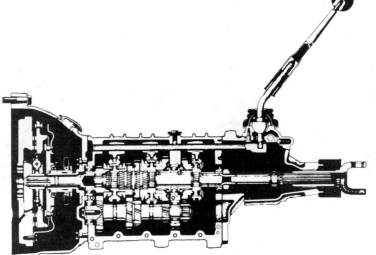

Fig. 6.3. Sectional view of Type T40 gearbox

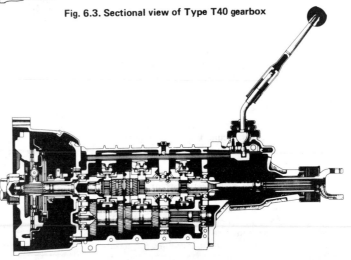

Fig. 6.4. Sectional view of Type T50 gearbox

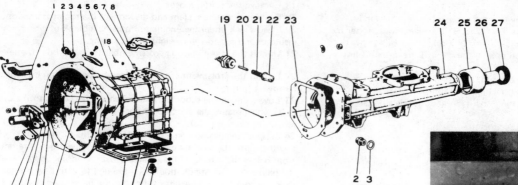

Fig. 6.5. Type K40 gearbox external components

1	Reinforcement plate	10	Gasket	19	Reverse light switch
2	Transmission case cover plug	11	Front bearing (input shaft retainer)	20	Pin
3	Gasket	12	Gasket	21	Spring
4	Clutch housing cover	13	Oil seal	22	Pin
5	Main casing	14	Plug	23	Gasket
6	Shift detent ball spring seat	15	Oil pan	24	Extension housing
7	Gasket	16	Gasket	25	Dust deflector
8	Transmission case cover	17	Drain plug	26	Bush
9	Countershaft cover plate	18	Bolt	27	Oil seal

2.22 Gearbox rear mounting bolts to crossmember

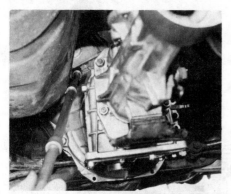

2.23 Unscrewing a clutch bellhousing upper bolt

2.24 Withdrawing the gearbox

3.3 Removing input shaft bearing retainer (K40 gearbox)

and a stiff brush or use a water soluble solvent (Figs. 6.5, 6.6 and 6.7).

2   Refer to Chapter 5 and remove the clutch release lever and bearing assembly.

3   Unscrew the bolts which secure the front bearing retainer to the inside of the clutch bellhousing. Slide the retainer from the input shaft (photo).

4   Remove the nuts and withdraw the cover and gasket from the top of the gear case. As the cover is withdrawn, carefully recover the three detent balls and their springs. Unscrew and remove the reversing lamp switch (photos).

5   Unbolt and remove the bottom cover and its gasket from the gear casing.

6   Unbolt and remove the speedometer driven gear from the extension housing then remove the nuts which secure the rear extension housing to the main gear casing.

7   Withdraw the extension housing and peel away its joint gasket (photo).

8   Remove the locking bolt and its washer which secures the reverse idler gear shaft to the main gear case (photo).

9   Withdraw the reverse idler shaft and lift off the idler gear (photo).

10   Remove the countershaft by first unscrewing the two bolts which secure the retaining plate to the front face of the gear case (photo).

11   Hold the countergear assembly steady and withdraw the countershaft rearwards (photo).

12   Lift the countergear assembly from the gearbox and recover the thrust washers (photo).

13   Remove the input shaft by tapping its bearing track towards the front of the gear case (photos).

14   The shift forks are secured to the selector shafts by roll (tension) pins which are accessible through the top cover aperture (photo).

15   Drive out the roll pins using a suitable drift.

16   The two selector shafts which are nearer the outside edge of the casing should be withdrawn first. When withdrawing a shaft, hold its shift fork steady and once it is removed, recover the interlock plungers (photos).

17   Remove the centre (3rd/4th) selector shaft last (photo).

18   Extract the 1st/2nd shift fork from the groove in the synchro unit sleeve (photo).

19   Extract the 3rd/4th shift fork from the groove in the synchro unit sleeve (photo).

20   Extract reverse shift fork (photo).

21   Withdraw the mainshaft assembly from the rear of the gear casing. If it is tight, tap it gently with a plastic faced mallet (photo).

22   The reverse selector arm can be removed if it is worn or damaged but this is not normally required (photo).

4   Gearbox components (Type K40) - inspection

1   It is assumed that the gearbox has been dismantled for reasons of excessive noise, lack of synchromesh action on certain gears or for

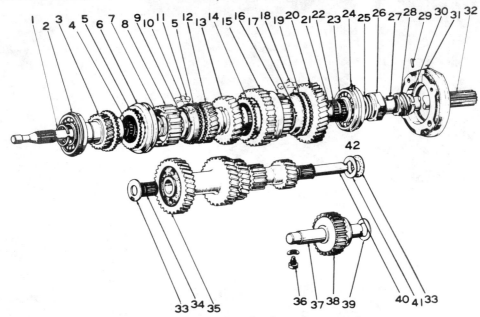

Fig. 6.6. Type K40 gearbox internal components

1 Circlip	11 Key	21 Locking ball	32 Mainshaft
2 Mainshaft front bearing	12 3rd gear	22 Bush	33 Thrust washer
3 Input shaft (top gear)	13 2nd gear	23 Rear bearing	34 Needle roller bearing
4 Needle roller bearing	14 Synchro. ring	24 Circlip	35 Countergear
5 Synchro. ring	15 Reverse gear	25 Shim	36 Lock bolt
6 Synchro. sleeve	16 1st/2nd synchro. unit	26 Nut	37 Reverse idler shaft
7 Circlip	17 Spring	27 Woodruff key	38 Reverse idler gear
8 3rd/4th synchro. unit	18 Key	28 Speedometer drive gear	39 Spacer
9 Spacer	19 Synchro ring	29 Roll pin	40 Countershaft
10 Spring	20 1st gear	30 Circlip	41 Thrust washer
		31 Bearing retainer	42 Needle roller bearing

3.4A Removing K40 type gearbox top cover

3.4B Detent springs (K40 gearbox)

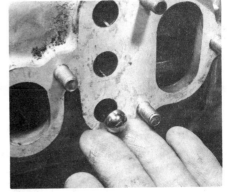

3.4C Detent ball (K40 gearbox)

3.7 Removing extension housing (K40 gearbox)

3.8 Removing reverse idler shaft lock bolt (K40 gearbox)

3.9 Removing reverse idler shaft and gear (K40 gearbox)

3.10 Countershaft front retaining plate (K40 gearbox)

3.11 Withdrawing countershaft (K40 gearbox)

3.12 Countergear thrust washers (K40 gearbox)

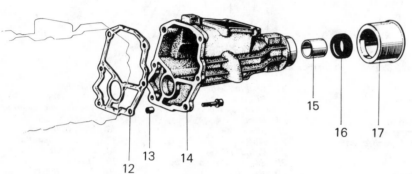

Fig. 6.7. Rear extension housing (K40 gearbox)

12 Gasket   13 Dowel   14 Housing   15 Bush   16 Oil seal   17 Dust deflector

3.13A Dislodging input shaft bearing (K40 gearbox)

Fig. 6.8. Gearshift components (K40 type gearbox)

1 1st/2nd shift fork
2 3rd/4th shift fork
3 Roll pin
4 Reverse shift fork
5 'E' ring
6 Circlip
7 Reverse shift arm
8 Shift arm pivot
9 Spring
10 Detent ball
11 Interlock pin
12 1st/2nd selector shaft
13 3rd/4th selector shaft
14 Reverse selector shaft
15 Circlip
16 Shift lever selector rod
17 Gearshift lever housing
18 Gasket
19 Gearshift lever retainer
20 Spring
21 Flexible boot
22 Gearshift lever
23 Knob

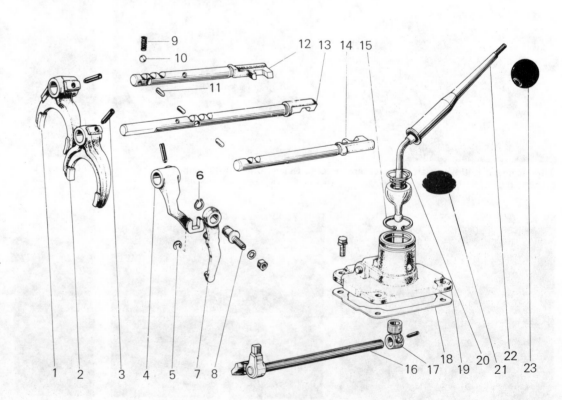

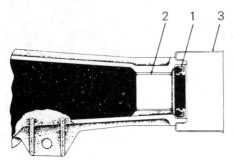

Fig. 6.9. Location of extension housing rear end components (K40 gearbox)

1 Oil seal
2 Bush

3 Dust deflector

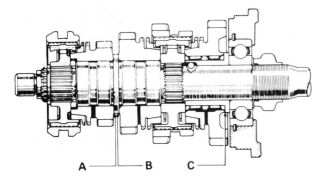

Fig. 6.10. Mainshaft gear thrust clearance (end-float) measurement diagram (K40 gearbox)

failure to stay in gear. If anything more drastic than this (total failure, seizure or main casing cracked) it would be better to leave well alone and look for a replacement, either secondhand or an exchange unit.

2 Examine all gears for excessively worn, chipped or damaged teeth. Any such gears should be renewed.

3 Check all synchromesh rings for wear on the bearing surfaces, which normally have clear machined oil reservoir lines in them. If these are smooth or obviously uneven, replacement is essential. Also when the rings are fitted to their gears - as they would be in operation - there should be no rock. This would signify ovality or lack of concentricity. One of the most satisfactory ways of checking is by comparing the fit of a new ring with an old one in the gearwheel cone.

The teeth and cut outs in the synchro rings also wear and for this reason also it is unwise not to fit new ones when the opportunity avails.

4 All ball race bearings should be checked for chatter and roughness after they have been washed out. It is advisable to renew these anyway even though they may not appear too badly worn.

5 Circlips which are all important in locating bearing; gears and hubs should be checked to ensure that they are undamaged and not distorted. In any case a selection of new circlips of varying thicknesses should be obtained to compensate for variations in new components fitted, and wear in old ones. The Specifications indicate what is available.

6 The thrust washers at the end of the countergear should be renewed as they will most certainly have worn if the gearbox is of any age.

7 Needle roller bearings between the input shaft and mainshaft are usually found to be in good order, but if in any doubt renew the needle roller bearings.

5 Extension housing (Type K40) - servicing

1 It is rarely necessary to dismantle the extension housing but if, due to wear or damage, this is essential, remove the gearshift lever retainer and then drive out the roll pin to release the selector control

3.13B Removing input shaft (K40 gearbox)

3.14 Shift fork securing roll pins (K40 gearbox)

3.15 Driving out a shift fork roll pin (K40 gearbox)

3.16A Withdrawing reverse selector shaft (K40 gearbox)

3.16B Withdrawing 1st/2nd selector shaft (K40 gearbox)

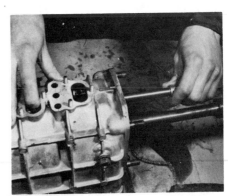

3.17 Withdrawing 3rd/4th selector shaft (K40 gearbox)

3.18 Removing 1st/2nd shift fork (K40 gearbox)

3.19 Removing 3rd/4th shift fork (K40 gearbox)

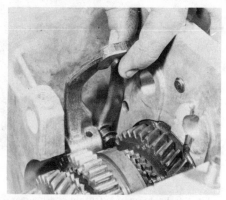
3.20 Removing reverse shift fork (K40 gearbox)

3.21 Removing mainshaft assembly (K40 gearbox)

3.22 Location of reverse selector arm (K40 gearbox)

5.1A Removing gearshift lever retainer (K40 gearbox)

5.1B Selector control rod and dogs in extension housing (K40 gearbox)

6.7 Input shaft needle roller bearing (K40 gearbox)

7.1 Extracting speedo. drive gear circlip from mainshaft (K40 gearbox)

7.2 Withdrawing speedo. drive gear (K40 gearbox)

7.4 Unscrewing mainshaft nut (K40 gearbox)

7.5 Mainshaft shims (K40 gearbox)

7.6 Removing mainshaft rear bearing retainer (K40 gearbox)

7.7 Removing 1st gear from mainshaft (K40 gearbox)

7.8 1st gear, bearing and bush (K40 gearbox)

7.9 1st gear bush and locking ball (K40 gearbox)

7.10 Removing reverse gear and synchro. unit (K40 gearbox)

7.11 Removing 2nd gear from mainshaft (K40 gearbox)

7.12 Mainshaft front circlip (K40 gearbox)

7.13 Removing 3rd/4th synchro unit from mainshaft (K40 gearbox)

7.14 Removing 3rd gear and thrust washer from mainshaft (K40 gearbox)

7.33 Refitting mainshaft rear bearing retainer (K40 gearbox)

7.40 Assembled mainshaft (K40 gearbox)

8.1 Countergear needle roller bearing (K40 gearbox)

rod from the gearshift lever housing (photos) (Fig. 6.8).
2   The oil seal in the end of the housing can be renewed by levering
out the old one and tapping in a new one using a piece of tubing as a
drift.
3   If the bush at the rear end of the extension housing requires
renewal then the oil seal must first be removed and then the extension
housing must be heated in boiling water. Extract the bush and press in
the new one keeping the extension housing at specified temperature.
Make sure that the butt joint of the bush is uppermost (when
extension housing is in its normal 'in vehicle' attitude).

6   Input shaft (Type K40 gearbox) - servicing

1   The shaft and bearing are located in the front of the main casing
by a large circlip in the outer track of the bearing.
2   To renew the bearing first remove the circlip from the front end
of the bearing.
3   Place the outer track of the race on the top of a firm bench vice
and drive the input shaft through the bearing. Note that the bearing is
fitted with the circlip groove towards the forward end of the input
shaft. Lift away the bearing.
4   The spigot bearing needle roller assembly may be slid out of the
inner end of the input shaft.
5   Using a suitable diameter tubular drift carefully drive the ball race
into position. The circlip in the outer track must be towards the front
of the input shaft.
6   Retain the bearing in position with a circlip. This is a selective
circlip which is available in two thicknesses to provide the closest fit.
7   Work some grease into the needle bearing assembly and insert into
the end of the input shaft (photo).

7   Mainshaft (Type K40 gearbox) - servicing

1   Remove the circlip from the rearmost end of the mainshaft (photo).
2   Slide off the speedometer drive gear and recover the key (photo).
3   Remove the second circlip from the rear end of the mainshaft.
4   Hold the mainshaft firmly in the vice, straighten the staking locking
the large nut and then remove the nut (photo).
5   Slide the shim(s) from the end of the mainshaft (photo).
6   Remove the rear bearing retainer from the end of the mainshaft
(photo).
7   Slide off the first speed gear noting which way round it is fitted.
Then remove the synchroniser ring (photo).
8   The first speed gear bush and needle roller bearing are next
removed from the mainshaft (photo).
9   The first speed gear bush is retained by a ball bearing that should be
lifted out from the mainshaft (photo).
10 The reverse gear and synchroniser assembly may next be removed
from the mainshaft (photo). Then remove the synchroniser ring.
11 Slide off the second speed gear (photo).
12 Turning to the front end of the mainshaft, remove the shaft snap
ring located at the end of the splines (photo).
13 Slide off the top/third synchromesh unit, noting which way round
it is fitted (photo). Remove the synchroniser ring.
14 Finally slide off the third speed gear and splined thrust washer
(photo).
15 Dismantling of the mainshaft is now complete.
16 The synchro hubs are only too easy to dismantle - just push the
centre out and the whole assembly flies apart. The point is to prevent
this happening, before you are ready. Do not dismantle the hub
without reason and do not mix up parts of the hubs.
17 It is most important to check backlash in the splines between the
outer sleeve and inner hub. If any is noticeable the whole assembly
must be renewed.
18 Mark the hub and sleeve so that you may reassemble them on the
same splines. With the hub and sleeve separated, the teeth at the end
of the splines which engage with corresponding teeth of the gearwheels,
must be checked for damage or wear.
19 Do not confuse the keystone shape at the ends of the teeth. This
shape matches the gear teeth shape and it is a design characteristic to
minimise jump-out tendencies.
20 If the synchronising cones are being renewed it is sensible also to
renew the sliding keys and springs which hold them in position.

21 The hub assemblies are not interchangeable so they must be
reassembled with their original or identical new parts (Fig. 6.11).
22 The pips on the keys are symmetrical so may be refitted either way
round into the hub.
23 One slotted key is assembled to each hub for locating the turned
out end of the key spring.
24 It should be noted that the keys for each synchromesh unit are of
different lengths.
25 The turned out end of each spring must locate in the slotted key
and be assembled to the hub in an anticlockwise direction as viewed
from either side of the hub.
26 Commence reassembly of the mainshaft by sliding 3rd speed gear
and the splined thrust washer onto the front end of the mainshaft.
27 Fit the third speed gear synchroniser ring onto the synchromesh
unit and slide the synchromesh unit onto the end of the mainshaft.
Ensure the ring grooves are aligned with the keys.
28 Refit the shaft snap ring located at the end of the mainshaft splines.
Measure the thrust clearance between the snap ring and synchromesh
unit hub. This should be less than 0.002 in (0.05 mm). A range of 8
snaprings is available to obtain the correct clearance (see Specifications
Section).
29 Slide the second speed gear onto the rear end of the mainshaft.
30 Fit the second speed gear synchroniser ring onto the second speed
synchromesh unit and slide the reverse gear and synchromesh unit
onto the mainshaft. Ensure the ring grooves are aligned with the keys.
31 Fit the first speed gear synchroniser ring onto the synchromesh
unit ensuring the ring grooves are aligned with the keys.
32 Insert the locking ball onto the mainshaft and assemble the first
speed gear bush, needle roller bearing and first speed gear onto the
mainshaft.
33 Refit the rear bearing retainer onto the end of the mainshaft and
follow this with the shim(s) previously removed (photo).
34 Hold the mainshaft firmly in the vice and refit the large nut. Do not
stake over yet.
35 Using feeler gauges measure the thrust clearance between the 3rd
gear and hub. This should be 0.002 - 0.006 inch (0.05 - 0.15 mm) and
is adjustable by a range of 3 different thicknesses of hub spacers (see
Specifications Section) (Fig. 6.10).
36 The following thrust clearances should also be checked using
feeler gauges as follows:
   a) 2nd gear to output shaft flange:
        0.004 - 0.012 in (0.10 - 0.25 mm)
   b) 1st gear to 1st gear bush flange:
        0.007 - 0.011 in (0.18 - 0.28 mm)
37 When all thrust clearances are correct ensure the mainshaft nut is
tight and stake the end into the slot in the mainshaft.
38 Fit the first speedometer drivegear circlip to the mainshaft.
39 Replace the Woodruff key and slide the speedometer drivegear
onto the mainshaft.
40 The mainshaft is now assembled and ready for refitting to the
gearbox (photo).

8   Countergear (Type K40 gearbox) - servicing

1   Dismantling of the countergear assembly simply entails the removal
of the needle roller bearing assemblies located at either end of the bore.

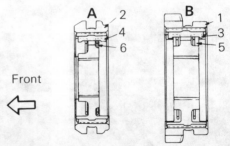

Fig. 6.11. Synchro. hub assembly and location on mainshaft (K40
gearbox)

A 3rd/4th synchro unit	B 1st/2nd synchro unit
1 Sleeve	4 Shift key
2 Sleeve	5 Spring
3 Shift key	6 Spring

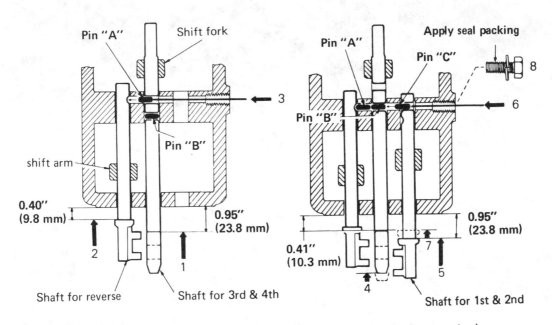

Pin "A"   Shift fork   Pin "A"   Pin "C"   Apply seal packing

Pin "B"

8

3   6

shift arm

0.40"
(9.8 mm)   0.95"   0.41"   0.95"
(23.8 mm)   (10.3 mm)   (23.8 mm)

2   1   4   5   7

Shaft for reverse   Shaft for 3rd & 4th   Shaft for 1st & 2nd

Fig. 6.12. Selector shaft setting diagram for insertion of interlock pins (K40 type gearbox)

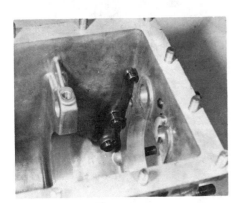

9.1 Interior of K40 type gearcase

9.2 Installing mainshaft assembly (K40 gearbox)

9.3 Mainshaft rear bearing retainer peg (K40 gearbox)

This is a straightforward operation and will present no problems (photo).
2   Refitting the needle roller bearings is the reverse sequence to removal.

9   Gearbox (Type K40) - reassembly

1   With all parts clean reassembly can be begun (photo).
2   First insert the mainshaft assembly into the gearbox casing (photo).
3   Make sure that the bearing retainer peg correctly engages in the cut out in the casing (photo).
4   Place a large washer and nut onto one of the extension housing securing studs to hold the mainshaft in position (photo).
5   Replace the 3rd/4th speed shift fork making sure it is the correct way round (photo).
6   Replace the 1st/2nd speed shift fork making sure it is the correct way round (photo).
7   Apply a little grease to the interlock pins and insert them into the selector shafts.
8   Insert the 1st/2nd speed selector shaft engaging it in the shift fork (photo).
9· Insert the 3rd/4th speed selector shaft engaging it in the shift fork (photo).
10 Hold the reverse selector fork in position and insert the reverse

selector shaft (photos).
11 Line up the selector shafts and insert plunger (photos and Fig. 6.12).
12 The shift fork securing roll pins should next be refitted. Make sure the hole in the fork and shaft line up and carefully drift the pins into position (photos).
13 Insert the three selector shaft detent balls and springs into the three holes (photo).
14 Refit the cover and gasket and secure with the five securing nuts and washers (photo).
15 Make sure the fourth speed synchroniser ring is in position and fit the input shaft into the front face of the main casing (photo).
16 Fit a new gasket and replace the input shaft bearing retainer. Secure with the four nuts and washers (photo).
17 The reverse idler is next to be refitted. Hold the gear in position (and the correct way round) and slide in the shaft making sure the dowel bolt hole lines up with the hole in the web (photo).
18 Refit the reverse idler shaft locking dowel bolt and washer (photo).
19 Smear some grease onto the faces of the countergear thrust washers and position them on the inside faces of the main casing. (photo).
20 Carefully lower the countergear into position so as not to dislodge the thrust washers (photo).
21 Slide the countershaft into position from the rear (photo).
22 The raised portion on the end of the countershaft must be

9.4 Method of temporarily securing mainshaft (K40 gearbox)

9.5 Fitting 3rd/4th shift fork (K40 gearbox)

9.6 Fitting 1st/2nd shift fork (K40 gearbox)

9.8 Installing 1st/2nd selector shaft (K40 gearbox)

9.9 Fitting 3rd/4th selector shaft (K40 gearbox)

9.10A Holding reverse shift fork ready for fitting of selector shaft (K40 gearbox)

9.10B Fitting reverse shift fork (K40 gearbox)

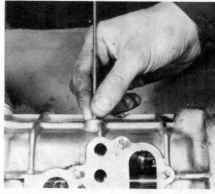

9.11A Aligning selector shafts (K40 gearbox)

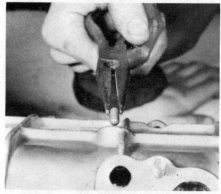

9.11B Inserting interlock plunger (K40 gearbox)

9.12A Driving in a shift fork roll pin (K40 gearbox)

9.12B Shift fork roll pin installed and next one ready for driving in (K40 gearbox)

9.12C Final shift fork roll pin ready for driving in (K40 gearbox)

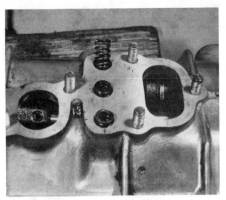

9.13 Selector shaft detent springs (K40 gearbox)

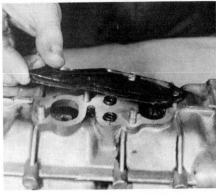

9.14 Fitting gearbox top cover (K40 gearbox)

9.15 Fitting input shaft (K40 gearbox)

9.16 Fitting input shaft retainer (K40 gearbox)

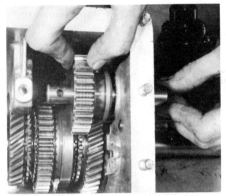

9.17 Fitting reverse idler shaft and gear (K40 gearbox)

9.18 Fitting reverse idler shaft lock bolt (K40 gearbox)

9.19 Countergear thrust washer correctly located (K40 gearbox)

9.20 Lowering countergear into gearbox (K40 type)

9.21 Fitting countershaft (K40 gearbox)

9.22 Correctly positioned countershaft rear end (K40 gearbox)

9.23 Extension housing gasket (K40 gearbox)

9.24 Installing extension housing (K40 gearbox)

9.26 Fitting bottom cover (K40 gearbox)

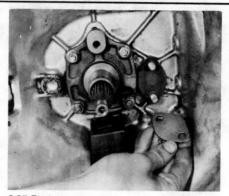

9.27 Fitting countershaft cover plate (K40 gearbox)

9.28 Refitting clutch release arm (K40 gearbox)

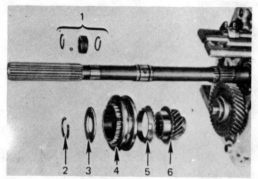

Fig. 6.13. Mainshaft rear end components (K50 type gearbox)

1 Speedometer drive gear circlips and locking ball
2 Circlip
3 Synchro. shift key retaining plate
4 5th gear synchro unit
5 Synchro. ring
6 5th gear

Fig. 6.15. Reverse idler components (K50 gearbox)

1 Lockbolt
2 Shaft
3 Gear

Fig. 6.16. Expanding countershaft rear bearing circlip (K50 type gearbox)

Circlip pliers arrowed

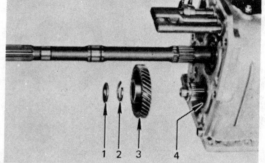

Fig. 6.14. Countershaft rear end components (K50 type gearbox)

1 Thrust washer
2 Circlip
3 Countershaft 5th gear
4 Countershaft rear bearing inner race

positioned as shown in these two photos so as to engage in the cut out in the front face of the extension housing.

23 Place the gearbox on end and fit a new gasket to the extension housing mating face. Do not forget to remove the nut and longer washer retaining the mainshaft (photo).

24 Carefully lower the extension housing into position ensuring that the gear selector lever shaft engages with the selector fork shafts (photo).

25 Secure the extension housing with the nuts and washers.

26 Fit a new bottom cover gasket and replace the oil pan. Secure with the twelve nuts and washers, tightening in a progressive and diagonal manner (photo).

27 Fit a new countergear shaft retaining plate gasket and refit the plate. Secure with the two nuts and washers (photo).

28 Refit the clutch release arm and bearing assembly as described in Chapter 5 (photo).

29 The gearbox is now ready for refitting to the car. Do not forget to refill the gearbox with the recommended grade of oil.

10 Gearbox (Type K50) - dismantling into major assemblies

1 Repeat the operations described in paragraphs 1 and 2 and 5 to 7 inclusive of Section 3. Treat the gearbox casing with respect as it is constructed entirely of light alloy.

2 Remove the shift arm bracket (Fig. 6.17).

3 From the rear end of the mainshaft extract the speedometer drive gear, circlip and locking ball.

4 Extract the second speedometer drive gear circlip.

5 Extract the spacer washer, the 5th gear synchro unit, synchro ring and 5th gear (Fig. 6.13).

6 From the end of the countershaft extract the countergear thrust washer, circlip, 5th gear and the countershaft bearing inner race (Fig. 6.14).

7 Remove the locking bolt and withdraw the reverse idler gear shaft and the gear itself (Fig. 6.15).

8 Prise open the circlip on the countershaft rear bearing outer track and drive the bearing track from the casing in an outward direction (Fig. 6.16).

9 Withdraw the countershaft from the rear of the gear case and then lift the countergear and thrust washers from the interior of the casing.

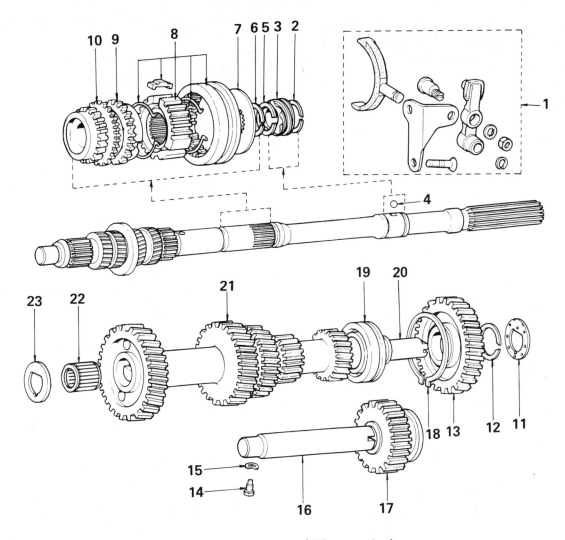

Fig. 6.17. Internal components (K50 type gearbox)

1	Shift arm bracket, 5th gear shift arm and 5th gear shift fork	6	Circlip
2	Circlip	7	Synchro. shift key retaining plate
3	Speedometer drive gear	8	5th gear synchro unit
4	Locking ball	9	5th gear synchro. ring
5	Circlip	10	5th gear
		11	Countergear thrust washer
12	Circlip	18	Circlip
13	5th gear	19	Countershaft bearing
14	Lockbolt	20	Countershaft
15	Lockwasher	21	Countergear
16	Reverse idler gear shaft	22	Needle roller bearing
17	Reverse idler gear	23	Countergear thrust washer

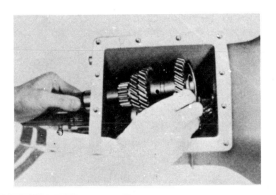

Fig. 6.18. Removing countershaft and countergear (K50 gearbox)

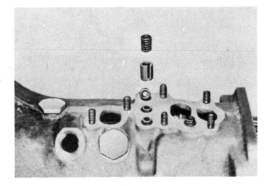

Fig. 6.19. Detent springs, sleeves and balls (K50 gearbox)

Note the needle roller bearings in each end of the countergear assembly.
10 Unbolt and remove the small cover plate from the top of the main gearcase. Extract the four springs, sleeves and detent balls (Fig. 6.19).
11 Push the 1st/2nd selector shaft fully in and then drive out the shift fork retaining roll pins. These are accessible through the aperture in the top surface of the gearcase.
12 Extract the blanking plug and remove the two interlock plungers from the gearcase.
13 Remove reverse shift fork.
14 Move the 1st/2nd shift fork towards second selector position and then withdraw the shift fork (Fig. 6.23).
15 Withdraw 3rd/4th shift fork from the gearcase.
16 Unscrew and remove the bolts which secure the front bearing retainer within the clutch bellhousing.
17 Withdraw the front bearing retainer complete with input shaft. If tight, tap out from inside the casing.
18 Remove the synchro ring and the needle rollers (Fig. 6.22).
19 Open the circlip and press or tap (soft faced mallet) the input shaft from the bearing retainer.
20 Withdraw the mainshaft from the front end of the gearcase.

11 Gearbox components (Type K50) - inspection

1 Refer to Section 4 of this Chapter.

12 Extension housing (Type K50) - servicing

1 Refer to Section 5 of this Chapter.

13 Input shaft (Type K50 gearbox) - servicing

1 Check the teeth of the gear and shaft splines for wear. If wear is evident, renew the shaft.
2 If the oil seal contact surface of the shaft is grooved then the shaft will have to be renewed.
3 The shaft bearing should be renewed if it is worn or noisy when spun with the fingers. Press the old one from the shaft and press the new one on until it is in full contact with the face of the gear. Make sure that the bearing outer track circlip groove is nearest the rear of the shaft (Fig. 6.24).
4 Select a bearing retaining circlip from the thicknesses listed in the Specifications which will eliminate any bearing endfloat on the shaft.
5 Renew the oil seal in the bearing retainer.

14 Mainshaft (Type K50 gearbox) - servicing

1 To dismantle the mainshaft, extract the circlip from the front end of the shaft, withdraw the 3rd/4th synchro assembly, the synchro hub spacer, the synchro ring and 3rd gear. Note carefully the location of each synchro ring; they are not interchangeable.
2 From the rear end of the mainshaft extract the circlip, and the bearing. To remove the latter, a press or puller will be required.
3 Now withdraw 1st gear bush, the needle roller bearing, 1st gear, the locking ball, synchro ring, 1st/2nd synchro unit, synchro ring and 2nd gear.
4 Servicing of the synchro units is as described in Section 7, paragraphs 16 to 25.
5 Commence reassembly of the mainshaft by installing onto the rear

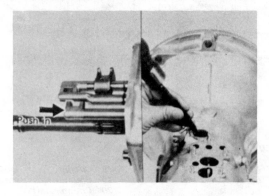

Fig. 6.20. Removing shift fork roll pins (K50 gearbox)

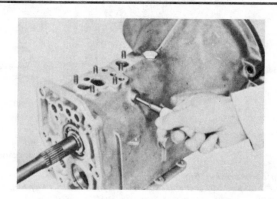

Fig. 6.21. Extracting interlock pins (K50 gearbox)

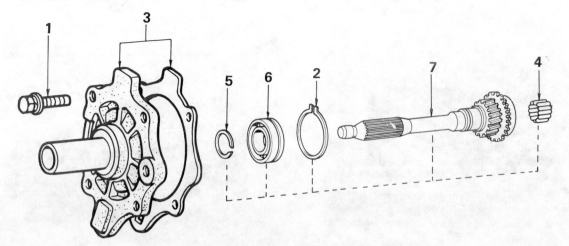

Fig. 6.22. Input shaft components (K50 gearbox)

| 1 Bolt | 3 Front bearing retainer and | 4 Needle rollers | 6 Bearing |
| 2 Circlip | gasket | 5 Circlip | 7 Input shaft |

end the following components; 2nd gear, synchro ring (with 9.0 mm wide cut-out), 1st/2nd synchro unit, locking ball, synchro ring (with 10 mm wide cut-out), 1st gear bush, needle roller bearing, 1st gear (Fig. 6.28).

6   Press on the mainshaft rear bearing so that the bearing outer track circlip groove is nearer the rear of the shaft.

7   Select a circlip which is the closest fit in the shaft groove from the thicknesses available (see the Specifications).

8   Using feeler blades check the 1st and 2nd gear endfloat is in accordance with that given in the Specifications.

9   To the front of the mainshaft fit 3rd gear and the synchro hub spacer. With 3rd gear pressed against the mainshaft flange, the selection of the correct spacer from those listed in Specifications can be determined by measuring the A to B dimension shown with a vernier gauge. A spacer should be selected which provides the smallest increment in thickness above the dimension measured (Fig. 6.31).

10 Fit the synchro ring and 3rd/4th synchro unit and then install a circlip from the range of thicknesses available (see the Specifications) which will eliminate any endfloat of the synchro hub.

11 Check 3rd gear endfloat is as specified using a feeler blade.

---

15 Countershaft and countergear (Type K50 gearbox) - servicing

1   Provided the gear teeth are not worn or chipped and the shaft is not grooved, the only items which can be renewed independently are the bearing at the rear end, the two sets of needle rollers and 5th gear.

2   The remainder of the assembly is only renewable complete.

---

16 Reverse shift and fifth gear shift arms (Type K50 gearbox) - servicing

1   Wear in these components can be rectified by dismantling and renewing the parts as necessary.

2   Dismantle the reverse shift arm by unscrewing the nut and extracting the circlip (Fig. 6.33).

3   Dismantle the fifth gear shift arm in similar manner (Fig. 6.34).

---

17 Reverse restrict pin and selector control rod (Type K50 gearbox) - servicing

1   The reverse restrict pin and the dog on the end of the selector

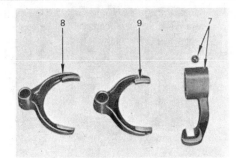

Fig. 6.23. Shift fork identification (K50 gearbox)

7   Reverse   9   3rd/4th
8   1st/2nd

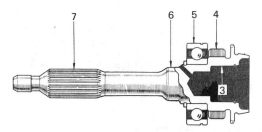

Fig. 6.24. Correct assembly of input shaft (K50 gearbox)

3   Needle rollers   6   Input shaft
4   4th gear   7   Splines (to engage with clutch
5   Front bearing   driven plate)

Fig. 6.25. Selecting an input shaft bearing circlip

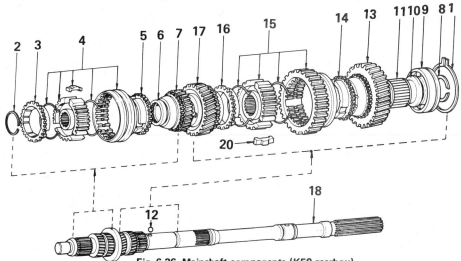

Fig. 6.26. Mainshaft components (K50 gearbox)

1 Circlip	5 Synchro ring	9 Bearing	14 Synchro. ring
2 Circlip	6 Spacer	10 1st gear bush	15 1st/2nd synchro with reverse gear
3 Synchro. ring	7 3rd gear	11 Needle roller bearing	16 Synchro. ring
4 3rd/4th synchro. unit	8 Circlip	12 Locking ball	17 2nd gear
		13 1st gear	18 Mainshaft

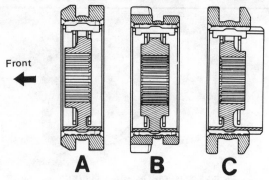

Fig. 6.27. Identification of synchro. units (K50 gearbox)

A 3rd/4th   C 5th gear
B 1st/2nd with reverse gear

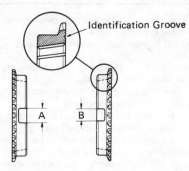

Fig. 6.28. Synchro. rings showing different cut-out widths

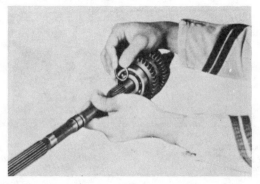

Fig. 6.29. Selecting mainshaft bearing circlip (K50 gearbox)

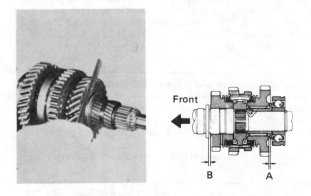

Fig. 6.30. Checking 1st/2nd gear end-float (K50 gearbox)

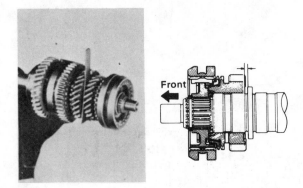

Fig. 6.31. 3rd gear synchro. hub spacer selection diagram (K50 gearbox)

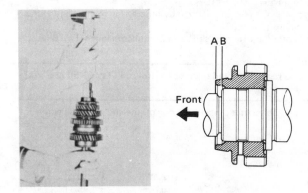

Fig. 6.32. 3rd gear end-float diagram (K50 gearbox)

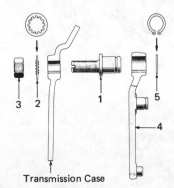

Transmission Case

Fig. 6.33. Reverse gear shift arm components (K50 gearbox)

1 Pivot   4 Shift arm
2 Lockwasher   5 Circlip
3 Nut

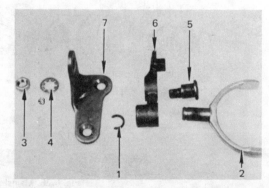

Fig. 6.34. 5th gear shift arm components (K50 gearbox)

1 Circlip   5 Pivot
2 5th gear shift fork   6 Shift arm
3 Nut   7 Shift arm bracket
4 Lockwasher

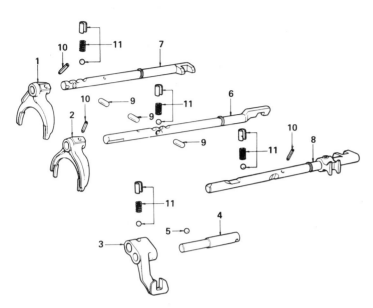

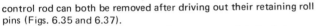

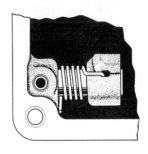

Fig. 6.36. Reverse restrict pin spring arrangement (K50 gearbox)

Fig. 6.35. Selector components (K50 gearbox)

1	1st/2nd shift fork	7	1st/2nd selector shaft
2	3rd/4th shift fork	8	5th gear selector shaft
3	Reverse shift fork	9	Interlock pin
4	Reverse selector shaft	10	Roll pin
5	Locking ball	11	Detent spring, sleeve and
6	3rd/4th selector shaft		ball

control rod can both be removed after driving out their retaining roll pins (Figs. 6.35 and 6.37).

2   Note the spring arrangement on the reverse restrict pin during reassembly.

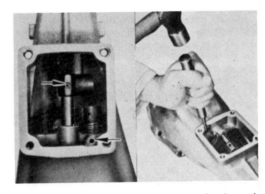

Fig. 6.37. Reverse restrict pin and selector control rod securing roll pins (K50 gearbox)

18 Gearbox (Type K50) - reassembly

1   Install the mainshaft assembly into the gearcase, entering it from the front end.

2   Secure it in position with a circlip.

3   Place a new gasket on the front face of the gearcase and install the input shaft assembly complete with bearing retainer. Smear the threads of the retainer bolts with jointing compound and tighten to specified torque.

4   Locate 1st/2nd shift fork in the synchro unit sleeve groove.

5   Move reverse gear so that 3rd/4th shift fork can be engaged in its synchro sleeve groove (Fig. 6.36).

6   Install reverse shift fork then align the groove in the fork tip with the pin on the reverse shift arm and insert the reverse shift fork shaft and ball. The ball is easily installed by coating it with grease and dropping it into position (Fig. 6.38).

7   Install the selector shafts, making sure that they pass through the holes in their respective shift forks and check that the ball is correctly located in its recess in the reverse selector shaft (Fig. 6.39).

8   Align the holes in the selector shafts using a thin screwdriver and then insert the interlock pins. Apply jointing compound to the hole and fit the plug (Fig. 6.40).

9   Secure the shift forks to their selector rods by driving in the tension pins. To do this, select 2nd gear and drive in the 1st/2nd fork pin. Shift the gears to neutral to drive in the remaining pins. When driving in the reverse fork roll pin, drive it in until it is quite flush with the upper surface of the shift fork.

10 Stick the needle rollers into the recesses in each end of the counter-gear and the thrust washers to the end faces of the countergear using thick grease. Note that the dimpled sides of the thrust washers are against the countergear.

11 Hold the countergear in position and pass the countershaft through it without displacing the needle rollers or thrust washers making sure that the key on the shaft is aligned with the cut-out on the front bearing retainer.

12 When correctly installed, the rear end of the countershaft should project by 0.374 in (9.5 mm).

13 Engage the reverse shift arm with the groove of the reverse idler gear and install the reverse idler shaft and gear assembly. Lock with the bolt, if necessary turn the idler shaft with a screwdriver engaged in the slot in the end of the shaft (Fig. 6.41).

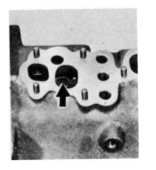

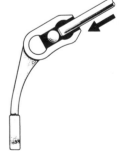

Fig. 6.38. Reverse shift fork rod arrangement (K50 gearbox)

14 To the rear end of the countershaft, fit the outer bearing track and retaining circlip.

15 Fit the needle roller bearing and the counter fifth gear. Make sure that the components are fitted the correct way round and then fit a circlip selecting a thickness to give the closest fit in its groove (Fig. 6.42).

16 The countergear thrust washer must now be selected and fitted. To do this, temporarily install the extension housing and a new gasket, tighten the securing bolts to specified torque. The thrust washer should be selected from the thicknesses available (see the Specifications) which will give a clearance (A) of between 0.0032 and 0.0016 in (0.08 and 0.04 mm) (Fig. 6.43).

17 To the rear end of the mainshaft now fit 5th gear, synchro ring, 5th gear synchro unit and the shift key retaining plate.

18 Select and fit a securing circlip. To do this, tap the mainshaft towards the front of the gearbox and press the shift key retainer hard against the synchro hub. From the circlip thicknesses available (see the Specifications) select one which will give a 5th gear endfloat (A) of between 0.008 and 0.012 in (0.2 and 0.3 mm).

19 Assemble the shift arm by first engaging the claw of the shift fork in 5th gear synchro sleeve groove, then engage the shaft of the shift arm in the selector shaft dog while the bracket connects with the reverse selector shaft groove.

20 To the rear end of the mainshaft fit a circlip, the locking ball, the speedometer drive gear and the second circlip.

21 Into the top face of the gearcase fit the four detent balls, the sleeves, the springs, gasket and the cover plate.

22 At this stage, adjust the reverse idler gear. To do this set the gearbox in neutral, slacken the pivot locknut and turn the pivot until dimension (A) is between 0.039 and 0.079 in (1.0 and 2.0 mm) when viewed through the bottom of the gearcase.

23 Now adjust 5th gear shift fork. To do this, set the 5th gears in engagement and turn the shift fork pivot until there is a clearance between the face of 5th gear synchro sleeve and the face of counter 5th gear (Fig. 6.48).

24 Offer up the extension housing to the main gearcase having already positioned a new flange gasket both sides coated with jointing compound.

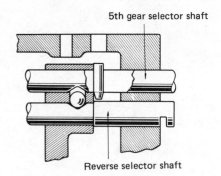

Fig. 6.39. Arrangement of reverse and 5th selector shafts showing ball (K50 gearbox)

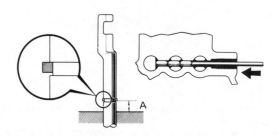

Fig. 6.40. Location of interlock pins (K50 gearbox)

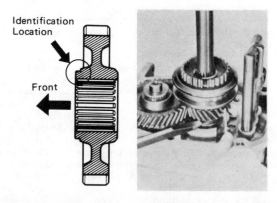

Fig. 6.42. Countershaft 5th gear installation diagram (K50 gearbox)

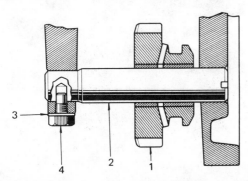

Fig. 6.41. Correct installation of reverse idler components (K50 gearbox)

1 Idler gear   3 Washer
2 Idler shaft   4 Lockbolt

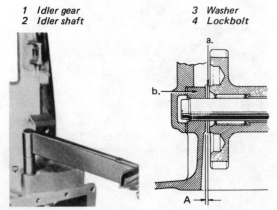

Fig. 6.43. Countergear thrust washer selection diagram (K50 gearbox)

    a   Thrust washer   A End-float
    b   Gearcase

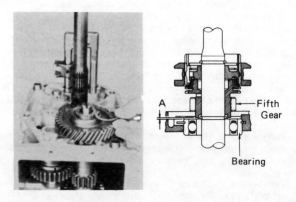

Fig. 6.44. 5th gear (end-float control) circlip selection diagram (K50 gearbox)

Fig. 6.45. Shift arm reassembly (K50 gearbox)

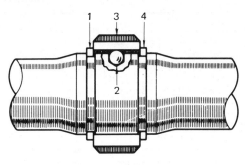

Fig. 6.46. Locking arrangement of speedometer drive gear (K50 gearbox)

1	Circlip	3	Speedometer drive gear
2	Locking ball	4	Circlip

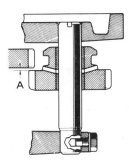

Fig. 6.47. Reverse idler gear adjustment (K50 gearbox)

A = 0.039 to 0.079 in (1.0 to 2.0 mm)

Fig. 6.48. 5th gear shift fork adjustment (K50 gearbox)

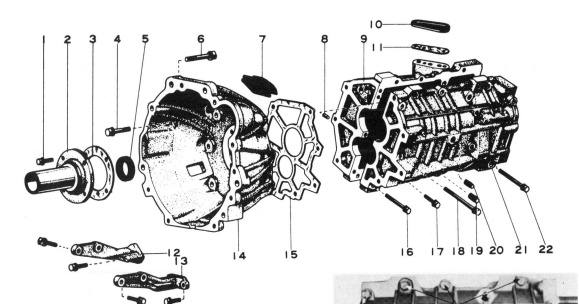

Fig. 6.49. External components (T40 type gearbox)

1	Bolt and washer	12	Reinforcement bracket
2	Front bearing retainer	13	Reinforcement bracket
3	Gasket	14	Clutch housing
4	Bolt and washer	15	Gasket
5	Oil seal	16	Bolt and washer
6	Bolt and washer	17	Bolt and washer
7	Clutch housing cover	18	Bolt and washer
8	Pin	19	Drain plug
9	Main casing (RH)	20	Filler plug
10	Cover	21	Main casing (LH)
11	Gasket	22	Bolt and washer

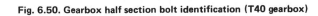

Fig. 6.50. Gearbox half section bolt identification (T40 gearbox)

25 Pull the selector rod as far as possible towards the front of the extension housing and engage it with the dogs on the selector shafts.

26 Install the extension housing and then coat the threads of the securing bolts with jointing compound and screw them into position and tighten to specified torque.

27 Fit the speedometer driven gear into the extension housing.

28 Fit the gearshift lever retainer and gasket.

29 Fit the bottom cover using a new gasket.

30 Fit the drain plug.

31 Install the reversing lamp switch.

32 Fit the clutch release bearing and lever as described in Chapter 5.

33 Fill the transmission with the correct quantity and grade of lubricant and screw in the filler plug.

34 The gearbox is now ready for installation.

19 Gearbox (Type T40) - dismantling into major assemblies

1 Drain the lubricant and clean the outside of the unit with paraffin and a stiff brush or use a water-soluble solvent (Figs. 6.49, 6.51 and 6.52).

2 Refer to Chapter 5 and remove the clutch release lever and bearing assembly.

3 Undo and remove the four bolts and spring washers securing the front bearing retainer to the inner face of the clutch bellhousing. Slide the retainer from the input shaft (photo).

4 Recover the paper gasket from the retainer or bellhousing face.

5 Undo and remove the bolts and spring washers that secure the clutch bellhousing to the front face of the main casing. Lift away the bellhousing (photo). Recover the gasket.

6 Note the location of the washers which will be exposed when the clutch bellhousing is removed (photo).

7 Undo and remove the four bolts and spring washers securing the gearchange lever retainer to the upper face of the extension housing. Lift away the retainer and recover the gasket. Note the two locating dowels (photo).

8 Undo and remove the bolt, spring washer and clip retaining the speedometer driven gear assembly to the extension housing.

9 Using a screwdriver carefully ease the assembly from its location in the extension housing (photos).

10 Undo and remove the bolts and spring washers securing the extension housing to the main casing. Draw the extension housing rearwards and recover the gasket (photo).

11 Undo and remove the bolts and spring washers securing the two halves of the gearbox main casing (Fig. 6.52).

12 Tap the joint to release the joint and lift away the upper main casing half (photo).

13 No gasket is used between these two mating faces.

14 This photo shows the layout of the main casing half with the gear trains, selector rods and forks fitted.

15 Carefully recover the locking ball located in the central web (photo).

16 Gently tap the countershaft assembly with a soft faced hammer and lift up from the main casing half.

17 Carefully remove the locking ball from the countershaft bearing outer track (photo).

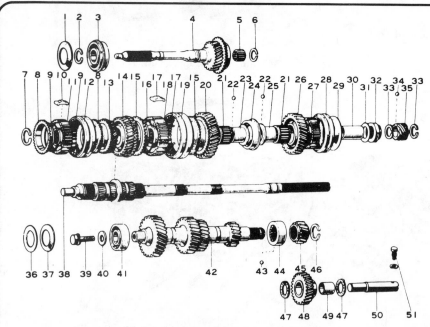

19.3 Removing front bearing retainer (T40 gearbox)

19.5 Separating gearcase from clutch bellhousing (T40 gearbox)

Fig. 6.51. Internal components (Type T40 gearbox)

1 Spring cone	19 Synchro sleeve	36 Shim
2 Circlip	20 1st gear	37 Spring
3 Bearing	21 Needle roller bearing	38 Mainshaft
4 Input shaft (4th gear)	22 Locking ball	39 Bolt
5 Needle rollers	23 1st gear bush	40 Washer
6 Circlip	24 Mainshaft bearing	41 Bearing
7 Circlip	25 Reverse gear bush	42 Countergear
8 Synchro. ring	26 Reverse gear (constant mesh)	43 Locking ball
9 Spring	27 Reverse synchro. unit	44 Bearing
10 Shift key	28 Synchro sleeve	45 Reverse gear (constant mesh type)
11 3rd/4th synchro hub	29 Spacer	46 Circlip
12 Synchro. sleeve	30 Spacer	47 Thrust washer
13 3rd gear	31 Shim	48 Reverse idler gear
14 2nd gear	32 Nut	49 Bush
15 Synchro. ring	33 Circlip	50 Reverse idler gear shaft
16 Spring	34 Locking ball	51 Locking bolt
17 Shift key	35 Speedometer drive gear	
18 1st/2nd synchro. unit		

19.6 Washers between gearcase and clutch bellhousing (T40 gearbox)

19.7 Removing gearshift lever retainer (T40 gearbox)

19.9A Prising speedometer drive gear from extension housing (T40 gearbox)

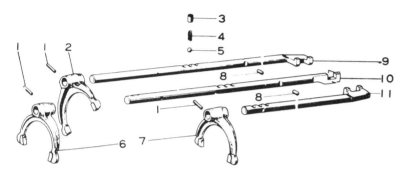

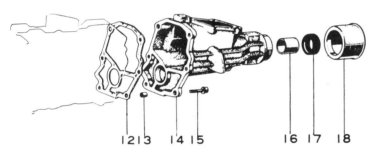

Fig. 6.52. Gear selector components (T40 gearbox)

1   Roll pin
2   1st/2nd shift fork
3   Detent sleeve
4   Detent spring
5   Detent ball
6   3rd/4th shift fork
7   Reverse shift fork
8   Interlock pin
9   1st/2nd selector shaft
10 3rd/4th selector shaft
11 Reverse selector shaft
12 Gasket
13 Dowel
14 Extension housing
15 Bolt
16 Bush
17 Oil seal
18 Dust deflector
19 Flexible boot
20 Threaded bush
21 Seal
22 Selector return plate
23 Lockbolt
24 Spring
25 Spring seat
26 Knob
27 Gearshift lever
28 Retainer
29 Spring
30 Ball
31 Pivot bolt
32 Dowel
33 Gasket

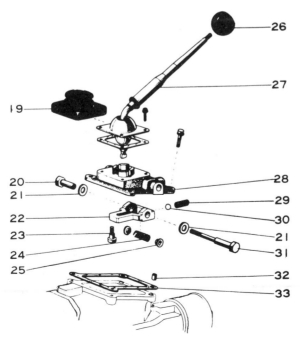

19.9B Withdrawing speedometer drive assembly (T40 gearbox)

19.10 Removing extension housing (T40 gearbox)

19.12 Separating two halves of T40 gearcase

19.14 Geartrain (T40 gearbox)

19.15 Locking ball in gearcase central web (T40 gearbox)

19.17 Countershaft bearing locking ball (T40 gearbox)

19.18 Removing countergear and shaft assembly (T40 gearbox)

19.19 Removing mainshaft/input shaft assemblies (T40 gearbox)

19.20 Reverse idler gear and shaft showing lock bolt (T40 gearbox)

20.3 Separating input shaft and mainshaft (T40 gearbox)

20.8 Needle rollers in end of input shaft (T40 gearbox)

21.1 Extracting mainshaft front circlip (T40 gearbox)

Fig. 6.53. Driving out a shift fork roll pin (T40 gearbox)

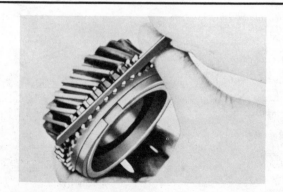

Fig. 6.54. Checking synchro. ring to cone clearance (T40 gearbox)

18 Lift away the countershaft assembly (photo).
19 The mainshaft and input shaft may now be lifted away from the main casing half (photo).
20 If necessary undo and remove the bolt and spring washer securing the reverse idler gearshaft (photo).
21 Carefully tap out the idler gearshaft and recover the gear and thrust washers.
22 The gearbox may now be considered to be dismantled into major assemblies. Normally it will not be necessary to remove the selector forks and rods. Should it be desirable to remove these parts mark the relative positions of the selector forks and rods and tap out the fork retaining roll pins using a suitable diameter parallel pin punch (Fig. 6.53).
23 Withdraw the selector shafts and recover the interlock pins, detent balls, spring and spring seat.
24 Clean out the casing and place it to one side ready for reassembly.
25 Inspect the gearbox components as described in Section 4.

20 Input shaft (Type T40 gearbox) - servicing

1 Take care not to let the synchromesh hub assemblies come apart before you want them to. It accelerates wear if the splines of the hub and sleeve are changed in relation to each other. As a precaution it is advisable to make a line up mark with a dab of paint.
2 Before finally going ahead with dismantling first ascertain the availability of spare parts - particularly shims, which could be difficult.
3 Draw the input shaft from the front of the mainshaft (photo).
4 The shaft and bearing are located in the front of the main casing by a large circlip in the outer track of the bearing.
5 To renew the bearing, first remove the circlip from the front end of the bearing.
6 Place the outer track of the race on the top of a firm bench vice and drive the input shaft through the bearing. Note that the bearing is fitted with the circlip groove towards the forward end of the input shaft. Lift away the bearing.
7 To remove the spigot bearing needle rollers, use a pair of circlip pliers or a small screwdriver and release the circlip.

8 Lift away the needle rollers from the end of the input shaft (photo).
9 Using a suitable diameter tubular drift carefully drive the ball race into position. The circlip in the outer track must be nearer the front of the input shaft.
10 Retain the bearing in position with a circlip. This is a selective circlip which is available in a range of 5 different sizes (see the Specifications).
11 Smear some grease onto the needle roller bore and insert the needle rollers. The best way to fit the needle rollers is to insert them into the base and push outwards.
12 Retain the needle rollers with the circlip.

21 Mainshaft (Type T40 gearbox) - servicing

1 Remove the circlip from the front of the mainshaft (photo).
2 Using a screwdriver, detach the top gear synchroniser assembly (photo).
3 Using a pair of circlip pliers remove the circlip from the rear end of the mainshaft (photo).
4 Carefully tap the speedometer drivegear from the mainshaft. Recover the locking ball from the hole in the mainshaft (photo).
5 Remove the second circlip from the rear end of the mainshaft.
6 Hold the mainshaft firmly in the vice and unscrew the large nut.
7 Slide the nut, shim and spacer from the end of the mainshaft (photo).
8 Slide the metal disc from the mainshaft noting which way round it is fitted (photo).
9 Hold the mainshaft as shown in this photo and tap the end with a soft faced hammer to release the reverse gear assembly from the mainshaft (photo).
10 Lift away the reverse gear assembly, needle roller race and bush (photo).
11 Remove the rear bearing ball race retaining ball bearing and slide off the rear bearing assembly, first gear assembly, needle roller race and bush (photo).
12 Slide off the thrust washer (photo).

21.2 Prising top gear synchro. unit from mainshaft (T40 gearbox)

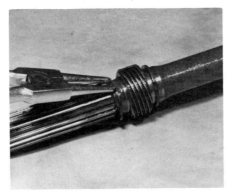
21.3 Extracting speedo. drive gear circlip (T40 gearbox)

21.4 Speedo. drive gear and locking ball (T40 gearbox)

21.7 Removing mainshaft nut, shim and spacer (T40 gearbox)

21.8 Removing disc from mainshaft (T40 gearbox)

21.9 Driving mainshaft out of reverse gear assembly (T40 gearbox)

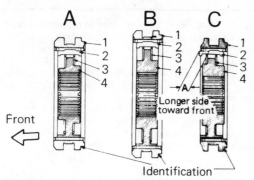

Fig. 6.55. Synchro. unit identification (T40 gearbox)

A 3rd/4th   *B 1st/2nd*   *C Reverse*

Front

Longer side toward front

Identification

21.10 Reverse gear, needle roller bearing and spacer on mainshaft of T40 gearbox

21.11 Removing mainshaft rear bearing and 1st gear assembly (T40 gearbox)

21.12 Removing thrust washer from mainshaft (T40 gearbox)

21.13 2nd gear removed from mainshaft (T40 gearbox)

21.25 Refitting mainshaft front circlip (T40 gearbox)

21.26 Refitting 2nd gear to mainshaft (T40 gearbox)

21.27 Fitting 1st/2nd synchro unit (T40 gearbox)

21.28 Fitting 1st gear to mainshaft (T40 gearbox)

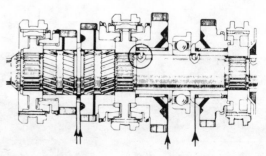

Fig. 6.56. Mainshaft gear end-float measurement points (T40 gearbox)

13 The second gear assembly can now be removed from the mainshaft (photo).

14 The synchro hubs are only too easy to dismantle - just push the centre out and the whole assembly flies apart. The point is to prevent this happening, before you are ready. Do not dismantle the hubs without reason and do not mix up the parts of the hubs.

15 It is most important to check backlash in the splines between the outer sleeve and inner hub. If any is noticeable the whole assembly must be renewed. Check the clearance between synchro ring and gear does not exceed 0.032 in (0.8 mm) (Fig. 6.54).

16 Mark the hub and sleeve so that you may reassemble them on the same splines. With the hub and sleeve separated, the teeth at the end of the splines which engage with corresponding teeth of the gearwheels, must be checked for damage or wear.

17 Do not confuse with wear, the keystone shape at the ends of the teeth. This shape matches the gear teeth shape and it is a design characteristic to minimise jump-out tendencies.

18 If the synchronising cones are being renewed it is sensible also to renew the sliding keys and springs which hold them in position.

19 The hub assemblies are not interchangeable so they must be reassembled with their original or identical new parts.

20 The pips on the sliding keys are symmetrical so may be refitted either way round into the hub.

21 One slotted key is assembled to each hub for locating the turned out end of the key spring.

22 It should be noted that the keys for each synchromesh unit are of different lengths (Fig. 6.55).

23 The turned out end of each spring must locate in the slotted key and be assembled to the hub in an anticlockwise direction as viewed from either side of the hub.

24 Slide the third speed gear assembly and synchromesh assembly onto the front end of the mainshaft.

25 Refit the circlip and check the endfloat which should be 0.024 in (0.6 mm). If the reading obtained is outside this limit a new circlip will be required (photo).

26 Slide the second gear assembly onto the mainshaft (photo).

27 Follow this with the synchromesh unit and needle roller bearing (photo).

28 Slide on the first gear assembly and bush. A locking ball must be fitted in the hole in the mainshaft between the synchromesh unit and first gear assembly (photo).

29 Slide on the ball race and push up to the back of the first gear assembly (photo).

30 Lock the ball race with a ball bearing in the first exposed hole in the mainshaft.

31 Refit the reverse gear and synchromesh unit together with bush and needle roller bearing (photo).

32 Slide on the metal disc with the disc located as shown in this photo. Follow this with the spacer, shim and nut.

33 Tighten the nut as tightly as possible. Ideally this should be set to a torque wrench setting of between 32 and 55 lb/ft (44 and 76 Nm).

34 Fit the first circlip to the end of the mainshaft. Insert the locking ball and slide on the speedometer drive gear.

35 Retain the speedometer drive gear with the second circlip.

36 The mainshaft is now reassembled.

37 Using feeler gauges or a dial gauge, measure the thrust clearances to ensure that they are within the manufacturer's recommended limits. If there is a significant difference the cause must be found and rectified (Fig. 6.56).

	New	Maximum
First gear	0.004 - 0.010 in. (0.10 - 0.25 mm)	0.020 in. (0.5 mm)
Second gear	0.006 - 0.010 in. (0.15 - 0.25 mm)	0.020 in. (0.5 mm)
Third gear	0.006 - 0.012 in. (0.15 - 0.30 mm)	0.024 in. (0.6 mm)
Reverse gear	0.008 - 0.012 in. (0.20 - 0.30 mm)	0.024 in. (0.6 mm)

22 Countershaft (Type T40 gearbox) - servicing

1 Undo and remove the bolt, spring washer and plain washer holding the ball race onto the end of the countershaft.

2 Using a universal puller and suitable thrust block draw the bearing

21.29 Fitting mainshaft bearing (T40 gearbox)

21.31 Fitting constant mesh reverse gear and synchro. unit (T40 gearbox)

21.32 Assembling disc, shims, spacer and nut to mainshaft (T40 gearbox)

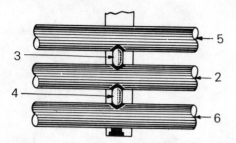

Fig. 6.57. Selector rod and interlock pin arrangement (T40 gearbox)

2	3rd/4th selector shaft	5	Reverse selector shaft
3	Interlock pin	6	1st/2nd selector shaft
4	Interlock pin		

Fig. 6.58. Measuring reverse idler gear end-float (T40 gearbox)

24.11 Fitting gearshift lever retainer (T40 gearbox)

24.15 Fitting input shaft bearing retainer (T40 gearbox)

24.17 Fitting clutch release arm (T40 gearbox)

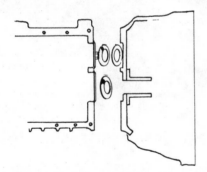

Fig. 6.59. Location of washers and spring cone between gearcase and clutch bellhousing

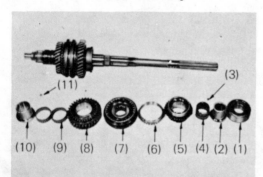

Fig. 6.60. Rear end of mainshaft dismantled (T50 gearbox)

1	Bearing	7	Reverse/5th synchro. unit
2	Bush	8	Reverse gear
3	Locking ball	9	Needle rollers
4	Needle roller bearing	10	Reverse gear bush
5	5th gear	11	Locking ball
6	Synchro. ring		

from the end of the countershaft. Note which way round the bearing is fitted.

3   Using a pair of circlip pliers remove the circlip retaining the reverse gear on the end of the countershaft.

4   Slide off the reverse gear.

5   Remove the ball bearing and ball race from the countershaft.

6   Refit the ball bearing and ball race to the splined end of the countershaft.

7   Slide the reverse gear onto the splines and push fully home.

8   Using feeler gauges measure the circlip groove width and select a new circlip. Two sizes are available:

   0.0709 - 0.0728 in. (1.80 - 1.85 mm)
   0.0728 - 0.0748 in. (1.85 - 1.90 mm)

9   Fit the new circlip and ensure that there is no gear endfloat.

10 Fit the ball race to the spigot end of the countershaft and retain in position with the bolt, spring and plain washer. Tighten the bolt to a torque wrench setting of between 22 and 36 lb/ft (30 and 50 Nm).

---

23 Extension housing (T40 type gearbox) - servicing

1   Refer to Section 5, the operations being similar.

---

24 Gearbox (Type T40) - reassembly

1   If the selector forks and rods have been removed they should be refitted. This is a direct reversal of the removal procedure (Fig. 6.57).

2   Hold the reverse idle and thrust washers in position in the half casing and slide in the reverse idler shaft. Line up the dowel bolt hole and refit the bolt and spring washer. Tighten the bolt to a torque wrench setting of between 10 and 13 lb/ft (14 and 18 Nm).

3   Check the reverse idler thrust clearance which should be 0.002 - 0.020 in (0.05 - 0.50 mm) with a maximum limit of 0.039 in (1.0 mm) (Fig. 6.58).

4   With the main casing halves clean, carefully lower the mainshaft into position.

5   Follow the mainshaft with the countershaft. Do not forget the ball

Fig. 6.61. Additional 5th gear components fitted to rear end of mainshaft on type T50 gearbox

26 Synchro. shift key spring
27 Shift key
28 Synchro. ring
29 5th gear

30 Needle roller bearing
31 Locking ball
32 Bush
33 Bearing

Fig. 6.62. Pressing off 5th gear from the countergear (T50 gearbox)

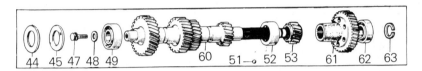

Fig. 6.63. Countergear arrangement on type T50 gearbox

44 Shim
45 Cone spring
47 Bolt

48 Washer
49 Bearing
51 Locking ball

52 Bearing
53 Counter reverse gear
60 Countergear

61 Counter 5th gear
62 Bearing
63 Circlip

race outer track locking ball.

6   Fit the locking ball to the hole in the central web.

7   Smear a little sealer to the mating face of the main gearbox casing with the exception of an area of 0.5 in (13 mm) around the reverse light switch.

8   Carefully fit the two halves of the main casing and refit the securing bolts and spring washers. Tighten in a progressive and diagonal manner to the specified torque wrench setting.

9   Fit a new gasket to the extension housing mating face and carefully lower into position. Tighten the securing bolts to the specified torque wrench setting.

10 Refit the speedometer driven assembly to the extension housing and retain with the bolt, spring washer and clip. Tighten the bolt to specified torque wrench setting.

11 Fit a new gasket to the gearchange lever retainer mating face and replace the retainer. Secure with the four bolts and spring washers which should be tightened to specified torque wrench setting (photo).

12 Turn the gearbox on end and position the washers and cone onto the end of the countershaft and input shaft (Fig. 6.59).

13 Fit a new gasket and replace the clutch bellhousing. Tighten the securing bolts to specified torque wrench setting.

14 Inspect the input shaft bearing retainer oil seal and if worn ease out the old seal. Fit a new seal using a drift of suitable diameter.

15 Fit a new gasket to the clutch bellhousing and refit the input shaft bearing retainer (photo).

16 Replace the four bolts and spring washers. Tighten to specified torque wrench setting.

17 Refit the clutch release arm and bearing carrier and secure with the two spring clips (photo).

18 The gearbox is now ready for refitting to the car. Do not forget to refill the gearbox with the recommended grade of oil.

25 Gearbox (Type T50) - dismantling, servicing, reassembly

1   The operations are almost identical with those described for the T40 unit except that 5th gear is located at the rear end of the mainshaft and a matching gear is fitted to the countergear (Fig. 6.61 and 6.63).

2   Selection of 5th speed is obtained through movement of the Reverse/5th selector rod and shift fork.

3   5th gear can be removed from the countergear if a press is available (Fig. 6.62).

4   The 5th gear endfloat on the mainshaft should be between 0.0059 and 0.0108 in (0.15 and 0.275 mm).

26 Fault diagnosis - manual gearbox

Symptom	Reason/s
Ineffective synchromesh on one or more gears	Worn baulk rings. Worn blocker bars.
Jumps out of one or more gears	Weak detent springs. Worn shift forks. Worn engagement dogs. Worn synchro hubs.
Whining, roughness, vibration allied to other faults	Bearing failure and/or overall wear.
Noisy and difficult gear engagement	Clutch not operating correctly.
Sloppy and impositive gear selection	Overall wear throughout the selector mechanism.

Chapter 6 Gearbox Part 2

Contents - Part 2 - Automatic transmission

Specifications - Part 2 - Automatic transmission

	A40	2-speed Toyoglide
Type	A-40 three speed and reverse 2-speed Toyoglide - two speeds and reverse	
Ratios		
1st	2.450 : 1	1.82 : 1
2nd	1.450 : 1	1.00 : 1
3rd	1.000 : 1	—
Reverse	2.220 : 1	1.82 : 1
Fluid capacity		
Fluid change (A40)	2.1 Imp. qts (2.5 US qts/2.4 litres)	
Refill (dry torque converter) (A40)	5.1 Imp. qts (6.1 US qts/5.8 litres)	
Refill (2-speed Toyoglide)	4.1 Imp. qts (5 US qts/4.7 litres)	

Torque wrench settings	lb/ft	Nm
Driveplate to crankshaft bolts	43	59
Driveplate to torque converter bolts	15	21
Torque converter housing to engine bolts (A40)	55	76
Torque converter housing to engine bolts (2-speed)	50	69
Oil pan bolts	8	11
Extension housing bolts (A40)	30	41
Extension housing bolts (2-speed)	11	16

27 General description

1 The optional automatic transmission (except UK) is the A40 type which is of Borg-Warner design manufactured in Japan (Fig. 6.68). In the UK a 2-speed Toyoglide is fitted.
2 The A40 is a fully automatic three forward and one reverse speed unit.
3 The A40 transmission is of bandless construction and requires no periodic adjustment apart from the control cables and selector rods.
4 No rear oil pump is incorporated in the A40 design and in the event of breakdown, the vehicle must not be towed in excess of 30 mph (48 km/h) or further than 50 miles (80 km) unless the propeller shaft is disconnected. Failure to observe this requirement may cause damage to the transmission due to lack of lubrication. Due to the complexities of dismantling and reassembly of automatic transmission units, the operations described in this Chapter are limited to maintenance, adjustment of the controls and removal and installation of the unit.

28 Maintenance

1 If the transmission fluid is cold, withdraw the dipstick, wipe it, re-insert it and withdraw it again. The fluid level should be within the cold range. If the vehicle has travelled at least 5 miles (8 km) the fluid level should be within the hot range of the dipstick when the same checking procedure is followed. Top-up with fluid of the specified grade (Fig. 6.64).
2 Keep the external surfaces of the transmission unit clean and free

COLD   HOT

Fig. 6.64. Dipstick markings

Fig. 6.65. Checking downshift cable length (crimped collar to end of outer cable threaded section)

Fig. 6.66. Releasing downshift cable locknuts

Fig. 6.67. Speed selector linkage swivel and pinch nut

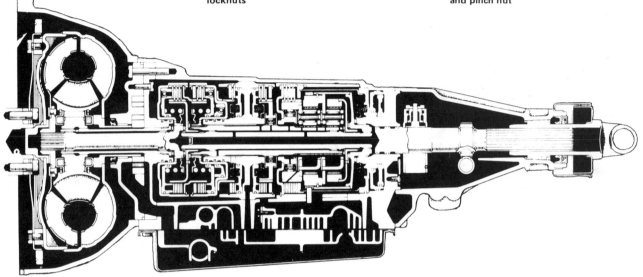

Fig. 6.68. Sectional view of A40 type automatic transmission

Fig. 6.69. Speed selector lever on side of transmission casing

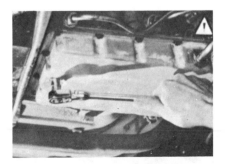

Fig. 6.70. Unscrewing fluid drain plug

from mud and grease to prevent overheating. An oil cooler is fitted, make sure that the connecting pipes are secure and in good condition.

3   The automatic transmission fluid normally only requires changing at 25,000 miles (40,000 km) intervals, but if the oil on the dipstick appears burned or discolored or if particularly arduous or dusty operating conditions prevail, the fluid should be drained by removing the plug, at more frequent intervals.

4   As the torque converter will not be drained by this method, the refill quantity of fluid will be only 2.1 Imp. qts (2.5 US qts/ 2.4 litres).

29 Downshift cable - adjustment

A40

1   To adjust the downshift cable, remove the air cleaner and fully depress the accelerator pedal (use a block or piece of wood) checking that the carburettor throttle valve is fully open. Hold the pedal depressed.

2   Measure the distance between the end of the accelerator outer cable and the stop collar which should be 2.05 in (52.0 mm). If necessary, adjust the outer cable by slackening the two locknuts on the support bracket (Fig. 6.65 and 6.66).

2-speed Toyoglide

3   Fully open the throttle valve and adjust the effective length of the downshift rod (by releasing the locknuts and turning the turnbuckle) until the throttle link indicator aligns with the mark on the transmission case.

30 Speed selector linkage - adjustment

A40

1   To adjust the speed selector linkage, slacken the swivel nut on the

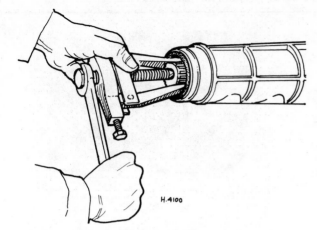

Fig. 6.71. Extracting rear extension housing oil seal

Fig. 6.72. Removing a starter motor bolt

Fig. 6.73. Disconnecting propeller shaft rear flange

Fig. 6.74. Disconnecting downshift cable

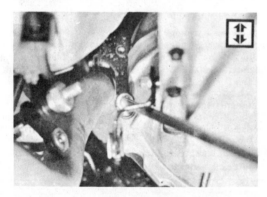

Fig. 6.75. Disconnecting exhaust pipe support bracket

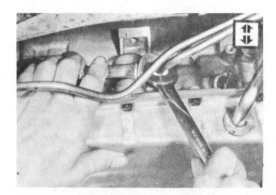

Fig. 6.76. Disconnecting fluid cooler pipes

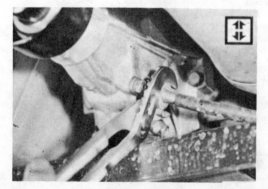

Fig. 6.77. Disconnecting speedometer drive cable

Fig. 6.78. Unbolting reinforcement bracket

control rod (Fig. 6.67).

2   Push the selector lever on the side of the transmission fully forward and then pull it back three notches to the 'N' position (Fig. 6.69).

3   Have an assistant hold the speed selector lever in 'N' and then retighten the swivel nut. Check the operation of the transmission in all positions of the speed range.

2-speed Toyoglide

4   Locate the manual valve control outer lever to 'N'.

5   Position the shift lever pin against the stop on the detent plate by loosening the nut on the control rod swivel and adjusting the effective length of the rod. Check all shift positions are obtainable.

31 Extension housing oil seal - renewal

1   Renewal of the oil seal may be carried out with the transmission unit in position in the vehicle.

2   Remove the propeller shaft as described in Chapter 7.

3   Knock off the dust deflector towards the rear and prise out the dust seal. Using a suitable extractor and levering against the end face of the mainshaft, extract the oil seal.

4   Drive in the new oil seal with a tubular drift, fit a new dust seal and refit the dust deflector (Fig. 6.70).

5   Refit the propeller shaft after first greasing the front sliding sleeve both internally and externally. Make sure that the propeller shaft and pinion driving flanges have their mating marks aligned.

32 Automatic transmission - removal and refitting

A40

1   It must be realised that the automatic transmission unit is of considerable weight and adequate assistance or the use of a trolley jack will be required for the following operations.

2   Disconnect the lead from the battery negative terminal.

Fig. 6.79. Unbolting under radiator splash shield

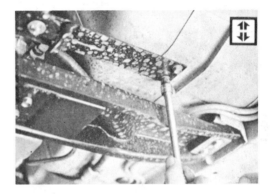

Fig. 6.80. Removing support plate for handbrake equaliser

Fig. 6.81. Extracting rubber plugs from front of converter housing

Fig. 6.82. Removing rear mounting crossmember

Fig. 6.83. Unscrewing a driveplate to torque converter bolt

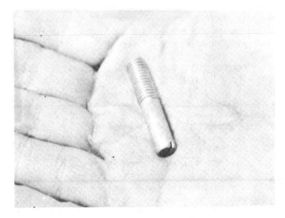

Fig. 6.84. Temporary guide pin

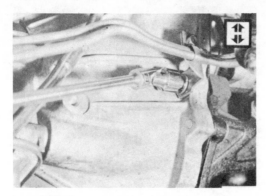

Fig. 6.85. Unscrewing a torque converter to engine bolt

Fig. 6.86. Levering against temporary guide pin

Fig. 6.87. Pulling torque converter forward out of transmission

Fig. 6.88. Driveplate bolted to crankshaft mounting flange showing starter ring gear and pilot hole

3   Drain the cooling system and disconnect the radiator top hose.

4   Remove the air cleaner and disconnect the throttle control at the carburettor.

5   Unless the vehicle is over a pit or raised on a hoist, jack-up the front and rear so that there is an adequate working clearance between the underside of the body floor and the ground to permit the torque converter housing to be withdrawn.

6   Drain the fluid from the transmission unit (Fig. 6.71).

7   Remove the starter motor (Fig. 6.72).

8   Disconnect the propeller shaft from the rear axle (see Chapter 7) and withdraw it from the transmission rear extension housing. (Fig. 6.73).

9   Disconnect the speed selector linkage at the transmission unit and the downshift cable at the engine end (Fig. 6.74).

10 Disconnect the exhaust downpipe from the manifold and remove the support bracket from the transmission unit (Fig. 6.75).

11 Disconnect the fluid cooler pipes from the transmission and plug them. Remove the pipe supports from the transmission (Fig. 6.76).

12 Disconnect the speedometer drive cable from the extension housing (Fig. 6.78).

13 Unbolt the two reinforcement brackets from the torque converter housing. Pull the fluid filler tube from the transmission and retain the 'O' ring seals (Fig. 6.79).

14 Remove the splash shield from below the radiator (Fig. 6.80).

15 Remove the support plate from the handbrake equaliser (Fig. 6.81).

16 Extract the two rubber plugs from the lower front face of the torque converter housing (Fig. 6.82).

17 Place a jack (preferably trolley type) under the transmission and unbolt the rear mounting and crossmember (Fig. 6.83).

18 Using a socket inserted through one of the holes in the lower front face of the torque converter housing, unscrew the bolts which hold the driveplate and torque converter together. The bolts can be brought into view one at a time by rotating the crankshaft with a ring spanner applied to the crankshaft pulley bolt (Fig. 6.84).

19 When all the bolts have been removed, screw in two guide pins (easily made from two old bolts) into two opposite bolt holes in the driveplate (Fig. 6.85). These bolts will actually pass through the drive-plate and screw into the blind holes of the torque converter (finger tight only). Position them horizontally by rotating the crankshaft, ready for them to act as leverage pins (see paragraph 20).

20 Place a jack under the engine sump (use a block of wood to protect it) and remove the bolts which secure the torque converter housing to the engine.

21 Lower both jacks progressively until the transmission unit will clear that lower edge of the engine rear bulkhead. Insert two levers between the engine rear plate and the temporary pivot bolts and prise the transmission unit from the engine. Catch the fluid which will run from the torque converter during this operation. **On no account should levers be placed between the driveplate and the torque converter as damage or distortion will result** (Fig. 6.86).

As the transmission moves away from the engine, the driveplate will remain bolted to the rear flange of the crankshaft.

22 The torque converter can now be pulled forward to remove it from the housing. The driveplate can be unbolted from the crankshaft flange if the plate has to be renewed because of worn starter ring gear. (Fig. 6.87).

23 Installation is a reversal of removal but tighten all bolts to the specified torque, apply grease to pilot hole in the centre of the drive-plate and carry out the adjustments described earlier in this Chapter according to type, after first having refilled the unit with the correct grade and quantity of fluid (Fig. 6.88).

2-speed Toyoglide

24 Removal and refitting of this type of transmission is very similar to the operations described for the A40 type except that it is recommended that the transmission case is withdrawn from the engine leaving the torque converter attached to the engine driveplate. The torque converter is then unbolted from the driveplate after the transmission has been removed.

33 Fault diagnosis - automatic transmission

Symptom	Reason/s
Oil on dipstick appears burned or discoloured	Transmission misused by towing overweight loads or by wheel spinning in mud or snow.
Water on dipstick	Leak in fluid cooler tube within radiator.
No vehicle movement in forward range, or reverse	Incorrectly adjusted selector linkage.
Harsh engagement when any drive range selected	Incorrectly adjusted downshift cable.
Screech or whine increasing with engine speed	Cracked driveplate. Oil pump screen (within oil pan) clogged.
Delayed upshifts or downshifts	Incorrectly adjusted downshift cable.
Slip on upshifts, downshifts squawk or shudder on take off	Incorrectly adjusted speed selector linkage or downshift cable.
Vehicle will not hold parked in 'P'	Incorrectly adjusted selector linkage.

Before carrying out any of the foregoing diagnosis checks always verify that the transmission fluid is at its correct level.

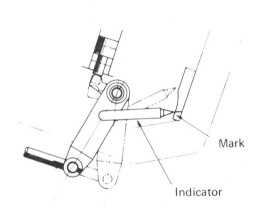

Fig. 6.89. Downshift rod indicator (2-speed Toyoglide)

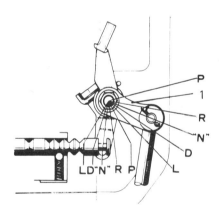

Fig. 6.90. Shift lever setting diagram (2-speed Toyoglide)

1   Outer lever

Chapter 7 Propeller shaft and universal joints

Refer to Chapter 13 for specifications and information applicable to 1979 US models.

Contents

Specifications

Type	Tubular, single piece with two universal joints and front sliding yoke

Length

1200E and 30 Series	46.38 in (1178.0 mm)
1600 models	45.20 in (1148.0 mm)

Shaft diameter

All models	2.95 in (75.0 mm)

Torque wrench setting

Rear flange coupling bolts:

	lb/ft	Nm
1200 and 30 Series models	20	28
1600 models	28	39

1 General description and maintenance

1 The drive from the gearbox to the rear axle is transmitted by the tubular propeller shaft. Due to the variety of angles caused by the up and down motion of the rear axle in relation to the gearbox, universal joints are fitted to each end of the shaft to convey the drive through the constantly varying angles. As the movement also increases and decreases the distance between the rear axle and the gearbox, the forward end of the propeller shaft is a splined sleeve which is a sliding fit over the rear of the gearbox splined mainshaft (Fig. 7.1).

2 The splined sleeve runs in an oil seal in the gearbox rear extension housing and is supported with the mainshaft on the gearbox rear bearing. The splines are lubricated by oil in the rear extension housing which comes from the gearbox.

3 The universal joints each comprise a four-way trunnion, or spider - each leg of which runs in a needle roller bearing race-preloaded with grease and fitted in the bearing journal yokes of the sliding sleeve and the propeller shaft and flange.

4 No maintenance is required except for occasionally checking the tightness of the propeller shaft rear flange bolts.

2 Propeller shaft - removal and refitting

1 Jack-up the rear of the car and support on firmly based axle stands.

2 The rear of the propeller shaft is connected to the rear axle pinion by a flange held by four nuts and bolts. Mark the position of both flanges relative to each other, and then undo and remove the nuts and bolts.

3 Move the propeller shaft forwards to disengage it from the pinion flange and then lower it to the ground (photo).

4 Draw the other end of the propeller shaft, that is the splined sleeve, out of the rear of the gearbox. The shaft is then clear for removal from

the underside of the car (photo).

5 Place a container under the gearbox rear extension housing to catch any oil which will certainly come out.

6 Refitting the propeller shaft is the reverse sequence to removal but the following additional points should be noted:

  a) *Ensure that the mating marks on the propeller shaft and differential pinion flanges are lined up.*
  b) *Don't forget to check the gearbox oil level and top-up if necessary.*
  c) *Tighten the bolts holding the flange to the differential to the specified torque wrench setting.*

3 Universal joints - inspection and repair

1 Wear in the needle roller bearings is characterised by vibration in the transmission, 'clonks' on taking up the drive and in extreme cases of lack of lubrication, metallic squeaking, and ultimately grating and shrieking sounds as the bearings break up.

2 It is easy to check if the needle roller bearings are worn, with the propeller shaft in position, by trying to turn the shaft with one hand, the other hand holding the rear axle flange. Any movement between the propeller shaft and the flange is indicative of considerable wear. If worn, the old bearings and spiders will have to be discarded and a repair kit comprising new universal joint spiders, bearings and oil seals purchased.

3 The front needle roller bearings should be tested for wear using the same principle as described in paragraph 2.

4 To test the splined coupling for wear, lift the end of the shaft and note any movement in the splines.

5 Check the splined coupling dust cover for signs of damage or looseness on the shaft.

4 Universal joints - dismantling and inspection

1 Clean away all traces of dirt and grease from the universal joint yoke. Using a pair of pliers compress the circlips and lift away. If the circlips are tight in their grooves tap the ends to shock move the bearing cups slightly.

2 Note that on 1200 and 30 Series models, the circlips are visible on the end faces of the bearing cups but on 1600 models the circlips are located inside the yokes (Figs. 7.4 and 7.5).

3 With the circlips removed, hold the propeller shaft and using a soft-faced hammer, tap the yoke to jar the bearing cups from the yoke (Fig. 7.6).

4 When a bearing cup has emerged, it can be gripped in the jaws of a vice and twisted out. As the cups are to be discarded, it does not matter if they are damaged (Fig. 7.7).

5 Remove all four bearing cups as described and then separate the yoke from the shaft *but not before marking their relationship.*

6 Clean all parts and thoroughly inspect for wear or damage.

7 If possible check the maximum runout at the centre using 'V' blocks and a dial indicator gauge. The runout should not exceed 0.010 in (0.254 mm).

8 Slide the yoke onto the gearbox mainshaft and check for spline wear both radially and vertically. Examine the expansion plug on the end of the yoke for signs of leakage. If leakage is evident, a new plug should be fitted.

9 If the needle bearings are worn it is probable that the spider trunnions are worn also, necessitating renewal.

10 Before obtaining new parts a check must be made to determine which sized parts are required as the trunnion bearings are available in different sizes.

11 *On 1200E and 30 Series models,* if a drill mark is to be seen on one side of the universal joint yoke, then the bearing on the side at which the mark is located is oversize and dimensions conform to the following. No drill mark is to be found on standard joint yokes and the bearing cups are painted red.

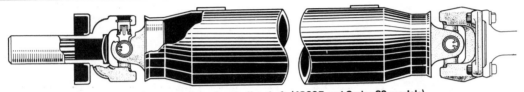

Fig. 7.1. Cut-away view of propeller shaft (1200E and Series 30 models)

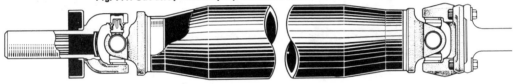

Fig. 7.2. Cut-away view of propeller shaft (1600 model)

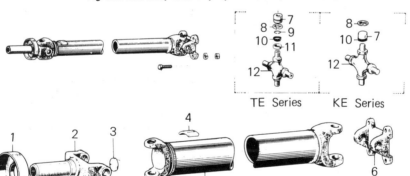

Fig. 7.3. Exploded view of propeller shaft showing different joint construction between 1200E/30 Series and 1600 models

1 Dust excluder	4 Balance weight	7 Bearing cup	10 Seal
2 Yoke	5 Tubular shaft	8 Circlip	11 Needle roller retaining cover
3 Plug	6 Yoke	9 'O' ring seal	12 Spider

2.3 Propeller shaft rear flange disconnected

Fig. 7.4. Extracting universal joint circlip (1200E and 30 Series models)

2.4 Propeller shaft front universal joint and sliding sleeve

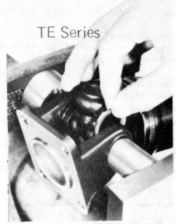

Fig. 7.5. Extracting universal joint circlip (1600 models)

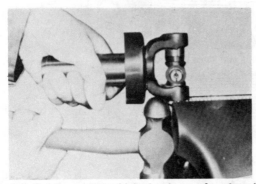

Fig. 7.7. Twisting a universal joint bearing cup from its yoke

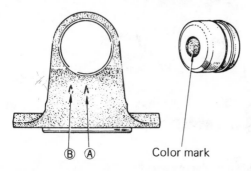

Fig. 7.9. Mark on yoke to indicate oversize bearing (1600 model)

A Indicates oversize bearing this side of yoke
B Indicates oversize bearing other side of yoke

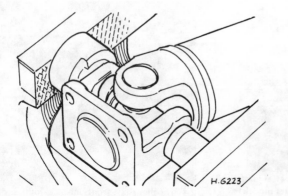

Fig. 7.11. Using sockets and distance piece to press in universal joint bearing cups

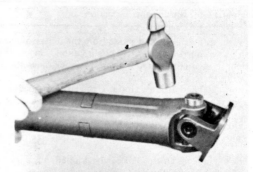

Fig. 7.6. Jarring out a universal joint bearing cup

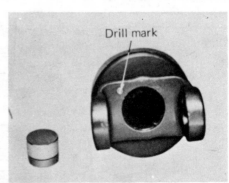

Fig. 7.8. Drill mark on yoke to indicate oversize bearing (1200E and 30 Series models)

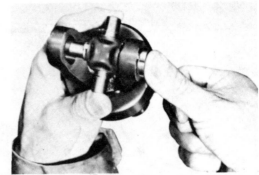

Fig. 7.10. Assembling universal joint spider and bearing cup

Oversize bearing cup outer diameter	0.7885 to 0.7891 in (20.029 to 20.042 mm)	Part No.
Oversize hole in yoke (diameter)	0.7882 to 0.7889 in (20.021 to 20.036 mm)	37402-10020

12 *On 1600 models,* no mark is made for standard bearings but oversize bearings are indicated by a yoke mark as shown in the illustration. Where the mark is located at A (centrally) then it indicates oversize bearings on the side nearest the mark. Where the mark is located at B then it indicates oversize bearings at the opposite side of the yoke.

Oversize bearing cup outer diameter	1.0250 to 1.0256 in (26.036 to 26.049 mm)
Oversize bearing hole in yoke (diameter)	1.0244 to 1.0253 in (26.021 to 26.042 mm)

13 It will be appreciated that a yoke may have one standard and one oversize bearing fitted in an attempt to improve propeller shaft balance, make sure that you renew bearings exactly as their originally selected sizes.

5 Universal joints - reassembly

1 Again clean out the yokes and trunnions and fit new oil seals to the spider journals.
2 Place the spider on the propeller shaft yoke and assemble the needle rollers into the bearing cups retaining them with some thick grease. Align the yoke and shaft mating marks made before dismantling.
3 Fill each bearing cup about ½ full with grease. Also fill the grease holes on the spider with grease taking care that all air bubbles are eliminated.
4 Press the bearing cups squarely into the yokes so that the needles are not displaced as the ends of the spiders pass into them. Use two suitably sized sockets in the jaws of a vice to do this (Fig. 7.10).

5 The cups should be pressed in until the axial movement of the spider is eliminated or is less than 0.0020 in (0.05 mm) then select suitable circlips and install them. *On 1200E and 30 Series models having circlips on the end faces of the bearing cups the circlips must be of the same thickness at each opposing end. On other models having internal circlips, it is permissible to use one of each pair of circlips one size thicker if necessary.*
6 Circlips are available in the following thicknesses.

1200E and	*0.0472 in (1.20 mm)*	*0.0492 in (1.25 mm)*
30 Series models	*0.051 in (1.30 mm)*	
1600 models	*0.0945 in (2.40 mm)*	*0.0965 in (2.45 mm)*
	0.0984 in (2.50 mm)	*0.1004 in (2.55 mm)*

6 Fault diagnosis - propeller shaft and universal joints

Symptom	Reason/s
Propeller shaft vibration	Universal joint spider bearing worn or damaged. Incorrect bearing cup circlip thickness. Bent propeller shaft. Propeller shaft out of balance. Worn gearbox extension housing bush. Universal joint mounting loose.
Noisy starting or while coasting	Universal joint spider bearing worn or damaged. Incorrect bearing cup circlip thickness. Slackness in the spider bearings. Universal joint mounting loose. No preload of the differential drive pinion bearing. Worn splines of drive pinion companion flange. Worn splines of universal joint sleeve yoke. Incorrect installation of splined coupling dust cover.

Chapter 8 Rear axle

Refer to Chapter 13 for specifications and information applicable to 1979 US models.

Contents

Specifications

Type ... ...   Rigid, semi-floating hypoid.

Ratios

1200E	4.300 : 1	
30 Coupe and Saloon	4.300 : 1	5.7 in
Wagon	4.556 : 1	6.0 in
Liftback	4.300 : 1	Differential
1975 Corolla 1600 Saloon and SR5	4.300 : 1	6.25 in
1976 on Corolla 1600 Saloon and SR5	3.900 : 1 or 4.100 : 1	6.38 in
		Differential
1977 Corolla 1600 Liftback, SR5 and Coupe	3.910 : 1	6.25 in
		6.38 in
		Differential

Oil capacity

6.0 and 6.38 in differential ... ...   0.9 Imp qt. 1.1 US qt. 1.0 litre
5.7 and 6.25 in differential ... ...   1.1 Imp qt. 1.3 US qt. 1.2 litre

Torque wrench settings

	lb f ft	Nm
Backplate to axle casing end flange bolt	50	69
Differential carrier bolts	28	39
Propeller shaft rear flange bolts (1200E and 30 series models)	20	28
(1600 models)	28	39
Pinion nut (initial setting before pre-load)	80	111

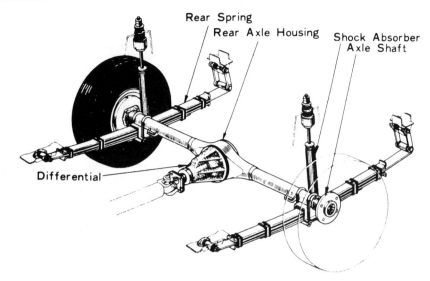

Fig. 8.1. Rear axle and suspension layout

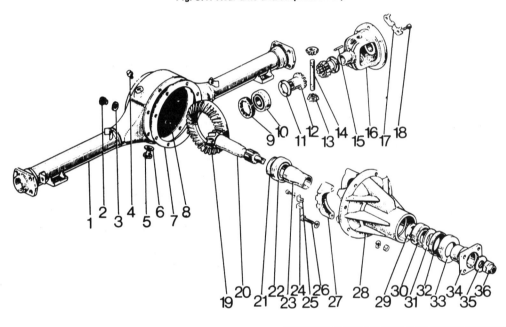

Fig. 8.2. Exploded view of typical fixed pinion shaft spacer type rear axle

1 Axle casing	19 Crownwheel
2 Filler plug	20 Drive pinion shaft
3 Gasket	21 Washer
4 Breather	22 Tapered roller bearing
5 Drain plug	23 Fixed spacer
6 Gasket	24 Adjusting nut lock plate
7 Gasket	25 Adjusting nut lock
8 Bolt	26 Bolt
9 Adjusting nut	27 Bearing cap
10 Tapered roller bearing	28 Differential carrier
11 Thrust washer	29 Shim
12 Side gear	30 Tapered roller bearing
13 Pinion gear	31 Oil slinger
14 Pinion	32 Oil seal
15 Pin	33 Dust deflector
16 Differential case	34 Drive pinion flange
17 Lockplate	35 Plain washer
18 Bolt	36 Nut

1 General description

1 The rear axle is of semi-floating hypoid type and is located to the upper surface of the rear semi-elliptic roadsprings by 'U' bolts (Fig. 8.1 and 8.2).

2 Various sizes of differential assembly are used according to vehicle model and date of production. The main difference between the 5.7 in, 6.0 in, 6.25 in and the 6.38 in differential units is that the 6.0 in and 6.38 in have collapsible type pinion bearing spacers.

3 The final drive ratio differs considerably between the models and according to date of production. Always consult the vehicle identification plate and the identifying tag on the rear axle differential unit to verify the exact type, if ordering a replacement differential or component for the axle assembly.

4 The axleshafts are splined at their inner ends to the differential side gears. At their outer ends, the shafts run in bearings mounted in the axle casing.

5 It is not recommended that the differential unit is dismantled or rebuilt by the home mechanic due to the need for special gauges and setting tools. The differential casing being mounted on the front face of the banjo axle housing is so easy to remove that it is recommended that the unit is removed and taken to your Toyota dealer, leaving the axle in position in the vehicle.

6 Restrict operations on the rear axle to those described in this Chapter.

2 Axleshafts, bearings and oil seals - removal and refitting

1 Jack up the rear axle and support it securely on axle stands (Fig. 8.4).
2 Remove the rear roadwheel.
3 Remove the brake drum.
4 Insert a socket and extension through one of the holes in the axle-shaft flange and unscrew the nuts which secure the brake backing plate to the axle casing (Fig. 8.6).
5 *On 1600 models*, remove the automatic brake shoe adjustment.
6 A slide hammer will now be required to extract the axleshaft from the axle casing. A slide hammer can easily be made up or if this is not possible, try bolting an old roadwheel onto the axle flange studs and striking two opposite points on the inner rim simultaneously to drive the axleshaft out of the axle casing. It is pointless to just try and pull the shaft out, you will only succeed in pulling the vehicle off the axle stands. (Fig. 8.7).
7 With the axleshaft removed, if it is only the oil seal that is leaking, lever the old one from the axle casing and drive a new one in using a piece of tubing as a drift. Make sure that the lips of the seal are facing inwards and that the end-face of the oil seal is 0.16 in (4.0 mm) below the end of the axle casing flange.

8 If the axleshaft bearing is rough or noisy when turned, it must be renewed.
9 To remove the old bearing, first grind a flat on one side of the bearing retaining collar and then split it with a sharp cold chisel. Take care not to damage the axleshaft (Fig. 8.8).
10 Remove the bearing from the shaft either by supporting the bearing and pressing the axleshaft from it or by drawing it off if a suitable extending leg extractor can be obtained (Fig. 8.9).
11 The new bearing should be pressed onto the shaft but don't forget to apply pressure to the bearing centre track only and make sure that the spacer bearing retainer plate and gaskets are in position on the shaft first.
12 With the bearing fitted, the bearing retaining collar must be pressed onto the shaft. Before pressing the collar onto the shaft it should be heated in an oven to between 572 and 608°F (140 to 160°C).
13 Pass the assembled axleshaft into the casing taking care not to damage the oil seal. Hold the shaft quite level and turn it gently until the splines on its inner end can be felt to pick up those in the differential side gears then push the shaft fully home (Fig. 8.10).
14 Refit the backplate bolts, the parking brake strut, the brake drum and the roadwheel.
15 Lower the vehicle to the ground.

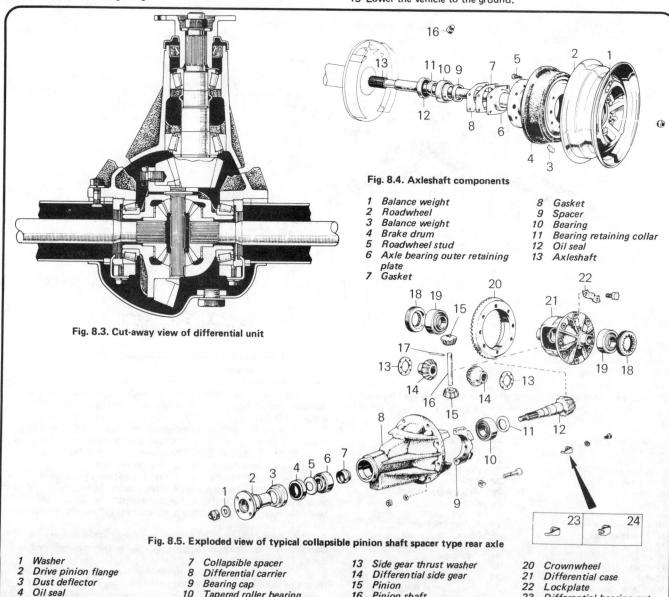

Fig. 8.3. Cut-away view of differential unit

Fig. 8.4. Axleshaft components

1	Balance weight	8	Gasket
2	Roadwheel	9	Spacer
3	Balance weight	10	Bearing
4	Brake drum	11	Bearing retaining collar
5	Roadwheel stud	12	Oil seal
6	Axle bearing outer retaining plate	13	Axleshaft
7	Gasket		

Fig. 8.5. Exploded view of typical collapsible pinion shaft spacer type rear axle

1	Washer	7	Collapsible spacer	13	Side gear thrust washer	20	Crownwheel
2	Drive pinion flange	8	Differential carrier	14	Differential side gear	21	Differential case
3	Dust deflector	9	Bearing cap	15	Pinion	22	Lockplate
4	Oil seal	10	Tapered roller bearing	16	Pinion shaft	23	Differential bearing nut lock plates
5	Oil slinger	11	Washer	17	Pin	24	Differential bearing nut lock plates
6	Tapered roller bearing	12	Drive pinion	18	Bearing adjusting nut		
				19	Tapered roller bearing		

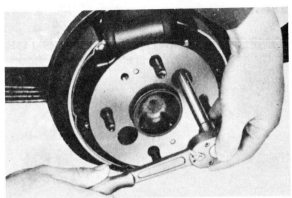

Fig. 8.6. Unscrewing backing plate to axle casing bolt

Fig. 8.8. Removing axleshaft bearing retaining collar

Fig. 8.7. Using a slide hammer to extract an axleshaft

Fig. 8.9. Pushing axleshaft out of bearing

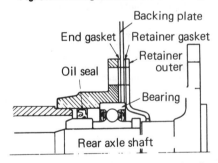

Fig. 8.10. Arrangement of axleshaft bearing, oil seal and gaskets

3 Pinion oil seal - renewal

1 The pinion oil seal may be renewed with the differential carrier still in position on the rear axle casing and the casing still attached to the rear suspension.

2 Jack up the rear of the vehicle and mark the edges of the propeller shaft rear flange and the pinion driving flange. Then disconnect the flanges and tie the propeller shaft up out of the way.

3 Ensure that the handbrake is fully off and then attach a spring balance to a length of cord wound round the pinion driving flange. Give an even pull and read off the bearing pre-load on the spring balance. Note the figure for later comparison (Fig. 8.11).

4 Mark the pinion coupling in relation to the pinion splines and knock back the staking on the pinion nut with a drift or narrow chisel.

5 Hold the pinion coupling quite still by bolting a length of flat steel to two of the coupling flange holes and then unscrew the pinion nut. A ring spanner of good length will be required for this.

6 Remove the lever from the coupling flange and withdraw the coupling. If it is tight, use a two or three legged puller but on no account attempt to knock it from the splined pinion. Withdraw the dust deflector.

7 Remove the defective oil seal using a two legged extractor (Fig. 8.12).

8 Refit the new oil seal first having greased the mating surfaces of the seal and the axle housing. The lips of the oil seal must face inwards. Using a piece of brass or copper tubing of suitable diameter, carefully drive the new oil seal into the axle housing recess until the face of the seal is flush with the housing. Make sure that the end of the pinion is not knocked during this operation.

9 Refit the coupling to its original position on the pinion splines after first having located the dust cover.

10 Fit a new pinion nut and holding the coupling still with the lever, tighten the nut until the pinion endfloat only just disappears. Do not overtighten. The torque wrench setting should not exceed 80 lb/ft (111 Nm).

11 Rotate the pinion to settle the bearings and then check the preload using the cord and spring balance method previously described and by slight adjustment of the nut and rotation of the pinion, obtain a spring preload figure to match that which applied before dismantling. Do not overtighten the nut as on later axles with compressible spacers, it

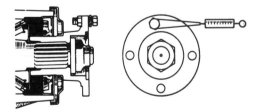

Fig. 8.11. Method of measuring rear axle pinion bearing pre-load using a spring balance

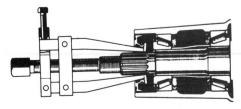

Fig. 8.12. Extracting a rear axle pinion oil seal

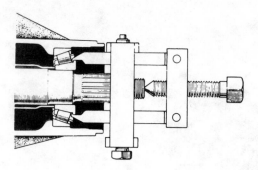

Fig. 8.13. Tool for extracting pinion front bearing inner race

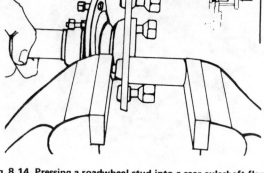

Fig. 8.14. Pressing a roadwheel stud into a rear axleshaft flange

cannot be backed off without having to renew the internal compressible spacer. To gain access to the spacer the bearing at the front of the pinion shaft must be removed (Fig. 8.13).

12 Stake the nut, refit the propeller shaft, making sure to align the mating marks.

13 Lower the vehicle and check the oil level in the axle.

4 Differential carrier - removal and refitting

1   Jack-up the car and support it on stands as for axle shaft removal. Drain the oil from the back axle by removing the drain plug. The axle shaft should then be removed sufficiently far for the inner ends to disengage from the differential side gears. The propeller shaft should then be dismantled from the rear axle pinion flange. It is not necessary to draw it out from the gearbox provided it can be conveniently rested out of the way on one side.

2   Undo the ten nuts and washers holding the differential carrier to the casing. The whole unit can be drawn forward off the studs and taken out.

3   When replacing the assembly ensure that the mating faces are perfectly clean and free from burrs. A new gasket coated with sealing compound should also be used. Otherwise refitting is a reversal of the removal operation. Tighten the nuts to the specified torque.

4   Refill the unit with the correct grade and quantity of oil.

5 Rear axle - removal and refitting

1   Jack-up the rear of the vehicle, place axle stands under the rear body frame side members and securely chock the front wheels. Place the jack under the differential and take its weight.

2   Remove the road wheels and disconnect the propeller shaft at the rear axle pinion coupling flange. Remember to mark the edges of the flange before disconnecting them so that they will be refitted in their original positions. Move the rear end of the propeller shaft to one side and support it.

3   Remove the brake drums and disconnect the handbrake cables from the actuating levers and then detach them from the brake backplate. Refit the drums to protect the brake shoe assemblies.

4   Disconnect the brake hydraulic line at the union on top of the axle casing. Plug both ends of the line to prevent loss of fluid or ingress of dirt.

5   Disconnect the rear shock absorber lower mountings from the road leaf spring support plates.

6   Unscrew and remove the four road spring 'U' bolts.

7   Remove each of the lower rear spring shackle bolts and lower the rear ends of the road springs to the ground.

8   Lower the jack previously placed under the differential until the rear axle assembly can be drawn out sideways from under the vehicle. Refitting is a reversal of removal but refer to Chapter 11, for details of loading/tightening conditions for the suspension components and to Chapter 9, for a description of bleeding the brake hydraulic system.

6 Roadwheel studs - renewal

1   Renewal of a sheared stud or one with a damaged thread is simply carried out by first removing the axleshaft as described in the preceding Section.

2   Adequately support the rear face of the hub flange and knock the old stud from its splined hole.

3   Press the new stud into position using a vice and a piece of tubing as a distance piece (Fig. 8.14).

7 Fault diagnosis - rear axle

Symptom	Cause
Noisy differential	
(a) During normal running	Lack of oil, damaged or worn gears, incorrect adjustment.
(b) During deceleration	Incorrect adjustment or damage to drive pinion bearings.
(c) During turning of vehicle	Worn or damaged axle-shaft bearing, worn differential gears.
Noisy rear hub	Worn axle-shaft bearings, buckled roadwheel, defective tyre, bent axle-shaft. ıxle-shaft.
Oil leakage at hub and pinion oil seals	May be caused by blocked breather plug on axle casing or over-filled unit.

Chapter 9 Braking system

Refer to Chapter 13 for specifications and information applicable to 1979 US models.

Contents

Specifications

Type	Four wheel hydraulic with handbrake mechanically operated on rear wheels Certain 1200 models have all drum otherwise all models use front disc with self-adjusting rear drum and vacuum servo booster unit. Dual circuit hydraulic system except with all drum.

Front drum brake
Two leading shoe
drum internal diameter	7.874 in (200 mm)
maximum (after refinishing)	7.953 in (202 mm)

Rear drum brake
Leading/trailing
drum internal diameter (1200E and 30 Series)	7.874 in (200 mm)
drum internal diameter (1600 models)	9.000 in (228.6 mm)
maximum (after refinishing - 1200E and 30 Series)	7.953 in (202 mm)
maximum (after refinishing - 1600 models)	9.079 in (230.6 mm)

Front disc brake
Disc thickness (PS and F type)	0.39 in (10 mm)
Minimum thickness (after refinishing)	0.35 in (9 mm)
Disc run-out (maximum)	0.0059 in (0.15 mm)

Torque wrench settings

	lb/ft	Nm
Single master cylinder		
Fluid outlet plug	58	80
Reservoir bolt	22	30
Tandem master cylinder		
Fluid outlet plug	50	69
Reservoir bolt	20	28
Mounting bolts to booster	12	16
Caliper (P5 type)		
Bridge bolts	60	83
Caliper mounting bolt	38	53
Caliper (F type)		
Caliper mounting bolt	50	69
Disc to hub bolts	65	90

1 General description

1 All vehicles have a four wheel hydraulically operated braking system with a mechanically operated handbrake on the rear wheels only.

2 Some saloon and wagon models destined for operation in countries where the latest safety regulations are not imposed are equipped with a single circuit system and have drum brakes all round.

3 Other models destined to meet more stringent requirements have disc brakes at the front, drum brakes at the rear, a dual circuit hydraulic system and a vacuum booster.

4 On dual circuit models, a pressure regulating valve is fitted to prevent the rear wheels locking during severe brake application.

2 Drum brakes - adjustment

1 Jack-up the front of the vehicle so that the roadwheels are off the ground.

2 Remove the plugs from the adjuster holes on the brake backplates.

3 Insert a suitable screwdriver into the first hole and rotate the adjuster wheel until the drum locks (Fig. 9.1).

4 Back off the adjuster until the roadwheel can be turned.

5 Depress the footbrake pedal hard and check the rotation of the roadwheel. If the brake is binding or scraping can be heard, back off the adjuster another 'click' or two until it is free.

6 Repeat the operations on the other adjuster on the same front brake and then carry out the same adjustment procedure on the opposite front brake.

7 *The rear brakes* are automatically adjusted by normal movement of the handbrake lever and require no manual adjustment.

3 Drum brake shoes - inspection and renewal

Front brakes

1 Jack-up the front of the vehicle and support it securely.

2 Remove the roadwheel.

3 Slacken the shoe adjuster wheels by inserting a screwdriver through the holes in the backplate.

4 Extract the drum securing screws and pull off the drum.

5 Brush away any dust from the shoes and the interior of the drum taking care not to inhale it.

6 With riveted linings, if the friction material has worn down to, or nearly down to, the rivet heads, the shoes should be renewed.

7 With bonded linings, the thickness of friction material remaining should not be less than 0.040 in (1.0 mm).

8 Always renew brake shoes in axle sets of four shoes. Purchase shoes ready lined, do not attempt to line the original shoes yourself.

9 Inspect the wheel cylinders, backplate and other internal components for signs of oil leakage. If any are evident, they must be rectified by renewing the hub oil seal or wheel cylinder seals, as appropriate.

10 Using a pair of pliers, depress and then rotate the shoe steady clips through $90°$ to release them from their 'T' headed pins (Fig. 9.3).

11 Note the holes in the shoe webs into which the shoe return springs are hooked and then disconnect one of the springs.

12 Pull the shoes against the tension of the remaining spring and remove the shoes from the backplate.

13 While the shoes are removed, do not touch the brake pedal or the wheel cylinder pistons will be ejected. It is recommended that a rubber band or a piece of wire is wrapped around the piston to stop it falling out.

14 Turn the adjuster wheel on both cylinders until the adjusting tappet

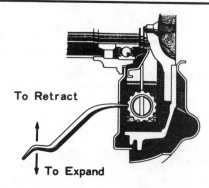

Fig. 9.1. Typical drum brake shoe adjustment

To Retract

To Expand

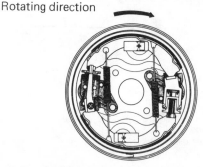

Rotating direction

Fig. 9.2. Front drum brake showing position of linings in relation to shoes

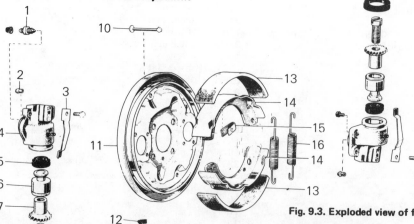

Fig. 9.3. Exploded view of front drum brake

1	Bleed screw	9	Dust excluder
2	Brake pipe union	10	Steady pin
3	Adjuster wheel locking clip	11	Backplate
4	Cylinder body	12	Backplate plug
5	Cup seal	13	Lining
6	Piston	14	Shoe
7	Adjuster wheel	15	Steady clip
8	Adjuster tappet	16	Shoe return spring

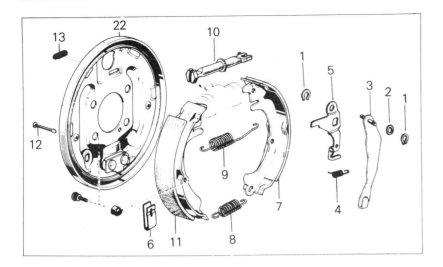

Fig. 9.4. Exploded view of rear drum brake

1 'C' washer
2 Shim
3 Handbrake lever on shoe
4 Return spring
5 Handbrake actuated automatic
   adjuster lever
6 Shoe steady clip
7 Shoe
8 Shoe return spring
9 Shoe return spring
10 Adjuster strut
11 Lining
12 Shoe steady pin
13 Backplate plug
14 Flexible boot
15 Piston
16 Cup seal
17 Brake pipe union
18 Cylinder body
19 Spring
20 Bleed screw
21 Dust cap
22 Backplate

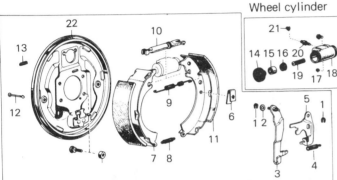

Wheel cylinder

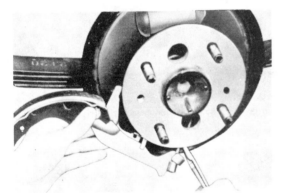

Fig. 9.5. Disconnecting handbrake cable from shoe lever

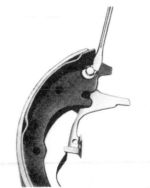

Fig. 9.6. Prising off 'C' washer from shoe automatic adjuster lever

is fully retracted.

15 Set the new shoes on the bench so that the leading and trailing ends of the shoes (lesser or greater exposed portions of the shoe web not covered by the lining material) are correctly located in respect of the direction of rotation of the drum (Fig. 9.2).

16 Connect one shoe return spring and then place the shoe assembly onto the backplate.

17 Reconnect the remaining shoe return spring and then fit the shoe steady pins and clips.

18 Fit the drum and adjust the shoes as described in the preceding Section.

Rear brakes

19 Jack-up the rear of the vehicle and fully release the handbrake.
20 Remove the roadwheel.
21 Extract the rubber plug from the brake backplate and insert a screwdriver to back off the toothed wheel on the automatic adjuster strut.
22 Extract the securing screws and pull off the brake drum. Inspect the shoes as described in paragraphs 5 to 9 (Fig. 9.4).
23 Depress the shoe steady springs with a pair of pliers and turn them through 90° to release them from their steady pins.
24 Disconnect the upper shoe return spring and expand the shoes and remove them from the backplate just far enough to be able to disconnect the handbrake cable from the lever on the shoe. Remove the shoe assembly completely (Fig. 9.5).
25 The 'C' washer must now be extracted so that the parking brake lever and the automatic adjuster lever can be removed and transferred to the new shoe (Fig. 9.6).
26 Lay the new shoes on the bench so that the leading and trailing ends of the shoes are correctly positioned with respect to the direction of travel of the drum (see paragraph 15) (Fig. 9.7/photo).
27 Turn the toothed wheel on the automatic adjuster strut so that the strut is fully retracted.
28 Reassemble the shoes to the backplate making sure that the handbrake cable is engaged in the groove in the shoe lever and that the automatic adjuster strut is fitted between the two shoes. The lower shoe return spring must be located below the anchor block on the backplate (photo).

29 Refit the shoe steady pins and clips.
30 Fit the brake drum and then adjust the toothed wheel on the automatic adjuster until the brake drum is locked. Back off the adjuster until the drum rotates freely.
31 Carry out all the operations on the opposite rear brake and when completed, operate the handbrake lever several times to bring the shoes into the closest permissible contact with the drums.
32 Refit the roadwheels and lower the vehicle.

4   Disc pads - inspection and renewal

1   No adjustment is required to the front disc brakes, the pads being kept in contact with the disc through the flexible characteristic of the cylinder boot and piston seal.
2   The single cylinder caliper units used on all vehicles differ in type between 1200 and 1600 '30' series models, the P5 caliper being fitted to the former while F type calipers are fitted to the latter.
3   Jack-up the front of the vehicle and support it securely.
4   Remove the roadwheels.
5   *On P5 type calipers,* extract the pad protection cover. The thickness of the friction material can now be seen. This must be at least 0.039 in (1.0 mm) in thickness. If it is not, the pads must be removed in the following way and new ones fitted (Fig. 9.8).
6   Prise off the anti-rattle springs.
7   Withdraw the retaining pins and extract the pads by gripping their ends with a pair of pliers (Fig. 9.9).
8   Brush away any dust from the caliper taking care not to inhale it.
9   The caliper piston should now be depressed fully into its cylinder in order to accommodate the new, thicker pads. Do this with a flat piece of metal or wood. Depressing the piston will cause the level of the fluid to rise in the brake reservoir and to prevent the fluid over-flowing, draw some off in anticipation using an old hydrometer or poultry baster.
10 Fit the new pads by reversing the removal operations and then operate the brake pedal several times to bring the pads into close contact with the disc.
11 *On F type calipers,* the thickness of the pad friction material can be seen through the inspection hole provided. The thickness must not be less than 0.04 in (1.0 mm) (Fig. 9.10 and 9.11).
12 If the pads must be renewed, pull out the clips with a pair of pliers and then remove the disc brake guides (front and rear) (photos).
13 Withdraw the cylinder and finally the disc pads (photos).
14 Repeat the operations described in paragraphs 9 and 10 of this Section.

5   Front drum wheel cylinder - overhaul

1   New seals can be fitted to the wheel cylinder without removing it

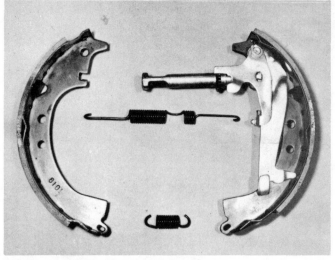

3.26 Rear drum brake components dismantled

3.27 Rear drum brake components assembled

4.12A Extracting clip (F type caliper)

4.12B Extracting a guide (F type caliper)

4.13A Withdrawing cylinder (F type caliper)

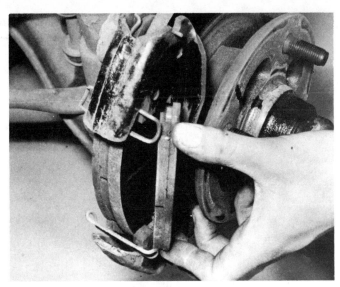

4.13B Removing a disc pad (F type caliper)

Rotating direction

Rotating direction

1200

1600

Fig. 9.7. Rear drum brake showing position of lining in relation to shoes

Fig. 9.8. Exploded view of PS type front disc brake

1	Complete caliper assembly	11	Dust excluder retainer
2	Cover	12	Torque plate
3	Cover plug	13	Disc pad
4	Cap	14	Pad shield
5	Cylinder body	15	Outer body
6	Dust seal	16	Retaining pin
7	Dust seal retainer	17	Anti-rattle spring
8	Piston seal	18	Bush
9	Piston	19	Bridge bolt
10	Dust excluder	20	Bleed screw
		21	Bleed screw cap

Fig. 9.9. Removing pad anti-rattle springs (PS type caliper)

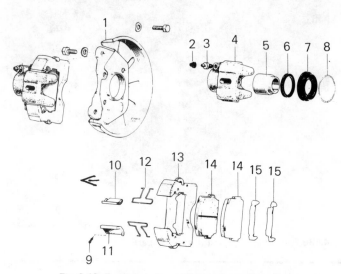

Fig. 9.10. Exploded view of F type front disc caliper

1   Cover   9   Clip
2   Bleed screw dust cap   10   Guide
3   Bleed screw   11   Guide
4   Cylinder body   12   Cylinder support springs
5   Piston   13   Cylinder mounting
6   Piston seal   14   Disc pad
7   Dust excluding boot   15   Support plates
8   Dust excluder retaining ring

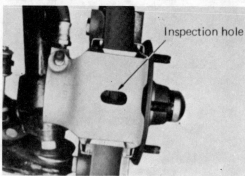

Fig. 9.11. Pad inspection hole (F type caliper)

from the backplate.

2   Remove the brake shoes as described in Section 3.

3   Pull out the adjuster tappet and toothed wheel.

4   Prise off the flexible boot.

5   Have an assistant *very gently* depress the brake pedal by hand until the piston is partially ejected from the cylinder and can be withdrawn by the fingers. Hold the opposite wheel cylinder components in position during this operation otherwise that piston too will be ejected.

6   Examine the condition of the piston and cylinder bore surfaces. If they are scored or scratched or show any 'bright' wear areas then the complete cylinder must be renewed after unbolting it from the backplate and disconnecting the fluid line union from it.

7   If the components are in good condition, remove the seals and discard them.

8   Obtain a wheel cylinder repair kit and manipulate the new seals into position using the fingers only.

9   Any cleaning must be done using hydraulic fluid or methylated spirit only, nothing else.

10 Dip the piston assembly in clean hydraulic fluid and insert it into the cylinder. Take care not to trap or bend back the lips of the seal.

11 Smear a little special rubber grease onto the adjuster assembly and install it together with the flexible boot.

12 Refit the brake shoes, drum and roadwheel.

13 Adjust the shoes and bleed the hydraulic circuit as described in Section 13.

6   Rear drum wheel cylinder - overhaul

1   The operations are similar to those described in the preceding Section for the front wheel cylinders except that a single cylinder is used which incorporates two pistons.

7   Front disc caliper (P5 type) - removal, overhaul and refitting

1   Jack-up the front of the vehicle and support it securely.

2   Remove the roadwheel.

3   Disconnect the flexible hose from the caliper. To do this, disconnect the hose at its union connector and then unscrew it from the caliper. Plug the open end of the fluid hose.

4   Remove the disc pads.

Fig. 9.12. Unscrewing a front disc caliper mounting bolt

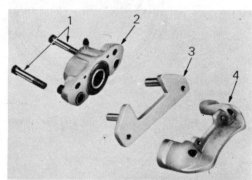

Fig. 9.13. PS type caliper dismantled into major components

1   Bridge bolts   3   Torque plate
2   Cylinder body   4   Outer body

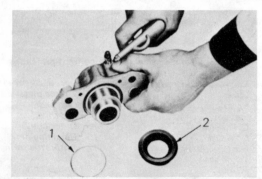

Fig. 9.14. Retaining ring (1) and dust excluder (2) removed from PS type caliper and piston being ejected by air pressure

Fig. 9.15. Master cylinder pushrod connected to brake pedal

Fig. 9.16. Unscrewing a master cylinder mounting bolt

Fig. 9.17. Extracting master cylinder pushrod retaining circlip

Fig. 9.18. Exploded view of single piston type master cylinder

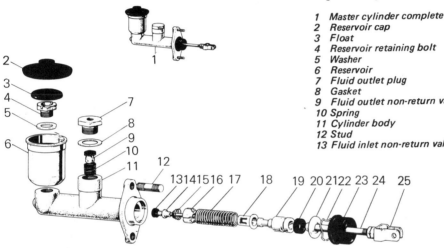

1 Master cylinder complete
2 Reservoir cap
3 Float
4 Reservoir retaining bolt
5 Washer
6 Reservoir
7 Fluid outlet plug
8 Gasket
9 Fluid outlet non-return valve
10 Spring
11 Cylinder body
12 Stud
13 Fluid inlet non-return valve

14 Inlet valve connecting rod
15 Spring
16 Inlet valve casing
17 Spring
18 Return spring retainer
19 Piston
20 Cup seal
21 Stop plate
22 Circlip
23 Flexible boot
24 Pushrod
25 Clevis

5   Unscrew and remove the two caliper mounting bolts, remove the caliper and clean its external surfaces (Fig. 9.12).
6   Unscrew the two bridge bolts (1) separate the cylinder body (2) from the outer body (4) and extract the torque plate (3). (Fig. 9.13).
7   Prise off the retaining ring (1) and remove the flexible boot (2).
8   The piston can now be ejected by applying air pressure from a tyre pump at the fluid entry port.
9   Inspect the surfaces of the piston and cylinder bore for scoring, scratching or 'bright' wear areas. If evident, renew the complete caliper unit.
10 If the components are in good condition, remove the seals, discard them and obtain a cylinder repair kit.
11 Reassemble the seals using the fingers only to manipulate them into position. Use only clean hydraulic fluid or methylated spirit for cleaning or lubrication purposes, nothing else.
12 Reassemble and refit by reversing the removal and dismantling operations. Tighten all bolts to specified torque.
13 Bleed the hydraulic system (see Section 13) on completion.

8   Front disc caliper (F type) - removal, overhaul and refitting

1   The operations are similar to those described in the preceding Section except that the cylinder body can be removed once the guides are withdrawn (see Section 4, paragraphs 11 to 14).
2   Overhaul the piston exactly as described for the P5 type.

9   Master cylinder (single type) - removal, overhaul and refitting

1   This type of master cylinder is encountered only where four wheel drum brakes are fitted.
2   Disconnect the pipe from the outlet port on the cylinder body.

3   Remove the split pin and clevis pin and disconnect the water cylinder pushrod from the brake pedal (Fig. 9.15).
4   Unbolt and remove the master cylinder from the engine compartment rear bulkhead. Take care not to spill any hydraulic fluid on the paintwork as it will act as an efficient paint stripper! (Fig. 9.16).
5   Unscrew the lid from the reservoir, tip out the fluid and then depress the pushrod several times to expel as much fluid as possible.
6   Clean away all external dirt.
7   Extract the flexible boot from the end of the cylinder and then prise out the circlip and remove the pushrod (Figs. 9.17 and 9.18).
8   Eject the piston assembly either by tapping the end of the cylinder on a block of wood or by applying air pressure at the fluid entry hole within the reservoir (Fig. 9.19).
9   Inspect the surfaces of the piston and cylinder bore, if they are scratched, scored or show any evidence of 'bright' wear areas then the master cylinder must be renewed complete.
10 If these components are in good condition, remove the seals and discard them. Obtain a repair kit which will contain the new seals and other renewable items.
11 If necessary, the inlet valve connecting rod can be disconnected from the piston return spring retainer by compressing the coil spring and depressing the small tag on the retainer with a thin screwdriver.
12 Reassemble by reversing the dismantling procedure. Fit the new seals using the fingers only. Use only clean hydraulic fluid or methylated spirit for cleaning or lubrication, nothing else.
13 Refit the master cylinder, bleed the hydraulic system and check the brake pedal setting (Sections 13 and 16 or 17).

10 Master cylinder (tandem type) - removal, overhaul and refitting

1   Disconnect the remotely sited reservoir hose from the master cylinder and let the fluid from this reservoir drain into a container. Do not allow the fluid to come in contact with the paintwork or it will

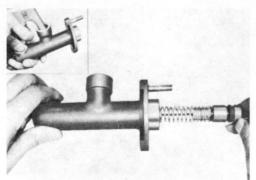

Fig. 9.19. Ejecting master cylinder piston
assembly

Fig. 9.20. Exploded view of tandem master cylinder

1   Fluid outlet plug
2   Gasket
3   Oil pressure switch
4   Fluid inlet banjo union
5   Hollow bolt
6   Fluid outlet non-return valve
7   Cylinder body
8   Piston stop
9   Spring
10 Circlip
11 Return spring retainer

12 Cup seal
13 Cup seal spacer
14 Secondary piston
15 Primary piston
16 Circlip
17 Flexible boot
18 Reservoir cap
19 Float
20 Filter
21 Reservoir
22 Stop bolt

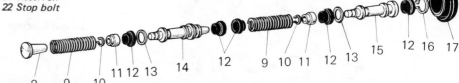

Fig. 9.21. Removing stop bolt (tandem master cylinder)

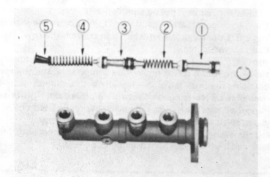

Fig. 9.22. Piston assemblies removed from tandem master cylinder

1   Primary piston
2   Spring
3   Secondary piston

4   Spring
5   Piston stopper

act as a paint stripper!

2   Disconnect the brake lines from the master cylinder outlet ports.

3   Unbolt and remove the master cylinder from the front face of the vacuum servo brake booster.

4   Clean away all external dirt.

5   With a rod, push in the primary piston until the pressure of the secondary piston on the stop bolt is relieved and then unscrew the stop bolt (Fig. 9.20 and 9.21).

6   Again depress the primary piston slightly and extract the circlip.

7   The internal piston assemblies will now be ejected under the action of their coil springs (Fig. 9.22).

8   Inspect the condition of the pistons and cylinder bores as described in paragraphs 11 and 12 of the preceding Section.

9   If necessary, the non-return valves, the warning switches and the rear reservoir can all be unbolted from the master cylinder body.

10 Reassembly is a reversal of dismantling. Fit the new seals using the fingers only to manipulate them into position. Use only hydraulic fluid or methylated spirit for cleaning or lubrication purposes. (Fig. 9.23).

11 When installing the secondary piston stop bolt, depress the primary piston fully with a rod to make sure that the secondary piston clears the bolt.

12 Tighten all components to the specified torque wrench settings.

13 When installation is complete, bleed both hydraulic circuits.

11 Flexible hoses - inspection, removal and refitting

1   Inspect the condition of the flexible hoses leading from under the front wings to the brackets on the front suspension units, and also the single hose on the rear axle casing. If they are swollen, damaged or chafed, they must be renewed.

2   Undo the locknuts at both ends of the flexible hoses and then, holding the hexagon nut on the flexible hose steady, undo the other union nut and remove the flexible hose and washer.

3   Refitting is a reversal of the removal procedure, but carefully check all the securing brackets are in a sound condition and that the locknuts are tight. Bleed the hydraulic system (Section 13).

12 Rigid brake lines - inspection and renewal

1 At regular intervals wipe the steel pipes clean and examine them for signs of rust or denting caused by flying stones.

2 Examine the securing clips. Bend the tongues of the clips if necessary to ensure that they hold the brake pipes securely without letting them rattle or vibrate.

3 Check that the pipes are not touching any adjacent components or rubbing against any part of the vehicle. Where this is observed, bend the pipe gently away to clear.

4 Any section of pipe which is rusty or chafed should be renewed. Brake pipes are available to the correct length and fitted with end unions from most Toyota dealers and can be made to pattern by many accessory suppliers. When installing the new pipes use the old pipes as a guide to bending and do not make any bends sharper than is necessary.

5 The system will of course have to be bled when the circuit has been reconnected.

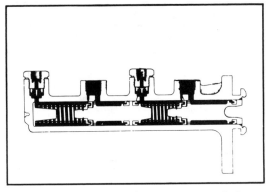

Fig. 9.23. Sectional view of tandem master cylinder

13 Hydraulic system - bleeding

1 Removal of all the air from the hydraulic system is essential to the correct working of the braking system, and before undertaking this, examine the fluid reservoir cap to ensure that both vent holes, one on top and the second underneath but not in line, are clear; check the level of the fluid and top up if required.

2 Check all brake line unions and connections for possible seepage, and at the same time check the condition of the rubber hoses, which may be perished.

3 If the condition of the wheel cylinders is in doubt, check for possible signs of fluid leakage.

4 If there is any possibility of incorrect fluid having been put into the system, drain all the fluid out and flush through with methylated spirit. Renew all piston seals and cups since these will be affected and could possibly fail under pressure.

5 Gather together a clean glass jar, a length of tubing which fits tightly over the bleed nipples, and a tin of the correct brake hydraulic fluid.

6 To bleed the system clean the areas around the bleed valves. *On single circuit systems,* start on the rear brakes by removing the rubber cup over the bleed valve, and fitting a rubber tube in position.

7 Place the end of the tube in a clean glass jar containing sufficient fluid to keep the end of the tube underneath during the operation.

8 Open the bleed valve with a spanner and quickly press down the brake pedal. After slowly releasing the pedal, pause for a moment to allow the fluid to recoup in the master cylinder and then depress again. This will force air from the system. Continue until no more air bubbles can be seen coming from the tube. At intervals make certain that the reservoir is kept topped-up, otherwise air will enter at this point again.

9 Once the rear brakes have been bled, bleed the front brake furthest from the master cylinder followed by the remaining front brake.

10 Tighten the bleed screws when the pedal is in the fully depressed position.

11 *On dual circuit systems,* the bleeding operations are similar to those just described but observe the following differences:

a) *Depress the brake pedal several times before commencing bleeding to destroy the vacuum in the booster.*

b) *Only one circuit need be bled if this is the only circuit which has been 'broken.'*

c) *Remember to top-up both reservoirs if both circuits are being bled.*

d) *Ignore brake warning lights, these will go out once the dual circuits have been bled and the master cylinder pressures are in balance.*

12 Use only clean fluid for topping-up purposes and discard fluid from the bleed jar. Fluid used for topping-up should have been kept in an air tight container and remained unshaken for the previous 24 hours.

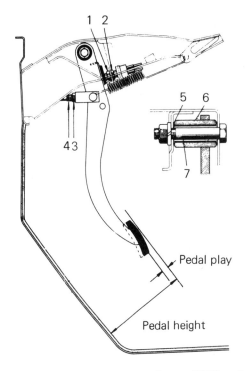

Fig. 9.24. Brake pedal adjustment diagram (1200 model)

1	Stop lamp switch locknut	5	Support bracket
2	Stop lamp switch locknut	6	Pedal
3	Pushrod locknut	7	Pivot bolt
4	Pushrod		

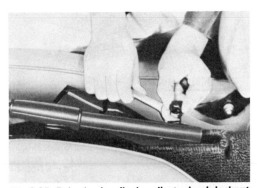

Fig. 9.25. Releasing handbrake adjuster knob locknut

14 Brake drum - examination and renovation

1   Whenever the brake drums are removed for inspection of the linings take the opportunity to check the internal shoe rubbing surface of the drum for scoring or grooving.
2   After a very high mileage, the drum internal diameter can wear oval in shape and this is often diagnosed by chatter when the brakes are applied.
3   The drums can be machined internally by your dealer provided their internal diameters do not exceed the maximum dimensions given in the Specifications. If they do, new drums will be required.

15 Brake disc - examination and renovation

1   Whenever the thickness of the front brake disc pads is being inspected, check the condition of the disc itself.
2   If deep grooves or scoring are visible then the disc will have to be machined provided it will not be reduced in thickness below that specified in the Specifications. If it will, then the disc will have to be renewed.
3   Also check the run-out (out of true) of the disc while turning it slowly. Ideally, a dial gauge should be used for this but feeler blades against a fixed point are a reasonable alternative.
4   To remove the disc/hub assembly refer to Chapter 11.
5   Unbolt the disc from the hub.
6   Refit the disc and hub then adjust the hub bearings as described in Chapter 11. Make sure that all bolts are tightened to the specified torque wrench settings.

16 Brake pedal (1200 models) - adjustment, removal and refitting

1   The distance of the upper surface of the brake pedal pad should be maintained at 6.65 in (169 mm) from the weatherproofed surface of the floor (Fig. 9.24).
2   To adjust, release the locknuts on the stop lamp switch and move the position of the switch. At the same time, release the pushrod

locknut and turn the pushrod in order to permit movement of the pedal arm.
3   Once the pedal height has been set, tighten the switch locknuts and then adjust the pushrod until there is a pedal free movement (when the pedal is depressed with the fingers) of between 0.02 and 0.20 in (0.5 to 5.0 mm).
4   Tighten the pushrod locknut.
5   If the pedal is to be removed, disconnect the pushrod from the pedal and then unscrew and remove the pedal pivot bolt.
6   Always lubricate the pivot bushes on reassembly and adjust the pedal height and free movement.

17 Brake pedal (1600 models) - adjustment, removal and refitting

1   The brake pedal is adjusted as described in the preceding Section but the free movement must be set to between 0.12 and 0.24 in (3 to 6 mm).
2   Removal and refitting of the pedal is described in Chapter 5 as it pivots on a common cross shaft with the clutch pedal.

18 Handbrake - adjustment

1   The handbrake should be fully applied after the control lever pawl has passed over 2 to 6 ('clicks') notches of the ratchet.
2   As the cable stretches, the need for adjustment will arise. Before carrying out any adjustment, jack-up the rear of the vehicle.
3   Release the locknut on the adjuster knob at the side of the handbrake lever. Turn the adjuster knob until the handbrake lever travel is to specification.
4   Now fully release the handbrake and check that the rear roadwheels turn without any tendency of the drums to bind or drag.
5   Tighten the adjuster locknut and lower the vehicle.
6   On some models, a handbrake 'ON' switch is fitted. The switch is retained by the handbrake lever mounting bolt. Adjust the position of the switch by releasing the mounting bolt so that as soon as the lever is pulled upwards the switch is actuated but the warning lamp is off when the lever is fully released.

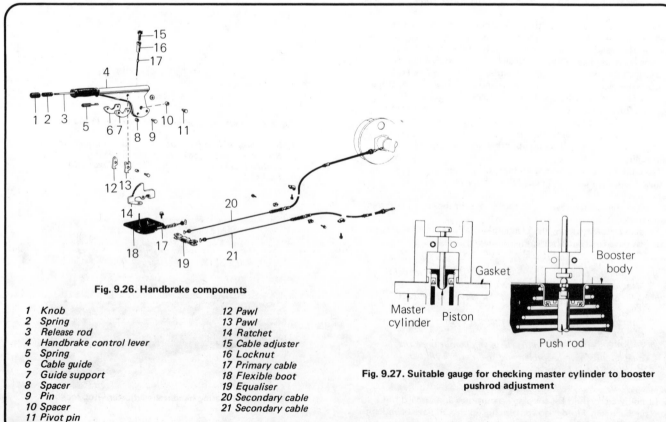

Fig. 9.26. Handbrake components

1 Knob
2 Spring
3 Release rod
4 Handbrake control lever
5 Spring
6 Cable guide
7 Guide support
8 Spacer
9 Pin
10 Spacer
11 Pivot pin
12 Pawl
13 Pawl
14 Ratchet
15 Cable adjuster
16 Locknut
17 Primary cable
18 Flexible boot
19 Equaliser
20 Secondary cable
21 Secondary cable

Fig. 9.27. Suitable gauge for checking master cylinder to booster pushrod adjustment

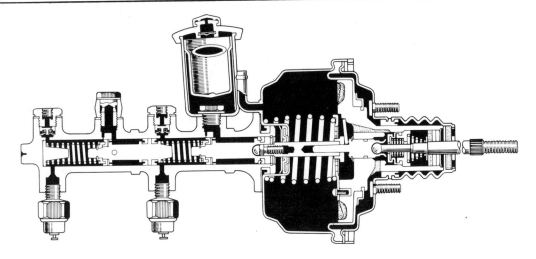

Fig. 9.28. Cut-away view of typical booster with tandem master cylinder

19 Handbrake cables - renewal

1   The handbrake cables comprise one primary and two secondary cables which can be renewed independently (Fig. 9.26).
2   To renew the primary cable, remove the rear section of the console from inside the vehicle and then release the adjuster locknut and unscrew the adjuster knob and then the locknut from the cable end.
3   Unbolt the parking brake control lever from the floor.
4   Disconnect the rear end of the primary cable from the equaliser. This is accessible from under the vehicle.
5   To remove one of the secondary cables, fully release the primary cable adjustment and disconnect the front of the secondary cable from the equaliser.
6   Remove the two secondary cable conduit clamps.
7   Disconnect the rear end of the secondary cable from the shoe lever as described in Section 3, paragraph 24.
8   Withdraw the cable from the hole in the brake backplate.
9   Refitting both types of cable is a reversal of removal.
10 Adjust the primary cable on completion as described in Section 18.

20 Vacuum servo (brake booster) unit - description

1   The vacuum servo unit is designed to supplement the effort applied by the driver's foot to the brake pedal.
2   The unit is an independent mechanism so that in the event of its failure the normal braking effort of the master cylinder is retained. A vacuum is created in the servo unit by its connection to the engine inlet manifold and with this condition applying on one side of the diaphragm, atmospheric pressure applied on the other side of the diaphragm is harnessed to assist the foot pressure on the master cylinder. With the brake pedal released, the diaphragm is fully recuperated and held against the rear shell by the return spring. The operating rod assembly is also fully recuperated and a condition of vacuum exists each side of the diaphragm.
3   When the brake pedal is applied, the valve rod assembly moves forward until the control valve closes the vacuum port. Amospheric pressure then enters the chamber to the rear of the diaphragm and forces the diaphragm plate forward to actuate the master cylinder pistons through the medium of the vacuum servo unit pushrod.
4   When pressure on the brake pedal is released, the vacuum port is opened and the atmospheric pressure in the rear chamber is extracted through the non-return valve. The atmospheric pressure inlet port remains closed as the operating rod assembly returns to its original position by action of the coil return spring.
5   The diaphragm then remains in its position with vacuum conditions on both sides until the next depression of the brake pedal when the cycle is repeated.

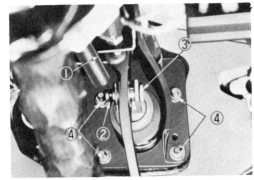

Fig. 9.29. Brake booster attachment, viewed from inside vehicle

1   Return spring
2   Groove for attachment of return spring
3   Clevis pin
4   Booster mounting bolts

21 Vacuum servo (booster) - removal and refitting

1   Destroy the vacuum in the unit by making repeated applications of the brake pedal (Fig. 9.28).
2   Disconnect the vacuum hose from the servo unit.
3   Disconnect the accelerator cable from the carburettor and its support bracket.
4   Disconnect the brake lines from the master cylinder. Plug or cap the open ends to prevent dirt entering.
5   Where a remote reservoir is fitted, disconnect the hose from the master cylinder and let the fluid drain into a container. Disconnect the master cylinder switch leads.
6   Working inside the vehicle, disconnect the brake pedal return spring and then disconnect the pushrod from the pedal arm by extracting the split pin and clevis pin (Fig. 9.29).
7   Unscrew the four booster mounting nuts and then lift the booster complete with master cylinder from the rear bulkhead of the engine compartment.
8   Unbolt and remove the master cylinder from the front face of the vacuum servo booster.
9   It is not recommended that the booster is dismantled but if faulty, replace it with a new or rebuilt unit. Several different makes and size of booster are used according to model so make sure that the correct type for your vehicle is ordered. Renewal of the servo air filter can be carried out (see Section 22).
10 Refitting is a reversal of removal but before assembling the master cylinder to the booster, check that there will be a clearance of 0.012 in (0.3 mm) between the end of the servo unit pushrod and the end of the master cylinder piston. Check by using the official tool or making up a depth gauge so that the projection of the servo unit pushrod can be compared with the depth of the recess to the end of the master

Fig. 9.30. Exploded view of AISIN type vacuum servo (booster) unit

1 Non-return valve
2 Grommet
3 Pushrod
4 Internal ring
5 Seal
6 Seal retainer
7 Front shell
8 Spring
9 Reaction retainer
10 Reaction plate
11 Reaction lever
12 Circlip
13 Plate washer
14 Piston
15 Diaphragm
16 Diaphragm retainer
17 Rear shell
18 Connector lock
19 Connector
20 Piston bearing
21 Air valve
22 Air filter separator
23 Air filter element
24 Internal ring
25 Silencer
26 Flexible boot

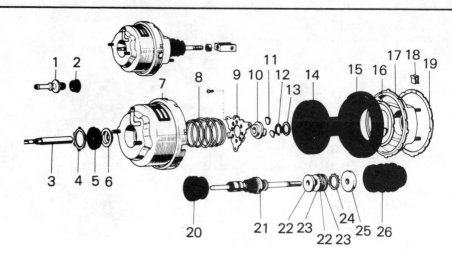

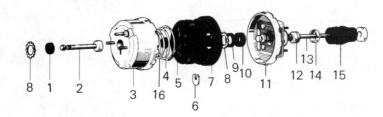

Fig. 9.31. Exploded view of JIDOSHA KIKI type booster

1 Plate and seal
2 Pushrod
3 Front shell
4 Reaction disc
5 Plate valve
6 Stop key
7 Diaphragm
8 Retainer
9 Bearing
10 Seal
11 Rear shell
12 Air filter
13 Valve rod/plunger
14 Air filter retainer
15 Flexible boot
16 Diaphragm return spring

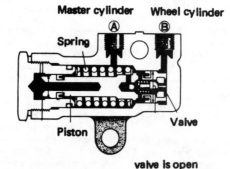

Fig. 9.32. Sectional view of pressure regulating valve

cylinder piston. Carry out any adjustment by loosening the locknut and rotating the front section of the vacuum servo nut pushrod. (Fig. 9.27).

11 When installation is complete, bleed the hydraulic system.

22 Vacuum servo (booster) air filter - renewal

1 At the specified intervals (see Routine Maintenance) the air filter disc which surrounds the pushrod should be renewed (Fig. 9.30).
2 To do this, disconnect the pushrod from the brake pedal (Fig. 9.31).
3 Pull back the dust excluding flexible boot.
4 Withdraw the silencer and retainer (AISIN type) or the retainer (JIDOSHA KIKI) to give access to the air filter element. To avoid dismantling the pushrod and the need for subsequent readjustment and pedal height setting, cut the air filter element from the pushrod hole to its edge, remove and discard it.
5 Cut the new element in a similar way and refit it together with

retainer and silencer.

23 Pressure regulating valve

1 As previously described, this valve is incorporated in the hydraulic circuit close to the master cylinder. It varies the hydraulic pressure between the front and rear circuits in order to prevent the rear wheels locking during heavy brake applications.
2 The valve cannot be adjusted or repaired and in the event of the valve leaking or a tendency for the rear wheels to lock, renew the valve complete (Fig. 9.32).
3 Disconnect the fluid pipes from the valve body by unscrewing the unions and then remove the valve securing bolts and lift the valve away.
4 Installation of the new valve is a reversal of removal but bleed the hydraulic system as described in Section 13.

24 Fault diagnosis - braking system

Symptom	Cause
Brake grab	Brake shoe linings or pads not bedded-in. Pads or linings contaminated with oil or grease. Scored drums or discs. Servo unit faulty.
Brake drag	Master cylinder faulty. Brake foot pedal return impeded. Blocked filler cap vent. Seized wheel caliper or cylinder. Incorrect adjustment of handbrake. Weak or broken shoe return springs. Crushed or blocked pipelines.
Brake pedal feels hard	Friction surfaces contaminated with oil or grease. Glazed friction material surfaces. Rusty disc surfaces. Seized caliper or wheel cylinder. Faulty servo unit.
Excessive pedal travel	Low fluid level in reservoir. Automatic rear shoe adjusters faulty. Excessive disc runout. Worn front wheel bearings. System requires bleeding. Worn pads or linings.
Pedal creep during sustained application	Fluid leak. Faulty master cylinder. Faulty servo.
Pedal 'spongy' or 'springy'	System requires bleeding. Perished flexible hose. Loose master cylinder. Cracked brake drum. Linings not bedded-in. Faulty master cylinder.
Fall in master cylinder fluid level	Normal disc pad wear. Leak. Internal fluid leak from master cylinder to servo.

Servo unit fault diagnosis

Symptom	Cause
Hard pedal, lack of assistance when engine running	Lack of vacuum due to: Loose connections. Restricted hose. Blocked air filter/silencer. Major fault in unit.
Slow action of servo	Faulty vacuum hose. Blocked air filter/silencer.
Lack of assistance during heavy braking	Air leaks in: Non-return valve grommet. Non-return valve Dust cover. Hoses and connections.
Loss of fluid	Major failure in unit
Brake pedal pushes back against foot pressure	Hydraulic inlet and outlet pipes incorrectly connected at regulator valve. Major fault in unit.

Chapter 10 Electrical system

Refer to Chapter 13 for specifications and information applicable to 1979 US models.

Contents

Specifications

System type	... ...	12 volt negative earth

Battery	... ...	12 volt, 32/40 or 60 AH depending upon vehicle model and operating territory

Alternator

Output current (3K series except 3K-H, 3K-B)		30A
(3K-H and 3K-B)		40A
(2T series)		40A
Rotor coil resistance		4.1 to 4.3 ohms
No load characteristic at normal temperature		14V at 800 to 1000 rev/min
Minimum brush length		0.217 in (5.5 mm)

Alternator regulator

Regulating voltage		13.8 to 14.8 volts
Relay operating voltage		4.5 to 5.8 volts

Starter motor

Type		dc series wound, pre-engaged with solenoid
Rating		0.6 or 0.8 kW (depending on vehicle model)
No load characteristic (0.6 kW type)		55A at 3500 rev/min at 11V
(0.8 kW)		50A at 5000 rev/min at 11V
Load characteristic (0.6 kW type)		450A at 8.0 lb/ft (1.1 kg/m) torque at 8.5V
(0.8 kW)		470A at 9.4 lb/ft (1.3 kg/m) torque at 7.7V
Minimum brush length (0.6 kW type)		0.47 in (12 mm)
(0.8 kW type)		0.39 in (10 mm)

Fuses (refer also to vehicle fuse block cover)
1200E until mid-1975

Fuse holder	Rating (A)	Circuit Protected
1	15	Tail, parking, instrument panel, heater control lamps
2	20	Horn, hazard warning, stop lamps
3	20	Cigar lighter, clock, interior lamp

4	15	Radio, stereo
5	20	Heated rear window, heater, reversing lamps instruments
6	15	Direction indicator lamp, voltage regulator (IG)
7	15	Ignition coil
8	15	Windscreen washer and wiper

1200E (mid-1975 on) 30 series and 1600 models

1	15	Stop lamps and hazard warning lamps
2	15	Tail, parking, rear number plate, side marker lamps, clock and ash tray illumination, cigar lighter, heater control, automatic transmission indicator illumination
3	15	Cigar lighter, interior lamp, clock
4	5	Radio, stereo tape player
5	15	Heater and air conditioner
6	15	Direction indicator lamps, windscreen wiper and washer, rear wiper and washer (Liftback)
7	15	Voltage regulator, fuel cut-out solenoid
8	15	Heated rear window, reversing lamps, brake warning lamp, parking brake warning lamp, oil temperature gauge, oil pressure gauge, low oil pressure warning lamp, fuel gauge, water temperature gauge, *ammeter, tachometer, ignition warning lamp

*On all models without an ammeter, the horn and headlight circuits are protected by a fusible link identified green

Bulbs

1200E, 30 series and 1600 (except N. America)

	Watts
Headlights (sealed beam)	50/40
(bulbs)	45/40
Front direction indicator lights	21
Parking lights	5
Side marker lights	5
Rear direction indicator lights	21
Stop and tail lights	21/5
Reversing lights	21
Rear number plate light	5
Interior light	10
Luggage area light (Liftback)	5

Corolla 1600 (N. America)

Location	Bulb type number	Wattage
Front turn signal and parking lights	1157	27/8
Front side marker lights	194	5
Rear side marker (Hardtop, Wagon) light	194	5
Rear side marker (Sedan) light	67	8
Rear turn signal light	1156	27
Stop and tail lights	1157	27/8
Back-up lights	1156	27
Rear license plate light	89	7.5
Interior light	12V-10CP	10
Luggage area (Liftback, Wagon) light	12V-10CP	5

1 General description

1 A 12 volt negative earth system is used on all models.

2 The main components of the electrical system comprise a battery, an alternator with separate voltage regulator and a pre-engaged starter motor.

3 The battery supplies a steady amount of current for the ignition, lighting, and other electrical circuits and provides a reserve of electricity when the current consumed by the electrical equipment exceeds that being produced by the alternator.

4 All electrical circuits are protected by fuses and the main power cable from the battery incorporates a fusible link.

2 Battery - maintenance

1 Once a week, check the level of electrolyte in the battery cells and top up if necessary with distilled or purified water.

2 Various types of battery may be encountered but of the two most popular types, one has a translucent case where the electrolyte level should be maintained between the two marks on the casing (Fig. 10.1).

3 Where a non-translucent battery case is used, the electrolyte level should be maintained at the bottom of the filler tubes.

4 The acid in a battery does not evaporate, it is only the water which requires replenishment. Acid is used in the electrolyte when the battery is first filled and charged and no acid should be needed throughout the life of the unit.

5 Periodically clean the top of the battery, check the tightness of the battery leads and apply petroleum jelly to the terminals to prevent corrosion.

6 If corrosion is evident (white fluffy deposits) on the battery tray or clamp, the battery should be removed as described in the next Section and the corrosion removed by wire brushing and by applying household ammonia. Paint the cleaned components with anti-corrosive paint.

7 To check the state of charge of the battery, use a hydrometer to draw up electrolyte from each of the cells in turn. The specific reading on the hydrometer should be in accordance with the following at an ambient temperature of 68°F (20°C).

Fully charged	1.260
Half charged	1.160
Discharged	1.060

8 Any variation in reading in excess of 0.025 between the cells will indicate an internal failure and battery renewal should be anticipated.

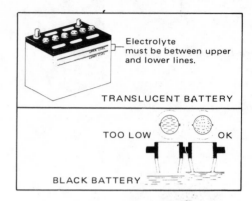

Fig. 10.1. Battery electrolyte filling details

4.3 Battery clamp

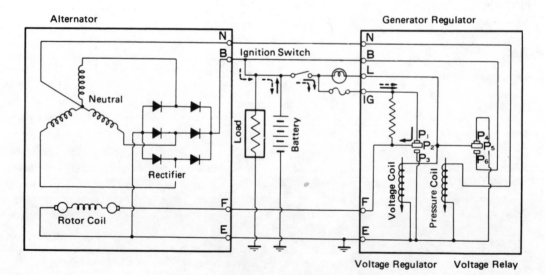

Fig. 10.2. Typical charging system circuit

3 Battery charging

1 In winter time when heavy demand is placed upon the battery, such as when starting from cold, and much electrical equipment is continually in use, it is a good idea to occasionally have the battery fully charged from an external source at the rate of 3.5 or 4 amps.
2 Continue to charge the battery at this rate until no further rise in specific gravity is noted over a four hour period.
3 Alternatively, a trickle charger charging at the rate of 1.5 amps can be safely used overnight.
4 Specially rapid 'boost' charges which are claimed to restore the power of the battery in 1 to 2 hours are not recommended as they can cause serious damage to the battery plates.
5 Before charging the battery from an external source always disconnect the battery leads to prevent damage to the alternator.

4 Battery - removal and refitting

1 The battery is located at the front left-hand corner within the engine compartment.
2 Disconnect the leads from the battery terminals.
3 Unbolt the battery hold down clamp and lift the battery from the battery support tray (photo).
4 Refitting is a reversal of removal.

5 Alternator - general description, maintenance and precautions

1 The alternator generates three-phase alternating current which is rectified into direct current by three positive and three negative silicone diode rectifiers installed within the end frame of the alternator. The in-built characteristics of the unit obviate the need for a cut-out or current stabiliser.
2 A voltage regulator unit is incorporated in the charging circuit to control the exciting current and the current applied to the voltage coil.
3 Check the drivebelt tension at the intervals specified in 'Routine Maintenance' and adjust, as described in Chapter 2, by loosening the mounting bolts. Pull the alternator body away from the engine block; do not use a lever as it will distort the alternator casing.
4 No lubrication is required as the bearings are grease sealed for life.
5 Take extreme care when making circuit connections to a vehicle fitted with an alternator and observe the following.

When making connections to the alternator from a battery always match correct polarity.
Before using electric-arc welding equipment to repair any part of the vehicle, disconnect the connector from the alternator and disconnect the positive battery terminal.
Never start the car with a battery charger connected.
Always disconnect the battery leads before using a mains charger.
If boosting from another battery, always connect in parallel using heavy cable.

6 Alternator - testing in vehicle

1 In the event of failure of the normal performance of the alternator, carry out the following test procedure paying particular attention to the possibility of damaging the charging and electrical system unless the notes (a) to (c) are observed.

    a) *The alternator output 'B' terminal must be connected to the battery at all times. When the ignition switch is operated, the 'F' terminal is also at battery voltage.*
    b) *Never connect the battery leads incorrectly or the rectifiers and flasher unit will be damaged.*
    c) *Never run the engine at high revs, with the alternator 'B' terminal disconnected otherwise the voltage at the 'N' terminal will rise abnormally and damage to the voltage relay will result.*

2 Check the security of the alternator mountings, the terminal leads and the drivebelt tension (Chapter 2).
3 Check the flasher fuse and the heater fuse and renew them if they

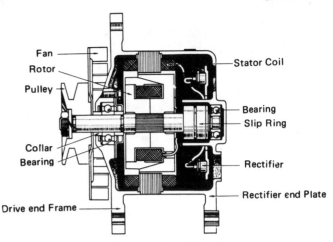

Fig. 10.3. Sectional view of the alternator

are blown.
4 Switch on the vehicle radio and tune into a local transmitter. Start the engine and increase its speed from idling to 2000 rev/min. If a distinct humming sound is heard from the radio speaker then this indicates that the alternator rectifier is shorted or open.
5 Connect a voltmeter and ammeter to the alternator 'B' terminal. Start the engine and gradually increase its speed to 2300 rev/min. The voltmeter should read between 13.8 and 14.8 volts and the ammeter under 10 amps. If the amperage is greater than the specified figure, the battery is either discharged or there is an internal short circuit. If the voltmeter needle fluctuates the regulator contacts may be dirty or arced or the alternator 'F' terminal may be loose.
6 If the voltage reading is too high then (i) the regulator contact gaps may be too wide (ii) there is an open circuit at the regulator and voltage relay coil, (iii) 'N' and 'B' regulator terminals are open and (iv) the regulator has a defective earth connection (Fig. 10.2).
7 Switch off the engine and disconnect the wiring harness connecting plug. Turn on the ignition switch and measure the voltage between the 'F' and 'E' sockets of the connecting plug. This should be 12 volts. If the reading is low or zero, check for (i) faulty fuse connection (ii) open circuit 'F' or 'IG' terminals (iii) regulator contact points fused together.
8 Repeat the tests described in the preceding paragraphs 5 and 6 but run the engine at only 1100 rev/min with all lights and accessories switched on; the ammeter reading should be in excess of 30 amps. If the reading is less than 30 amps it is indicative of open rectifiers, stator coil circuit or short circuited rectifiers.

7 Alternator - removal and refitting

1 Disconnect the cable from the battery negative terminal.
2 Loosen the alternator mounting bracket bolts and the adjustment strap bolts and then push the alternator in towards the engine block so that the driving belt can be removed from the pulley.
3 Disconnect the electrical plug from the alternator terminals, remove the mounting bolts and lift the unit from its location.
4 Refitting is a reversal of removal but adjust the driving belt tension, as described in Chapter 2.

8 Alternator - dismantling, servicing and reassembly

1 Remove the three tie bolts which secure the two end frames together. (Fig. 10.3).
2 Insert screwdrivers in the notches in the drive end frame and separate it from the stator (Fig. 10.4).
3 Hold the front end of the rotor shaft still with an Allen key and remove the securing nut, pulley, fan and spacer. If an Allen key and socket is not provided, grip the rotor between wooden blocks in the jaws of a vice (Fig. 10.5).
4 Press the rotor shaft from the drive end frame.
5 Remove the bearing retainer, bearing, cover and felt ring from the drive end frame.

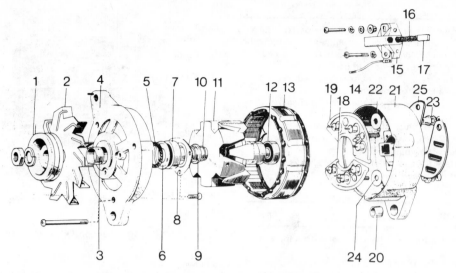

Fig. 10.4. Exploded view of the alternator

1 Pulley	8 Bearing retainer	14 Lead	20 Bush
2 Fan	9 Spacer	15 Brush holder	21 Rectifier and frame
3 Spacer	10 Circlip	16 Brush spring	22 Insulating washer
4 Drive end frame	11 Rotor	17 Brush	23 'B' terminal insulator
5 Felt washer	12 Bearing	18 Rectifier (−) holder	24 Insulating washer
6 Felt retainer	13 Stator	19 Rectifier (+) holder	25 End cover plate
7 Bearing			

Fig. 10.5. Levering off alternator drive end frame

Fig. 10.6. Removing alternator brush holder

6   Remove the rectifier holder and brush holder securing screws and detach the stator from the rectifier end frame (Fig. 10.6).

7   Remove the brush lead and stator coil 'N' terminals from the brush holder by prising with a small screwdriver.

8   Test the rotor coil for an open circuit by connecting a circuit tester between the two slip rings located at the rear of the rotor. The indicated resistance should be from 4.1 to 4.3 ohms but if there is no conductance then the coil is open and the rotor must be renewed as an assembly (Fig. 10.7).

9   Now conduct the tester between each slip ring in turn and the rotor shaft. If the tester needle moves then the rotor must be renewed as it is earthed (Fig. 10.8).

10 Inspect the rotor bearing for wear and renew if necessary by removing it from the shaft with a two legged puller (Fig. 10.9).

11 Clean the slip rings and rotor surfaces with a solvent moistened cloth.

12 Test the insulation of the stator coil by connecting the tester between the stator coil and the stator core. If the tester needle moves then the coil is earthed through a breakdown in the insulation and must be renewed (Fig. 10.10).

13 To test the stator coil for open circuit, the coil leads must be disconnected from the rectifier leads. Apply the soldering iron to the joint for the minimum time to prevent any heat travelling to the rectifier which is easily damaged (Fig. 10.11 and 10.12).

14 Check the four stator coil leads for conductance. If the tester needle does not flicker then the coil has an open circuit and it must be renewed.

15 The testing of the rectifiers should be limited to measuring the resistance between their leads and holders in a similar manner to that described in paragraph 13. These tests will indicate short or open circuited diodes but not rectifying or reverse flow characteristics which can only be checked with specialised equipment.

16 If more than one of the preceding tests proves negative then it will be economically sound to exchange the alternator complete for a factory reconditioned unit rather than renew more than one individual component.

17 Finally, examine the brushes for wear. If they are less than 0.34 in (8.5 mm) in length renew them. Remove the old brushes and insert the new ones in their holders, checking to see that they slide freely. Ensure that the brush does not project more than 0.5 in (12.5 mm) from its holder and then solder the brush lead, cutting off any surplus wire (Fig. 10.13 and 10.14).

18 Commence reassembly of the alternator by fitting the stator coil 'N' terminal to the brush holder, then a terminal insulator followed by

the brush negative lead.

19 Fit the two insulating washers between the rectifier positive holder and the end frame and install the 'B' terminal and the retaining bolt insulators and secure the holder with its four retaining nuts. Secure the negative rectifier holder with its four nuts.

20 Fit the brush holder with its insulating plate and tighten the securing screws passing them through the terminal insulators. Locate the stator coil in the rectifier end frame (Fig. 10.15).

21 To the drive end frame fit the felt ring, cover (convex face to pulley) bearing (packed with multi-purpose grease) and bearing retainer (3 screws).

22 Fit the spacer ring to the rotor shaft and then press the drive end frame onto the shaft. Fit the collar, fan and pulley and tighten the securing nut to a torque of 35 lb/ft (48 Nm).

23 Connect the drive end frame assembly to the rectifier end frame assembly and secure with the three tie bolts. Use a piece of wire to support the brushes in the raised position during this operation (Fig. (Fig. 10.16).

9 Alternator regulator - testing and adjustment

1 Testing of the relay operating voltage and the regulator output voltage and amperage levels should be left to an auto-electrician as special equipment is needed. However, circuit testing and mechanical adjustments may be carried out in the following manner:

2 Disconnect the regulator connector plug. Remove the cover from the regulator unit and inspect the condition of the points. If they are pitted, clean with very fine emery cloth otherwise clean them with methylated spirit (photo).

3 Connect a circuit tester between the 'IG' and 'F' terminals of the connector plug when no resistance should be indicated. If a resistance is shown, then the regulator points assembly P1 is making poor contact. Now press down the regulator armature and check the resistance which should be about 10 ohms. If it is much higher, the control resistance is defective and must be renewed (Fig. 10.17).

4 Connect the circuit tester between the connector plug 'L' and 'E'

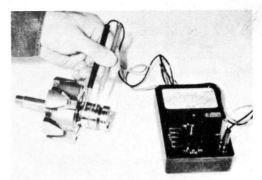
Fig. 10.7. Checking alternator rotor coil for open circuit

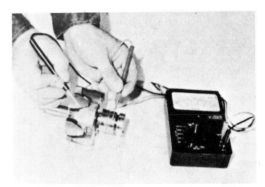
Fig. 10.8. Checking alternator rotor coil for earthing

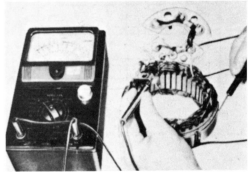
Fig. 10.10. Testing alternator stator coil for earthing

Fig. 10.9. Withdrawing alternator rotor bearing

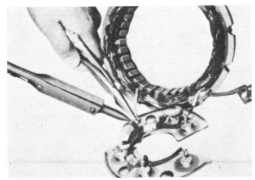
Fig. 10.11. Unsoldering alternator rectifier holder

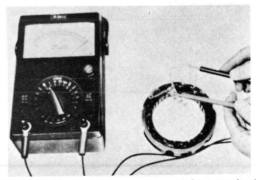
Fig. 10.12. Checking alternator stator coil for open circuit

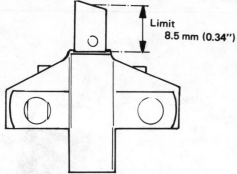

Limit
8.5 mm (0.34")

Fig. 10.13. Alternator brush wear diagram

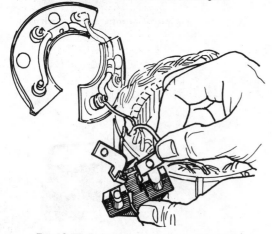

Fig. 10.15. Refitting alternator brush holder

"IG" terminal   "N" terminal   "F" terminal

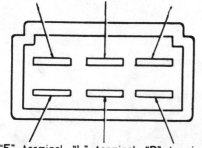

"E" terminal   "L" terminal   "B" terminal

Fig. 10.17. Identification of alternator connecting plug terminals

9.2 Voltage regulator

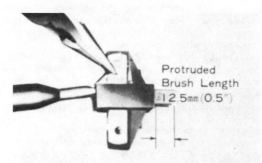

Protruded
Brush Length
12.5mm (0.5")

Fig. 10.14. Alternator brush projection after installation

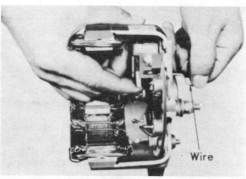

Wire

Fig. 10.16. Supporting brushes during refitting of alternator drive end frame

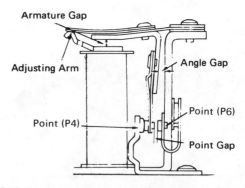

Armature Gap

Adjusting Arm

Angle Gap

Point (P4)

Point (P6)

Point Gap

Fig. 10.18. Alternator voltage relay - identification of components

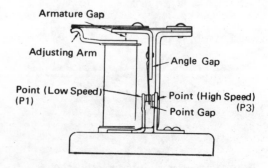

Armature Gap

Adjusting Arm

Angle Gap

Point (Low Speed) (P1)

Point (High Speed) (P3)

Point Gap

Fig. 10.19. Alternator voltage regulator - identification of components

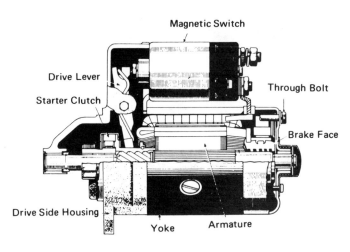

Fig. 10.20. Cut-away view of starter motor

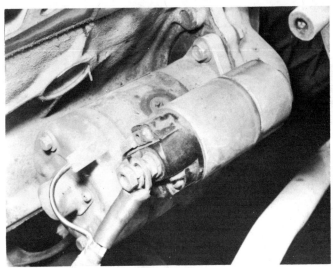

12.2 Disconnecting starter motor cables

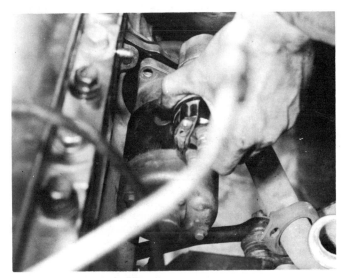

12.3 Removing starter motor

terminals when no resistance should be indicated. If a resistance is shown then the contact point 'P4' is making poor contact. Press down the relay armature and check the resistance which should be about 100 ohms. If it is higher, the voltage coil has an open circuit or if lower, the points 'P4' are fused together or the coil is shortened (Fig. 10.18).

5   Connect the circuit tester between the 'N' and 'E' terminals when a resistance of 23 ohms should be indicated. If the resistance is much higher, the pressure coil has an open circuit, if lower then it is short circuited.

6   Connect the circuit tester between the 'B' and 'L' terminals and depress the voltage relay armature. There should be no indicated resistance but if there is this will show that the contact of the points assembly 'P6' is poor (Fig. 10.19).

7   Connect the circuit tester between the 'B' and 'E' terminals when the indicated resistance should be infinity. Where this is not so, the points assembly 'P6' are fused together. Depress the relay armature and check the resistance which should be about 100 ohms. If the resistance is higher then the voltage coil has an open circuit and if lower it has a short circuit.

8   With the connector plug still disconnected carry out the following mechanical checks. Refer to illustration and depress the voltage relay armature. Using a feeler gauge check the deflection gap between the contact spring and its supporting arm. This should be between 0.008 and 0.024 in (0.20 and 0.60 mm) if not, bend the contact point holder (P6). Release the armature and check the point gap which should be between 0.016 and 0.047 in (0.4 to 1.2 mm) if not bend the contact point holder (P4).

9   Check the armature gap on the voltage regulator which should be in excess of 0.012 in (0.30 mm) otherwise bend the contact point holder P1 to adjust the gap. Check the voltage regulator point gap which should be between 0.012 and 0.018 in (0.30 and 0.45 mm) otherwise bend the contact point holder 'P3' to adjust. Depress the voltage regulator armature and check the deflection gap between the contact spring and its supporting arm. This should be between 0.008 and 0.014 in (0.2 and 0.6 mm). If not renew the regulator as an assembly. Finally depress the voltage regulator armature and check the angle gap at its narrowest point. This gap should not exceed 0.008 in (0.2 mm) otherwise renew the unit as an assembly.

10 Starter motor - general description

The starter operates on the principle of pre-engagement which, through the medium of a solenoid switch, meshes the starter drive gear with the ring gear on the flywheel (or torque convertor - automatic transmission) fractionally in advance of the closure of the main starter motor contacts. This slight delay in energising the starter motor does much to extend the life of the starter drive and ring gear components. As soon as the engine fires and its speed or rotation exceeds that of the armature shaft of the starter motor, a built-in clutch mechanism prevents excessive rotation of the shaft and the release of the starter

switch key causes the solenoid and drive engagement fork to return to their de-energised positions. The armature shaft is fitted with rear and central rotational speed retarding mechanisms to stop its rotational movement rapidly after the starter has been de-energised (Fig. 10.20).

11 Starter motor - testing in vehicle

1   If the starter motor fails to operate, test the state of charge of the battery by checking the specific gravity with a hydrometer or switching on the headlamps. If they glow brightly for several seconds and then gradually dim, then the battery is in an uncharged state.

2   If the test proves the battery to be fully charged, check the security of the battery leads at the battery terminals, scraping away any deposits which are preventing a good contact between the cable clamps and the terminal posts.

3   Check the battery negative lead at its body frame terminal, scraping the mating faces clean if necessary.

4   Check the security of the cables at the starter motor and solenoid switch terminals.

5   Check the wiring with a voltmeter for breaks or short circuits.

6   Check the wiring connections at the ignition/starter switch terminals.

7   If everything is in order, remove the starter motor as described in the next Section and dismantle, test and service as described in Section 14.

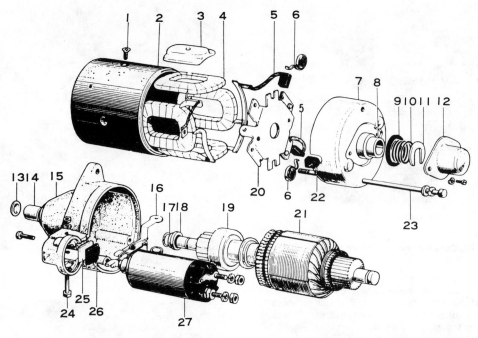

Fig. 10.21. Exploded view of starter motor

1 Pole shoe screw	8 Bush	15 Pinion housing	22 Grommet
2 Yoke	9 Ring	16 Pinion engagement lever	23 Tie bolt
3 Pole core	10 Spring	17 Circlip	24 Pivot bolt
4 Field coil	11 Lockplate	18 Stop	25 Plate
5 Brush	12 Cover	19 Clutch assembly	26 Flexible plug
6 Brush spring	13 Plug	20 Brush holder	27 Solenoid switch
7 Commutator end frame	14 Bush	21 Armature	

12 Starter motor - removal and installation

1 Disconnect the lead from the battery negative terminal.
2 Disconnect the cables from the starter solenoid terminals (photo).
3 Unscrew and remove the starter motor securing bolts and withdraw
the unit from the clutch bellhousing (or torque converter housing -
automatic transmission) (photo).
4 Installation is a reversal of removal.

13 Starter motor - dismantling

1 Disconnect the field coil lead from the starter solenoid main
terminal (Fig. 10.21).
2 Remove the two securing screws from the solenoid and withdraw the
the solenoid far enough to enable it to be unhooked from the drive
engagement lever fork (Fig. 10.22).
3 Remove the end frame cover, the lockplate, washer, spring and seal.
4 Unscrew and remove the two tie bolts and withdraw the commutator
end frame.
5 Pull out the brushes from their holders and remove the brush holder
assembly (Fig. 10.23).
6 Pull the yoke from the drive end frame.
7 Remove the engagement lever pivot bolt from the drive end frame
and detach the rubber buffer and its backing plate. Remove the armature,
complete with drive engagment lever from the drive end frame.
8 With a piece of tubing, drive the pinion stop collar up the armature
shaft far enough to enable the circlip to be removed and then pull the
stop collar from the shaft together with the pinion and clutch assembly.
(Fig. 10.24).

14 Starter motor - servicing and testing

1 Check for wear in the armature shaft bearings. The specified
clearance between shaft and bearing is between 0.037 and 0.053 in
(0.095 and 0.135 mm) with a maximum of 0.008 in (0.2 mm).

Fig. 10.22. Removing starter solenoid

Fig. 10.23. Removing starter brush holder

Normally the bearings will require renewal by pressing out the old ones from the end frames and pressing in the new but before doing this check the diameter of the armature shaft which should be 0.492 in (12.50 mm). If this is worn then a new armature will be required and it will be more economical to exchange the starter complete for a reconditioned unit.

2 Armature shaft bearings are available in standard sizes and under-sizes where it is decided to have the original shaft turned down as the method of renovation.

3 Check the armature shaft for bend or ovality and renew if evident.

4 Check the commutator segments and undercut the mica insulators if necessary, using a hacksaw blade ground to correct thickness. If the commutator is burned or discoloured, clean it with a piece of fine glass paper (not emery or carborundum) and finally wipe it with a solvent moistened cloth (Fig. 10.25).

5 To test the armature is not difficult but a voltmeter or bulb and 12 volt battery are required. The two tests determine whether there may be a break in any circuit winding or if any wiring insulation is broken down. The illustration shows how the battery, voltmeter and probe connectors are used to test whether (a) any wire in the windings is broken or (b) whether there is an insulation breakdown. In the first test the probes are placed on adjacent segments of clean commutator. All voltmeter readings should be similar. If a bulb is used instead it will glow very dimly or not at all if there is a fault. For the second test any reading or bulb lighting indicates a fault. Test each segment in turn with one probe and keep the other on the shaft. Should either test indicate a faulty armature the wisest action in the long run is to obtain a new starter. The field coils may be tested if an ohmmeter or ammeter can be obtained. With an ohmmeter the resistance (measured between the terminal and the yoke) should be 6 ohms. With an ammeter, connect it in series with a 12 volt battery again from the field terminal to the yoke. A reading of 2 amps, is normal. Zero amps or infinity ohms indicate an open circuit. More than 2 amps or less than 6 ohms indicates a break-down of the insulation. If a fault in the field coils is diagnosed then a reconditioned starter should be obtained as the coils can

only be removed and refitted with special equipment.

6 Check the insulation of the brush holders and the length of the brushes. If these have worn to below 0.47 in (12 mm), renew them. Before fitting them to their holders, dress them to the correct contour by wrapping a piece of emery cloth round the commutator and rotating the commutator back and forth (Fig. 10.27).

7 Check the starter clutch assembly for wear or sticky action, or chipped pinion teeth and renew the assembly if necessary.

15 Starter motor - assembly

1 Fit the clutch assembly to the armature shaft followed by a new pinion stop collar and circlip. Pull the stop collar forward and stake the collar rim over the circlip. Grease all sliding surfaces.

2 Locate the drive engagement lever to the armature shaft as shown in Fig. 10.28 with the spring towards the armature and the steel washer up against the clutch.

3 Apply grease to all sliding surfaces and locate the armature assembly in the drive end frame. Insert the drive engagement lever pivot pin, well greased.

4 Fit the rubber buffer together with its backing plate and then align and offer into position the yoke to the drive end frame.

5 Fit the brush holder to the armature and then insert the brushes.

6 Grease the commutator end frame bearing and then fit the end frame into position. Insert and tighten the two tie bolts.

7 Fit the seal, washer lockplate and end cover (half packed with multi-purpose grease). Check the armature shaft endfloat, if this exceeds 0.03 in (0.8 mm) remove the end cover and add an additional thrust washer. (Fig. 10.29).

8 Install the solenoid switch making sure that its hook engages **under** the spring of the engagement lever fork (Fig. 10.30).

9 Set up a test circuit similar to the one shown in Fig. 10.31, and check that the motor rotates smoothly at a current loading of 45 amps. With the solenoid switch energised, insert a feeler gauge between the

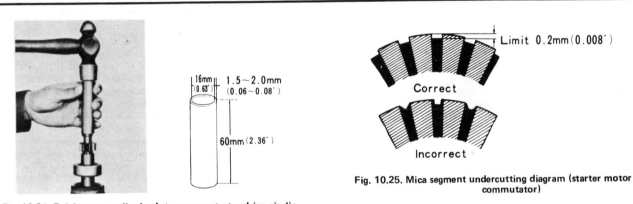

Fig. 10.24. Driving stop collar back to expose starter drive circlip

16mm (0.63") 1.5~2.0mm (0.06~0.08")
60mm (2.36")

Limit 0.2mm (0.008")

Correct

Incorrect

Fig. 10.25. Mica segment undercutting diagram (starter motor commutator)

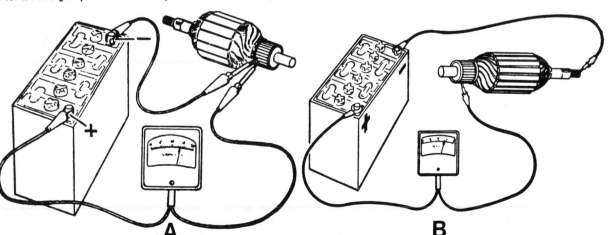

A   B

Fig. 10.26. Testing the starter motor armature (A) for open circuit and (B) for breakdown of wiring insulation

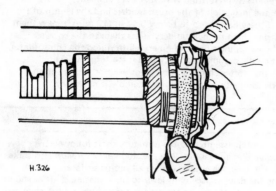

Fig. 10.27. Dressing starter motor brushes to correct shape

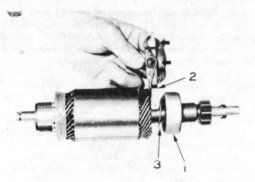

Fig. 10.28. Fitting starter drive engagement lever

1   Clutch   3   Steel washer
2   Lever

Fig. 10.29. Fitting starter motor lockplate

Fig. 10.30. Installing cover to starter motor end frame

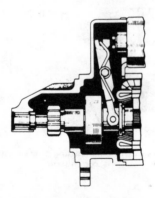

Fig. 10.31. Correct installation of solenoid to starter motor drive engagement lever

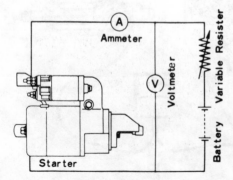

Fig. 10.32. Starter motor test circuit used after reassembly is complete

end face of the clutch pinion and the pinion stop collar. There should be a clearance of between 0.04 to 0.16 in (1 to 4 mm). If the clearance is incorrect, remove the solenoid switch and adjust the length of the adjustable hooked stud by loosening its locknut (Figs. 10.32 and 10.33).

16 Fuses and fusible link

1   The fuse block is located under the facia panel. The fuse ratings and circuits protected vary according to model and date of manufacture but the fuse block is clearly marked and the cover incorporates two spare spare fuses (photo).
2   In the event of a fuse blowing, always find the reason and rectify the trouble before fitting the new one. Always renew a fuse with one of the same amperage rating as the original.
3   A double protection is provided for the electrical harness by a fusible link installed in the lead running from the battery positive terminal. The fusible link must never be by-passed and should it melt, the cause of the circuit overload must be established before renewing the link with one of similar type and rating (Figs. 10.35 and 10.36).

Note: The electrical equipment described in the remainder of this Chapter may only be fitted in part to vehicles according to date of manufacture and operating territory. Only the very latest vehicles marketed in North America are equipped with the more sophisticated warning devices. Readers should check the specifications of their particular vehicle to ascertain which Sections of this Chapter are relevant.

17 Relays

1   The number of relays fitted to individual vehicles depends upon the equipment and the operating territory.
2   Two examples of relay locations are shown and they may be positioned under the instrument panel or within the engine compartment (Fig. 10.34).

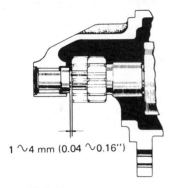

Fig. 10.33. Starter motor pinion to stop
collar clearance

1 ∿4 mm (0.04 ∿0.16")

16.1 Removing cover from fuse block

Fig. 10.34. Typical location of relays and
switches (except North America)

1 Stop lamp switch
2 Stop lamp bulb failure relay
3 Starter relay
4 Direction indicator and hazard warning relay
   relay
5 Coolant temperature switch
6 Oil temperature sender unit
7 Oil pressure switch
8 Oil pressure sender unit
9 Voltage regulator
10 Head and tail light relay

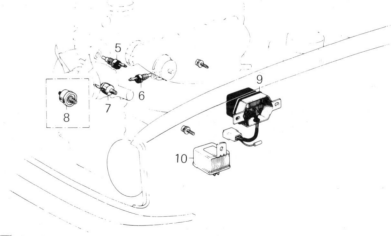

Fig. 10.35. Location and types of fusible link (except SR-5)

Fig. 10.36. Fusible link (SR-5)

18.2 Removing headlight trim

18.4 Removing headlight retaining ring

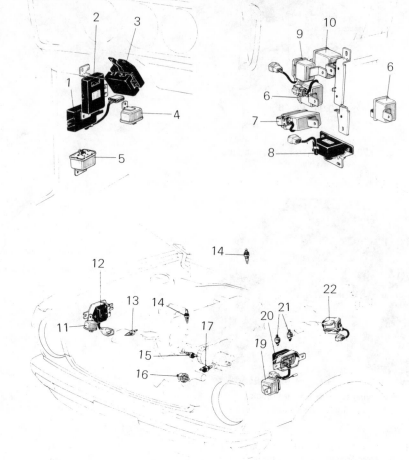

Fig. 10.37. Typical location of relays and switches (North America)

1	Seat belt computer	7	Starter relay
2	Emission control computer	8	Safety belt lock (G) sensor
3	Fuse box	9	Choke control relay
4	Warning buzzer	10	Stop lamp
5	Turn signal and hazard warning relay	11	Horn
6	Ignition control relay	12	Igniter

13	Thermo switch (electric raditor fan)	16	Oil pressure sender
14	Thermo switch (emission control or dual points distributor)	17	Oil temperature sender
		19	Head and tail light relay
15	Coolant temperature sender unit	20	Alternator regulator
		21	Brake warning light
		22	Starter interlock cancel switch

3   In the event of failure of an electrical component, first check the fuse and then the bulb (where applicable).

4   Check the security of all connecting wires and terminals.

5   If all these are in order then the relay is probably faulty and as they are all sealed units, it must be renewed as a unit.

18 Headlight sealed beam units and bulbs - renewal

1   The headlamp may be of sealed beam or separate bulb type according to operating territory.

2   *To renew a sealed beam unit,* extract the screws which secure the headlamp trim or the radiator grille according to model and date of production (photo).

3   If the radiator grille must be removed and inspection will determine this, open the bonnet as some screws are accessible along the top edge of the grille.

4   With the headlamp trim or radiator grille removed, unscrew the sealed beam unit retaining ring screws and withdraw the ring. Do not touch the adjuster screws. On some models, only release the retaining ring screws and turn the ring clockwise (photo).

5   Pull the lamp unit for enough forward to be able to disconnect the electrical plug from the rear and then remove the unit (photo).

6   Refitting is a reversal of removal and provided the adjuster screws have not been touched, the headlamp beam alignment should remain unaltered. It is a wise precaution however to have them checked at your local service station.

7   Some models are equipped with semi-sealed headlamps which use a bulb. Access is as described for sealed beam units but once removed, pull off the rubber cover from the back of the lamp and turn the bulb holder in an anti-clockwise direction (Fig. 10.39).

8   When fitting a new bulb make sure that the projection on the bulb holder fits into the groove in the back of the lamp reflector (Fig. 10.40).

9   Refit the rubber cover, connect the electrical plug and refit the lamp.

19 Light bulbs - renewal

1   Aecess to most bulbs is obtained simply by extracting the lens securing screws and removing the lens. (photo).

2   Bulbs for most lights are of bayonet fixing type and they should always be renewed by ones of similar type.

3   On Hardtop, Saloon and Liftback versions, the rear light bulbs are accessible from within the luggage boot or luggage compartment (photos).

4   Remove the panel and withdraw the bulb holder from the back of the light.

Fig. 10.38. Headlamp adjuster screws (B) Retaining ring screw (A)

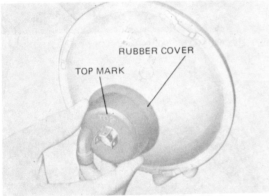

Fig. 10.39. Rear view of bulb type headlamp

5 The rear side marker light bulb is also accessible from within the luggage boot by pulling the holder from the back of the light (Fig. 10.42).
6 The interior light bulb is of festoon type and can be reached by pinching the sides of the lens inwards and withdrawing it. On Liftback versions, the luggage compartment light lens is held by two screws (photo).
7 Indicator and warning light bulbs can be renewed if the instrument panel is withdrawn as described in Section 30. The bulb holders are twisted out of the rear of the panel and the capless bulbs removed.

20 Ignition switch and lock cylinder - removal and refitting

1 Remove the upper shroud from the steering column.
2 Insert the ignition key into the lock and turn it to the 'ACC' position (Fig. 10.43).
3 Insert a probe into the hole at the side of the lock cylinder and while depressing the pin, withdraw the lock cylinder.
4 The ignition switch can be removed from the opposite end of the lock in the following way.
5 Disconnect the wiring harness plug from its position near the switch.
6 Unscrew and remove the ignition switch securing screw and withdraw the switch (photos).
7 Refitting is a reversal of removal.

21 Steering column switch - removal and refitting

1 Disconnect the battery.
2 Disconnect the wiring connector plugs at the side of the steering column.
3 Remove the steering wheel crash pad and the steering wheel as described in Chapter 11.
4 Remove the steering column shrouds.
5 Release the switch securing screws and remove it.
6 Refitting is a reversal of removal.

18.5 Removing headlight sealed beam unit

19.1A Removing direction indicator/parking light lens

19.1B Removing side marker light lens

19.3A Rear light cluster cover panel (Liftback)

19.3B Removing a rear light bulb (Liftback)

19.6 Removing interior lamp lens

Press and turn counterclockwise

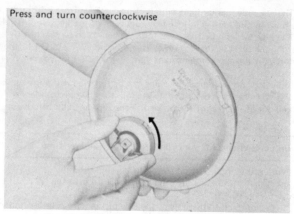

Fig. 10.40. Removing headlamp bulb holder

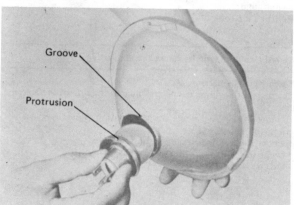

Fig. 10.41. Headlamp bulb holder alignment points

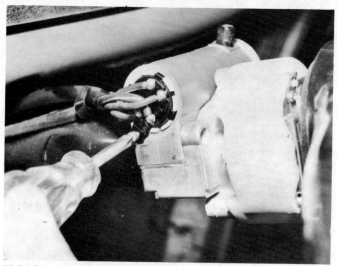

20.6A Removing ignition switch securing screw

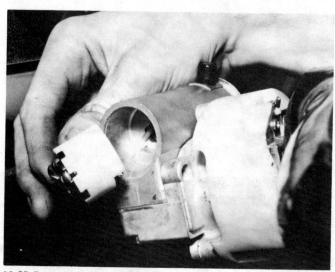

20.6B Removing ignition switch

22 Horns and horn switch

1   If a horn works badly or fails completely, first check the wiring leading to it for short circuits, blown fuse or loose connections. Also check that the horn is firmly secured and there is nothing lying on the horn body (Fig. 10.45).

2   If a horn loses its adjustment it will not alter the pitch as the tone of a horn depends on the vibration of an air column. It will however, give a softer or more harsh sound. Also excessive current will be required which can cause fuses to blow.

3   The horn should never be completely dismantled but it is possible to adjust it. This adjustment is to compensate for wear only and will not affect the tone. Two types of horns can be fitted to models covered by this manual:

Vibrator type horn

4   Disconnect the wires from each horn that lead to the horn button.

5   Slacken the adjustment screw locknuts.

6   Connect an ammeter to the horn terminal as shown in Fig. 10.44 and make any adjustment necessary.

7   As the adjusting screw is turned anticlockwise the pitch and current will increase. Too great a current (over 2.5 amps) will burn the contact points so do not exceed this figure.

Trumpet type horn

8   Adjustment for this type of horn is basically identical to that for the vibrator type horn.

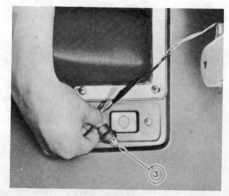

Fig. 10.42. Removal of rear side marker bulb (3) on Hardtop

9 Remove the cover to gain access to the adjustment nut.
10 Connect an ammeter as shown in Fig. 10.46 and make any adjustments that are necessary.
11 The horn switch arrangement on the steering wheel is shown in Chapter 11.

23 Windscreen wiper blades and arms - removal and refitting

1 To remove a blade from the wiper arm on 1200E models, pull down the small tag with the thumb nail and withdraw the blade from the arm (photo).
2 On 1600 and 20 Series models, the blade is attached to the arm with two screws (photo).
3 To remove a wiper arm, unscrew and remove the domed nut which secures the arm to the splined driving spindle. Make sure that the wipers have been switched off by means of the wiper switch (not the ignition key) and are in their true parked position.
4 Pull the arm from the driving spindle (photo).
5 Refit the blade and arm by reversing the removal operations. Check the wiping arc of the wiper blades on a wet screen and adjust the position of the arms if necessary by removing them and moving one or more splines in the appropriate direction.

24 Windscreen wiper motor and linkage - removal and refitting

1 *On 1200E models,* the wiper motor and linkage are removable from below the instrument panel within the vehicle.
2 Disconnect the battery, remove the wiper arms and blades.
3 Disconnect the electrical leads from the wiper motor.
4 Disconnect the wiper motor crank arm from the linkage by prising with a screwdriver.
5 Unbolt and remove the wiper motor and its mounting bracket.

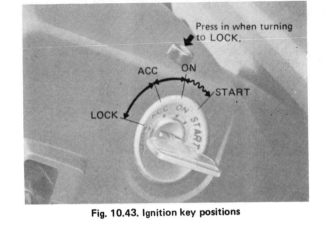

Fig. 10.43. Ignition key positions

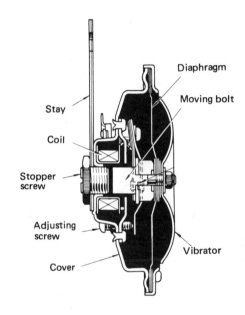

Fig. 10.45. Sectional view of vibrator type horn

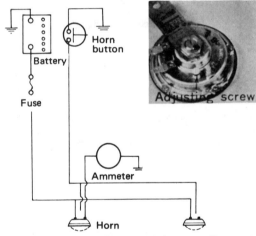

Fig. 10.44. Horn test circuit for note adjustment

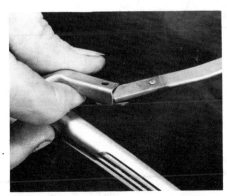

23.1 Removing wiper blade from arm (1200E)

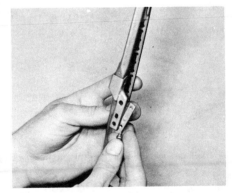

23.2 Removing wiper blade from arm (30 Series and 1600)

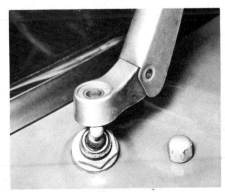

23.4 Removing a wiper arm

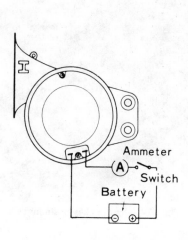

Fig. 10.46. Trumpet type horn adjustment circuit

24.8 Removing cover plate from engine compartment rear bulkhead

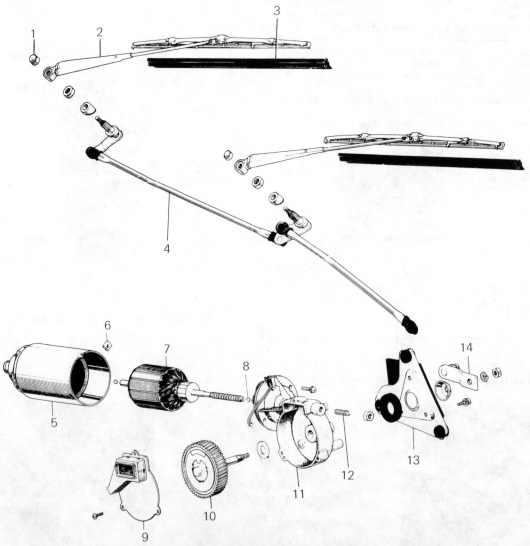

Fig. 10.47. Exploded view of wiper motor and linkage (typical)

1	Dome nut	5	Stator	9	Gear housing cover plate	12	Adjuster screw
2	Wiper arm	6	Tie bolt nut	10	Gear	13	Mounting bracket
3	Wiper blade	7	Armature	11	Gear housing	14	Crankarm
4	Link	8	Ball				

Fig. 10.48. Wiper motor withdrawn to disconnect crankarm from linkage (30 series and 1600 models)

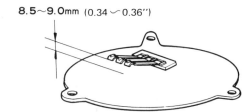

8.5~9.0mm (0.34 ~ 0.36'')

Fig. 10.49. Wiper motor contact point adjustment diagram

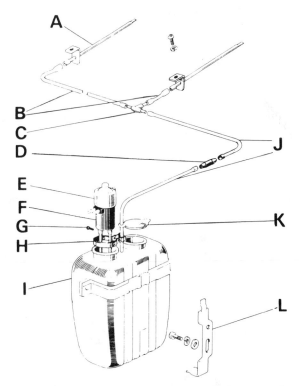

Fig. 10.50. Windscreen washer arrangement (1600E models)

A	Nozzle	G	Screw
B	Hose	H	Support ring
C	T-joint	I	Reservoir
D	Connector	J	Hose
E	Cap	K	Cap
F	Motor/pump assembly	L	Bracket

Removal of the parcel shelf may facilitate this operation.

6 Remove the demister hose and outlet nozzle, unscrew and remove the driving spindle nuts and withdraw the linkage from under the instrument panel.

7 *On 30 series and 1600 models,* the wiper motor and linkage are accessible from under the bonnet (Fig. 10.47).

8 Unbolt and remove the cover plate from the rear bulkhead (photo).

9 Remove the wiper arms and blades.

10 Disconnect the electrical harness plug from the wiper motor.

11 Remove the wiper motor mounting screws and withdraw the motor just enough to be able to prise the linkage from the wiper motor crank arm (Fig. 10.48).

12 Withdraw the linkage and driving spindles from the aperture in the engine compartment rear bulkhead.

13 Refitting is a reversal of removal.

25 Windscreen wiper motor - overhaul

1 It is recommended that when a fault occurs in a wiper motor that a new unit is obtained.

2 If it is essential that the original unit is overhauled then make sure that the necessary spares are available first.

3 Dismantling is carried out by removing the gearbox cover plate, the crank arm and the gear housing to stator housing screws.

4 Renew the brushes if worn and clean the commutator.

5 Note the position of the two armature endfloat balls.

6 Lubricate the bearings and bushes on reassembly and tighten the armature endfloat adjuster screw and locknut to give an almost imperceptible end movement of the armature. Check and adjust the parking switch contacts on the gear housing cover as shown in the illustration (Fig. 10.49).

7 When refitting the crank arm, temporarily connect the wiper motor and switch it on, then off, through its control switch. With the motor in its automatic parked position, refit the crank arm in accordance with the diagram (Fig. 10.51).

26 Windscreen washer - general

1 The washer reservoir is located within the engine compartment.

2 1200E models have the washer pump integral with the reservoir while 30 series and 1600 models have a separately mounted pump (Fig. 10.50) (photo).

3 Always keep the fluid reservoir filled and do not operate the electric pump with a dry reservoir. In any case, operation of the washer pump should be limited to periods not exceeding 20 seconds.

4 It is recommended that a proprietary screen cleaning solvent is used in the reservoir and during very cold weather add some methylated spirit *but never anti-freeze,* as this will damage the vehicle paintwork.

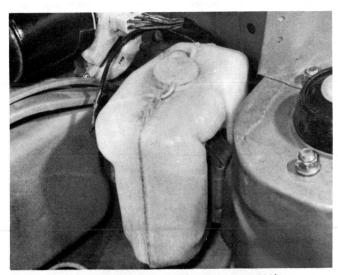

26.2 Windscreen washer fluid reservoir (30 Series and 1600)

27 Rear wiper (Liftback) - removal, overhaul and refitting

1   The wiper motor is mounted at the base of the glass within the tail-gate (photo).
2   To remove the wiper motor assembly, unscrew the domed nut and withdraw the wiper arm.
3   Unscrew the plastic moulded cover from the wiper motor and then disconnect the wiring connector plug.
4   Unscrew and remove the wiper motor mounting bolts and withdraw the motor complete with bracket.
5   To dismantle the assembly, remove the mounting bracket from the motor (Fig.10.52).
6   Extract the circlip from the now exposed crank arm (Fig. 10.53).
7   Withdraw the gear from the gear housing after extracting the three cover screws.
8   Unscrew and remove the two tie bolts and nuts and withdraw the gear housing from the stator/armature. Take care to keep the armature engaged in the stator during this operation otherwise the brushes may slip off the commutator and become damaged by the worm gear.
9   Withdraw the armature from the stator, retrieving the two steel balls, one from each end of the armature shaft.
10 Renew the brushes if they are less than 0.24 in (6 mm) in length.
11 Clean the commutator with a fuel socket cloth. If it is badly burned or scored then it will have to be renewed or a complete unit obtained either new or reconditioned.
12 Reassembly is a reversal of dismantling but check the height of the automatic stop switch lever. Use a straight edge to do this as shown and bend the switch lever if necessary (Fig. 10.54).
13 On completion, adjust the armature shaft endfloat using the adjuster screw and locknut until the endfloat just disappears.
14 Fit the mounting bracket and install the wiper assembly. Note the earth lead under one of the bracket bolts.
15 With the wiper motor switched off in its parked position, refit the wiper arm so that it is parallel with the bottom edge of the rear screen.

28 Rear washer (Liftback) - removal and refitting

1   The rear screen washer fluid reservoir and pump are located behind the right-hand trim panel within the luggage compartment (photo).
2   Access to the reservoir is obtained by prising away the small cover which is located just below and to the right of the luggage compartment interior lamp.
3   To remove the pump and reservoir, withdraw the trim panel and also the floor covering from the luggage area (Fig. 10.56).
4   Remove the jack, the jack carrier and then unbolt the reservoir bracket bolts (photo).
5   Disconnect the hoses and electrical leads and remove the reservoir and pump.
6   The washer jet assembly can be removed by prising it out of the tailgate with two large screwdrivers but protect the paint surface before doing this (photo).

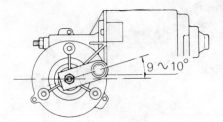

Fig. 10.51. Wiper motor crankarm installation diagram

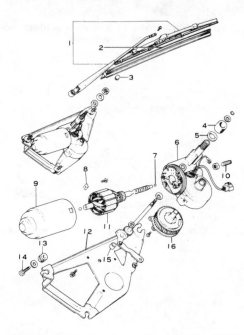

Fig. 10.52. Exploded view of rear wiper assembly (Lift-back)

1	Arm and blade	9	Stator
2	Blade	10	Adjuster screw
3	Domed nut	11	Armature
4	Spacer	12	Mounting bracket
5	Washer	13	Bush
6	Gear housing	14	Bolt
7	Ball	15	Stop
8	Tie bolt nut bracket	16	Gear

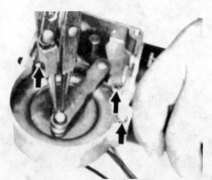

Fig. 10.53. Extracting crankarm circlip (Lift-back rear wiper) lower screws (arrowed)

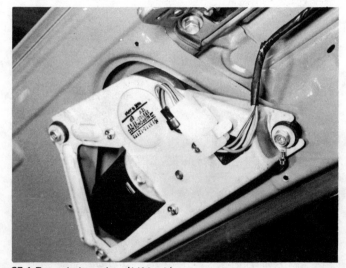

27.1 Rear window wiper (Liftback)

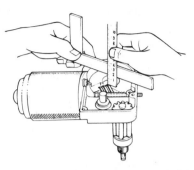

Fig. 10.54. Checking height of automatic stop switch lever (Lift-back rear wiper motor)

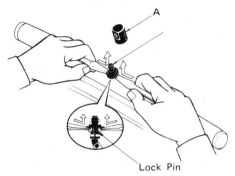

Fig. 10.55. Removing washer nozzle (A) and jet (Lift-back)

Lock Pin

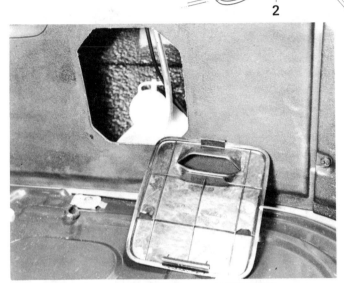

28.1 Location of rear window washer reservoir (Liftback)

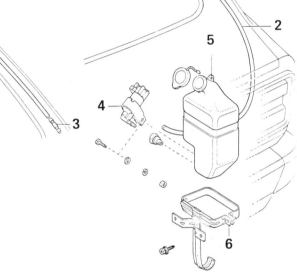

Fig. 10.56. Rear washer components (Lift-back)

1 Jet	4 Motor/pump
2 Hose	5 Reservoir
3 Connector	6 Mounting bracket

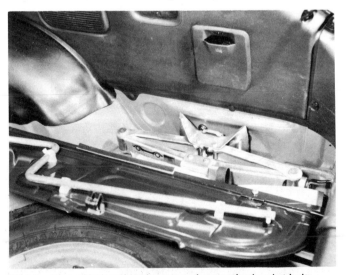

28.4 Location of jack and washer reservoir mounting bracket bolts

29 Speedometer cable - removal and refitting

1 Withdraw the instrument panel far enough (see next Section) for the cable assembly to be disconnected from the rear of the speedometer. To disconnect, depress the locking tab on the side of the cable attachment sleeve and pull the outer cable conduit away.

2 If the inner cable is not broken, grip the end of it with a pair of pliers and withdraw it.

3 If the inner cable is broken, withdraw the upper section as just described and then disconnect the cable from the transmission and withdraw the lower section of cable. Take care not to lose the felt washers.

4 Install a new cable from the speedometer end of the outer conduit. Smear the lower two thirds of the inner cable with multi-purpose grease.

30 Instrument panel - removal and refitting

1 On 1200E models, disconnect the battery.

2 Reach up behind the instrument panel and disconnect the speedometer cable from the speedometer.

3 Remove the moulding from the lower face of the instrument panel upper crash pad.

4 Extract the screws now exposed which retain the instrument trim

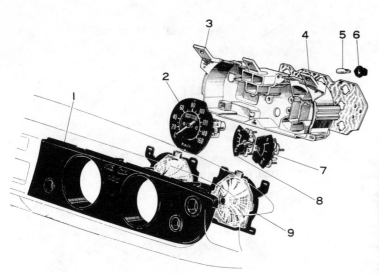

Fig. 10.57. Instrument panel components (1200E)

1   Trim panel
2   Speedometer
3   Casing
4   Printed circuit board
5   Instrument illuminating bulb
6   Holder
7   Fuel contents gauge
8   Water temperature gauge
9   Instrument lens

Fig. 10.58. Removing instrument trim panel (1200E)

panel. Remove the panel (Figs. 10.57 and 10.58).

5   Unscrew and remove the two nuts which secure the instrument cluster in position. These are accessible from behind the instruments.

6   Pull the instrument cluster far enough towards you to be able to disconnect the electrical leads and then withdraw the instruments completely.

7   *On 30 series and 1600 models,* remove the moulding from the lower face of the instrument upper crash pad (Fig. 10.59).

8   Remove the instrument trim panel (Fig. 10.60).

9   Reach round with the hand and disconnect the speedometer cable from the back of the speedometer.

10 Extract the screws which hold the instrument cluster, withdraw the cluster just far enough to be able to disconnect the electrical wiring harness plugs and then remove the cluster.

11 If for any reason, the complete fascia assembly is to be removed on 30 series and 1600 models, continue by removing the radio, the ashtray, the heater control panel, the glove compartment and choke control knob.

12 The steering column upper bracket must also be unbolted (see Chapter 11) and the column lowered.

13 The twelve securing bolts can then be unscrewed and the complete fascia assembly removed from the vehicle (Fig. 10.61).

14 On all cars, once the instrument cluster has been removed, the individual instruments can be removed for renewal or repair.

15 Refitting is a reversal of removal.

Fig. 10.59. Instrument panel moulding screws (30 Series and 1600)

31 Instruments - testing

1   If a fault occurs in the water temperature gauge, refer to Chapter 2, Section 13.

2   If a fault occurs in the fuel level contents gauge, refer to Chapter 3, Section 9.

3   If an oil pressure warning light is fitted, if the light fails to illuminate when the ignition key is first turned 'ON', check the bulb and the electrical connections.

4   If the light comes on when the engine is running or fails to go out once the engine has started, immediately switch off and trace the cause. The sender switch which is screwed into the outlet port of the oil filter is designed to operate at an oil pressure of between 2.8 and 5.7 lb/in^2 (0.2 and 0.4 kg/cm^2). At this pressure, the circuit is broken by the switch contacts and the warning lamp should be out.

5   Provided the engine is in good condition, renew the sender switch and test again by starting the engine. If the light still remains on, the engine oil level may be low, the oil pump worn or drive sheared or the oil filter clogged.

6   If an oil pressure gauge is fitted and a low or very high reading is observed and yet the engine is known to be in good condition, pull the lead from the terminal on the back of the gauge and earth the terminal using a piece of cable with a 3.4 W bulb incorporated in it. Turn the ignition switch 'ON' when the bulb should light and the

Fig. 10.60. Instrument trim panel screws (30 Series and 1600)

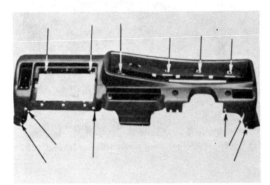

Fig. 10.61. Fascia panel securing screws (30 Series and 1600)

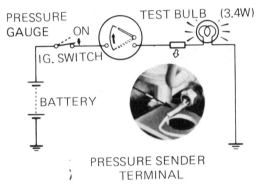

Fig. 10. 62. Oil pressure gauge test circuit

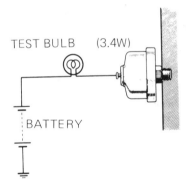

Fig. 10.63. Oil pressure sender unit test circuit

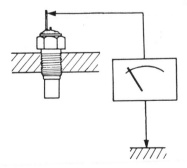

Fig. 10.65. Oil temperature sender unit test circuit

gauge needle should deflect. If this does not happen, renew the gauge (Fig. 10.62).

7   To check the oil pressure sender unit, pull off the lead from it and connect battery (+) voltage to it but passing it through a 3.4 W bulb. With the engine stationary, the test bulb should be out, with the engine running, the bulb should flash and the number of flashes increase with the engine speed. Renew the sender unit if it does not behave in this way (Fig. 10.63).

8   If the oil pressure gauge and sender unit are proved to be satisfactory, then if the engine is generally in good condition, the cause of very low reading will be due to low oil level or the oil pump drive sheared. Exceptionally high readings may be caused by a seized pressure relief valve or clogged filter.

9   If an oil temperature gauge is fitted and very high readings are being obtained, carry out the following tests: Pull the lead from the temperature gauge terminal and earth it through a piece of cable into which a 3-4 W bulb has been connected. The bulb should light as soon as the ignition is switched 'ON' and then start to flash after a few seconds. The gauge needle should deflect to near centre of its scale (Fig. 10.64).

10 To test the temperature sender unit, an ohmmeter should be used to measure the resistance between its terminal and earth. At varying temperature levels, the resistance values should be in accordance with the following table (Fig. 10.65).

Temperature	Resistance (ohms)
122°F (50°C)	154
176°F (80°C)	52
212°F (100°C)	27.5
248°F (120°C)	16

32 Radio - removal and refitting

1   On 1200E models, remove the two main control knobs from the radio.
2   Unscrew the nuts from the spindles which are now visible. These

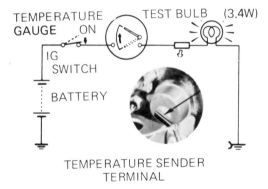

Fig. 10.64. Oil temperature gauge test circuit

Fig. 10.66. Removing the radio (1200E)

Fig. 10.67. Removing radio aerial

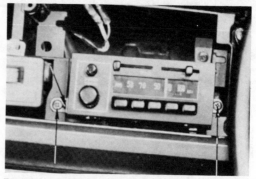

Fig. 10.68. Radio securing screws (Series 30 and 1600)

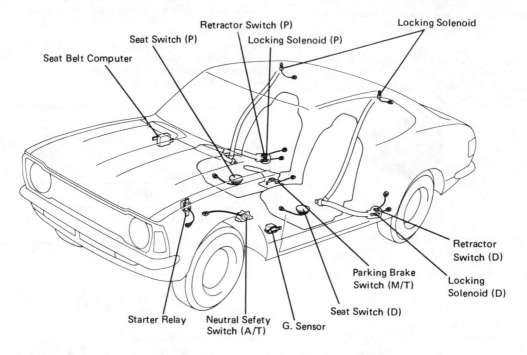

Retractor Switch (P)
Seat Switch (P)
Locking Solenoid (P)
Locking Solenoid
Seat Belt Computer
Retractor Switch (D)
Locking Solenoid (D)
Parking Brake Switch (M/T)
Seat Switch (D)
Starter Relay
Neutral Safety Switch (A/T)
G. Sensor

Fig. 10.69. Seat belt interlock system - location of components

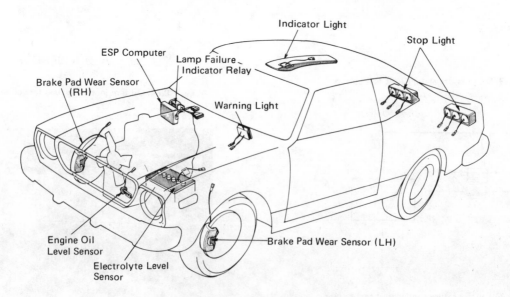

Indicator Light
Stop Light
ESP Computer
Lamp Failure Indicator Relay
Brake Pad Wear Sensor (RH)
Warning Light
Engine Oil Level Sensor
Electrolyte Level Sensor
Brake Pad Wear Sensor (LH)

Fig. 10.70. Electro Sensor Panel (ESP) components

nuts act as retainers for the radio. Disconnect the support bracket at the rear of the radio.

3   Disconnect the aerial lead from the radio.

4   Disconnect the ventilator duct and withdraw the radio until the speaker leads and power lead can be disconnected (Fig. 10.66).

5   The speaker can be removed if necessary after unscrewing the securing nuts accessible through the glove compartment upper service hole.

6   The aerial is removable from under the left front wing but first the splash shield will have to be detached (Fig. 10.67).

7   *On 30 series and 1600 models,* the radio securing screws are accessible after first withdrawing the instrument trim panel (Fig. 10.68).

33   Seat belt electrical interlock system

1   Vehicles produced for operation in North America are fitted with an elaborate warning and safety interlock system. Basically, if either of the two front seats are occupied but the respective seat belt is not fastened, the following system functions are actuated.

   a) A warning buzzer and lamp actuate if the ignition key is turned to the 'START' position.
   b) The starter will not operate if the key is turned. The starter will operate if the driver's seat belt is connected

and there is no weight on the passenger front seat also if the seat belt on the unoccupied front seat is fully retracted.

2   The engine can be started for repairs, tuning etc. by reaching in through one of the side windows to turn the ignition key. Although the seat belts are not fastened neither is there any weight on the front seats to actuate the interlock system devices.

3   On vehicles equipped with automatic transmission, a neutral safety switch is fitted to the transmission.

4   A deceleration (G) sensor is incorporated which locks the inertia type seat belts in advance of impact should a collision occur.

5   Individual components of the system are sealed units and they can only be renewed as such. Any maintenance should be limited to checking the security of the connecting wires.

6   On vehicles operating in Canada, the system is similar except that the starter interlock capabillty is excluded.

7   An overriding emergency system cancel switch is located in the engine compartment.

34   Electro Sensor Panel - description, removal and refitting

1   This device is fitted to late model vehicles operating in North America.

Fig. 10.71. Electro Sensor Panel check button

Fig. 10.72. Removing interior rear view mirror

Fig. 10.73. Removing interior light unit

Fig. 10.74. Removing - roof console retaining screw

Fig. 10.75. ESP computer location (1) Computer (2) Relay

Fig. 10.76. ESP computer removed

180

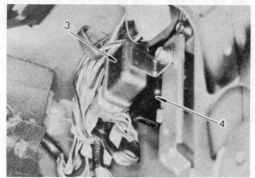

Fig. 10.77. Location of choke control relay (3) and stop lamp failure relay (4)

Fig. 10.78. Stop lamp failure relay removed

Fig. 10.79. Disc pad wear sensor

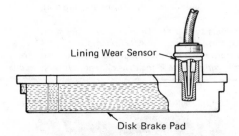

Lining Wear Sensor

Disk Brake Pad

Fig. 10.80. Cut-away view of disc pad wear sensor

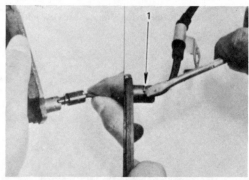

Fig. 10.81. Detaching sensor wire clamp (1) from disc pad

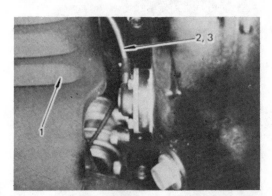

Fig. 10.82. Location of engine oil level (1) Under shield (2) Cable connector (3) Cable clamp

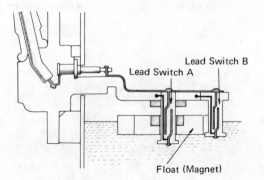

Lead Switch B

Lead Switch A

Float (Magnet)

Fig. 10.83. Diagrammatic view of engine oil level sensor

Fig. 10.84. Turning engine oil level sensor prior to removal

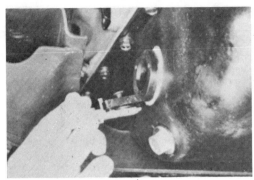

Fig. 10.85. Withdrawing engine oil level sensor and float from engine sump

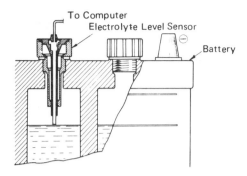

Fig. 10.86. Battery electrolyte sensor

2   It is designed to monitor the following components and in the event of a fault occurring or wear having taken place, the appropriate indicator message will illuminate on the roof interior mounted console.

    a) *Brake stop lamps (fuse or bulb failure)*
    b) *Engine oil level (level too low)*
    c) *Disc brake pads (thickness of friction material below specification)*
    d) *Battery electrolyte level (lower than specified level).*

3   In addition, warning lights are fitted to the instrument panel to draw attention to the fact that one of the indicator lights on the roof console is illuminated.
4   When the ignition key is turned 'ON', the warning lights of the system should come on. Periodically check the indicator panel lights. To do this, depress the check button while the ignition is switched 'ON'. The console indicator message will now light up in succession. If one does not, check the bulb and wiring connections (Fig. 10.71).
5   The individual components of the circuit should be removed in the following manner; if the fault arises in one particular circuit, have the component tested by your dealer and if faulty renew it by installing a new part.
6   **The roof-mounted console** can be removed after disconnecting the main battery fusible link and the interior rear view mirror. Remove the interior light and the indicator console from the roof. Disconnect the wiring and renew any bulbs as necessary (Figs. 10.72, 10.73 and 10.74).

7   **The computer** can be removed after first lifting out the windscreen washer reservoir and the relay adjacent to it to give access to the computer securing bolt. This work is carried out within the engine compartment.
  Working under the instrument panel disconnect the electrical wiring from the computer and then remove it (Figs. 10.75 and 10.76).
8   **The brake stoplight failure indicator relay** is removable after first withdrawing the computer and the side trim panel from under the instrument panel. Now the stoplamp failure relay and the choke control relay can be removed together by unscrewing the mounting bracket bolts (Figs. 10.77 and 10.78).
9   **The disc pad wear sensor,** can be removed after jacking up the front of the vehicle, removing the roadwheel and withdrawing the pad wear sensor wiring clamp. Disconnect the lead at the connector plug, remove the caliper cylinder and the brake pads. Detach the sensor from the pad (Figs. 10.79, 10.80 and 10.81).
10 **The engine oil level sensor,** can be removed after draining the engine oil and removing the engine undershield. Disconnect the lead to the sensor at the connector plug. Remove the lead clamp and unscrew the three securing bolts from the sensor. Turn the sensor through 180° (½ turn) in an anticlockwise direction and then withdraw it carefully taking care not to catch the float mechanism on the sump (Figs. 10.82, 10.83, 10.84 and 10.85).
11 **The battery electrolyte sensor** is removed simply by pulling it from the cell plug hole (Fig. 10.86).
12 Refitting in all cases is a reversal of removal.

Fault diagnosis overleaf

35 Fault diagnosis - electrical system

Symptom	Cause
Starter motor fails to turn engine	
No electricity at starter motor	Battery discharged.
	Battery defective internally.
	Battery terminal leads loose or earth lead not securely attached to body.
	Loose or broken connections in starter motor circuit.
	Starter motor switch or solenoid faulty.
Electricity at starter motor: faulty motor	Starter brushes badly worn, sticking or brush wires loose.
	Commutator dirty, worn or burnt.
	Starter motor armature faulty.
	Field coils earthed.
Starter motor turns engine very slowly	
Electrical defects	Battery in discharged condition.
	Starter brushes badly worn, sticking or brush wires loose.
	Loose wires in starter motor circuit.
Starter motor operates without turning engine	
Mechanical damage	Pinion or flywheel gear teeth broken or worn.
Starter motor noisy or excessively rough engagement	
Lack of attention or mechanical damage	Pinion or flywheel gear teeth broken or worn.
	Starter motor retaining bolts loose.
Battery will not hold charge for more than a few days	
Wear or damage	Battery defective internally.
	Electrolyte level too low or electrolyte too weak due to leakage.
	Plate separators no longer fully effective.
	Battery plates severely sulphated.
Insufficient current flow to keep battery charged	Battery plates severely sulphated.
	Drive belt slipping.
	Battery terminal connections loose or corroded.
	Alternator not charging.
	Short in lighting circuit causing continual battery drain.
	Regulator unit not working correctly.
Ignition light fails to go out, battery runs flat in a few days	
Alternator not charging	Drive belt loose and slipping or broken.
	Brushes worn, sticking, broken or dirty.
	Brush springs weak or broken.
Regulator fails to work correctly	Regulator incorrectly set.
	Open circuit in wiring of regulator unit.

Failure of individual electrical equipment to function correctly is dealt with alphabetically, item-by-item, under the headings listed below:

Horn	
Horn operates all the time	Horn push either earthed or stuck down.
	Horn cable to horn push earthed.
Horn fails to operate	Blown fuse.
	Cable or cable connection loose, broken or disconnected.
	Horn has an internal fault.
Horn emits intermittent or unsatisfactory noise	Cable connections loose.
	Horn incorrectly adjusted.
Lights	
Lights do not come on	If engine not running, battery discharged.
	Light bulb filament burnt out or bulbs broken.
	Wire connections loose, disconnected or broken.
	Light switch shorting or otherwise faulty.
Lights come on but fade out	If engine not running battery discharged.
	Light bulb filament burnt out or bulbs or sealed beam units broken.
	Wire connections loose, disconnected or broken.
	Light switch shorting or otherwise faulty.

Symptom	Cause
Lights give very poor illumination	Lamp glasses dirty. Lamps badly out of adjustment. Incorrect bulb with too low wattage fitted. Existing bulbs old and badly discoloured.
Lights work erratically - flashing on and off, especially over bumps	Battery terminals or earth connection loose. Lights not earthing properly. Contacts in light switch faulty.

Wipers

Symptom	Cause
Wiper motor fails to work	Blown fuse. Wire connections loose, disconnected, or broken. Brushes badly worn. Armature worn or faulty. Field coils faulty.
Wiper motor works very slowly and takes excessive current	Commutator dirty, greasy or burnt. Armature bearings dirty or unaligned. Armature badly worn or faulty. Armature thrust adjuster screw overtightened.
Wiper motor works slowly and takes little current	Brushes badly worn. Commutator dirty, greasy or burnt. Armature badly worn or faulty.

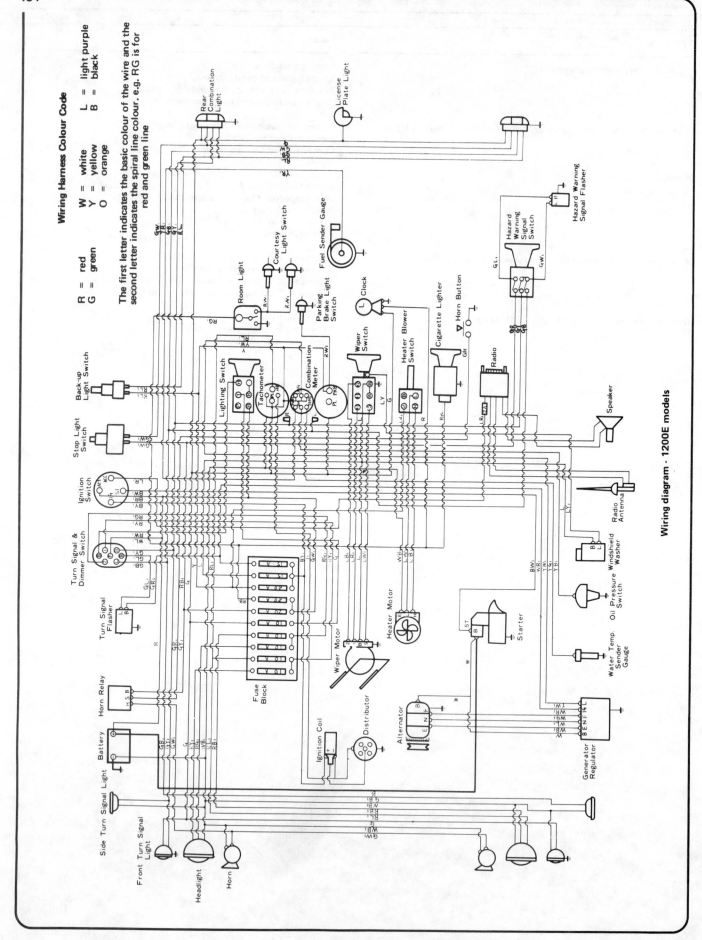

Wiring diagram - 1200E models

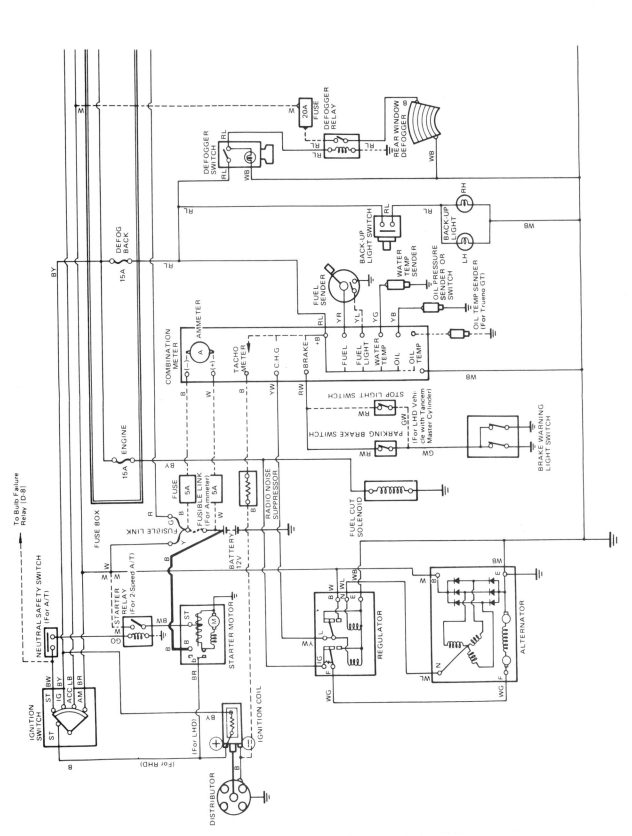

Wiring diagram - 30 Series and 1600 models (1975 on) except North America

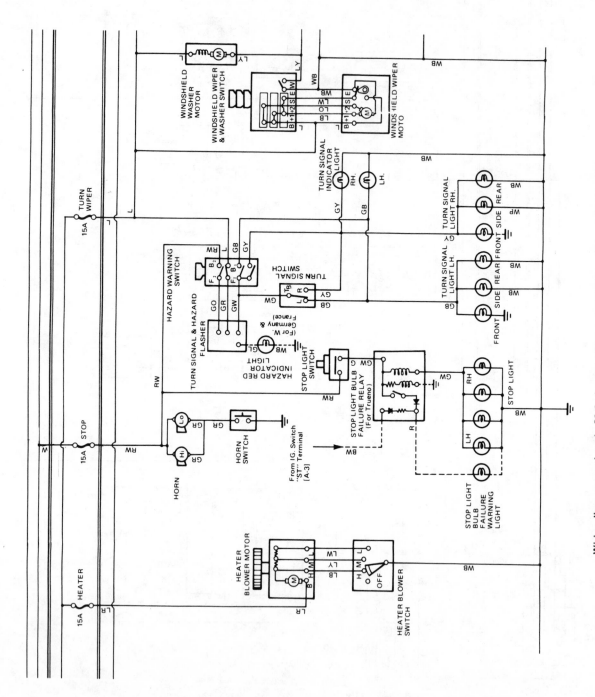

Wiring diagram continued - 30 Series and 1600 models (1975 on) except N. America

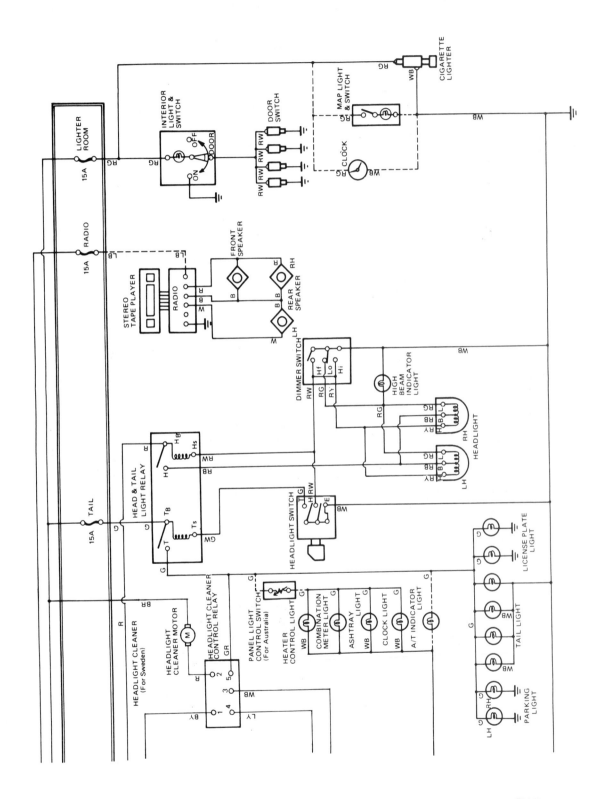

Wiring diagram continued - 30 Series and 1600 models (1975 on) except N. America

GRID LOCATION	COMPONENTS
E-2	ALTERNATOR
B-4	AMMETER
C-3	BATTERY
E-16	CIGARETTE LIGHTER
D-15	CLOCK
B-4	COMBINATION METER
D-6	DEFOGGER, REAR WINDOW
C-1	DISTRIBUTOR
C-9	FLASHER, TURN SIGNAL & HAZARD
D-3	FUEL CUT SOLENOID
D-4	FUEL GAUGE
D-5	FUEL SENDER
A-3	FUSE BOX
B-3	FUSIBLE LINK
C-8	HORN, LO · HI
C-1	IGNITION COIL
	LIGHTS:
D-12	ASHTRAY
E-12	AUTOMATIC T/M INDICATOR
E-5	BACK-UP, LH · RH
C-4	BRAKE WARNING
D-12	CLOCK
D-12	COMBINATION METER
C-4	DISCHARGE WARNING
D-4	FUEL LEVEL
C-8	HAZARD RED INDICATOR
E-13	HEADLIGHT, LH · RH
D-12	HEATER CONTROL
E-14	HIGH BEAM INDICATOR
C-16	INTERIOR
F-12	LICENSE PLATE
D-16	MAP
D-4	OIL PRESSURE WARNING
F-11	PARKING
F-8	STOP, LH · RH
F-7	STOP LIGHT BULB FAILURE WARNING
F-12	TAIL, LH · RH
E-9	TURN SIGNAL, LH
E-10	TURN SIGNAL, RH
D-10	TURN SIGNAL INDICATOR, LH · RH
	MOTORS:
B-12	HEADLIGHT CLEANER (For Sweden)
C-7	HEATER BLOWER

GRID LOCATION	COMPONENTS
C-2	STARTER
C-10	WINDSHIELD WASHER
E-10	WINDSHIELD WIPER
D-4	OIL PRESSURE GAUGE
E-5	OIL PRESSURE SENDER
D-4	OIL TEMP GAUGE (For Trueno GT)
E-4	OIL TEMP SENDER (For Trueno GT)
C-14	RADIO
C-3	RADIO NOISE SUPPRESSOR
D-2	REGULATOR
	RELAYS:
D-6	DEFOGGER
C-12	HEADLIGHT CLEANER CONTROL (For Sweden)
B-13	HEAD & TAIL LIGHT
B-2	STARTER (For 2-Speed A/T)
D-8	STOP LIGHT BULB FAILURE (For Trueno)
C-15	SPEAKER, FRONT
D-14	SPEAKER, REAR (OPT)
B-14	STEREO TAPE PLAYER (OPT)
	SWITCHES:
D-5	BACK-UP LIGHT
F-4	BRAKE WARNING LIGHT
C-6	DEFOGGER
D-14	DIMMER
D-16	DOOR
C-9	HAZARD WARNING
D-13	HEADLIGHT
E-7	HEATER BLOWER
C-8	HORN
A-1	IGNITION
C-16	INTERIOR LIGHT
D-16	MAP LIGHT
A-2	NEUTRAL SAFETY (For A/T)
E-5	OIL PRESSURE
C-12	PANEL LIGHT CONTROL (For Australia)
D-4	PARKING BRAKE
D-4, D-9	STOP LIGHT
D-9	TURN SIGNAL
C-11	WINDSHIELD WIPER AND WASHER
C-4	TACHOMETER
D-4	WATER TEMPERATURE GAUGE
D-5	WATER TEMPERATURE SENDER

— Note —

When reading the wiring diagram, following would be noted.

1. WIRING COLOR CODE IS SHOWN WITH ALPHABETICAL LETTER/S.
   THE FIRST LETTER INDICATES THE BASIC COLOR FOR THE WIRE, AND THE SECOND LETTER INDICATES THE SPIRAL LINE COLOR.

   B=BLACK   O=ORANGE   W=WHITE
   G=GREEN   R=RED   Y=YELLOW
   L=LIGHT BLUE

   EXAMPLE : RG, IS FOR RED AND A GREEN LINE.

2. LEGEND IN THE BRACKET [ ] OF THE WIRING DIAGRAM SHOWS THE GRID LOCATION OF MATING CONNECTION.

3. BROKEN LINES IN THE WIRING DIAGRAM ARE FOR VARIED MODELS OR OPTIONAL EQUIPMENT.

Wiring diagram - 30 Series and 1600 models (1975 on) except North America

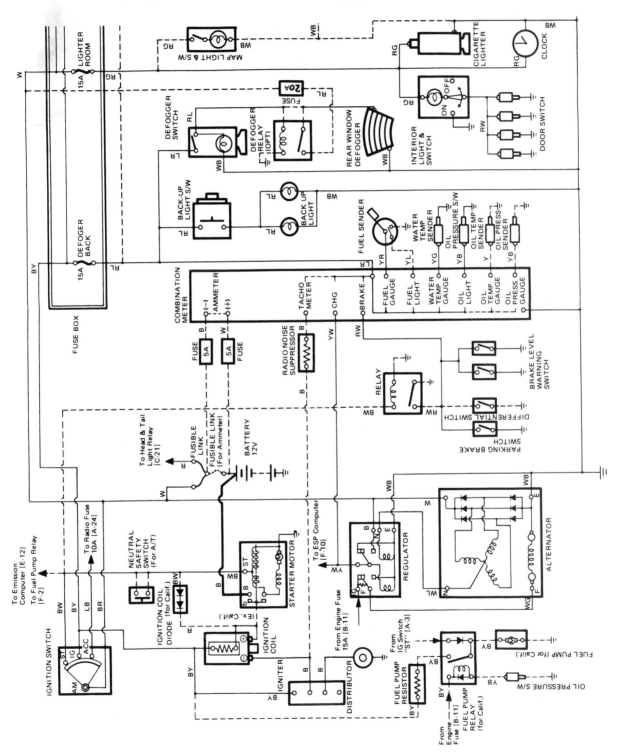

Wiring diagram - Corolla (North America) 1975 to 1977

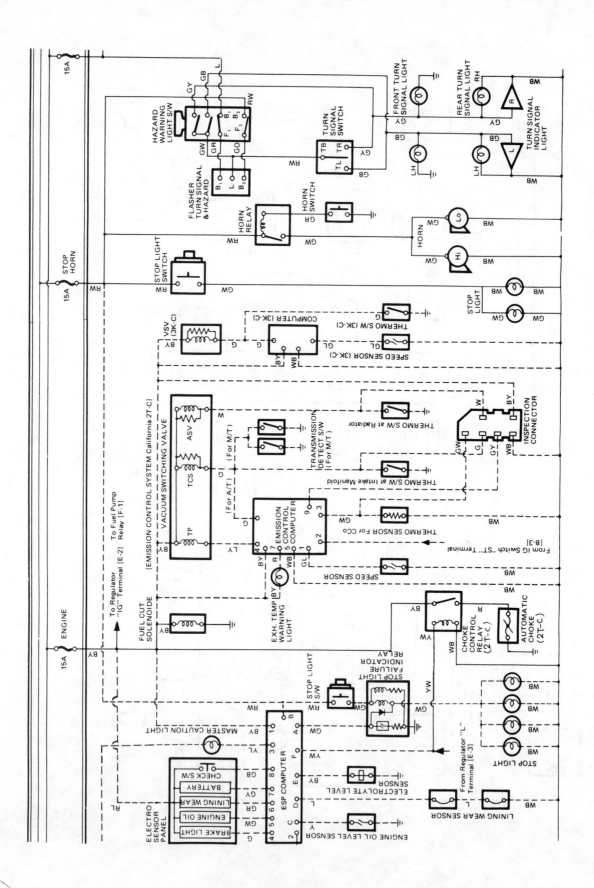

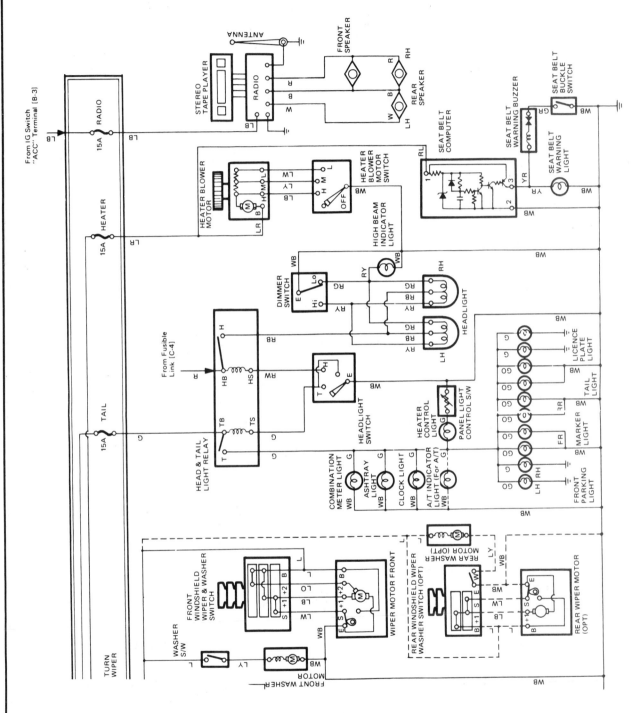

Wiring diagram continued - N. America 1975 - 1977

GRID LOCATION	COMPONENTS	GRID LOCATION	COMPONENTS
G-3	ALTERNATOR	G-22	LICENSE PLATE
D-6	AMMETER	F-6	LOW OIL PRESSURE WARNING
D-25	ANTENNA	C-9	MAP (For TE37)
G-11	AUTOMATIC CHOKE	G-21	MARKER, FRONT SIDE, LH. RH.
		G-21	MARKER, REAR SIDE, LH. RH.
D-4	BATTERY	G-20	PARKING, LH. RH.
		G-15	STOP, LH. RH.
G-9	CIGARETTE LIGHTER	G-21	TAIL, LH. RH.
G-9	CLOCK	F-17	TURN SIGNAL, LH. Front & Rear
C-6	COMBINATION METER	F-17	TURN SIGNAL, RH. Front & Rear
		H-17	TURN SIGNAL INDICATOR, LH. RH.
E-8	DEFOGGER, REAR WINDOW		MOTORS:
E-1	DISTRIBUTOR	C-23	HEATER BLOWER
	EMISSION CONTROL SYSTEM (For California 2T-C):	D-2	STARTER
D-13	EMISSION CONTROL COMPUTER	D-18	WINDSHIELD WASHER, Front
E-12	EXH. TEMP WARNING LIGHT	F-19	WINDSHIELD WASHER, Rear (OPT)
G-14	INSPECTION CONNECTOR	E-19	WINDSHIELD WIPER, Front
F-12	SPEED SENSOR	G-19	WINDSHIELD WIPER, Rear (OPT)
F-13	THERMO SENSOR For CCo		
F-13	THERMO SWITCH at INTAKE MANIFOLD	G-6	OIL PRESSURE GAUGE (For TE37)
F-14	THERMO SWITCH at RADIATOR	G-7	OIL PRESSURE SENDER (For TE37)
C-13	VACUUM SWITCHING VALVE	G-6	OIL TEMPERATURE GAUGE (For TE37)
	EMISSION CONTROL SYSTEM (For Canada 3K-C):	F-7	OIL TEMPERATURE SENDER (For TE37)
E-15	EMISSION CONTROL COMPUTER	D-25	RADIO
F-15	SPEED SENSOR	D-5	RADIO NOISE SUPPRESSOR
F-15	THERMO SWITCH	F-3	REGULATOR
C-15	VACUUM SWITCHING VALVE		RELAYS:
	ESP (For TE 37):	G-11	CHOKE CONTROL
D-10	CHECK SWITCH	D-8	DEFOGGER (OPT)
C-9	ELECTRO SENSOR PANEL	F-1	FUEL PUMP (For California)
F-10	ELECTROLYTE LEVEL SENSOR	C-20	HEAD & TAIL LIGHT
F-9	ENGINE OIL LEVEL SENSOR	D-16	HORN
E-9	ESP COMPUTER	E-5	RELAY for PKB Light Inspection
G-9	LINING WEAR SENSOR		SEAT BELT SYSTEM:
D-10	MASTER CAUTION LIGHT	H-25	SEAT BELT BUCKLE SWITCH
G-10	STOP LIGHT	F-24	SEAT BELT COMPUTER
F-11	STOP LIGHT FAILURE INDICATOR RELAY	G-24	SEAT BELT WARNING BUZZER
F-11	STOP LIGHT SWITCH	H-24	SEAT BELT WARNING LIGHT
C-16	FLASHER, TURN SIGNAL & HAZARD	E-25	SPEAKER, FRONT
C-11	FUEL CUT SOLENOID	E-25	SPEAKER, REAR LH. RH.
E-6	FUEL GAUGE	C-25	STEREO TAPE PLAYER
G-2	FUEL PUMP (For California)		SWITCHES:
F-1	FUEL PUMP RESISTOR (For California)	C-7	BACK-UP LIGHT
E-7	FUEL SENDER	G-5	BRAKE LEVEL WARNING
B-5	FUSE BOX	C-8	DEFOGGER, REAR WINDOW
F-11	FUSE, EXTERNAL (For Automatic Choke)	G-4	DIFFERENTIAL
D-8	FUSE, EXTERNAL (For Defogger)	D-22	DIMMER
C-5	FUSES, EXTERNAL (For Ammeter)	G-8	DOOR
C-4	FUSIBLE LINKS	C-17	HAZARD WARNING LIGHT
C-4	FUSIBLE LINK, SHUNT (For Ammeter)	E-21	HEADLIGHT
F-16	HORNS, LO·HI.	E-24	HEATER BLOWER MOTOR
D-2	IGNITION COIL	E-16	HORN
C-2	IGNITION COIL DIODE (For California)	A-1	IGNITION
D-1	IGNITER	F-8	INTERIOR LIGHT
	LIGHTS:	C-9	MAP LIGHT (For TE37)
E-20	ASHTRAY	B-3	NEUTRAL SAFETY
F-20	AUTOMATIC TRANSMISSION INDICATOR	F-7,G-1	OIL PRESSURE
D-7	BACK-UP, LH. RH.	F-21	PANEL LIGHT CONTROL
E-6	BRAKE WARNING	G-4	PARKING BRAKE
E-20	CLOCK	C-15	STOP LIGHT
E-20	COMBINATION METER	E-17	TURN SIGNAL
E-6	DISCHARGE WARNING	C-19	WINDSHIELD WIPER AND WASHER, Front
F-6	FUEL REMAINING WARNING (For California)	F-19	WINDSHIELD WIPER AND WASHER, Rear (OPT)
F-22	HEADLIGHT, LH. RH.	D-6	TACHOMETER
F-21	HEATER CONTROL	F-6	WATER TEMPERATURE GAUGE
E-23	HIGH BEAM INDICATOR	F-7	WATER TEMPERATURE SENDER
F-8	INTERIOR		

~ Note ~

When reading the wiring diagram, following should be noted.

1. WIRING COLOR CODE IS SHOWN WITH ALPHABETICAL LETTER/S.
    THE FIRST LETTER INDICATES THE BASIC COLOR FOR THE WIRE, AND THE SECOND LETTER INDICATES THE SPIRAL LINE COLOR.

B=BLACK	O=ORANGE	W=WHITE
G=GREEN	R=RED	Y=YELLOW
L=LIGHT BLUE		

    EXAMPLE : RG, IS FOR RED AND A GREEN LINE.

2. LEGEND IN THE BRACKET [ ] OF THE WIRING DIAGRAM SHOWS THE GRID LOCATION OF MATING CONNECTION.

3. BROKEN LINES IN THE WIRING DIAGRAM ARE FOR VARIED MODELS OR OPTIONAL EQUIPPMENT.

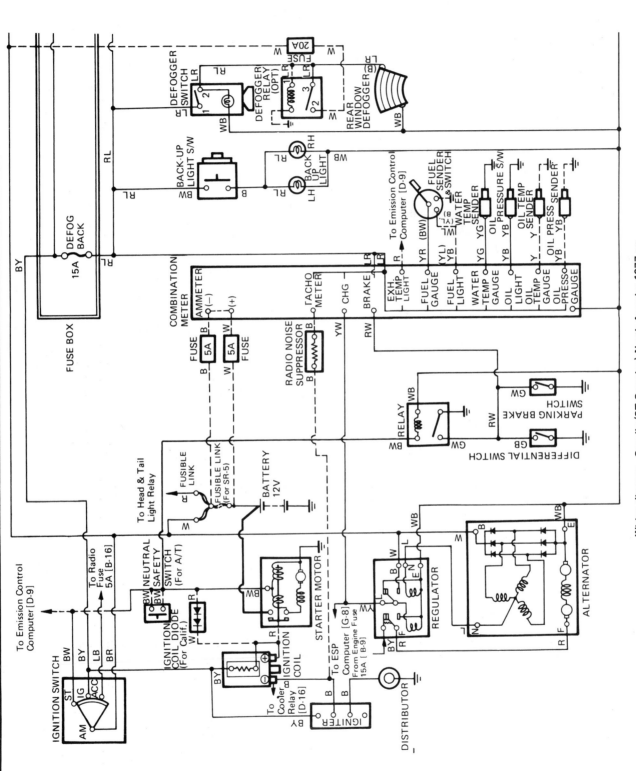

Wiring diagram - Corolla (2T-C engine) North America 1977 on

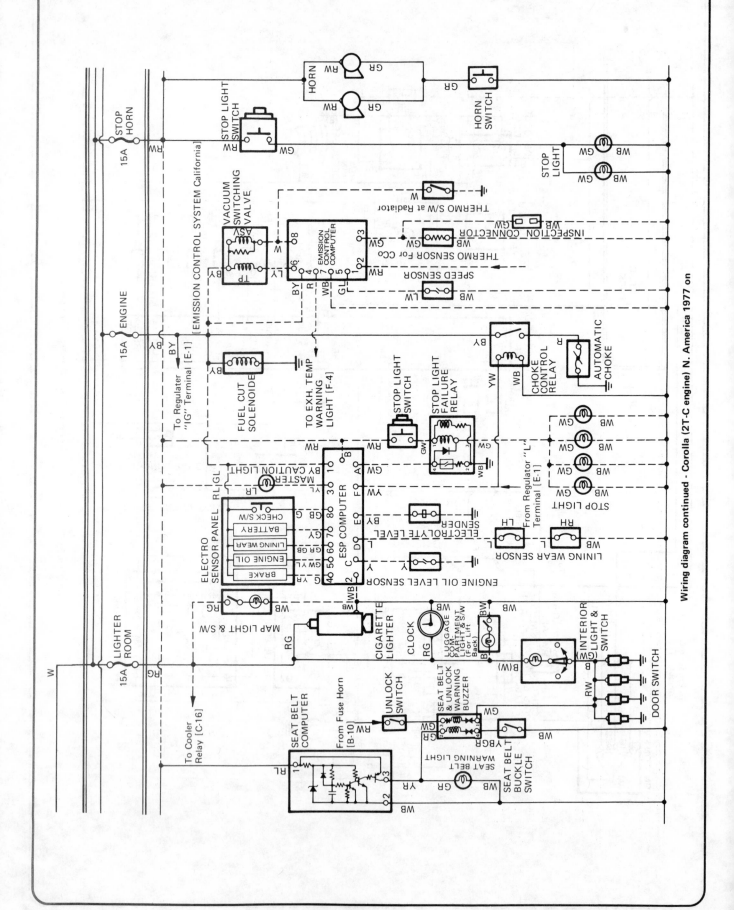

Wiring diagram continued - Corolla (2T-C engine) N. America 1977 on

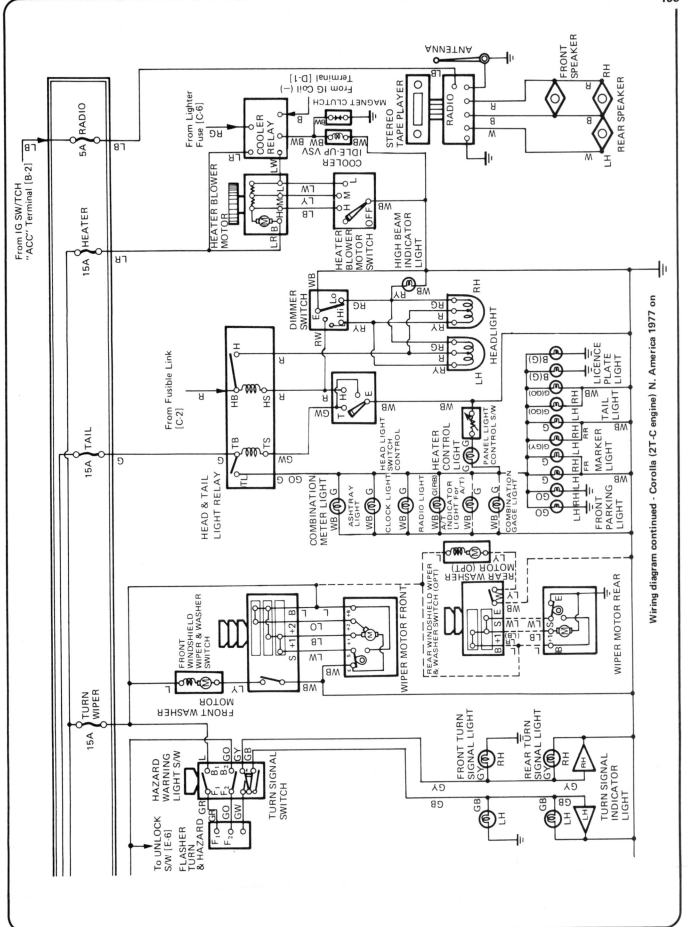

Wiring diagram continued - Corolla (2T-C engine) N. America 1977 on

Group 1

FIG. 1	FIG. 2	FIG. 3	COMPONENTS
G-2	G-3	A	ALTERNATER
C-4	G-8	E	AMMETER (For Hardtop, SR-5 Only)
C-4	D-7-8	E	AMMETER (For Coupe & Lift Back, SR-5 Only)
F-16	–	E	ANTENNA
G-9	C-3	D	AUTOMATIC CHOKE
D-2	E-2	A	BATTERY
D-16	A-3	B	COOLER IDLE-UP VSV (For Cooler)
D-7	G-8	E	CIGARETTE LIGHTER (For Sedan, Hardtop & Wagon)
D-7	C-6	E	CIGARETTE LIGHTER (For Coupe & Lift Back)
F-7	F-8	E	CLOCK (For Sedan, Hardtop & Wagon)
F-7	F-9	E	CLOCK (For Hardtop SR-5)
F-7	D-7	E	CLOCK (For Coupe & Lift Back)
C-4	D~G 7~9	E	COMBINATION METER
E-5	B-10	I·J	DEFOGGER, REAR WINDOW (For Sedan & Hardtop)
E-5	C-13	I·J	DEFOGGER, REAR WINDOW (For Wagon)
E-5	E-12	I·J	DEFOGGER, REAR WINDOW (For Coupe)
E-5	G-13	I·J	DEFOGGER, REAR WINDOW (For Lift Back)
E-1	–	B	DISTRIBUTOR
			EMISSION CONTROL SYSTEM (For California)
D-9	F-5	E	EMISSION CONTROL COMPUTER
F-4	F-7	E	EXH. TEMP WARNING LIGHT (For Sedan, Hardtop, Wagon)
F-4	F-8	E	EXH. TEMP WARNING LIGHT (For Hardtop SR-5)
F-4	E-9	E	EXH. TEMP WARNING LIGHT (For Coupe, Lift Back)
F-10	F-5	E	INSPECTION CONNECTOR
E-9	F-8	E	SPEED SENSOR (For Sedan, Hardtop, Wagon)
E-9	F-9	E	SPEED SENSOR (For Hardtop SR-5)
E-9	E-7	E	SPEED SENSOR (For Coupe & Lift Back)
E-9	C-4	E	THERMO SENSOR (For CCo)
E-10	D-1	E	THERMO SWITCH
C-9	C-2	B	VACUUM SWITCHING VALVE
			ESP SYSTEM (For Hardtop SR-5):
C-7	B-7	E·F	CHECK SWITCH
C-7	B-7	E·F	ELECTRO SENSOR PANEL
E-8	H-1	A	ELECTROLYTE LEVEL SENSOR
F-7	D-3	B	ENGINE OIL LEVEL SENSOR
D-8	A-6	F	ESP COMPUTER
F-7	H-3	A	LINING WEAR SENSOR, LH
G-7	B-3	B	LINING WEAR SENSOR, RH
D-8	F-8	E	MASTER CAUTION LIGHT
G-8	B-13	I	STOP LIGHT, LH
G-8	A-13	J	STOP LIGHT, RH
E-8	B-7	F	STOP LIGHT FAILURE INDICATOR RELAY
E-8	F-5	E	STOP LIGHT SWITCH
C-11	H-6	E	FLASHER, TURN SIGNAL & HAZARD
C-9	C-3	D	FUEL CUT SOLENOID
F-4	E-8	E	FUEL GAUGE (For Sedan, Hardtop & Wagon)
F-4	F-8	E	FUEL GAUGE (For Hardtop SR 5)
F-4	E-8	E	FUEL GAUGE (For Coupe & Lift Back)
F-4	A-12	I	FUEL SENDER (For Sedan, Hardtop)
F-4	D-13	I·J	FUEL SENDER (For Wagon)
F-4	F-11	I·J	FUEL SENDER (For Coupe)
F-4	G-14	I·J	FUEL SENDER (For Lift Back)
B-3	F-4	E	FUSE BOX
E-5	A-7	F	FUSE, EXTERNAL (For Defogger)
C-3	F-1	A	FUSES, EXTERNAL (For Ammeter)
C-2	F-2	A	FUSIBLE LINKS
D-11	E-1	A	HORN, LH
D-11	D-1	B	HORN, RH
D-1	A-2	B	IGNITION COIL
C-2	A-2	B	IGNITION COIL DIODE (For California)
E-1	–	B	IGNITER
			LIGHTS:
E-13	H-8	E	ASHTRAY INDICATOR (For Sedan, Hardtop & Wagon)
E-13	C-6	E	ASHTRAY INDICATOR (For Coupe, Lift Back)
F-13	C-5	E	AUTOMATIC TRANSMISSION INDICATOR
D-5	B-13	I	BACK-UP, LH (For Sedan & Hardtop)
D-5	D-12	I	BACK-UP, LH (For Wagon)
D-5	F-13	I	BACK-UP, LH (For Coupe)
D-5	H-13	I	BACK-UP, LH (For Lift Back)
D-5	A-13	J	BACK-UP, RH (For Sedan & Hardtop)
D-5	C-12	J	BACK-UP, RH (For Wagon)
D-5	E-13	J	BACK-UP, RH (For Coupe)
D-5	G-13	J	BACK-UP, RH (For Lift Back)
E-4	E-7	E	BRAKE WARNING (For Sedan, Hardtop & Wagon)
E-4	F-8	E	BRAKE WARNING (For Hardtop SR-5)
E-4	E-9	E	BRAKE WARNING (For Coupe & Lift Back)
F-13	D-7	E	CLOCK
G-13	G-8	E	COMBINATION GAUGE (For Hardtop SR-5)
G-13	D-8	E	COMBINATION GAUGE (For Coupe & Lift Back SR-5)
E-13	F-7	E	COMBINATION METER (For Sedan, Hardtop & Wagon)

Group 2

FIG. 1	FIG. 2	FIG. 3	COMPONENTS
E-13	E-8	E	COMBINATION METER (For Hardtop SR-5)
E-13	E-9	E	COMBINATION METER (For Coupe & Lift Back)
C-4	E-8	E	DISCHARGE WARNING (For Sedan, Hardtop & Wagon)
C-4	F-8	E	DISCHARGE WARNING (For Hardtop SR-5)
C-4	E-9	E	DISCHARGE WARNING (For Coupe & Lift Back)
F-4	E-7	E	FUEL REMAINING WARNING (Sedan, Hardtop & Wagon for Calif.)
F-4	E-8	E	FUEL REMAINING WARNING (Hardtop SR-5)
F-4	E-8	E	FUEL REMAINING WARNING (Coupe, Lift Back For Calif.)
F-14	F-1	A	HEADLIGHT, LH
F-15	C-1	B	HEADLIGHT, RH
E-15	H-7	E	HEATER CONTROL (For Sedan, Hardtop & Wagon)
E-15	D-6	E	HEATER CONTROL (For Lift Back & Coupe)
E-15	F-7	E	HIGH BEAM INDICATOR (For Sedan, Hardtop & Wagon)
E-15	F-9	E	HIGH BEAM INDICATOR (For Hardtop SR-5)
E-15	F-9	E	HIGH BEAM INDICATOR (For Lift Back & Coupe)
G-7	C-7	E·F	INTERIOR
G-7	B-8	E·F	INTERIOR (For Hardtop SR-5)
F-7	H-12	J	LUGGAGE COMPARTMENT (For Lift Back)
G-14	B-14	I·J	LICENSE PLATE (For Sedan, Hardtop)
G-14	C-14	I·J	LICENSE PLATE (For Wagon)
G-14	F-12	I·J	LICENSE PLATE (For Coupe)
G-14	G-14	I·J	LICENSE PLATE (For Lift Back)
G-4	E-7	E	LOW OIL PRESSURE WARNING (For Sedan, Hardtop & Wagon)
G-4	E-8	E	LOW OIL PRESSURE WARNING (For Lift Back & Coupe)
D-7	C-8	E·F	MAP (For Hardtop SR-5)
G-13	E-1	A	MARKER, FRONT SIDE, LH
G-13	C-2	B	MARKER, FRONT SIDE, RH
G-13	B-14	I	MARKER, REAR SIDE, LH (For Sedan & Hardtop)
G-13	D-12	I	MARKER, REAR SIDE, LH (For Wagon)
G-13	F-14	I	MARKER, REAR SIDE, LH (For Coupe)
G-13	A-14	J	MARKER, REAR SIDE, RH (For Sedan & Hardtop)
G-13	C-12	J	MARKER, REAR SIDE, RH (For Wagon)
G-13	E-14	J	MARKER, REAR SIDE, RH (For Coupe)
G-13	G-14	J	MARKER, REAR SIDE, RH (For Lift Back)
G-13	G-2	A	PARKING, LH
G-13	C-3	B	PARKING, RH
F-13	H-7	E	RADIO INDICATOR (For Sedan, Hardtop & Wagon)
F-13	D-7	E	RADIO INDICATOR (For Lift Back & Coupe)
G-10	B-13	I	STOP, LH (For Sedan & Hardtop)
G-10	D-12	I	STOP, LH (For Wagon)
G-10	F-13	I	STOP, LH (For Coupe)
G-10	H-13	I	STOP, LH (For Lift Back)
G-10	A-13	J	STOP, RH (For Sedan & Hardtop)
G-10	C-12	J	STOP, RH (For Wagon)
G-10	E-13	J	STOP, RH (For Coupe)
G-10	G-13	J	STOP, RH (For Lift Back)
G-14	B-13	I	TAIL, LH (For Sedan & Hardtop)
G-14	D-12	I	TAIL, LH (For Wagon)
G-14	F-13	I	TAIL, LH (For Coupe)
G-14	H-13	I	TAIL, LH (For Lift Back)
G-14	A-13	J	TAIL, RH (For Sedan & Hardtop)
G-14	C-12	J	TAIL, RH (For Wagon)
G-14	E-13	J	TAIL, RH (For Coupe)
G-14	G-13	J	TAIL, RH (For Lift Back)
F-11	G-2	A	TURN SIGNAL, FRONT, LH
F-11	C-3	B	TURN SIGNAL, FRONT, RH
G-11	B-13	I	TURN SIGNAL, REAR, LH (For Sedan & Hardtop)
G-11	D-12	I	TURN SIGNAL, REAR, LH (For Wagon)
G-11	F-13	I	TURN SIGNAL, REAR, LH (For Coupe)
G-11	H-13	I	TURN SIGNAL, REAR, LH (For Lift Back)
G-11	A-13	J	TURN SIGNAL, REAR, RH (For Sedan & Hardtop)
G-11	C-12	J	TURN SIGNAL, REAR, RH (For Wagon)
G-11	E-13	J	TURN SIGNAL, REAR, RH (For Coupe)
G-11	G-13	J	TURN SIGNAL, REAR, RH (For Lift Back)
H-11	E-7	E	TURN SIGNAL INDICATOR, LH (For Sedan, Hardtop & Wagon)
H-11	E-8	E	TURN SIGNAL INDICATOR, LH (For Hardtop SR-5)
H-11	E-9	E	TURN SIGNAL INDICATOR, LH (For Lift Back & Coupe)
H-11	F-7	E	TURN SIGNAL INDICATOR, RH (For Sedan, Hardtop & Wagon)
H-11	F-9	E	TURN SIGNAL INDICATOR, RH (For Hardtop SR-5)

Group 3

FIG. 1	FIG. 2	FIG. 3	COMPONENTS
H-11	D-8	E	TURN SIGNAL INDICATOR, RH (For Lift Back & Coupe)
D-16	D-3	B	MAGNET CLUTCH (For Cooler, OPT)
			MOTORS:
C-15	D-4	E	HEATER BLOWER
D-2	G-1	A	STARTER
C-12	B-4	D	WINDSHIELD WASHER, FRONT
F-13	D-12	I	WINDSHIELD WASHER, REAR (For Wagon, OPT)
F-13	H-11	J	WINDSHIELD WASHER, REAR (For Lift Back, OPT)
E-12	A-4	D	WINDSHIELD WIPER, FRONT
G-12	D-13	I·J	WINDSHIELD WIPER, REAR (For Wagon, OPT)
G-12	H-11	I·J	WINDSHIELD WIPER, REAR (For Lift Back, OPT)
G-4	G-8	E	OIL PRESSURE GAUGE (For Hardtop SR-5)
G-4	D-9	E	OIL PRESSURE GAUGE (For Lift Back & Coupe SR-5)
G-4	D-3	D	OIL TEMPERATURE SENDER (For SR-5)
F-14	H-7	E	RADIO (For Sedan, Hardtop & Wagon)
F-14	D-7	E	RADIO (For Coupe, Lift Back)
E-3	A-3	E	RADIO SUPPRESSOR (Only SR-5)
F-2	H-2	A	REGULATOR
			RELAYS:
F-9	B-6	F	CHOKE CONTROL
D-16	D-4	F	COOLER (OPT)
D-5	A-7	F	DEFOGGER (OPT)
C-14	H-2	A	HEAD & TAIL LIGHT CONTROL
F-3	B-7	A	RELAY (For Brake Warning Light Inspection)
			SEAT BELT SYSTEM:
D-6	C-4	E	SEAT BELT BUCKLE SWITCH
F-6	H-6	E	SEAT BELT WARNING BUZZER
D-6	H-6	E	SEAT BELT WARNING COMPUTER
F-6	E-7	E	SEAT BELT WARNING LIGHT (For Sedan, Hardtop & Wagon)
F-6	F-9	E	SEAT BELT WARNING LIGHT (For Hardtop SR-5)
F-6	E-8	E	SEAT BELT WARNING LIGHT (For Lift Back & Coupe)
G-16	–	E	SPEAKER, FRONT
H-16	B-11	I	SPEAKER, REAR (For Sedan & Hardtop)
H-16	E-10	I	SPEAKER, REAR (For Coupe)
H-16	H-11	I	SPEAKER, REAR (For Lift Back)
E-16	D-5	E	STEREO TAPE PLAYER
			SWITCHES:
C-5	F-3	F	BACK-UP LIGHT
C-5	G-7	E	DEFOGGER, REAR WINDOW (For Sedan, Hardtop & Wagon)
C-5	E-6	E	DEFOGGER, REAR WINDOW (For Coupe & Lift Back)
G-3	D-4	D	DIFFERENTIAL
D-14	E-4	E	DIMMER
G-6	H-7	E	DOOR, LH
G-6	A-5	F	DOOR, RH
F-4	A-12	I·J	FUEL REMAINING WARNING (For Sedan & Hardtop)
F-4	D-13	I·J	FUEL REMAINING WARNING (For Wagon)
F-4	F-11	I·J	FUEL REMAINING WARNING (For Coupe)
F-4	G-4	I·J	FUEL REMAINING WARNING (For Lift Back)
C-11	E-4	E	HAZARD WARNING LIGHT
E-14	E-4	E	HEADLIGHT CONTROL
E-15	C-5	E	HEATER BLOWER MOTOR
F-11	E-5	E	HORN
A-1	F-5	E	IGNITION
G-7	C-7	E·F	INTERIOR LIGHT
G-7	B-8	E·F	INTERIOR LIGHT (For Hardtop SR-5)
F-7	H-12	J	LUGGAGE COMPARTMENT
D-7	C-8	J	MAP LIGHT (For Hardtop SR-5)
C-2	E-3	F	NEUTRAL SAFETY (For A/T)
G-4	D-3	D	OIL PRESSURE
F-14	G-7	E	PANEL LIGHT CONTROL (For Sedan, Hardtop & Wagon)
F-14	D-7	E	PANEL LIGHT CONTROL (For Coupe & Lift Back)
G-3	C-4	E	PARKING BRAKE
C-10	F-5	E	STOP LIGHT (Exc. Hardtop SR-5)
C-11	E-4	E	TURN SIGNAL
D-12	E-5	E	UNLOCK WARNING
F-12	C-9	E	WINDSHIELD WIPER AND WASHER, FRONT
F-12	G-9	E	WINDSHIELD WIPER AND WASHER, REAR (OPT. For Wagon)
F-12	G-9	E	WINDSHIELD WIPER AND WASHER, REAR (OPT. For Lift Back)
E-4	E-8	E	TACHOMETER (For Hardtop SR-5)
E-4	E-9	E	TACHOMETER (For Coupe & Lift Back SR-5)
F-6	H-6	E	UNLOCK WARNING BUZZER
F-4	F-8	E	WATER TEMPERATURE GAUGE (For Sedan, Hardtop & Wagon)
F-4	D-8	E	WATER TEMPERATURE GAUGE (For Coupe & Lift Back)
F-4	G-3	A	WATER TEMPERATURE SENDER

Corolla (2T-C engine) North America 1977 on

Colour code:

B	=	Black	O =	Orange
Br	=	Brown	R =	Red
G	=	Green	W =	White
Gr	=	Grey	Y =	Yellow
L	=	Light Blue		

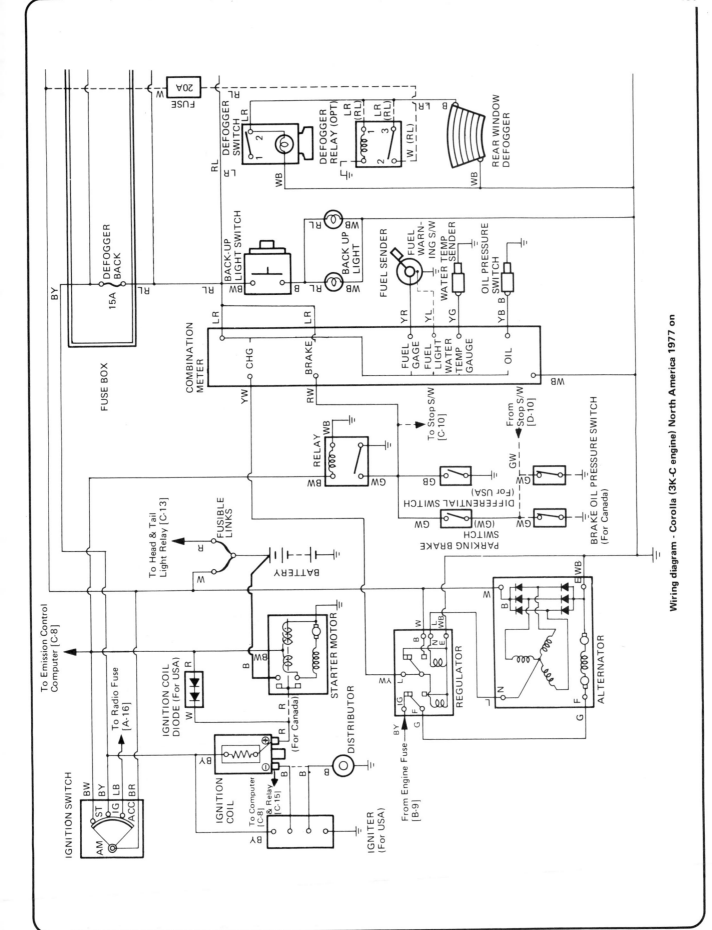

Wiring diagram - Corolla (3K-C engine) North America 1977 on

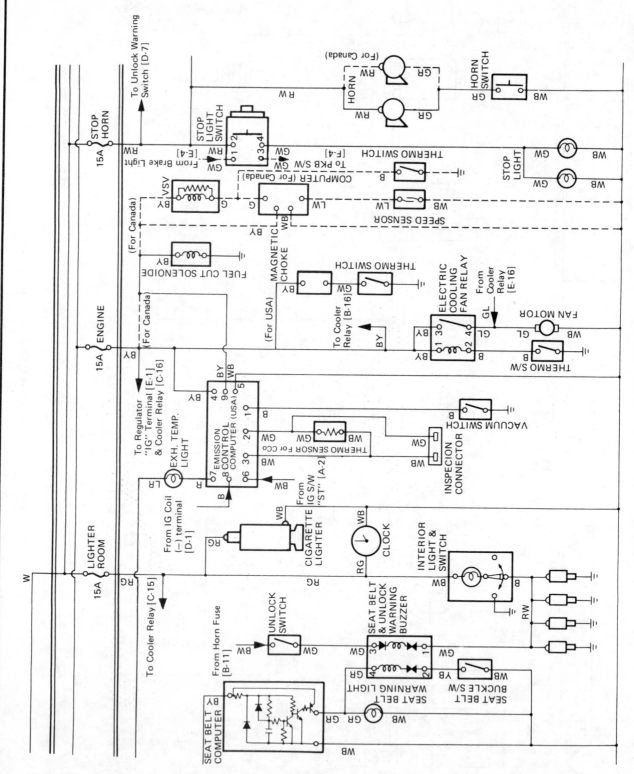

Wiring diagram continued - Corolla (3K-C engine) N. America 1977 on

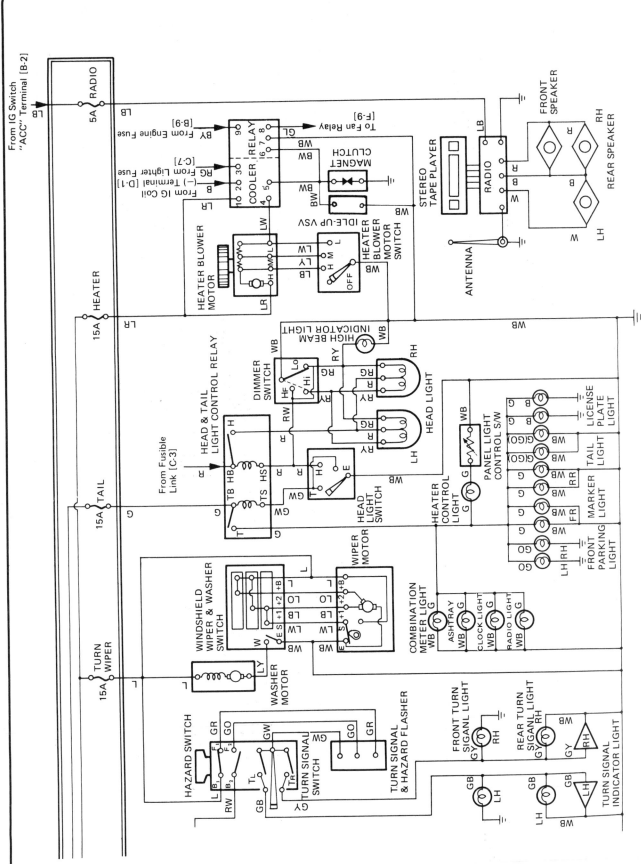

Wiring diagram continued - Corolla (3K-C engine) N. America 1977 on

GRID LOCATION			COMPONENTS
FIG. 1	FIG. 2	FIG. 3	
G-2	D-2	A	ALTERNATOR
F-15	—	E	ANTENNA
D-3	H-3	A	BATTERY
D-8	G-13	E	CIGARETTE LIGHTER
E-8	H-11	E	CLOCK
C-4	F-10	E	COMBINATION METER
	H-10		
F-6	D-12	I · J	DEFOGGER, REAR WINDOW
E-1	—	B	DISTRIBUTOR
			EMISSION CONTROL SYSTEM (U.S.A.):
D-8	G-6	E	EMISSION CONTROL COMPUTER
C-8	H-10	E	EXH. TEMP WARNING LIGHT
F-8	F-7	E	INSPECTION CONNECTOR
D-8	E-5	E	THERMO SENSOR (For CCo)
F-8	H-3	A	VACUUM SWITCH
			EMISSION CONTROL SYSTEM (Canada):
D-10	G-6	E	EMISSION CONTROL COMPUTER
F-10	H-11	E	SPEED SENSOR
F-10	E-4	B	THERMO SWITCH
F-11	E-6	E	FLASHER, TURN SIGNAL & HAZARD
C-10	G-5	C	FUEL CUT SOLENOID
F-4	G-10	E	FUEL GAUGE
E-5	A-12	I · J	FUEL SENDER
B-4	F-8	E	FUSE BOX
C-6	A·C-9	F	FUSE EXTERNAL (For Defogger, OPT)
C-3	H-3	A	FUSIBLE LINKS
E-11	C-1	B	HORN, LH (Canada only)
	E-1	A	HORN, RH
E-15	A-3	B	IDLE UP VSV (For Cooler)
C-1	D-2	D	IGNITION COIL
C-2	D-3	D	IGNITION COIL DIODE (For U.S.A.)
D-1	—	D	IGNITER (For U.S.A.)
			LIGHTS:
F-12	G-12	E	ASHTRAY
E-5	G-14	I	BACK-UP, LH
E-5	D-14	J	BACK-UP, RH
D-4	G-9	E	BRAKE WARNING
F-12	H-10	E	CLOCK
F-12	H-10	E	COMBINATION METER
D-4	G-10	E	DISCHARGE WARNING
F-4	G-10	E	FUEL WARNING
F-14	F-1	A	HEADLIGHT, LH
F-14	C-1	B	HEADLIGHT, RH
F-13	H-12	E	HEATER CONTROL
E-14	H-10	E	HIGH BEAM INDICATOR
F-7	B-6	E · F	INTERIOR
H-14	E-13	I · J	LICENSE PLATE
F-4	F-10	E	LOW OIL PRESSURE WARNING
H-13	G-1	A	MARKER, FRONT SIDE, LH
H-13	A-1	B	MARKER, FRONT SIDE, RH
H-13	H-14	I	MARKER, REAR SIDE, LH
H-13	C-14	J	MARKER, REAR SIDE, RH
H-13	F-2	I	PARKING, LH
H-13	C-3	J	PARKING, RH
G-12	G-11	E	RADIO
G-10	G-14	I	STOP, LH
G-10	D-14	J	STOP, RH
H-14	G-14	I	TAIL, LH
H-14	D-14	J	TAIL, RH
F-11	F-2	A	TURN SIGNAL, FRONT, LH
F-12	C-3	B	TURN SIGNAL, FRONT, RH
G-11	G-14	I	TURN SIGNAL, REAR, LH
G-12	D-14	J	TURN SIGNAL, REAR, RH
H-11	G·H-10	E	TURN SIGNAL INDICATOR, LH, RH
E-15	A-3	B	MAGNET CLUTCH
D-9	G-7	E	MAGNETIC CHOKE

GRID LOCATION			COMPONENTS
FIG. 1	FIG. 2	FIG. 3	
			MOTORS:
G-9	F-4	B	ELECTRIC COOLING FAN (For U.S.A.)
C-15	D-11	F	HEATER BLOWER
D-2	E-3	C	STARTER
D-12	B-4	D	WINDSHIELD WASHER
E-12	A-4	D	WINDSHIELD WIPER
G-15	G-11	E	RADIO
F-2	B-3	B	REGULATOR
			RELAYS:
D-15	D-10	F	COOLER (RELAY)
	E-10		
	C-8		
E-6	B-10	F	DEFOGGER (OPT. For U.S.A.)
E-6	D-8	F	DEFOGGER (OPT. For Canada)
F-9	D-9	F	ELECTRIC COOLING FAN
C-14	G-2	A	HEAD & TAIL LIGHT CONTROL (RELAY)
E-4	D-9	F	RELAY (For Brake Warning Light Inspection U.S.A. only)
			SEAT BELT SYSTEM:
F-7	F-5	G	SEAT BELT BUCKLE SWITCH
D-6	E-6	E	SEAT BELT COMPUTER
E-7	F-7	E	SEAT BELT WARNING BUZZER
E-6	G-9	E	SEAT BELT WARNING LIGHT
G-16	—	E	SPEAKER, FRONT
H-15	E-12	I	SPEAKER, REAR, LH
H-16	E-13	J	SPEAKER, REAR, RH
F-15	D-8	E	STEREO TAPE PLAYER
			SWITCHES:
D-5	C-5	E	BACK-UP LIGHT
G-3	G-4	C	BRAKE OIL PRESSURE (For Canada)
D-6	H-11	E	DEFOGGER, REAR WINDOW
F-3	A-4	D	DIFFERENTIAL (For U.S.A.)
E-14	E-10	E	DIMMER
G-7	E-7	E · G	DOOR, LH
G-7	B-8	F · H	DOOR, RH
F-5	A-12	I · J	FUEL WARNING
C-11	F-10	E	HAZARD WARNING LIGHT
E-13	E-11	E	HEADLIGHT
E-15	C-6	E	HEATER BLOWER MOTOR
G-11	E-11	E	HORN
A-1	F-9	E	IGNITION
F-7	B-6	E · F	INTERIOR LIGHT
F-5	D-4	D	OIL PRESSURE
G-13	H-11	E	PANEL LIGHT CONTROL
F-3	D-7	E · F	PARKING BRAKE
D-10	E-8	E	STOP LIGHT
E-11	F-11	E	TURN SIGNAL
G-9	C-1	B	THERMO (For Cooling Fan)
E-9	E-4	B	THERMO (For Magnetic Choke)
D-7	E-9	E	UNLOCK WARNING
C-12	F-11	E	WINDSHIELD WIPER AND WASHER
F-7	F-7	E	UNLOCK WARNING BUZZER
F-4	G-10	E	WATER TEMPERATURE GAUGE
F-5	E-4	B	WATER TEMPERATURE SENDER

Colour code:

B	=	Black	
Br	=	Brown	O = Orange
G	=	Green	R = Red
Gr	=	Grey	W = White
L	=	Light Blue	Y = Yellow

Corolla (3K-C engine) North America 1977 on

Chapter 11 Suspension and steering

Refer to Chapter 13 for specifications and information applicable to 1979 US models.

Contents

Specifications

Front suspension
Type ... ...   MacPherson struts, with stabiliser bar

Rear suspension
Type ... ...   Semi-elliptic leaf springs and telescopic shock absorbers

Steering
Type ... ...   Recirculating ball with collapsible type column
Oil capacity ... ...   ½ Imp. pt, ½ US pt, 0.25 litre

Steering angles (1200E)
Toe-in ... ...   0 to 0.08 in (0 to 2.0 mm)
Camber ... ...   50' positive
Castor ... ... 2° 0' positive
Steering axis inclination ... ... 7° 55'
Turning circle ... ...   29 ft 7 in (8.99 m)

Steering angles (30 Series and 1600 models)
Toe-in ... ...   0 to 0.08 in (0 to 2.0 mm)
Camber ... ... 0° 30' to 1° 30' positive
Castor ... ... 1° 20' to 2° 20' positive
Steering axis inclination ... ... 7° 20' to 8° 20'
Turning circle ... ...   31 ft (9.45 m)

Steering (full lock) angles
1200E
   Inner ... ... 38° 30' to 41° 30'
   Outer ... ... 30° 00' to 36° 00'
30 Series and 1600
   Inner ... ... 37° to 39°
   Outer ... ... 29° 25' to 33° 25'
Steering gear ratio
   1200E ... ...   18.1 : 1
   30 Series and 1600 ... ...   18.0 : 1

Roadwheels and tyres
Wheel size
   1200E ... ...   4J x 12
   30 Series, 1600 ... ...   4½J x 13
Tyre type ... ...   Radial ply

*Tyre sizes

	Standard
1200E	155 SR 12
30 Series, 1600	155 SR 13
SR5	165 SR 13

*Tyre pressures

	Front	Rear
1200E	24 lb/in^2 (1.68 kg/cm^2)	24 lb/in^2 (1.68 kg/cm^2)
30 Series and 1600	24 lb/in^2 (1.68 kg/cm^2)	24 lb/in^2 (1.68 kg/cm^2)
Saloon and Hardtop	24 lb/in^2 (1.68 kg/cm^2)	24 lb/in^2 (1.68 kg/cm^2)
Wagon	28 lb/in^2 (1.96 kg/cm^2)	28 lb/in^2 (1.96 kg/cm^2)
Liftback (SR5)	26 lb/in^2 (1.82 kg/cm^2)	26 lb/in^2 (1.82 kg/cm^2)

Also consult the vehicle sticker. Check pressures cold. For continuous high speeds, inflate 4 lb/in^2 (0.28 kg/cm^2) higher.

Torque wrench settings

	lb/ft	Nm
1200E		
Front suspension		
Front strut spindle to top mounting nut	38	53
Front strut top mounting to body nuts	15	21
Front strut to steering arm bolts	60	83
Strut bar (drag link) bracket bolts to body	30	41
Strut bar nuts to bracket	60	83
Strut bar bolts to track control arm	35	48
Track control arm pivot bolt to body crossmember	60	83
Track control arm balljoint to steering arm	60	83
Stabiliser bar drop link to track control arm (upper nut)	15	21
(lower nut)	10	14
Crossmember to bodyframe bolts	38	53
Engine mountings to crossmember nuts	38	53
Steering lock control bolt locknuts	15	21
Trackrod end locknuts	50	69
Balljoint taper pin nuts	50	69
Rear suspension		
Rear leaf spring front pivot bolt	20	28
Rear leaf spring rear shackle bolts	20	28
Rear spring 'U' bolt nuts	30	41
Rear shock absorber mounting bolts and nuts	20	28
Steering		
Steering wheel nut	22	30
Steering column upper clamp	30	41
Gearbox to bodyframe bolts	30	41
Drop arm to sector shaft nut	80	111
Idler arm bracket to bodyframe bolts	30	41
Idler arm pivot pin nut	50	69
Roadwheel nuts	65	90

30 Series and 1600 models

The torque wrench settings are similar to those for the 1200E except for the following variations.

Front suspension

Bolts are not used on the strut bar bracket to bodyframe

Rear suspension	lb/ft	Nm
Rear leaf spring front pivot bolt	38	53
Rear leaf spring rear shackle bolts	38	53

Steering		
Trackrod end clamp pinch bolt	15	21
Column upper bracket (break-away type)		
Upper bolts	10	14
Lower bolts	30	41
Steering flexible coupling pinch bolt	20	28
Idler arm pivot pin nut	60	83
Idler arm bracket to bodyframe bolts	40	55

1 General description

1 *The front suspension* fitted to all models is of MacPherson strut type. The struts are secured at their upper ends to reinforced areas under the wings and attached at their lower ends to balljoints at the outer ends of the track control arms (Fig. 11.1).

2 A drag strut (radius rod) is fitted between the track control arm and the bodyframe to positively locate the suspension track control arm.

3 A stabiliser bar is fitted.

4 *The rear suspension* is of semi-elliptic leaf spring type secured with 'U' bolts below the rear axle casing. Telescopic shock absorbers are fitted but the spring setting and the shock absorber mountings differ between the Wagon and other versions (Fig. 11.2).

5 *The steering gear* is of recirculating ball type with collapsible steering column (Fig. 11.3).

2 Maintenance and inspection

1 Refer to 'Routine Maintenance' Section at the front of the manual and carry out the checks and lubrication operations at the specified mileage intervals.

2 The most important job is inspection of all the steering and suspension components at regular intervals.

3 First check the condition of the dust excluding gaiters on the front suspension struts.

4 Inspect the condition of the balljoints dust excluding boots. If these are split, they must be renewed.

5 At the specified intervals, check all the steering and suspension nuts and bolts and tighten if necessary to the specified torque wrench settings.

6 With the help of an assistant, jack-up the front of the vehicle and move the steering linkage while checking for lost motion or slackness in the balljoints (refer to Section 9 - paragraph 15).

7 Grip the roadwheels top and bottom and attempt to rock them. Any movement may indicate incorrectly adjusted hub bearings, worn bearings or worn track control arm bushes.

8 Now watch the rear spring shackles and shock absorber mountings. Any slackness in these will necessitate their renewal.

3 Shock absorbers - removal, testing and refitting

1 At the specified intervals (see the Routine Maintenance Section at the beginning of this manual), the rear shock absorbers should be removed and tested in the following way.

2 The lower mounting on all vehicles is of the pivot bolt type and this should be removed from the shock absorber mounting eye (Fig. 11.4).

3 *On Saloon and Hardtop models,* remove the rear seat and unscrew

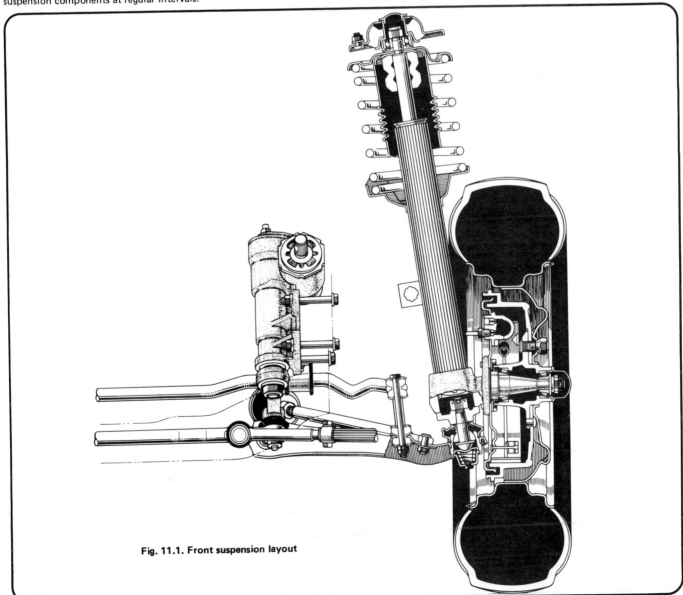

Fig. 11.1. Front suspension layout

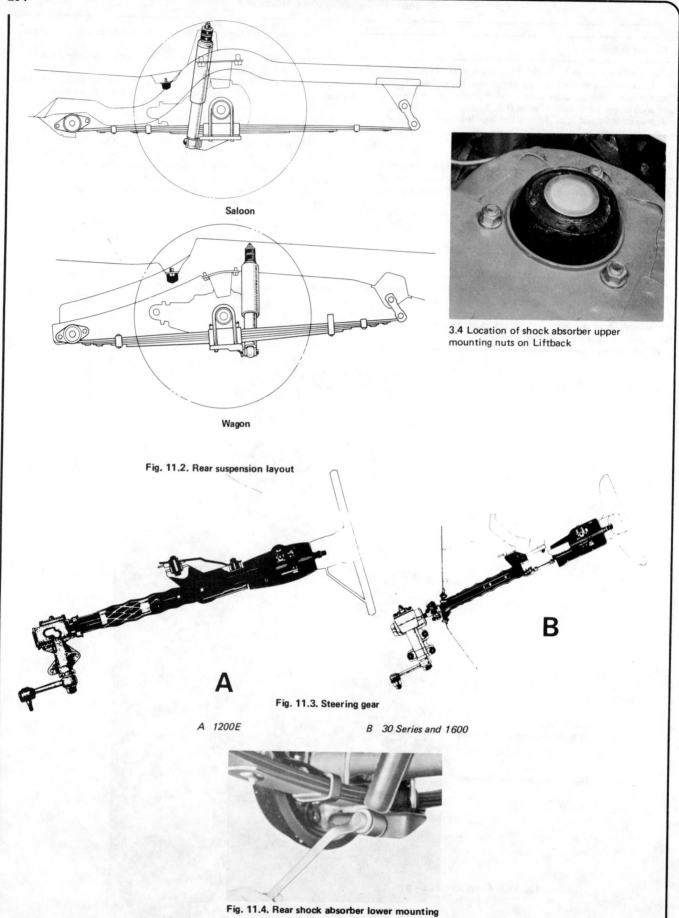

Saloon

Wagon

Fig. 11.2. Rear suspension layout

3.4 Location of shock absorber upper
mounting nuts on Liftback

A

B

Fig. 11.3. Steering gear

A   1200E   B   30 Series and 1600

Fig. 11.4. Rear shock absorber lower mounting

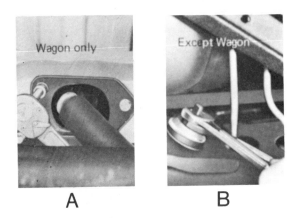

Fig. 11.5. Rear shock absorber upper mounting

A   Wagon   B   Other models

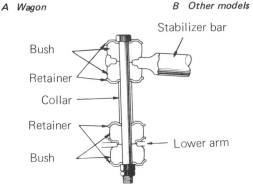

Fig. 11.6. Stabiliser bar attachment to track control arm

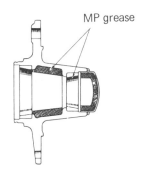

Fig. 11.7. Front hub grease packing diagram

and remove the nut and locknut from the shock absorber upper spindle and remove the shock absorber. Retain the washers and rubber cushions in their correct fitted order.

4   *On Liftback models,* remove the floor covering from the luggage area to gain access to the upper mounting nuts (photo).

5   *On Wagon models,* working under the vehicle, unbolt the upper mounting bracket and withdraw it complete with shock absorber. The bracket can be unbolted from the shock absorber spindle once the assembly is removed (Fig. 11.5).

6   With the shock absorber removed, grip its lower mounting eye in the jaws of a vice so that it is supported in a vertical attitude. Now fully extend and compress the shock absorber ten or twelve times. If there is any jerkiness, lack of resistance or seizure during these operations, renew the unit.

7   Refitting is a reversal of removal but do not overtighten the upper mounting nut or the rubber cushions will be overcompressed. Hold the spindle of the shock absorber with a spanner fitted to the flats on its upper end while the mounting nut and locknut are tightened.

4   Front suspension stabiliser bar - removal and refitting

1   Jack-up the front of the vehicle and support it on axle stands.

2   Remove the engine under shield.

3   Unscrew and remove the bolts which secure the ends of the stabiliser bar to the track control arm. Note the arrangement of rubber bushes, retainers and spacers (Fig. 11.6).

4   Unbolt the stabiliser brackets from the bodyframe.

5   Now unbolt both ends of one of the strut bars (unbolt the bracket from the bodyframe at one end) and remove the strut bar complete with bracket still attached to it at one end. Do not disturb the strut bar to bracket setting.

6   Remove the stabiliser bar.

7   Refitting is a reversal of removal but tighten all nuts and bolts to the specified torque wrench settings.

5   Front hub bearings - maintenance, adjustment and renewal

Vehicles with front drum brakes

1   At the intervals specified in the Routine Maintenance Section at the beginning of this manual, jack-up the front of the vehicle and remove the roadwheels.

2   Remove the securing screws holding the drum and withdraw it. If the drum is tight, release the shoe adjusters as described in Chapter 9.

3   Prise off the grease cap and extract the split pin (Fig. 11.8).

4   Remove the nut retainer and unscrew and remove the nut and thrust washer.

5   Pull the hub assembly from the stub axle.

6   If there is any evidence of grease contamination on the brake backplate, the oil seal must be renewed. If the bearings are noisy when turned with the fingers they must be renewed. If the components are in good condition, pass to paragraph 11. Wipe away all the old grease

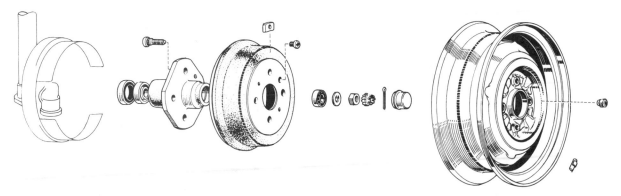

Fig. 11.8. Front hub components (drum brakes)

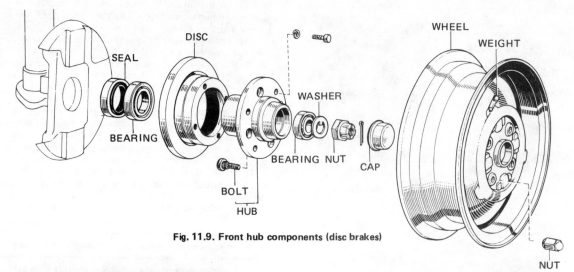

Fig. 11.9. Front hub components (disc brakes)

Fig. 11.10. Tightening front hub bearing nut using socket wrench

Fig. 11.11. Method of suspending disc brake caliper prior to hub/disc
removal

from the bearings and hub interior.

7   To renew the oil seal, drive it from the inner end of the hub using
a suitable drift. Tap the new seal carefully into position until it is
flush with the end of the hub.

8   To renew the inner and outer hub bearings, first remove the oil
seal as described in the preceding paragraph. Drive out the bearings
with a drift inserted from either end in turn. Never be tempted to
renew only the bearing inner race to avoid removing the old outer
tracks. All bearings are made as matched components.

9   Drive in the new bearing outer tracks and fit the new oil seal.

10 If the oil seal or bearings have now been renewed, wipe away any
dirt and then proceed as described in the next paragraph.

11 Pack the bearings and interior of the hub as shown in the diagram
with fresh wheel bearing grease (Fig. 11.7).

12 Refit the hub, taking care not to damage the oil seal, fit the thrust
washer and nut.

13 Tighten the nut to 23 lb/ft (32 Nm) at the same time turning the
hub in both directions to settle the bearings.

14 Now release the nut until it can be easily turned with the fingers.
Retighten the nut using a socket wrench and tightening with hand
pressure only (Fig. 11.10).

15 Fit the nut retainer in such a way that one pair of cut-outs in the
retainer are in alignment with the hole in the stub axle.

16 Fit a new split pin and bend the ends over neatly, half fill the
grease cap and tap it into position.

17 Refit the brake drum, the roadwheel and repeat the operations
on the opposite hub.

Vehicles with front disc brakes

18 The operations are identical with those described in the earlier
paragraphs of this Section except that the caliper must be removed
before the disc/hub assembly can be withdrawn. There is no need to
disconnect the hydraulic hose but simply tie the caliper assembly to
the front suspension strut using a piece of wire (Figs. 11.9 and 11.11).

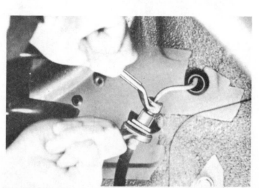

Fig. 11.12. Disconnecting flexible from rigid brake line

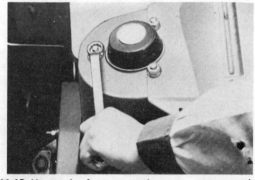

Fig. 11.13. Unscrewing front suspension strut upper mounting nut

6 Front suspension strut - removal

1 Jack-up the front of the vehicle and support the bodyframe on axle stands.
2 Remove the roadwheel.
3 Disconnect the flexible brake hose from the rigid brake line at the support bracket union connection (Fig. 11.12).
4 Unscrew and remove the three nuts from the strut upper mounting (Fig. 11.13).
5 Unscrew and remove the two bolts which secure the steering arm to the base of the strut. Once the bolts are removed, depress the track control arm to release the steering arm positioning dowels (Fig. 11.14).
6 Withdraw the suspension strut from under the front wing.

7 Front suspension strut - overhaul

1 In the event of failure of a front suspension strut it is recommended that a reconditioned or new unit is obtained or a cartridge is fitted in accordance with the particular manufacturer's recommendations.
2 Whichever recommendation it is decided to follow, the following operations will have to be carried out as new units are not supplied with hub, brake or coil spring components.
3 Remove the hub and brake components as described in Section 5.
4 Using a suitable compressor, compress the coil spring. Remove the bearing dust cap.
5 Insert a screwdriver in the hole in the spring upper seat and holding the seat steady, unscrew the nut from the top of the piston rod (Fig. 11.15).
6 Slowly release the spring compressor and remove the upper mounting, spring seat and coil spring components (Figs. 11.16 and 11.17).
7 When reassembling the spring, seat and mounting to the new or reconditioned strut again use the coil spring compressor and tighten the piston rod nut to the specified torque wrench setting.

8 Front suspension strut - refitting

1 Refit the strut by reversing the removal operations given in Section 6.
2 Tighten all nuts and bolts to specified torque wrench settings.
3 Refit the hub/brake assembly and adjust the hub bearings as described in Section 5.
4 Reconnect the brake hose and bleed the hydraulic circuit.
5 Pack some grease into the bearing at the upper mounting and refit the dust cap (photo).
6 Refit the roadwheel and lower the vehicle to the ground.

8.5 Front suspension strut upper bearing

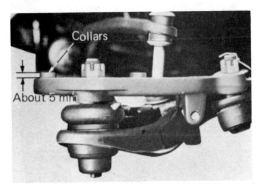

Fig. 11.14. Steering arm and suspension swivel joint showing locating dowels (collars)

Fig. 11.15. Unscrewing front suspension strut piston nut

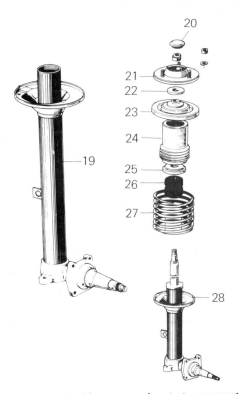

Fig. 11.16. Typical front suspension strut components

19 Strut shell
20 Cap
21 Mounting plate
22 Dust seal
23 Spring upper seat
24 Dust excluding gaiter
25 Bumper
26 Spring buffer
27 Coil spring
28 Suspension strut complete

Fig. 11.17. Removing spring upper seat

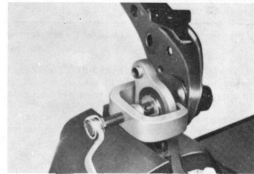

Fig. 11.18. Separating track control arm balljoint from steering arm

Fig. 11.19. Removing dust excluder and retaining ring from track control arm balljoint

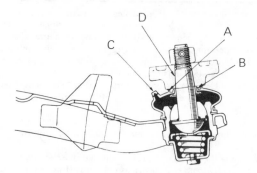

Fig. 11.20. Cut-away view of track control arm balljoint

A Grease application point   C Vent
B Grease application point   D Taper pin

9 Front suspension track control arm balljoint dust excluder - renewal

1   To renew one of the track control arm balljoint flexible dust excluders, raise the front of the vehicle and support it on axle stands.
2   Remove the roadwheel.
3   Extract the bolts which secure the base of the suspension strut to the steering arm. Depress the track control arm to release it from the suspension strut hollow positioning dowels.
4   Disconnect the trackrod end from the eye in the steering arm. Use a balljoint separator for this or forked wedges. Although a balljoint can be released by unscrewing the nut from its taper pin and striking both sides of the eye into which the taper pin engages with two large hammers simultaneously, this is not to be recommended due to the possibility of damaging adjacent components.
5   Extract the split pin and unscrew the castellated nut from the balljoint taper pin at the end of the track control arm.
6   Using a suitable extractor, press the balljoint taper pin out of the steering arm (Fig. 11.18).
7   There is now sufficient working room to be able to prise off the dust cover and retaining ring from the balljoint (Fig. 11.19).
8   Fit the new dust cover and always use a new retaining ring. Apply grease to the parts of the cover 'A' and 'B' and ensure that the vent in the cover is towards the rear of the vehicle (Fig. 11.20).
9   Unscrew the plug from the balljoint and substitute a grease nipple. Inject grease and then refit the plug.
10 Reconnect the balljoint to the steering arm and tighten the nut to the specified torque wrench setting. Insert a new split pin.
11 Reconnect the steering arm to the base of the suspension strut.
12 Reconnect the trackrod end balljoint to the steering arm eye.
13 Refit the roadwheel and lower the vehicle.
14 It should be noted that if the track control arm balljoint is worn, it can only be renewed complete with the control arm as an assembly.
15 A more important fact is that the track control arm balljoint is designed to have a vertical movement of between 0.06 and 0.069 in (1.5 and 1.75 mm). This is a manufacturing tolerance and in the event of a vehicle failing its roadworthiness test because of this movement being detected and not understood, the vehicle examiner should be

referred to the Toyota Technical Department.

10 Front suspension track control arm - removal, renovation and refitting

1   Repeat the operations described in paragraphs 2, 3 and 4 of the preceding Section.
2   Disconnect the strut bar (drag link) and the stabiliser bar from the track control arm (Figs. 11.21 and 11.22).
3   Unscrew and remove the pivot bolt which secures the inner end of the track control arm to the bodyframe crossmember (Fig. 11.23).
4   The track control arm can now be withdrawn from the vehicle.
5   If the bushes are worn at the inner end of the arm, they can be removed and new ones fitted either using a press or a long bolt, nuts, washers and distance pieces of suitable diameter.
6   If the track control arm balljoint is worn, it can only be renewed as part of a complete new arm assembly - refer to paragraph 15 of the preceding Section.
7   Refit the track control arm by reversing the removal operations. Tighten all nuts and bolts to the specified torque wrench settings **except** the control arm inner pivot bolt. Screw this up only finger tight until the vehicle is on the ground again with the jacks removed. Bounce the body up and down two or three times and then tighten the bolt to the specified torque wrench setting (Fig. 11.24).

11 Strut bar (drag link) - removal and refitting

1   To remove this component, raise the front of the vehicle and remove the roadwheel.
2   Unbolt the bar from the track control arm and from the bodyframe attachment bracket. The backing nut at the bracket is staked in position and should not be removed so that refitting is not complicated. However, where a new bar is to be fitted, tighten the nuts at the bracket end in accordance with the appropriate diagram and then stake the new backing nut (Figs. 11.25 and 11.26).
3   Refit the roadwheel and lower the vehicle.

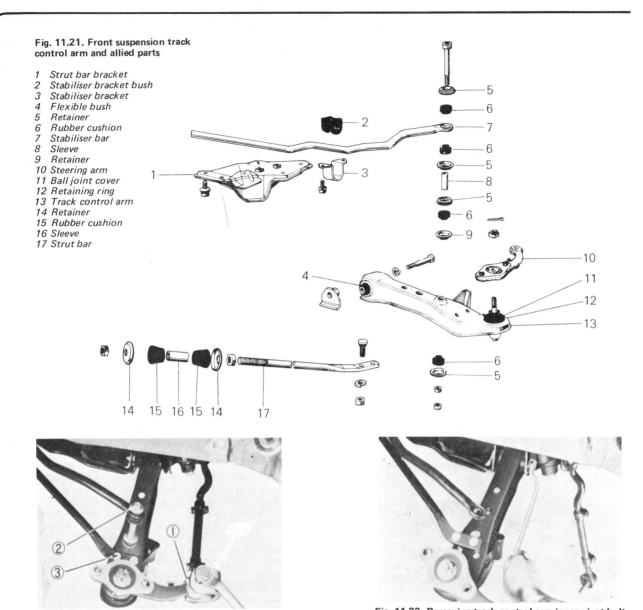

Fig. 11.21. Front suspension track control arm and allied parts

1 Strut bar bracket
2 Stabiliser bracket bush
3 Stabiliser bracket
4 Flexible bush
5 Retainer
6 Rubber cushion
7 Stabiliser bar
8 Sleeve
9 Retainer
10 Steering arm
11 Ball joint cover
12 Retaining ring
13 Track control arm
14 Retainer
15 Rubber cushion
16 Sleeve
17 Strut bar

Fig. 11.22. Connection of (1) track rod to steering arm, (2) stabiliser bar to track control arm, (3) strut bar

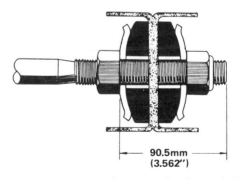

Fig. 11.23. Removing track control arm inner pivot bolt

Fig. 11.24. Refitting track control arm inner pivot bolt

Fig. 11.25. Strut bar to bracket connecting diagram (1200E)

90.5mm (3.562")

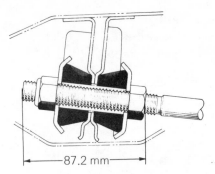

Fig. 11.26. Strut bar to bracket connecting diagram (30 Series and 1600 models)

87.2 mm

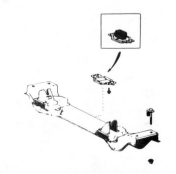

Fig. 11.27. Suspension/bodyframe crossmember

Fig. 11.28. Unscrewing a rear spring 'U' bolt nut

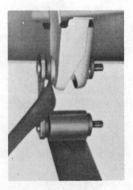

Fig. 11.29. Disconnecting rear spring shackle

12 Front bodyframe crossmember - removal and refitting

1 This operation is normally only called for in exceptional cases of damage or severe corrosion.
2 Remove the engine undershield.
3 Support the weight of the engine either by attaching a hoist to it or by supporting it on a jack and a block of wood placed under the sump (Fig. 11.27).
4 Disconnect the engine mountings from the crossmember brackets.
5 Remove the pivot bolts from the inner ends of the lower track control arms.
6 Unscrew and remove the bolts which hold the crossmember to the bodyframe side members. Do not attempt to move the vehicle while the track control arms are disconnected.
7 Refit the new crossmember by reversing the removal operations. Tighten all bolts to specified torque.
8 *On 1200E models,* adjust the steering lock bolts as described in Section 21.

13 Rear leaf spring - removal and refitting

1 Raise the rear of the vehicle and support it securely on stands placed under the bodyframe and rear axle casing.
2 Remove the roadwheel.
3 Disconnect the shock absorber lower mounting (photo).
4 Unscrew the nuts from the spring securing 'U' bolts (Fig. 11.28).
5 Unscrew the two nuts from the rear shackle, remove the shackle plate and prise out the shackle/pin assembly (Fig. 11.29).
6 Unscrew the nut from the front pivot pin, remove the bolts from the pin bracket and withdraw the pin (Fig. 11.30).
7 The spring can now be removed from the vehicle.
8 Wire brush the spring and inspect the leaves for cracks. If any are found the spring should be renewed complete or repaired professionally.
9 The silencer pads can be renewed if the leaves are prised open far enough to remove the old ones and the leaf clips bent aside carefully.
10 Split type flexible bushes are used at all spring attachment points and these are easily renewed. Use a little brake fluid if necessary when fitting the new bushes, to ease their insertion into the spring eyes and shackle pin holes in the bodyframe.
11 Refitting is a reversal of removal but tighten all nuts to the specified torque wrench setting after the vehicle has been lowered to the ground and the weight of the vehicle is on the springs.

14 Steering wheel - removal and refitting

1 Set the roadwheels in the straight ahead position.
2 Remove the steering wheel pad. This is attached by screws entered

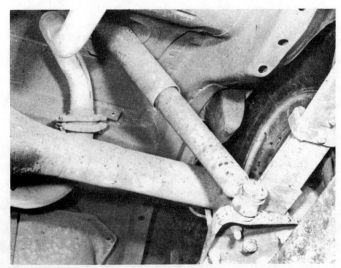

13.3 Rear shock absorber lower mounting

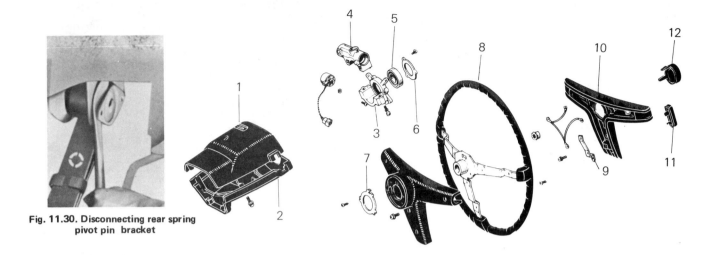

Fig. 11.30. Disconnecting rear spring
pivot pin bracket

Fig. 11.31. Typical steering wheel components

1 Steering column upper shroud   7 Horn contact ring
2 Steering column lower shroud   8 Steering wheel
3 Steering column lock assembly   9 Horn button plate
4 Steering column lock assembly   10 Safety pad
5 Bearing   11 Horn button
6 Bearing retainer   12 Motif

15.2 Removing steering column lower shroud

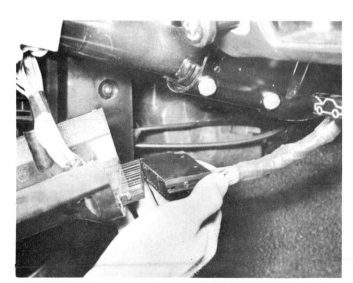

15.3 Disconnecting steering column switch harness plug

from the rear face of the steering wheel spokes. On SR5 models having
a four spoke steering wheel, prise out the central motif for access to
the steering wheel retaining nut (Fig. 11.31). Hold the wheel steady
and unscrew and remove the nut.
3 All models are fitted with a collapsible type safety steering
column, so on no account try to thump the wheel from the shaft,
always use a suitable extractor.
4 Refitting is a reversal of removal but make sure that the roadwheels
are in the straight ahead position when refitting. Tighten the securing
nut to the specified torque wrench setting.

15 Steering column lock - removal and refitting

1 This is an operation which will only normally be required if, the
vehicle keys have been lost without any record of their number having
been kept.
2 Remove the steering wheel as described in Section 14.
3 Remove the upper and lower steering column shrouds (photo).
4 Remove the combination switch connector plug (photo).
5 Remove the combination switch from the column.
6 Extract the now exposed circlip (Fig. 11.32).
7 Centre punch the ends of the shear bolts and then drill them out
using a twist drill 0.8 to 0.12 in (3.0 to 4.0 mm) in diameter. Extract
the remains of the bolts using a bolt (easy out) extractor. Alternatively,
if the lock is to be destroyed, use a hacksaw at each side of the lock
(between the section halves) to cut through the bolts (Fig. 11.33).
8 Refit the new lock assembly but only lightly tighten the shear
bolts until the cylinder lock has been fitted and the new key inserted
and removed several times to test that the tongue of the lock engages
correctly in the shaft cut-out. The steering may have to be turned
slightly once the key has been removed to engage the lock tongue in
the cut-out.
9 The original ignition switch can be fitted to the new lock assembly.
10 When correct alignment of the lock has been verified, fully tighten
the shear bolts until their heads break off (Fig. 11.34).
11 Refit the circlip, switch, connector plug, column shrouds and
steering wheel by reversing the removal operations.

16 Steering gear (1200E) - removal, overhaul and refitting

1 Remove the steering wheel (Section 14) and column switches (see Chapter 10).

2 Peel back the floor covering from the area around the steering column.

3 Unbolt the cover plate from around the steering column.

4 Remove the clutch pedal (see Chapter 5).

5 Remove the steering column shrouds and disconnect the wiring harness plug.

6 Working under the vehicle, remove the engine undershield.

7 Unscrew the nut which retains the steering drop arm to the sector shaft.

8 Using a substantial puller, extract the drop arm from the splined sector shaft (Fig. 11.35).

9 Unscrew the bolts which secure the steering box to the bodyframe within the engine compartment and disconnect the steering column upper bracket.

10 Withdraw the complete steering gear into the vehicle interior and remove it from the vehicle.

11 Clean away all external dirt, remove the filler plug and drain away all the lubricant.

12 Release the adjuster screw locknut, remove the sector shaft end cover retaining screws and remove the cover. To do this unscrew the adjuster screw, so winding it out of the cover.

13 Release the worm bearing adjuster locknut and then using a pin wrench, unscrew the worm bearing adjusting screw.

14 Extract the 'O' ring and lower worm bearing.

15 Withdraw the steering shaft complete with worm nut. Do not allow the nut to run down the worm and to stop abruptly, otherwise the balls may be damaged.

16 Extract the upper worm bearing and its outer track from the housing.

17 Extract the steering gear housing cover.

18 Remove the sector shaft oil seal.

19 With the steering gear dismantled, inspect each component for.

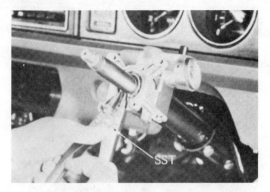

Fig. 11.32. Extracting steering column upper circlip

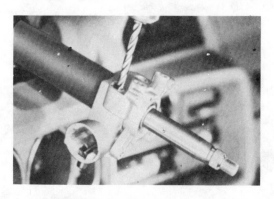

Fig. 11.33. Drilling out steering lock shear bolts

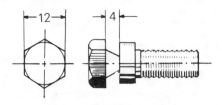

Fig. 11.34. Steering column lock shear bolts

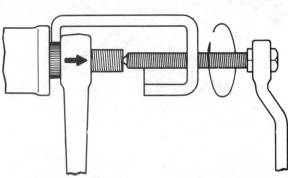

Fig. 11.35. Using an extractor to remove steering drop arm

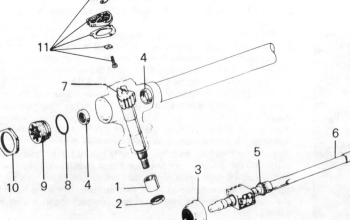

Fig. 11.36. Steering gear components (1200E)

1 Bush
2 Oil seal
3 Cover
4 Lower bearing
5 Upper bearing inner race
6 Collapsible type steering shaft
7 Sector shaft
8 'O' ring
9 Adjuster
10 Locknut
11 Cover plate components

wear or damage and renew as necessary. Always renew oil seals and 'O' rings. If the sector shaft bush is worn, leave renewal to your dealer as the new one will have to be reamed when fitted. Examine the steering shaft to see that the safety shear pins are intact (Fig. 11.36).
20 Commence reassembly by fitting the outer track for the upper bearing.
21 Fit the steering shaft/worm nut and the lower shaft bearing.
22 Fit the 'O' ring, worm bearing, adjuster and locknut, the last two items only finger tight.
23 Wind a cord round the upper end of the steering shaft and attach a spring balance to the end of the cord. The pre-load (starting torque) is correct when the pull on the spring balance is between 5.5 and 14 lb (2.5 and 6.3 kg). Adjust as necessary with the bearing adjuster and when correct, lock it with the locknut (Fig. 11.37).
24 Fit the adjuster screw into the sector shaft. There should be a clearance at the base of the screw not exceeding 0.002 in (0.05 mm) when the screw is pulled upwards with the fingers. Correct this clearance if necessary by selecting a suitable thrust washer from the five available thicknesses and place it under the head of the adjuster screw

(Figs. 11.38 and 11.39).
25 Set the nut at its centre position and then fit the sector shaft by engaging the centre tooth of the shaft with the centre groove of the worm nut (Fig. 11.40).
26 Fit the sector shaft end cover and gasket by unscrewing the adjuster screw through the cover. Fit the cover bolts.
27 Again wind the cord round the splined upper end of the steering shaft and attach it to a spring balance. Check the starting torque (pre-load) with the worm nut in its centre position. The spring balance should show a pull of between 14 and 22 lbs (6.3 and 10 kg). Adjust by turning the sector shaft adjuster screw. When correct, lock the adjuster screw with the locknut. When the adjustment has been correctly carried out, the sector shaft should have no backlash when moved through 5° from its centre position, in either direction (Fig. 11.41).
28 Install the steering gear into the vehicle and insert the steering box bolts, finger tight.
29 Reconnect the column upper bracket. If a break-away type bracket is fitted, insert and tighten the upper bolts first (Fig. 11.42).

Fig. 11.37. Checking worm bearing preload (1200E)

Fig. 11.38. Checking adjuster screw clearance in sector shaft (1200E)

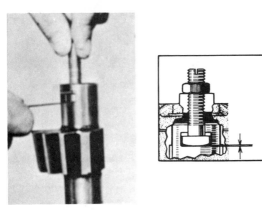

Fig. 11.39. Sector shaft adjuster screw clearance diagram (1200E)

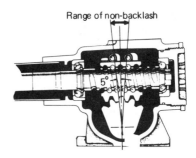

Fig. 11.40. Sector shaft engaged with steering worm in central position (1200E)

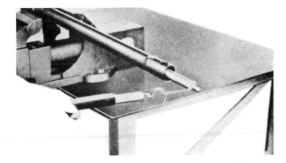

Fig. 11.41. Checking sector shaft adjustment (1200E)

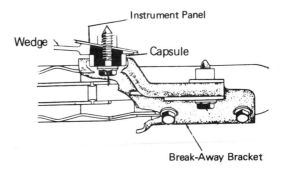

Fig. 11.42. Steering column upper breakaway bracket

30 Fit the castor wedge between the instrument panel and the
bracket and insert the lower bolt. Tighten both bolts to 30 lb/ft (41
Nm) torque.
31 Tighten the steering box to bodyframe bolts.
32 Refit the steering drop arm, making sure that the sector shaft and
drop arm alignment marks are in alignment. Set the roadwheels in the
straight ahead position and the steering column shaft in approximately
the centre position of its travel before attempting this, otherwise it is
possible to misalign the drop arm by 180°. Fit the nut and tighten to
the specified torque.
33 Fit the column switch and steering wheel and tighten its retaining
nut to the specified torque.
34 Fit the steering column upper shrouds and reconnect the wiring
harness plug.
35 Fill the steering box to the level of the filler plug with the specified
lubricant.

---

17 Steering column (30 Series and 1600 models) - removal, overhaul, refitting

---

1   Set the roadwheels in the straight ahead position.
2   Working within the engine compartment, mark the relationship of
the steering shaft flexible coupling to the pinion shaft of the steering
box (Fig. 11.43).
3   Unscrew and remove the coupling pinch bolt.
4   Working inside the vehicle remove the steering wheel and the
combination switch (see Chapter 10).
5   Remove the cover plate which surrounds the lower end of the
steering column (Fig. 11.44).
6   Unscrew and remove the column upper shrouds.
7   Unscrew and remove the bolts from the column upper break-away
type bracket (Fig. 11.45).
8   Draw the steering column into the vehicle interior and then remove
it.
9   To dismantle the steering column, unbolt the upper bracket, pull
the steering shaft from the column tube and extract the dust seal
(Fig. 11.46).
10 Unbolt and remove the flexible coupling from the steering shaft.
11 Unbolt the column cover plate, twist the column tube and remove
the cover plate (Fig. 11.47).
12 Inspect all the components for damage or wear. If the plastic shear
pins are deformed or partially collapsed, renew the shaft assembly.
Check the upper mounting bracket for any sign of strain or collapse,
if evident renew it. Renew the dust seal and 'O' ring if they show signs
of deterioration.
13 Reassemble by reversing the dismantling operations but only
tighten the column cover plate bolts finger tight.
14 Refit the column assembly from inside the vehicle. Align the
coupling with the steering gear pinion shaft, insert the pinch bolt and
tighten it.
15 Attach the break-away bracket tightening the bolts only finger
tight.
16 Fit the column hole cover plate, the 'O' ring and bolt to the floor
and column flange.
17 Push the column as far down as possible, tighten the bracket upper
bolts only. Insert the castor wedge between the pedal support and
bracket and tighten the lower bolts. The castor wedge is not used on
vehicles destined for operation in North America (Fig. 11.48).
18 Check that the column cover plate positioning lug is engaged as
shown in the diagram (Fig. 11.49).

---

18 Steering gear (30 Series and 1600 models) - removal, overhaul and refitting

---

1   Working within the engine compartment, mark the alignment of
the flexible coupling yoke to the pinion shaft of the steering gear and
then unscrew the coupling pinch bolt and remove it. It is best to have
the front roadwheels in the straight ahead position before carrying out
this work.
2   Disconnect the steering relay rod balljoint from the steering drop
arm using a suitable extractor or forked wedges (Fig. 11.50).
3   Unbolt the steering gear from the bodyframe and remove it
downwards from the vehicle.
4   Using a substantial puller, draw off the steering drop arm, having

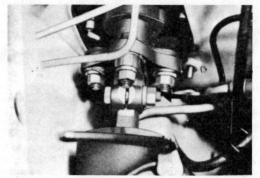

Fig. 11.43. Steering shaft flexible coupling (30 Series and 1600)

Fig. 11.44. Steering column cover plate and screws (arrowed) on 30
Series and 1600

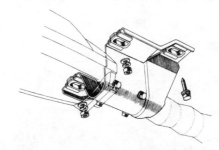

Fig. 11.45. Steering column upper breakaway bracket (30 Series and
1600 models)

Fig. 11.46. Removing steering shaft from column (30 Series and 1600)

Fig. 11.47. Removing column cover plate (30 Series and 1600)

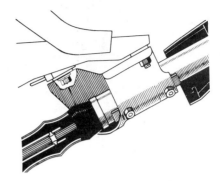

Fig. 11.48. Column breakaway bracket bolts (30 Series and 1600)

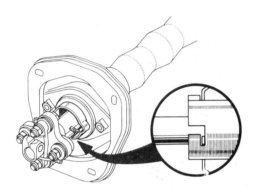

Fig. 11.49. Steering column cover plate positioning lug

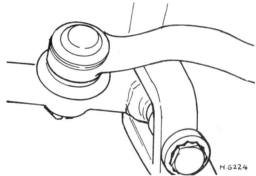

Fig. 11.50. Disconnecting relay rod balljoint from steering drop arm
(30 Series and 1600)

first removed the retaining nut (Fig. 11.51).

5   Drain the oil from the gear housing.

6   Release and remove the sector shaft adjuster screw locknut, remove the sector shaft end cover bolts and remove the cover by winding the adjuster screw out of it with a screwdriver.

7   Withdraw the sector shaft.

8   Release the worm bearing adjuster locknut and then using a pin wrench, unscrew and remove the bearing adjuster from the gear housing (Figs. 11.52 and 11.53).

9   Withdraw the worm assembly complete with the bearing races (Fig. 11.54).

10 Do not dismantle the ball nut but if defective, renew the complete worm/nut assembly.

11 On some models, needle roller type bearings are used for the sector shaft. In this case, any wear must be rectified by renewal of the bearings, gear case and sector shaft as a matched assembly (Fig. 11.54A).

12 On vehicles with bushes in which the sector shaft runs, have your dealer renew them if they are worn as they will require reaming after fitting and a new matching sector shaft to go with them.

13 Check the gap between the end face of the sector shaft adjuster screw and the recess in the shaft. This should not exceed 0.0020 in (0.05 mm). Adjustment can be made if necessary by fitting a thrust washer from the six different thicknesses available and locating it under the head of the adjuster screw (see Fig. 11.39).

14 New worm bearing outer tracks should be **pressed** into the gear housing, not drifted into position.

15 Commence reassembly by installing the worm/nut, adjuster screw (finger tight) and locknut.

16 Wind a cord round the splines of the pinion shaft and attach it to a spring balance. The pinion shaft should start to turn when the spring balance records a pull in accordance with the following:

   30 Series models   *4 to 9 lb (1.8 to 4.1 kg)*
   1600 models   *9 to 11 lb (4.1 to 5.0 kg)*

17 Adjust by means of the bearing adjuster and then tighten the locknut.

18 Move the ball nut to the centre position on the worm and insert the sector shaft so that its centre tooth meshes with the centre groove of the ball nut (Fig. 11.56).

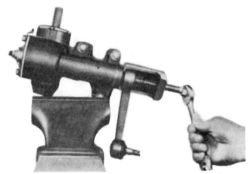

Fig. 11.51. Removing steering drop arm (30 Series and 1600)

Fig. 11.52. Removing worm adjuster locknut (30 Series and 1600)

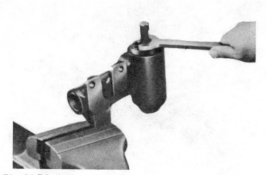

Fig. 11.53. Removing worm adjuster (30 Series and 1600)

Fig. 11.54. Withdrawing worm assembly (30 Series and 1600)

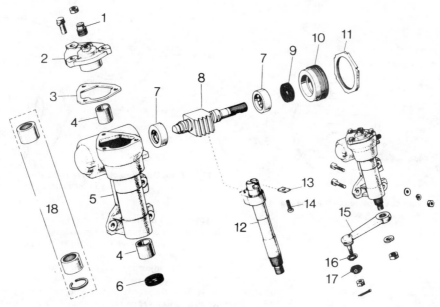

Fig. 11.54A. Steering box components (30 Series and 1600)

1	Breather	6	Oil seal	11	Lock nut
2	Cover	7	Bearing	12	Sector shaft
3	Gasket	8	Worm/nut	13	Shim
4	Bush	9	Oil seal	14	Adjuster screw
5	Housing	10	Worm bearing adjuster	15	Drop arm

16	Dust cover retainer
17	Dust cover
18	Alternative sector shaft needle roller bearings

19 Fit the sector shaft adjuster screw and fit the end cover with a new gasket, winding the adjuster screw into the cover with a screwdriver. Secure with the three bolts.

20 Again wind a cord round the splined end of the pinion shaft and adjust the starting torque (pre-load) using the spring balance method and the sector shaft at its centre position. Turn the adjuster screw until the pinion shaft starts to turn when the reading on the spring balance is in accordance with the following:

    30 Series models   *11 to 18 lb (5.0 to 8.1 kg)*
    1600 models   *18 to 24 lb (8.1 to 10.9 kg)*

21 If correctly adjusted, there should be no backlash when at the centre position, the sector shaft is turned 5° in either direction. Tighten the sector shaft adjuster screw locknut.

22 Refit the drop arm, aligning the mating marks. To avoid refitting the arm 180° out, set the steering worm to the centre of its travel and make sure that the drop arm is pointing away from the pinion shaft (Fig. 11.59).

23 Refit the steering gear to the vehicle by reversing the removal operations, tighten all bolts to specified torque.

24 Reconnect the relay rod balljoint to the drop arm and fit and tighten the taper pin nut.

25 Fill the steering box to the level of the filler plug with the correct specified grade of oil.

Fig. 11.55. Checking worm bearing preload (Series 30 and 1600)

19 Steering linkage, balljoints and idler arm

1   The steering linkage comprises a central relay rod, two outer track-rods and an idler arm assembly (photos).

2   The design of the components differs slightly between the 1200E and the 30 Series and 1600 models, the main difference being that the trackrod ends on the 1200E are secured by locknuts while on the other models, clamps are used (Figs. 11.58 and 11.61).

3   The steering lock angles on 1200E models are controlled by stop bolts which can be adjusted to limit the movement of the stop plate on the relay rod.

4   On other models, the steering lock angles are adjusted by means of the stop bolts on the steering arms at the base of the suspension struts (see Section 21).

5   The steering linkage can be removed in part or complete by unscrewing the nuts from the balljoint taper pins and then separating the taper pins from the eye of the connecting component. To do this, use a balljoint separator or a pair of forked wedges.

6   If any part of the steering linkage is renewed, always have the front wheel alignment checked. (See Section 20).

7   The trackrod ends are not adjustable and if any wear is evident, renew them. If the dust excluder is split, renew it and pack its interior with multipurpose grease (Fig. 11.60).

8   Any slackness in the idler arm will be due to wear in the internal flexible bushes. To remove the idler arm, disconnect it from the relay rod by separating the balljoint. Unbolt the idler arm support bracket from the bodyframe.

9   Unscrew the idler arm pivot nut and dismantle the components.

10 On 1200E models, the idler arm bush is of rubber. It should be renewed using only a little brake hydraulic fluid if necessary to fit it. Tighten the pivot nut to the specified torque while the idler arm is held parallel with the support bracket (Figs. 11.62 and 11.63).

11 On other models, the idler arm bushes are of the split type and should be greased when fitted. Tighten the idler arm pivot nut to specified torque with the arm in any position.

Fig. 11.56. Sector shaft engaged with worm in central position (30 Series and 1600)

Fig. 11.57. Checking sector shaft preload (30 Series and 1600)

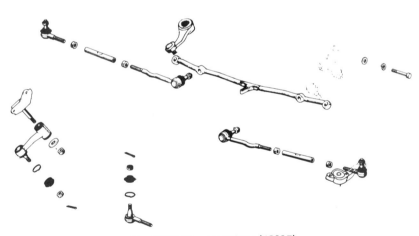

Fig. 11.58. Steering linkage (1200E)

Fig. 11.59. Drop arm and sector shaft alignment marks (30 Series and 1600)

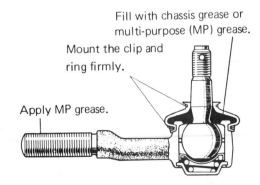

Fill with chassis grease or multi-purpose (MP) grease.

Mount the clip and ring firmly.

Apply MP grease.

Fig. 11.60. Cutaway view of trackrod end balljoint (1200E)

19.1A Steering box sector shaft drop arm and outer track rod (30 Series and 1600 models)

19.1B Steering idler and outer trackrod (30 Series and 1600 models)

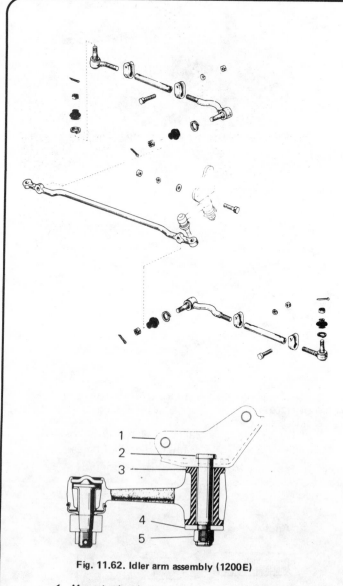

Fig. 11.61. Steering linkage (30 Series and 1600)

Fig. 11.62. Idler arm assembly (1200E)

1 Mounting bracket   4 Washer
2 Pivot pin   5 Nut
3 Flexible bush

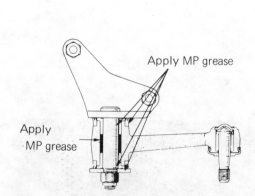

Fig. 11.63. Idler arm assembly (30 Series and 1600) showing multi-purpose grease application points

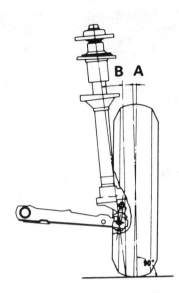

Fig. 11.64. Diagram showing (A) Camber, (B) Steering axis inclination

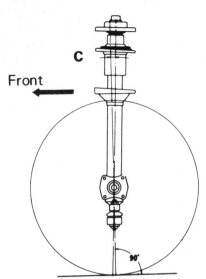

Fig. 11.65. Diagram showing (C) Castor

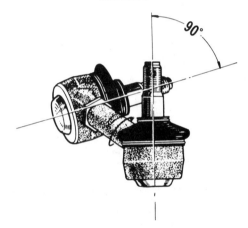

Fig. 11.66. Correct setting of balljoints at opposite ends of track rod

Fig. 11.67. Rotating a track rod (30 Series and 1600)

20 Steering angles and front wheel alignment

1 Accurate front wheel alignment is essential for good steering and even tyre wear.

2 The steering angles consist of the following:

Camber, which is the angle at which the front roadwheels are inclined from the vertical when viewed from the front of the vehicle. The camber is regarded as positive (degrees) if the wheels are tilted outwards at the top (Fig. 11.64).

Castor, is the angle between the steering axis and a vertical line when viewed from each side of the vehicle. Castor is regarded as positive when the steering axis is inclined rearwards (Fig. 11.65).

Steering axis inclination, is the angle, when viewed from the front of the vehicle between the vertical and an imaginary line drawn between the upper and lower suspension strut bearing points.

Toe-in (front wheel alignment or tracking) is the amount by which the distance between the front inside edges of the roadwheels (measured at hub height) is less than the diametrically opposite distance measured between the rear inside edges of the front roadwheels.

3 All steering angles except toe-in are set in production and cannot be adjusted but if a front end collision has occurred always have the angles checked after repairs are completed in case the angles have been altered by body distortion.

4 Although it is preferable to have front wheel alignment (toe-in) carried out by your dealer, using special tracking equipment, it is possible to do this work yourself in the following way.

5 Place the vehicle on level ground with the roadwheels in the straight ahead attitude.

6 Obtain or make a toe-in gauge. This can easily be made from a length of tubing, cranked to clear the sump and bellhousing, having an adjustable nut and setscrew at one end.

7 With the gauge, measure the distance between the two roadwheel inner rims (at hub height) at the rear of the wheels.

8 Push or pull the vehicle so that the roadwheel rotates through 180° (half a turn) and measure the distance between the wheel inner rims (again at hub height) at the front of the roadwheels. This distance should be less by an amount which corresponds to the toe-in specified for the particular vehicle model. (See the Specifications Section at the beginning of this Chapter).

9 Where the toe-in is found to be incorrect, adjust in the following way according to the model.

10 *On 1200E models* hold the flats on the trackrod ends steady with one spanner while releasing the locknuts with another. Note that the locknut on the left-hand trackrod end is a left-hand thread, while the right-hand one has a normal right-hand thread. This applies to both trackrods.

11 With all the four trackrod ends free, mark the position of the rods and then turn each rod about one quarter of a turn so that the mark moves in the same direction. If the toe-in is to be increased, turn the rods so that their effective lengths are increased. If the toe-in is to be decreased, turn the rods so as to decrease their effective lengths.

12 If new components have been fitted or one trackrod is greater in length than the other, set both rods so that their 'between balljoint

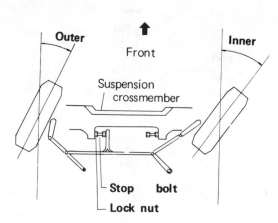

Fig. 11.68. Steering lock angles showing stop bolts (1200E)

21.3 Steering lock stop bolt (30 Series and 1600 models)

centres' is 13.2 in (335.6 mm). This will provide a starting point for adjustment.

13 When the adjustment has been carried out, re-check the alignment as previously described. Re-adjust if necessary until the toe-in is correct.

14 Without moving the position of the trackrods, the trackrod end locknuts should be tightened while the balljoints are held in relationship to each other as shown in the diagram (Fig. 11.66).

15 *On 30 Series and 1600 models,* adjustment of the toe-in is almost identical to that just described but the trackrods are movable after releasing the clamp pinch bolts. Refer to the Specifications for toe-in and on completion tighten the clamps so that their openings are in line with the slots in the trackrod tubes. Make sure that the balljoints are set in relation to each other as shown in Fig. 11.66 (Fig. 11.67).

21 Steering lock adjustment

1 The maximum angles to which the front roadwheels turn are controlled by stop bolts (Fig. 11.68).

2 *On 1200E models,* the bolts are located on the front crossmember.

3 *On 30 Series and 1600 models,* the stop bolts are located on the steering arms at the base of the front suspension struts (photo).

4 Adjust the stop bolts so that at full lock, the wheel angles are as specified when measured by drawing a line on the ground and compar-

ing it with the centre line of the vehicle.

22 Roadwheels and tyres

1 Pressed steel wheels are fitted with radial ply tyres.

2 Regularly check the tyre pressures including the spare.

3 Periodically, jack-up the vehicle and spin the roadwheels to check for out of true (buckle). At the same time examine the sidewalls for cuts or bulges and remove any flints which are in the tread.

4 *If the wheels have been balanced on the vehicle,* never remove a roadwheel unless you have first marked the relationship of the wheel to the mounting studs, otherwise the balance will be upset. Do not move the position of roadwheels in order to even out the tread wear.

5 *If the wheels have been balanced off the vehicle,* then they can be interchanged from front to rear periodically but only on the same side of the vehicle not from opposite sides. With radial tyres, moving them from one side of the vehicle to the other will create disconcerting steering and roadholding characteristics.

6 When the tyre treads have worn to the minimum safety level, have new tyres fitted complete with new valves and make sure that the wheels are balanced.

7 In the event of a puncture, have it professionally repaired and re-balanced as soon as possible.

8 Oversize tyres may be fitted provided their sizes are in accordance with those officially recommended in the Specifications Section.

23 Fault diagnosis - suspension and steering

Before diagnosing faults from the following chart, check that any irregularities are not caused by:
1 *Binding brakes*
2 *Incorrect tyre pressures*
3 *Misalignment of the bodyframe*

Symptom	Reason/s
Steering wheel can be moved considerably before any sign of movement of the wheels is apparent	Wear in the steering linkage, gear and column coupling.
Vehicle difficult to steer in a consistent straight line - wandering	As above. Wheel alignment incorrect (indicated by excessive or uneven tyre wear). Front wheel hub bearings loose or worn. Worn suspension unit swivel joints.
Steering stiff and heavy	Incorrect wheel alignment (indicated by excessive or uneven tyre wear). Excessive wear or seizure in one or more of the joints in the steering linkage or suspension unit balljoints. Excessive wear in the steering gear unit.
Wheel wobble and vibration	Roadwheels out of balance. Roadwheels buckled. Wheel alignment incorrect. Wear in the steering linkage, suspension unit bearings or track control arm bushes. Broken front coil spring.
Excessive pitching and rolling on corners and during braking	Defective shock absorbers and/or broken spring.

Chapter 12 Bodywork and underframe

Contents

1 General description

1 The body and underframe is of a unitary, all steel welded construction.

2 The body type varies according to model and date of production and reference should be made to the introductory section at the beginning of this manual.

3 In the interest of economy of repair, the front wings are detachable, otherwise, the body panels are not renewable without cutting and welding.

2 Maintenance - bodywork exterior

1 The general condition of a car's bodywork is the one thing that significantly affects its value. Maintenance is easy but needs to be regular and particular. Neglect - particularly after minor damage - can quickly lead to further deterioration and costly repair bills. It is important also to keep watch on those parts of the bodywork not immediately visible, for example the underside, inside all the wheelarches and the lower part of the engine compartment.

2 The basic maintenance routine for the bodywork is washing - preferably with a lot of water from a hose. This will remove all the loose solids which may have stuck to the car. It is important to flush these off in such a way as to prevent grit from scratching the finish. The wheelarches and underbody need washing in the same way, to remove any accumulated mud which will retain moisture and tend to encourage rust. Paradoxically enough, the best time to clean the underbody and wheelarches is in wet weather when the mud is thoroughly wet and soft. In very wet weather the underbody is usually cleared of large accumulations automatically and this is a good time for inspection.

3 Periodically, it is a good idea to have the whole of the underside of the car steam cleaned, engine compartment included, so that a thorough inspection can be carried out to see what minor repairs and renovations are necessary. Steam cleaning is available at many garages and is

necessary for removal of accumulations of oily grime which sometimes collects thickly in areas on and near the engine, gearbox and back axle. If steam cleaning facilities are not available there are several excellent grease solvents available which can be brush applied. The dirt can then be simply hosed off.

4 After washing the paintwork wipe it off with a chamois leather to give a clean unspotted finish. A coat of clear wax polish will give added protection against chemical pollutants in the air and will survive several subsequent washings. If the paintwork sheen has dulled or oxidised use a cleaner/polish combination to restore the brilliance of the shine. This requires a little more effort but is usually caused because regular washing has been neglected! Always check that door and ventilator drain holes and pipes are completely clear so that water can drain out. Brightwork should be treated in the same way as the paintwork. Windscreens and windows can be kept clear of the smeary film which often appears, if a little ammonia is added to the water. If glass work is scratched a good rub with a proprietary metal polish will often clean it. Never use any form of wax or other paint/chromium polish on glass.

3 Maintenance - bodywork interior

Mats and carpets should be brushed or vacuum cleaned regularly to keep them free of grit. If they are badly stained, remove them from the car for scrubbing or sponging and make quite sure that they are dry before refitting. Seat and interior trim panels can be kept clean with a wipe over with a damp cloth. If they do become stained, (which can be more apparent on light coloured upholstery) use a little liquid detergent and a soft nailbrush to scour the grime out of the grain of the material. Do not forget to keep the headlining clean in the same way as the upholstery. When using liquid cleaners inside the car do not over-wet the surfaces being cleaned. Excessive damp could get into the upholstery seams and padded interior, causing stains, offensive odours or even rot. If the inside of the car gets wet accidentally it is worthwhile taking some trouble to dry it out properly, particularly where carpets are involved. **Do not** leave oil or electrical heaters inside the car for this purpose.

4   Minor body damage - repair

See also the photo sequences on pages 230 and 231

Repair of minor scratches in the car's bodywork

If the scratch is very superficial, and does not penetrate to the metal of the bodywork - repair is very simple. Lightly rub the area of the scratch with a paintwork renovator or a very fine cutting paste, to remove loose paint from the scratch and to clear the surrounding bodywork of wax polish. Rinse the area with clean water.

Apply touch-up paint to the scratch using a thin paint brush; continue to apply thin layers of paint until the surface of the paint in the scratch is level with the surrounding paintwork. Allow the new paint at least two weeks to harden; then blend it into the surrounding paintwork by rubbing the paintwork in the scratch area with a paint-work renovator or a very fine cutting paste. Finally apply wax polish.

Where a scratch has penetrated right through to the metal of the bodywork, causing the metal to rust, a different repair technique is required. Remove any loose rust from the bottom of the scratch with a penknife; then apply rust inhibiting paint to prevent the formation of rust in the future. Using a rubber or nylon applicator fill the scratch with body-stopper paste. If required this paste can be mixed with cellulose thinners to provide a very thin paste which is ideal for filling narrow scratches. Before the stopper-paste in the scratch hardens, wrap a piece of smooth cotton rag around the tip of a finger,dip the finger in cellulose thinners and then quickly sweep it across the surface of the stopper-paste in the scratch; this will ensure that the surface of the stopper-paste is slightly hollowed. The scratch can now be painted over as described earlier in this Section.

Repair of dents in the car's bodywork

When deep denting of the car's bodywork has taken place, the first task is to pull the dent out, until the affected bodywork almost attains its original shape. There is little point in trying to restore the original shape completely, as the metal in the damaged area will have stretched on impact and cannot be reshaped fully to its original contour. It is better to bring the level of the dent up to a point which is about 1/8 in (3 mm) below the level of the surrounding bodywork. In cases where the dent is very shallow anyway, it is not worth trying to pull it out at all.

If the underside of the dent is accessible, it can be hammered out gently from behind, using a mallet with a wooden or plastic head. Whilst doing this, hold a suitable block of wood firmly against the outside of the dent. This block will absorb the impact from the hammer blows and thus prevent a large area of bodywork from being 'belled-out'.

Should the dent be in a section of the bodywork which has a double skin or some other factor making it inaccessible from behind, a different technique is called for. Drill several small holes through the metal inside the dent area - particularly in the deeper sections. Then screw long self-tapping screws into the holes just sufficiently for them to gain a good purchase in the metal. Now the dent can be pulled out by pulling on the protruding heads of the screws with a pair of pliers.

The next stage of the repair is the removal of the paint from the damaged area, and from an inch or so of the surrounding 'sound' bodywork. This is accomplished most easily by using a wire brush or abrasive pad on a power drill, although it can be done just as effectively by hand using sheets of abrasive paper. To complete the preparations for filling, score the surface of the bare metal with a screwdriver or tang of a file, or alternatively, drill small holes in the affected area. This will provide a really good key for the filler paste.

To complete the repair see the Section on filling and respraying.

Spray the whole repair area with a light coat of grey primer - this will show up any imperfections in the surface of the filler. Repair these imperfections with fresh filler paste or body-stopper, and once more smooth the surface with abrasive paper. If bodystopper is used, it can be mixed with cellulose thinners to form a really thin paste which is ideal for filling small holes. Repeat this spray and repair procedure until you are satisfied that the surface of the filler, and the feathered edge of the paintwork are perfect. Clean the repair area with clean water and allow to dry fully.

Repair of rustholes or gashes in the car's bodywork

Remove all paint from the affected area and from an inch or so of the surrounding 'sound' bodywork, using an abrasive pad or a wire brush on a power drill. If these are not available, a few sheets of abras-

ive paper will do the job just as effectively. With the paint removed you will be able to gauge the severity of the corrosion and therefore decide whether to renew the whole panel (if this is possible) or to repair the affected area. New body panels are not as expensive as most people think and it is often quicker and more satisfactory to fit a new panel than to attempt to repair large areas of corrosion.

Remove all fittings from the affected area, except those which will act as a guide to the original shape of the damaged bodywork (eg; head-lamp shells etc). Then, using tin snips or a hacksaw blade, remove all loose metal and any other metal badly affected by corrosion. Hammer the edges of the hole inwards in order to create a slight depression for the filler paste.

Wire brush the affected area to remove the powdery rust from the surface of the remaining metal. Paint the affected area with rust inhibiting paint; if the back of the rusted area is accessible treat this also.

Before filling can take place it will be necessary to block the hole in some way. This can be achieved by the use of one of the following materials: Zinc gauze, Aluminium tape or Polyurethane foam.

Zinc gauze is probably the best material to use for a large hole. Cut a piece to the approximate size and shape of the hole to be filled, then position it in the hole so that its edges are below the level of the surrounding bodywork. It can be retained in position by several blobs of filler paste round its periphery. Aluminium tape should be used for small or very narrow holes. Pull a piece off the roll and trim it to the approximate size and shape required, then pull off the backing paper (if used) and stick the tape over the hole; it can be overlapped if the thickness of one piece is insufficient. Burnish down the edges of the tape with the handle of a screwdriver or similar, to ensure that the tape is securely attached to the metal underneath.

Polyurethane foam is best used where the hole is situated in a section of bodywork of complex shape, backed by a small box section (eg. where the sill panel meets the rear wheelarch - most cars). The usual mixing procedure for this foam is as follows: Put equal amounts of fluid from each of the two cans provided in the kit, into one container. Stir until the mixture begins to thicken, then quickly pour this mixture into the hole, and hold a piece of cardboard over the larger apertures. Almost immediately the polyurethane will begin to expand, gushing out of any small holes left unblocked. When the foam hardens it can be cut back to just below the level of the surrounding bodywork with a hacksaw blade.

Having blocked off the hole the affected area must now be filled and sprayed - see Section on Bodywork repairs - filling and respraying.

Bodywork repairs - filling and re-spraying

Before using this Section, see the Sections on dent, deep scratch, rust hole and gash repairs.

Many types of bodyfillers are available, but generally speaking those proprietary kits which contain a tin of filler paste and a tube of resin hardener are best for this type of repair. A wide, flexible plastic or nylon applicator will be found invaluable for imparting a smooth and well contoured finish to the surface of the filler.

Mix up a little filler on a clean piece of card or board - use the hardener sparingly (follow the maker's instructions on the packet), otherwise the filler will set very rapidly.

Using the applicator apply the filler paste to the prepared area; draw the applicator across the surface of the filler to achieve the correct contour and to level the filler surface. As soon as a contour that approximates the correct one is achieved, stop working the paste - if you carry on too long the paste will become 'tacky' and begin to 'pick-up' on the applicator. Continue to add thin layers of filler paste at twenty-minute intervals until the level of the filler is just 'proud' of the surrounding bodywork.

Once the filler has hardened, excess can be removed using a metal plane or file. From then on, progressively finer grades of abrasive paper should be used, starting with a 40 grade production paper and finishing with 400 grade 'wet-and-dry' paper. Always wrap the abrasive paper around a flat rubber, cork, or wooden block - otherwise the surface of the filler will not be completley flat. During the smoothing of the filler surface the 'wet-and-dry' paper should be periodically rinsed in water - this will ensure that a very smooth finish is imparted to the filler at the final stage.

At this stage the 'dent' should be surrounded by a ring of bare metal, which in turn should be encircled by the finely 'feathered' edge of the good paintwork. Rinse the repair area with clean water, until all of the dust produced by the rubbing-down operation is gone.

The repair area is now ready for spraying. Paint spraying must be carried out in a warm, dry, windless and dust free atmosphere. This condition can be created artificially if you have access to a large indoor working area, but if you are forced to work in the open, you will have to pick your day very carefully. If you are working indoors, dousing the floor in the work area with water will 'lay' the dust which would otherwise be in the atmosphere. If the repair area is confined to one body panel, mask off the surrounding panels; this will help to minimise the effects of a slight mis-match in paint colours. Bodywork fittings (eg; chrome strips, door handles etc.) will also need to be masked off. Use genuine masking tape and several thickness of newspaper for the masking operation.

Before commencing to spray, agitate the aerosol can thoroughly, then spray a test area (an old tin, or similar) until the technique is mastered, Cover the repair area with a thick coat of primer; the thickness should be built up using several thin layers of paint rather than one thick one. Using 400 grade 'wet-and-dry' paper, rub down the surface of the primer until it is really smooth. While doing this, the work area should be thoroughly doused with water, and the wet-and-dry paper periodically rinsed in water. Allow to dry before spraying on more paint.

Spray on the top coat, again building up the thickness by using several thin layers of paint. Start spraying in the centre of the repair area and then, using a circular motion, work outwards until the whole repair area and about 2 inches of the surrounding original paintwork is covered. Remove all masking material 10 to 15 minutes after spraying on the final coat of paint

Allow the new paint at least 2 weeks to harden fully; then, using a paintwork renovator or a very fine cutting paste, blend the edges of the new paint into the existing paintwork. Finally apply wax polish.

5 Major body damage - repair

Where serious damage has occurred or large areas of the body need renewal due to rusting it means certainly that complete new sections or panels will need welding in and this is best left to the professionals. If the damage is due to impact it will also be necessary to completely check the alignment of the body shell structure. Due to the principle of construction the strength and shape of the whole car can be affected

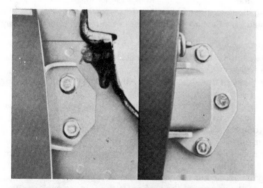

Fig. 12.1. Door hinge attachment to body pillar

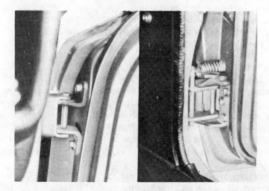

Fig. 12.2. Door hinge attachment to door frame

by damage to a relatively small area. In such instances the services of a Toyota garage with specialist jigs are essential. If a body is left misaligned it is first of all dangerous as the car will not handle properly, and secondly, uneven stresses will be imposed on the steering, engine and transmission, causing abnormal wear or complete failure. Tyre wear may also be excessive.

6 Maintenance - hinges, door catches and locks

1   Oil the hinges of the bonnet, boot and doors with a drop or two of light oil periodically. A good time is after the car has been washed.
2   Oil the bonnet safety catch thrust pin periodically.
3   Do not over-lubricate door latches and strikers. Normally one or two drops regularly applied is better than a lot at one go.

7 Doors - tracing of rattles and their rectification

1   Check first that the door is not loose at the hinges and that the latch is holding the door firmly in position. Check also that the door lines up with the aperture in the body.
2   If the hinges are loose or the door is out of alignment it will be necessary to reset the hinge position as described in Section 8.
3   If the latch is holding the door properly it should hold the door tightly when fully latched and the door should line up with the body. If it is out of alignment it needs adjustment as described in Section 9. If loose some part of the lock mechanism must be worn out and requiring renewal.
4   Other rattles from the door would be caused by wear or looseness in the window winder, the glass channels and sill strips or the door buttons and interior latch release mechanism. All these are dealt with in subsequent Sections.

8 Door alignment - hinge adjustment

1   The hinges are adjustable both on the door and pillar mountings. Access to some of the bolts will require removal of trim and the use of a spanner.
2   When re-aligning is necessary first slacken the bolts holding the hinge to the door and reposition the door as required and make sure the bolts are thoroughly tightened up again. If the amount of movement on the door half of the hinge is insufficient it may be adjusted at the door pillar (Fig. 12.1).
3   If the hinges themselves are worn at the hinge pin the door should be detached from the hinges, the hinges removed and new ones fitted (Fig. 12.2).

9 Door latch striker - alignment

1   Assuming that the door hinges are correctly aligned but the trailing edge of the door is not flush with the body when the door is fully latched, then the striker plate needs adjusting.
2   Slacken the two crosshead screws holding the striker plate to the door pillar just enough to hold the striker plate in position and then push the plate to the inner limit of its position. Try and shut the door,

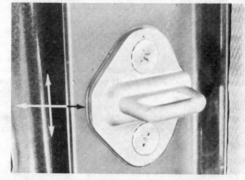

Fig. 12.3. Door lock striker

moving the striker plate outwards until the latch is able to engage fully. (Fig. 12.3).

3 Without pulling on the release handle but working inside the car push the door outwards until it is flush with the bodywork. This will move the striker plate along with the latch.

4 Release the latch very carefully so as not to disturb the striker plate and open the door. Tighten down the striker plate securing screws.

10 Door lock components - removal and refitting

1 The operations are similar on all models but reference should be made to the appropriate illustrations for exact details of individual components (Figs. 12.4, 12.5 and 12.6).

2 Unscrew the armrest securing screws and remove the armrest (photo).

3 Press the door interior trim panel away from the window regulator handle and insert a piece of wire with a hook to engage in the regulator handle spring clip. Pull the clip and remove the regulator handle (photo).

4 Pinch the frame of the door interior lock handle escutcheon plate and withdraw it from the trim panel. Some models also have a central securing screw in the escutcheon plate. (photo).

5 Insert the fingers or a blade between the edge of the trim panel and the door frame and jerk the panel securing clips from their holes. Work round the edge of the panel until it can be removed from the door (photo).

6 Carefully peel away the waterproof sheeting from the door and place it to one side (photo).

7 To remove the lock assembly, temporarily refit the window regulator handle and raise the glass fully.

8 Disconnect the linkage from the lock.

9 Extract the lower frame mounting bolt (1) and the lock screws (2).

10.2 Removing a door armrest securing screw

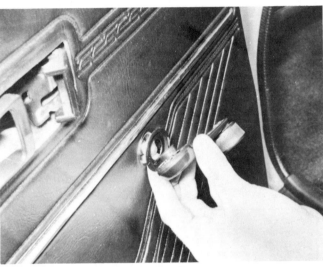

10.3 Removing a window regulator handle

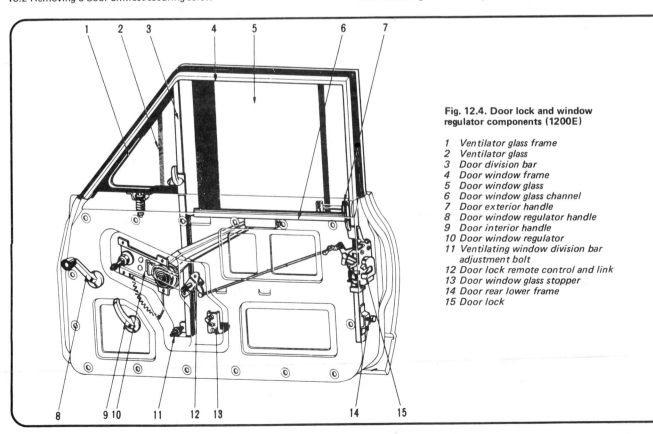

Fig. 12.4. Door lock and window regulator components (1200E)

1 Ventilator glass frame
2 Ventilator glass
3 Door division bar
4 Door window frame
5 Door window glass
6 Door window glass channel
7 Door exterior handle
8 Door window regulator handle
9 Door interior handle
10 Door window regulator
11 Ventilating window division bar adjustment bolt
12 Door lock remote control and link
13 Door window glass stopper
14 Door rear lower frame
15 Door lock

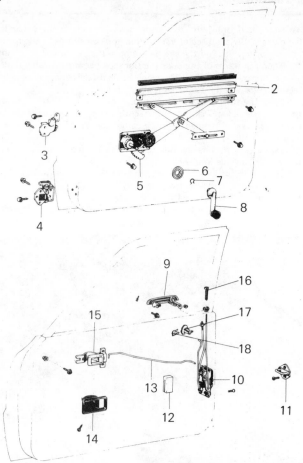

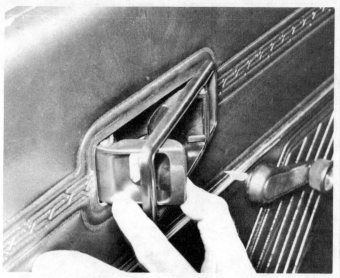

10.4 Removing door interior lock handle escutcheon plate

Fig. 12.5. Front door lock and regulator components (30 Series and 1600)

1	Glass weatherstrip	10	Door lock assembly
2	Glass channel	11	Striker plate
3	Door upper hinge	12	Anti-rattle clip
4	Door lower hinge	13	Link rod
5	Regulator assembly	14	Interior handle escutcheon plate
6	Regulator handle escutcheon plate	15	Door interior handle
7	Winder handle clip	16	Door lock plunger
8	Window winder handle	17	Lock cylinder
9	Exterior handle	18	Lock cylinder retainer

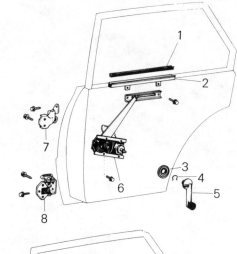

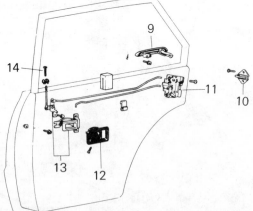

Fig. 12.6. Rear door lock and regulator components (30 Series and 1600)

1	Glass weatherstrip	8	Door lower hinge
2	Glass channel	9	Exterior handle
3	Escutcheon plate	10	Striker plate
4	Window winder handle clip	11	Lock assembly
5	Winder handle	12	Interior handle escutcheon plate
6	Window regulator assembly	13	Lock interior handle
7	Door upper hinge	14	Door lock plunger

10.5 Removing door interior trim panel

Withdraw the lock through the access hole in the door panel (Fig. 12.7).

10 The exterior handle can be removed after disconnecting the control link at the securing bolts. The latter are accessible from inside the door (Fig. 12.8).

11 The key-operated lock cylinder can be removed once its securing circlip and clamp have been extracted (Fig. 12.9).

12 The interior remote control handle can be removed if the link rod is detached and the handle mounting screws extracted (Fig. 12.10).

13 Refitting is a reversal of removal but the following adjustments must be carried out.

14 When refitting the interior lock control handle, insert the securing screws finger tight initially and push the control (with link rod attached) towards the front of the vehicle until resistance is felt and then move it back between 0.02 and 0.04 in (0.5 and 1.0 mm).

15 The exterior handle link rod should be adjusted so that there is a clearance of between 0.02 and 0.04 in (0.5 and 1.0 mm) before the handle actuates the lock mechanism (Fig. 12.11).

11 Door window regulator - removal and refitting

1 Remove the door interior trim as previously described and lower the glass fully.

2 Support the glass and remove the lower stop.

3 Unscrew the regulator securing bolts and turn the unit to release its rollers from the glass channel. On some models, the regulator arm is attached to the glass channel by two bolts which should be removed (Fig. 12.12).

4 Withdraw the regulator from the door cavity.

5 Refitting is a reversal of removal but apply grease to all moving parts of the regulator and to the glass channel slides.

6 Refit the regulator handle at the angle shown when the glass is fully raised. When refitting the regulator handle, engage its securing spring clip in the grooves in the handle, position it on the spindle of the regulator unit and give the handle a sharp blow with the hand to drive it into position. As this happens, the spring clip will expand momentarily and then lock the handle to the spindle (Fig. 12.13).

12 Door glass (1200E) - removal and refitting

1 Refer to Section 10 and remove the door interior trim panel.

2 Lower the glass fully and then using a screwdriver carefully ease out the door window glass inner weatherstrip.

3 Remove the door window glass outer weatherstrip using a wide bladed screwdriver. Be careful not to chip the paintwork.

4 Remove the division bar adjustment bolts and then remove the door window glass run from the division bar.

10.6 View of door (1600 Liftback) trim panel removed

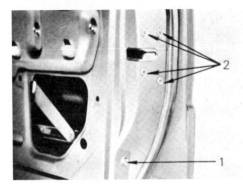

Fig. 12.7. Door lock attachment

1 Lower frame mounting bolt   2 Lock securing screws

Fig. 12.8. Door exterior handle securing screws (1)

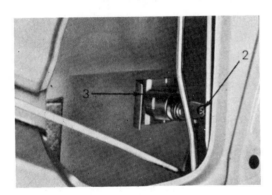

Fig. 12.9. Door lock cylinder securing circlip (2) and clamp (3)

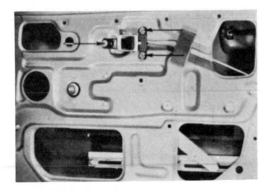

Fig. 12.10. Door lock remote control interior handle securing screws

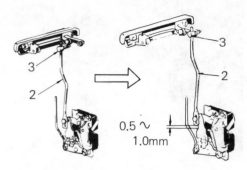

Fig. 12.11. Door exterior handle adjustment diagram

2   Link rod   3   Swivel clamp

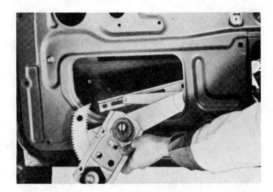

Fig. 12.12. Removing window regulator mechanism

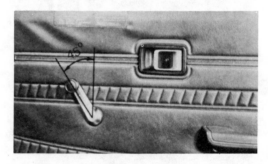

Fig. 12.13. Window regulator handle correctly installed (glass fully up)

Fig. 12.14. Removing door glass division bar (1200E)

5   Undo and remove the three screws that secure the division bar to the door and move the division bar rearwards, whilst tilting the top of the ventilator assembly rearwards. Lift away the assembly (Fig. 12.14).
6   The door window glass can now be removed from the door.
7   It is possible to detach the channel from the bottom of the glass using a soft faced hammer.
8   To refit the channel onto the glass, position the glass channel with weatherstrip on the glass so that it is central and tap the channel base with a soft faced hammer. If it is tight lubricate with a concentrated soap and water solution or washing up liquid (Fig. 12.15).
9   If necessary the ventilator window glass can be removed from the frame. First remove the upper pivot bracket securing screw (Fig. 12.16).
10 The glass can now be removed from the frame.
11 To refit the glass apply a little adhesive to the glass frame and install the frame strip.
12 Apply a little adhesive to the frame strip and fit the glass to the glass frame.
13 The glass frame may now be fitted to the division frame. Adjust the ventilator window tension by resetting the compression spring nut and then lock the nut with a lockplate.
14 To reassemble first insert the door glass into the door.
15 Fit the door window glass run to the door division bar.
16 Insert the door division bar assembly into the door and locate the division bar on the glass. Fit the three securing screws.
17 Fit the door window glass inner weatherstrip and then the outer weatherstrip.
18 Raise the glass and support in this position.
19 Position the window regulator in the door and insert the regulator roller into the glass channel. Apply a little grease onto the glass channel.
20 Secure the regulator to the door.
21 Fit the door window glass stopper.
22 Fit the division bar adjustment bolt and adjust the location of the division bar to give a smooth, even movement without rattling (Fig. 12.18).
23 Replace the service hole cover and then the door trim panel and handles.

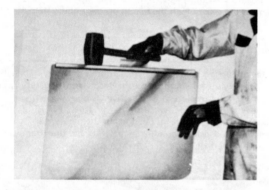

Fig. 12.15. Refitting channel to door glass (1200E)

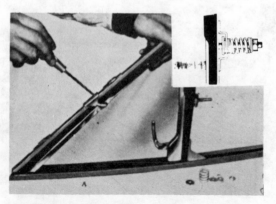

Fig. 12.16. Removing ventilator upper pivot (1200E)

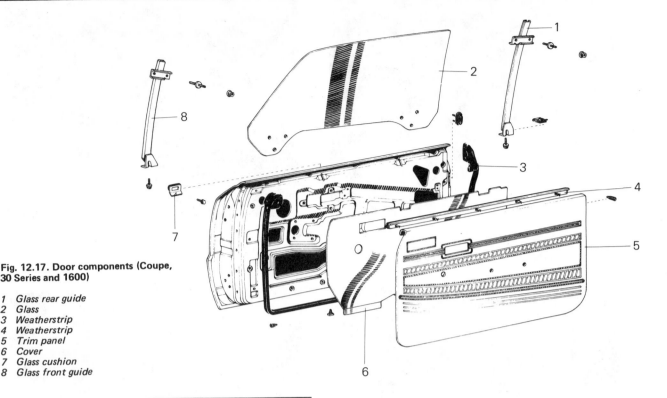

Fig. 12.17. Door components (Coupe, 30 Series and 1600)

1   Glass rear guide
2   Glass
3   Weatherstrip
4   Weatherstrip
5   Trim panel
6   Cover
7   Glass cushion
8   Glass front guide

13 Front door glass (Saloon, Wagon, 30 Series, 1600) - removal and refitting

1   Remove the door interior trim as previously described in Section 10.
2   Lower the glass fully and extract the two bolts which secure the regulator arm to the glass channel (Fig. 12.19).
3   Withdraw the glass with channel attached.
4   The channel can be removed from the glass if necessary by tapping it off with a hammer and thin piece of hardwood.
5   When fitting the glass channel to the glass, set it as shown in the diagram. Tap the channel into position using a soft faced hammer and apply soapy water to the rubber to ease its installation (Fig. 12.20).
6   Refitting is a reversal of removal but adjust the glass side guides to give smooth operation.

14 Front door glass (Coupe, 30 Series and 1600) - removal and refitting

1   The operations are very similar to those described in the preceding Section for other body versions but the different method of securing the glass to the regulator mechanism by means of retaining plates will be seen from the illustration (Fig. 12.17).
2   Correct adjustment of the glass can be carried out by means of the many adjustment screws accessible from the door interior panel.

15 Rear door glass (Saloon, Wagon, 30 Series, 1600) - removal and refitting

1   Refer to Section 10 and remove the door interior trim panel.
2   Lower the glass fully.
3   Unscrew and remove the glass division bar by extracting the bolt (4), the screws (5) (Fig. 12.21).
4   Unscrew and remove the two bolts which attach the window regulator arm to the glass channel.
5   Remove the glass out of the top of the door.
6   If the glass is to be renewed, set the channel to the new glass as shown in the diagram (Fig. 12.22).
7   The quarter window glass can be removed towards the front of the vehicle (Fig. 12.23).
8   Refitting is a reversal of removal.

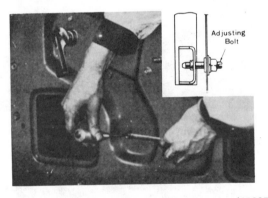

Fig. 12.18. Adjusting position of door glass division bar (1200E)

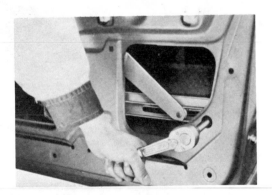

Fig. 12.19. Unscrewing regulator arm to glass channel bolt (30 Series and 1600)

This sequence of photographs deals with the repair of the dent and paintwork damage shown in this photo. The procedure will be similar for the repair of a hole. It should be noted that the procedures given here are simplified — more explicit instructions will be found in the text

In the case of a dent the first job — after removing surrounding trim — is to hammer out the dent where access is possible. This will minimise filling. Here, the large dent having been hammered out, the damaged area is being made slightly concave

Now all paint must be removed from the damaged area, by rubbing with coarse abrasive paper. Alternatively, a wire brush or abrasive pad can be used in a power drill. Where the repair area meets good paintwork, the edge of the paintwork should be 'feathered', using a finer grade of abrasive paper

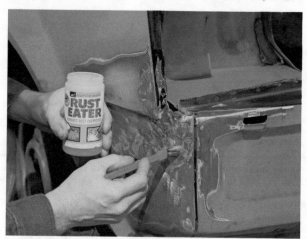

In the case of a hole caused by rusting, all damaged sheet-metal should be cut away before proceeding to this stage. Here, the damaged area is being treated with rust remover and inhibitor before being filled

Mix the body filler according to its manufacturer's instructions. In the case of corrosion damage, it will be necessary to block off any large holes before filling — this can be done with aluminium or plastic mesh, or aluminium tape. Make sure the area is absolutely clean before ...

... applying the filler. Filler should be applied with a flexible applicator, as shown, for best results; the wooden spatula being used for confined areas. Apply thin layers of filler at 20-minute intervals, until the surface of the filler is slightly proud of the surrounding bodywork

Initial shaping can be done with a Surform plane or Dreadnought file. Then, using progressively finer grades of wet-and-dry paper, wrapped around a sanding block, and copious amounts of clean water, rub down the filler until really smooth and flat. Again, feather the edges of adjoining paintwork

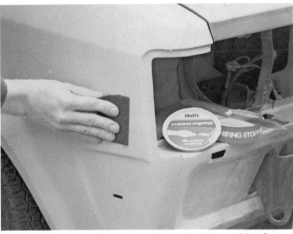

Again, using plenty of water, rub down the primer with a fine grade wet-and-dry paper (400 grade is probably best) until it is really smooth and well blended into the surrounding paintwork. Any remaining imperfections can now be filled by carefully applied knifing stopper paste

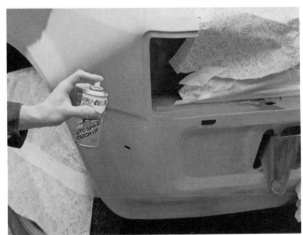

The top coat can now be applied. When working out of doors, pick a dry, warm and wind-free day. Ensure surrounding areas are protected from over-spray. Agitate the aerosol thoroughly, then spray the centre of the repair area, working outwards with a circular motion. Apply the paint as several thin coats

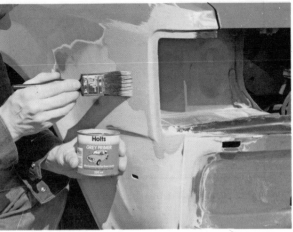

The whole repair area can now be sprayed or brush-painted with primer. If spraying, ensure adjoining areas are protected from over-spray. Note that at least one inch of the surrounding sound paintwork should be coated with primer. Primer has a 'thick' consistency, so will find small imperfections

When the stopper has hardened, rub down the repair area again before applying the final coat of primer. Before rubbing down this last coat of primer, ensure the repair area is blemish-free — use more stopper if necessary. To ensure that the surface of the primer is really smooth use some finishing compound

After a period of about two weeks, which the paint needs to harden fully, the surface of the repaired area can be 'cut' with a mild cutting compound prior to wax polishing. When carrying out bodywork repairs, remember that the quality of the finished job is proportional to the time and effort expended

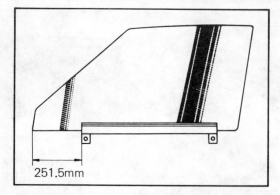

Fig. 12.20. Channel to front door glass fixing diagram (30 Series and 1600)

251.5mm

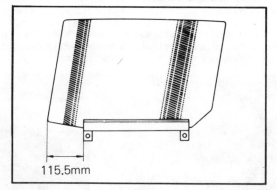

Fig. 12.22. Channel to rear door glass fixing diagram (30 Series and 1600)

115.5mm

Fig. 12.21. Rear door glass division bar removal (30 Series, 1600)

4   Lower securing bolt   6   Division bar
5   Upper screws

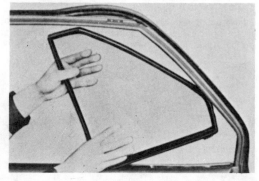

Fig. 12.23. Removing quarter window glass (30 Series and 1600)

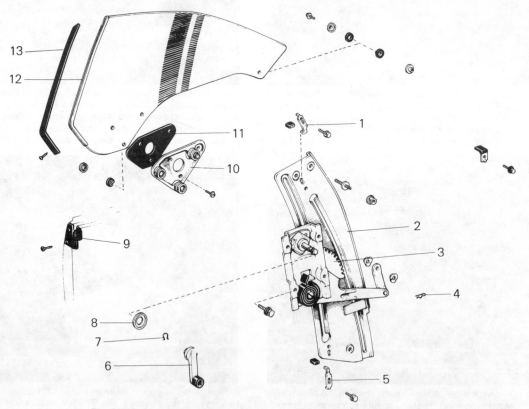

Fig. 12.24. Rear quarter window components (Coupe 30 Series and 1600)

1 Upper stop	5 Glass lower stop	8 Escutcheon plate	11 Glass bracket plate
2 Glass guide	6 Window regulator handle	9 Corner weatherstrip	12 Glass
3 Regulator assembly	7 Regulator handle securing clip	10 Glass holder spacer	13 Front weatherstrip
4 Clip			

16 Rear Quarter window regulator and glass (Coupe, 30 Series and 1600) - removal and refitting

1   Remove the rear seat and seat belt retractor.
2   Remove a section of the rear scuff plate to permit withdrawal of the quarter trim panel (Fig. 12.24).
3   Extract the spring clip which secures the window regulator handle and remove the handle (see Section 10).
4   Remove the trim panel securing screws and withdraw the panel.
5   Release the nuts (1) the pin (2) and bolts (3) and withdraw the regulator unit (Fig. 12.26).
6   To remove the glass, extract the screws which hold the bolt moulding to the body and remove the moulding.
7   Remove the rear upper stopper (4) and the front upper stopper (5).
8   Withdraw the glass.
9   Refitting is a reversal of removal, any adjustment required to provide smooth operation of the glass can be carried out by moving the position of some or all of the bolts shown in Fig. 12.26.

17 Opening quarter window (1200E and Liftback) - removal and refitting

1   To remove the glass assembly undo and remove the screws that secure the hinges and lock assembly to the window aperture (Fig. 12.27).
2   Lift away the glass assembly.
3   To remove the hinges and lock from the glass undo and remove the securing bolts. Take care not to lose or damage the rubber packing pieces.
4   Reassembly and refitting is the reverse sequence to removal. To adjust the glass location slacken the hinge and lock securing bolts and reposition the glass. Retighten the securing bolts.
5   To adjust the quarter window for correct contact with the weather-strip increase or decrease the number of shims at the window lock.

18 Doors - removal and refitting

1   Open the door to its fullest extent and support its lower edge on jacks or blocks covered with rag to prevent damage to the paintwork.
2   Mark the position of the hinge plates on the edges of the doors.
3   Have an assistant support the door in the vertical position and unscrew and remove the hinge bolts from the door side.
4   Lift the door away.
5   If the hinges must be removed from the door pillars, again mark their position before unbolting them.
6   Refit the door by reversing the removal operations, adjust if necessary after reference to Section 8.

19 Windscreen - removal and refitting

1   Windscreen refitting is no light task. Leave this to a specialist if possible. Instructions are given below for the more ambitious.
2   Remove the windscreen wiper arms and blades and also the interior mirror.
3   If the screen is of non-laminated type and has already shattered and been knocked out, use a vacuum cleaner to pick up as much as possible of the glass crystals.
4   Switch on the heater boost motor and adjust the controls to 'Screen Defrost' but watch out for flying pieces of glass which might be blown out of the ducting.
5   If the screen is unbroken or is of the laminated type, carefully ease out the windscreen mouldings from the weatherstrip.
6   The assistance of a second person should now be enlisted, ready to catch the glass when it is released from its aperture.
7   Using a screwdriver break the seal between the weatherstrip and the aperture taking care not to scratch the paintwork.
8   Working from inside the car, commencing at one top corner, press the glass and ease it and the rubber weatherstrip from the aperture lip.
9   Remove the rubber weatherstrip from the glass.
10 Now is the time to remove all pieces of glass if the screen has shattered (toughened type glass).
11 Carefully inspect the rubber weatherstrip for signs of splitting or

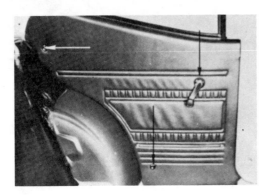

Fig. 12.25. Rear quarter trim panel securing screws and window winder handle

Fig. 12.26. Rear quarter trim panel removed showing (1) glass guide bolts (2) regulator to equaliser arm pin (3) window regulator bolts (4) rear upper stop (5) front upper stop

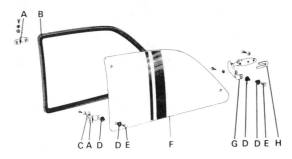

Fig. 12.27. Components of opening quarter window (1200E and Liftback)

A   Hinge plate   E   Screw
B   Weatherstrip   F   Glass
C   Boss   G   Lock
D   Grommet   H   Spacer

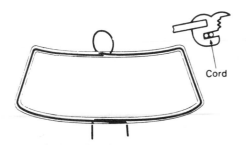

Fig. 12.28. Cord fitting diagram for windscreen installation

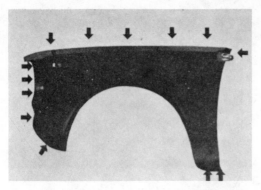

Fig. 12.29. Front wing securing bolts (1200E)

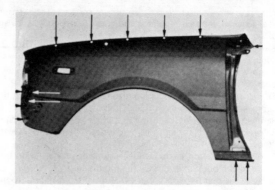

Fig. 12.30. Front wing securing bolts (30 Series and 1600)

Fig. 12.31. Removing a front wing (30 Series and 1600)

Fig. 12.32. Front wing splash shield securing screws (30 Series and 1600)

Fig. 12.33. Stone deflector panel securing screws (1200E)

Fig. 12.34. Stone deflector panel securing screws (30 Series and 1600)

other deterioration. Clean all traces of sealing compound from the weatherstrip and windscreen aperture flange.

12 To refit the glass first place the rubber weatherstrip onto the glass edge.

13 Place a piece of cord onto the body flange groove of the weatherstrip and cross the ends at the top centre of the weatherstrip (Fig. 12. 28).

14 Offer up the glass and weather strip to the aperture and using the cord pull the rubber lip over the body flange. Whilst this is being done a person outside the car must apply firm pressure to the glass to ensure that the weatherstrip seats correctly onto the body flange.

15 If the weatherstrip is new, or stiff, lubricate the aperture and weatherstrip flanges with a little concentrated soap and water solution or washing-up liquid.

16 Apply some adhesive cement between the weatherstrip and the body and also between the weatherstrip and the glass.

17 Carefully refit the weatherstrip moulding using a screwdriver or special fitting tool and finally refit the interior mirror and the wiper arms.

20 Rear window - removal and refitting

1   The operations are almost identical with those described for the windscreen, except that the leads to the heater element should be disconnected before removal of the glass.

21 Front wing - removal and refitting

1   *On 1200E models,* for safety reasons, disconnect the battery.

2   Remove the windscreen wiper arm assemblies and then the cowl ventilator louvre located at the base of the windscreen.

3   Remove the rocker panel moulding.

4   Remove the wing splash shield.

5   Refer to Chapter 10, and remove the headlight assembly and then the radiator grille.

6   Refer to Section 27, and remove the front bumper.

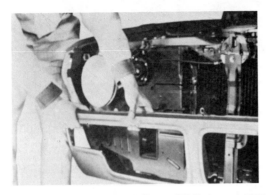

Fig. 12.35. Removing stone deflector (30 Series and 1600)

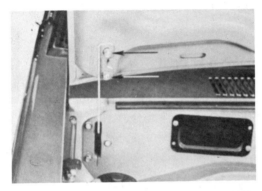

Fig. 12.36. Bonnet hinge bolts (30 Series and 1600)

Fig. 12.37. Adjusting bonnet lock dowel (1200E)

Fig. 12.38. Bonnet lock (30 Series and 1600)

7   Undo and remove the 13 nuts, bolts and screws securing the front wing to the body (Fig. 12.29). Lift away the front wing panel. When removing the left-hand wing do not forget to disconnect the radio aerial.

8   Refitting the front wing is the reverse sequence to removal. Do not tighten the wing securing nuts, bolts and screws until its final fitted position has been adjusted at the bonnet aperture and leading edge of the front door. Then tighten the attachments.

9   *On 30 series and 1600 models,* the operations are similar to those just described except that the wiper arms and louvre need not be removed.

10   Observe also the different locations of the bolts at the front edge of the wing and remember to disconnect the leads to the side marker light.

22 Stone deflector - removal and refitting

1   The stone deflecting panel is located beneath the radiator grille.
2   Refer to Chapter 10 and remove the headlight units and the radiator grille.
3   Remove the front bumper (Section 27).
4   Disconnect the leads from the front direction indicator and parking lights.
5   Unscrew and remove the securing bolts and screws which hold the stone deflector panel in position and remove (Figs. 12.33, 12.34 and 12.35).
6   Refitting is a reversal of removal but do not fully tighten the securing bolts until the panel has been aligned with the surrounding bodywork surfaces.

23 Bonnet - removal and refitting

1   With the bonnet open, use a soft pencil and mark the outline position of both hinges on the bonnet to act as a guide to refitting (Fig. 12.36).
2   With the help of an assistant to support the front of the bonnet undo and remove the hinge securing bolts.
3   Undo and remove the two bolts and washers securing the bonnet to each hinge. Lift away the bonnet from over the front of the car.
4   *On 1200E models,* removal of the hinges themselves can be carried out after first unscrewing the air intake grille at the base of the windscreen.
5   *On 30 series and 1600 models,* the hinges can be unbolted and removed after the cover plates have been removed from the engine compartment rear bulkhead.
6   *On 1200E models,* the removal of the bonnet lock and release lever is a straightforward operation and will not present any problems. The battery should be disconnected to prevent accidental short circuiting.
7   Reassembly and refitting as applicable is the reverse sequence to removal. Several adjustments are necessary and should be carried out as follows:
8   Adjustment of the bonnet in the aperture is effected by slackening the bonnet to hinge securing bolts and repositioning the bonnet in the aperture. To lift the rear edge of the bonnet, the hinge can be raised once the securing bolts to the body have been slackened. To

Fig. 12.39. Adjusting a bonnet bump stop

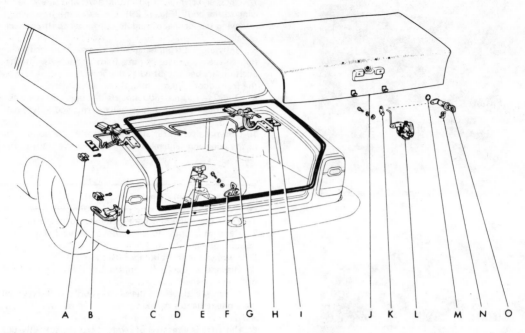

Fig. 12.40. Rear boot lid components (1200E)

A Jack handle clamp   E Weatherstrip   I Spacer   M Circlip
B Jack carrier   F Striker plate   J Boot lid   N Lock cylinder retainer
C Spare wheel clamp screw   G Torsion bar   K Clip   O Lock cylinder
D Spare wheel clamp plate   H Hinge   L Lock

lift the front edge of the bonnet slacken the bonnet lock securing nut and screw out the dowel by the required amount. Tighten the
locknut. The bump stops at the front of the engine compartment
should also be adjusted to be compatible with the new setting of the
lock dowel (Fig. 12.37).
9 *On 30 series and 1600 models,* the lock mechanism which is
attached to the crossmember above the radiator is adjustable for
position to ensure positive closure of the bonnet, otherwise the bonnet
hinges and bump stops should be adjusted as described for 1200E
models (Figs. 12.38 and 12.39).

24 Luggage boot lid - removal and refitting

1 With the boot lid open, mark the fitted position of the hinge
relative to the boot lid (Fig. 12.40).
2 An assistant should now support the weight of the boot lid and then
undo and remove the four bolts and washers securing the boot lid to
the hinges (Fig. 12.41).
3 Lift away the boot lid and recover the hinge spacers.
4 If necessary the torsion bar may be removed by detaching at one
end to release the tension and then lifting away (Fig. 12.42).
5 To remove the lock cylinder release the spring retainer with a pair
of pliers, detach the pull rod and lift away the lock cylinder.
6 To remove the lock from the boot lid undo and remove the
securing bolts and washers (Fig. 12.43).
7 Reassembly and refitting of the boot lid, lock and hinges is the
reverse sequence to removal.
8 The following adjustments may be required if the hinge to body
bolts have been disturbed or new components fitted.
9 Adjustment of the boot lid in the aperture is effected by slackening
the boot lid to hinge securing bolts and repositioning the boot lid in
the aperture.
10 To lift or lower the hinge end of the boot lid fit or remove hinge
spacers as necessary.
11 To adjust the lock slacken the lock striker securing bolts and
move the striker as necessary. Tighten the securing bolts (Fig. 12.45).

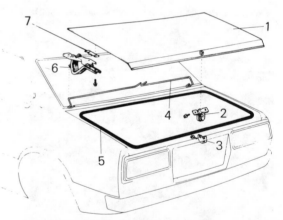

Fig. 12.41. Rear boot lid components (30 Series and 1600)

1 Boot lid   5 Weatherstrip
2 Lock   6 Hinge
3 Striker plate   7 Spacer
4 Torsion bar

Fig. 12.42. Removing luggage boot lid torsion bar

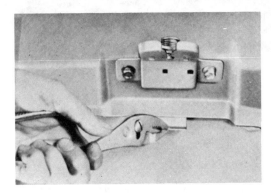

Fig. 12.43. Extracting luggage boot lid lock cylinder clamp

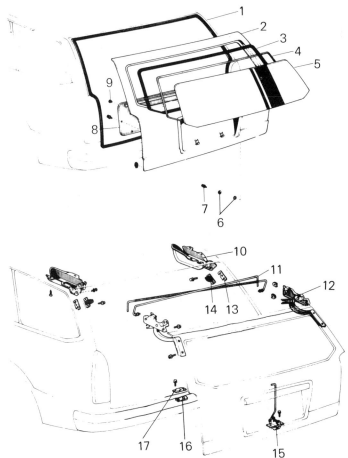

Fig. 12.44. Estate wagon tailgate components (30 Series, 1600)

1	Weatherstrip	10	Hinge cover
2	Tailgate	11	Torsion bar
3	Glass surround	12	Hinge
4	Weatherstrip	13	Spacer plate
5	Glass	14	Upper stop
6	Lockwashers	15	Lock assembly
7	Door stop	16	Shim
8	Trim panel	17	Striker assembly
9	Panel clip		

25 Tailgate (Wagon) - removal and refitting

1   Open the tailgate fully, disconnect the leads from the heated rear window and the wiper motor. Disconnect the tubing to the rear washer (Fig. 12.44).
2   With an assistant supporting the weight of the tailgate, mark the position of the hinge plates on the underside of the tailgate, unscrew the bolts and lift the tailgate from the vehicle.
3   If the hinges must be removed from the body shell, first extract the screws and covers from the hinges (Fig. 12.46).
4   A suitable lever will now be required to relieve the force of the torsion bars and release them from their anchorages. Take care with this job as the torsion bars exert a considerable tension (Fig. 12.47).
5   Unscrew and remove the hinge bolts and remove the hinges (Fig. 12.49).
6   Refitting is a reversal of removal. If the tailgate must be adjusted to make its outer surface flush with those of the rear body panels, loosen the bolts which secure the hinges to the body. If the tailgate requires adjustment up or down, loosen the bolts which secure it to the hinges.
7   The lock striker plate and the bump stops are all adjustable (the latter with shims or screws) to provide a secure, rattle free closure of the tailgate.

26 Liftback - removal and refitting

1   Open the door fully and disconnect the leads from the heating element, wiper motor and the tubing from the washer jet (Fig. 12.48).
2   Disconnect the stays.
3   Have an assistant support the door and disconnect the hinges from it. Lift the door from the vehicle.
4   On no account attempt to dismantle the gas-filled stays. Renew them if they are faulty.
5   Refitting is a reversal of removal, adjust if necessary by moving the position of the door on the hinges and by adjustment of the lock striker.
6   Refer to Chapter 10 for details of the washer and wiper mechanism.

27 Bumpers - removal and refitting

1   On vehicles without impact absorbing bumpers, removal is simply a matter of either unbolting the bumper bar from the brackets or unbolting the brackets from the bodyframe side members and withdrawing the complete assembly (Fig. 12.50).
2   On vehicles equipped with impact absorbing bumpers, the multi-component construction of the bumper bar should be noted. The bumper bar can be unbolted from the silicone-filled shock absorbing pistons.
3   The pistons can be unbolted either complete with or separately from their support brackets.
4   The piston assemblies should slowly return to their normal state after being compressed by impact or during test. If they do not, renew them.
5   Refitting is a reversal of removal.

Fig. 12.45. Luggage boot lid striker plate

238

Fig. 12.46. Wagon tailgate hinge cover and retaining screws

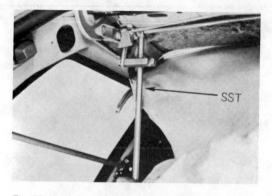

Fig. 12.47. Using a lever to release tailgate torsion bar

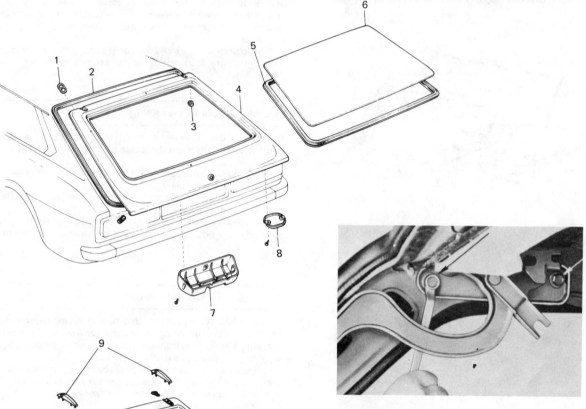

Fig. 12.49. Unscrewing tailgate hinge bolt from body

Fig. 12.48. Liftback door components

1	Grommet	8	Inspection plate
2	Weatherstrip	9	Hinges
3	Grommet	10	Lock
4	Door	11	Stay
5	Weatherstrip	12	Pivot pin
6	Glass	13	Bracket
7	Wiper motor cover	14	Striker plate

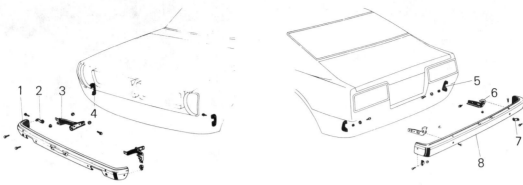

Fig. 12.50. Bumper components (non-impact absorbing)

| 1 Bumper bar | 3 Strengthener | 5 Protector | 7 Side clip |
| 2 Mounting bracket | 4 Protector | 6 Strengthener | 8 Bumper bar |

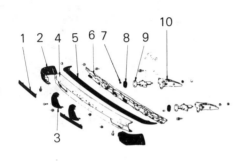

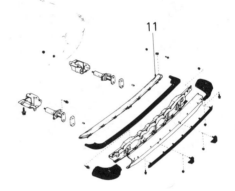

Fig. 12.51. Bumper components (impact absorbing)

1 Pad	4 Bar	7 Spacer	10 Mounting bracket
2 Extension	5 Filler	8 Insulator	11 Stone deflector
3 Overriders	6 Reinforcement	9 Shock absorbing piston	

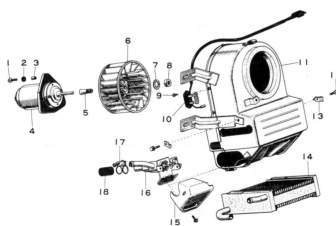

Fig. 12.52. Exploded view of heater (1200E)

1 Screw	10 Resistor
2 Extension	11 Heater casing
3 Bush	12 Bolt
4 Blower motor	13 Clamp
5 Adaptor	14 Matrix
6 Blower fan	15 Cover
7 Lock washer	16 Water valve
8 Nut	17 Hose clips
9 Screw	18 Hose

28 Heater (1200E) - removal, dismantling and refitting

1 Each of the following major components can be removed independently (Fig. 12.52).

Control panel
2 Remove the instrument panel as described in Chapter 10. It is recommended that the battery is first disconnected.
3 Disconnect the control cables and rod from the heater assembly.
4 Disconnect the leads from the heater blower switch and from the cigar lighter.
5 Disconnect the leads from the radio and remove it as described in Chapter 10.
6 Pull off the heater control knob by following the directions given in the accompanying diagram (Fig. 12.53).
7 Remove the heater control panel from the central embellishment of the fascia extracting the three securing screws.

Blower switch
8 Remove the ash-tray and the ash-tray housing.
9 Disconnect the leads from the switch (Fig. 12.54).
10 Remove the switch after extracting the single retaining screw.

Heater unit
11 Drain the cooling system as described in Chapter 2.
12 Remove the parcels tray from under the instrument panel.
13 Disconnect the heater hoses from the side of the heater. Mark their positions before removal and be prepared to catch any coolant which may run out (Fig.12.55).

240

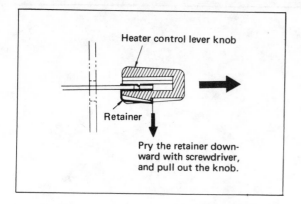

Fig. 12.53. Removal diagram for heater control knob

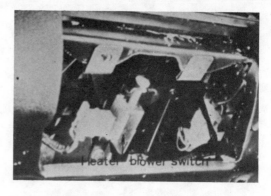

Fig. 12.54. Location of heater blower switch (1200E)

Fig. 12.55. Hose connections to heater (1200E)

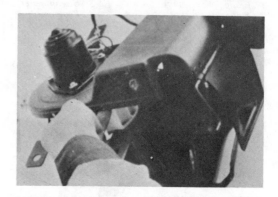

Fig. 12.56. Cowl ventilator and side ventilator (1200E)

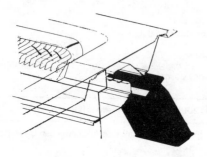

Fig. 12.57. Dismantling heater casing (1200E)

Fig. 12.58. Removing heater matrix (1200E)

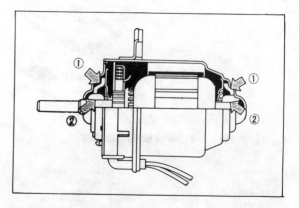

Fig. 12.59. Heater blower motor lubrication points (1200E)

14 Disconnect the demister hose from the heater.

15 Disconnect the heater control cable.

16 Remove the cowl ventilator duct by disconnecting the control rod and extracting the two ventilator securing bolts. Withdraw the ventilator duct from under the instrument panel (Fig. 12.57).

17 Disconnect the leads from the blower motor.

18 Unscrew and remove the four heater mounting bolts and withdraw the complete heater assembly from inside the vehicle.

19 If the heater is to be dismantled, remove the water valve and resistor and then extract the heater casing screws (Fig. 12.56).

20 Pull out the matrix. If this is leaking, renew it. If it is clogged, try reverse flushing it with a cold water hose. If this does not clear it, renew it (Fig. 12.58).

21 Unscrew the blower fan nut and tap the end of the motor shaft lightly, the fan can then be removed after unscrewing and removing the nut and lockwasher.

22 Remove the motor.

23 Extract the two stator securing screws and withdraw the armature from the stator. The brushes must be held aside with two pieces of wire during this operation.

24 The brushes should be renewed if they have worn to 0.275 in (7.0 mm) or less in length.

25 Inspect and renovate the commutator in the same way as described for the starter motor in Chapter 10.

26 Reassembly and refitting are reversals of removal and dismantling but observe the following.

27 Lubricate the motor at the points indicated (Fig. 12.59).

28 Set the adaptor on the motor shaft so that when the fan is fitted it will not touch the heater casing. Do this on a trial and error basis before fully tightening the fan securing nuts (Fig. 12.60).

29 Remember to fill the cooling system when fitting is complete.

29 Heater (30 series and 1600) - removal, dismantling and refitting

1 Drain the cooling system.

2 Disconnect the heater hoses at the rear bulkhead of the engine compartment.

3 Working under the instrument panel disconnect the demister hose (1) and the air duct (2). Disconnect the heater control cables from the heater unit (Fig. 12.61).

4 Pull off the heater control lever knobs.

5 Remove the heater blower switch.

6 Extract the two screws and remove the heater control panel complate with the control cables (Fig. 12.62).

7 Disconnect the heater leads at the connector plug.

8 Remove the three mounting bolts and remove the heater from the vehicle (Fig. 12.63).

9 If the heater is to be dismantled, remove the water valve and resistor. Withdraw the cover and matrix and the motor. Renovation of the matrix and motor is as described in the preceding Section.

10 The blower motor can be removed without having to withdraw the heater assembly complete. Simply disconnect the electrical leads, remove the right-hand demister hose and release the three motor mounting screws (Fig. 12.64).

11 Reassembly and refitting are reversals of removal and dismantling.

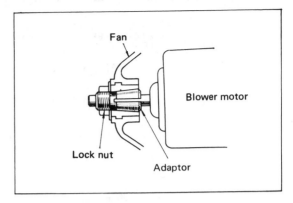

Fig. 12.60. Heater fan with adaptor assembled to blower fan spindle (1200E)

Fig. 12.61. Demister hose (1) and air duct (2) on 30 Series and 1600 heater

Fig. 12.62. Heater control panel disconnection points (30 Series and 1600)

Fig. 12.63. Heater (30 Series and 1600) showing hose clamp and electrical wiring connector plug

Fig. 12.64. Blower motor mounting bolts (30 Series, 1600 heater)

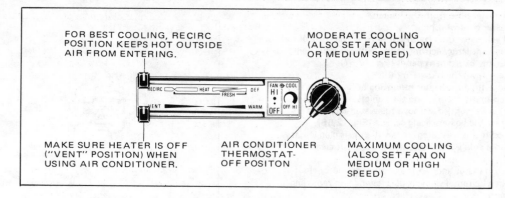

FOR BEST COOLING, RECIRC POSITION KEEPS HOT OUTSIDE AIR FROM ENTERING.

MODERATE COOLING (ALSO SET FAN ON LOW OR MEDIUM SPEED)

MAKE SURE HEATER IS OFF ("VENT" POSITION) WHEN USING AIR CONDITIONER.

AIR CONDITIONER THERMOSTAT-OFF POSITON

MAXIMUM COOLING (ALSO SET FAN ON MEDIUM OR HIGH SPEED)

Fig. 12.65. Heater control panel showing additional knob for air conditioning unit

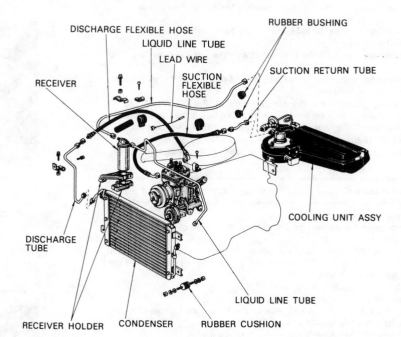

DISCHARGE FLEXIBLE HOSE
LIQUID LINE TUBE
LEAD WIRE
SUCTION FLEXIBLE HOSE
RUBBER BUSHING
SUCTION RETURN TUBE
RECEIVER
COOLING UNIT ASSY

Fig. 12.66. Main components of air conditioning system

DISCHARGE TUBE
RECEIVER HOLDER
CONDENSER
RUBBER CUSHION
LIQUID LINE TUBE

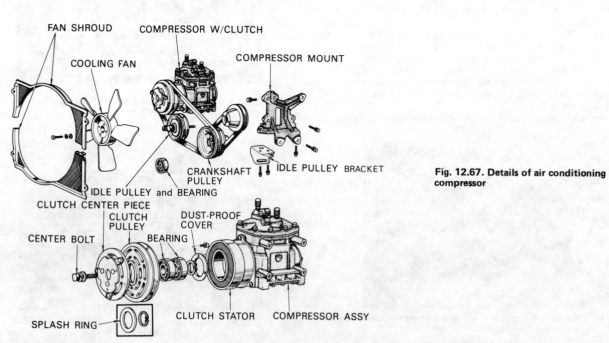

FAN SHROUD
COOLING FAN
COMPRESSOR W/CLUTCH
COMPRESSOR MOUNT

CRANKSHAFT PULLEY
IDLE PULLEY and BEARING
IDLE PULLEY BRACKET

CLUTCH CENTER PIECE
CLUTCH PULLEY
DUST-PROOF COVER
CENTER BOLT
BEARING

Fig. 12.67. Details of air conditioning compressor

SPLASH RING
CLUTCH STATOR
COMPRESSOR ASSY

30 Air conditioning unit

1   An under-dashboard type air conditioning unit can be optionally specified on vehicles destined for operation in North America.

2   Where this system is fitted, an additional control knob is added to the heater control panel. This knob switches the unit on and off and controls the thermostat which adjusts the temperature level of the cooled air (Figs. 12.65 and 12.66).

3   In addition to the thermostat control, the system comprises a condenser mounted in front of the radiator, a belt-driven compressor, a receiver and the necessary connecting hoses and pipework.

4   The oil filled compressor is driven from the crankshaft pulley and incorporates a magnetic type clutch (Fig. 12.67).

5   Servicing of the system is outside the scope of the home mechanic as special equipment is needed to purge or recharge the system with refrigerant gas and dismantling of any part of the system must not be undertaken, in the interest of safety, without first having discharged the system pressure.

6   To maintain optimum performance of the system, the owner should limit his operations to the following:

   i)   *Checking the tension of the compressor driving belt. The total deflection of this belt should be ½ in (12.7 mm) at the centre of its longest run. Adjust by moving the idler pulley.*
   ii) *Checking the security of all hoses and unions.*
   iii) *Always keeping the ignition timing correctly set.*
   iv) *Checking the security of the electrical connections.*

7   Use a soft brush to remove accumulations of dust and flies from the condenser fins.

8   During the winter months, operate the air conditioning system for a few minutes each week to lubricate the interior of the compressor pumps as lack of use may cause deterioration in the moving parts.

9   If a pool of water is observed under the vehicle when it has been standing in hot weather, this is normal and is condensation from the air conditioning unit drain tube.

Chapter 13 Supplement:
Revisions and information on later USA models

Contents

---

1 Introduction

This supplement contains specifications and service procedure changes that apply to Corolla models produced for sale in the US during the 1979 model year. Also included is information related to previous models that was not available at the time of the original publication of this manual.

Where no differences (or very minor differences) exist between the 1979 models and previous models, no information is given. In such instances, the original material included in Chapters 1 through 12 should be used.

---

2 Specifications

Note: *The specifications listed here include only those items which differ from those listed in Chapters 1 through 12. For information not specifically listed here, refer to the appropriate Chapter.*

Engine

Piston pin installation temperature (3K-C engine only). . . 158 to 176°F (70 to 80°C)

Cam lobe height
Intake . . . . 1.4358 to 1.4397 in (36.469 to 36.569 mm)
Exhaust . . . . 1.4319 to 1.4358 in (36.369 to 36.469 mm)

Valve face angle (intake and exhaust) . . . . 44.5°

Valve length
Intake . . . . 3.93 in (99.9 mm)
Exhaust . . . . 3.94 in 100.1 mm)

Cooling system

Coolant capacity (3K-C engine) . . . . 5.8 US qts

Thermostat
Starts to open at . . . . 187 to 194°F
Fully open at . . . . 212°F

Carburetion, fuel and emissions control systems

3K-C engine
Idle speed . . . . 750 rpm
Idle mixture speed . . . . 830 rpm

2T-C engine
Idle speed . . . . 850 rpm
Idle mixture speed
   California . . . . 910 rpm
   All others . . . . 920 rpm
Throttle positioner setting speed
   Manual transmission . . . . 1400 rpm
   Automatic transmission . . . . 1200 rpm

Ignition system

Distributor air gap . . . . 0.008 to 0.016 in (0.2 to 0.4 mm)

Ignition timing
3K-C engine . . . . 8° BTDC @ 900 rpm
2T-C engine . . . . 10° BTDC @ 900 rpm

Coil
Primary coil resistance
   3K-C engine . . . . 1.3 to 1.7 ohms
   2T-C engine . . . . 1.3 to 1.5 ohms
Secondary coil resistance . . . . 12 000 to 16 000 ohms

Spark plug type

	2T-C engine	3K-C engine
US		
ND	W14EX-U/W16EX-U	W16EX-U
NGK	BP5EA/BP5EA-L	BP5EA-L
Canada		
ND	W16EPR/W16EXR-U	W16EPR/W16EXR-U
NGK	BPR5ES/BPR5EA-L	BPR5ES/BPR5EA-L

Clutch and actuating mechanism

Pedal height
Cable-operated clutch . . . . 6.65 in (169 mm)
Hydraulically-operated clutch . . . . 6.46 in (164 mm)

Pedal free play
Hydraulically-operated clutch . . . . 0.20 to 0.59 in (5 to 15 mm)

Propeller shaft and universal joints

Torque specifications
Center bearing-to-body . . . . 22 to 32 ft-lb
Center bearing-to-insulator . . . . 7 to 12 ft-lb
Intermediate shaft-to-center bearing flange
   First step . . . . 123 to 144.7 ft-lb
   Second step . . . . Loosen nut
   Third step . . . . 18.1 to 25.3 ft-lb

Rear axle

Pinion oil seal recess dimensions
6 in differential . . . . 0.040 in (1 mm)
6.38 in differential . . . . 0 to 0.020 in (0 to 0.5 mm)
6.7 in differential . . . . 0.160 in (4 mm)

Pinion nut torque (6 in differential) . . . . 68.7 ft-lb

Oil capacity (6.7 in differential) . . . . 1.3 US qts

Braking system

Brake fluid type . . . . DOT 3

Brake pedal reserve travel
With vacuum booster . . . . 3.35 in (85 mm) minimum
Without vacuum booster . . . . 2.87 in (73 mm) minimum

Electrical system

Starter motor
Commutator runout
    Direct drive motor (3K-C) . . . . 0.010 in (0.3 mm)
    Reduction gear motor (2T-C) . . . . 0.002 in (0.05 mm)
Commutator diameter
    Direct drive motor (3K-C) . . . . 1.22 in (31.0 mm) minimum
    Reduction gear motor (2T-C) . . . . 1.10 in (29 mm) minimum
Brush wear limit. . . . . 0.400 in (10 mm)
Armature shaft thrust clearance (direct drive motor - 3K-C). . . . . . . 0.004 to 0.040 in (0.01 to 1.0 mm)
No-load current draw
    0.6 kW direct drive motor . . . . Less than 55 amps
    0.8 kW direct drive motor . . . . Less than 50 amps
    Reduction gear motor . . . . Less than 80 amps

Suspension and steering

Steering angles
Toe-in
    Radial tires. . . . . 0.040 in (1 mm)
    Bias ply tires. . . . . 0.120 in (3 mm)
Camber
    KE30R(L) and KE35R(L). . . . . 20' to 1°20'
    KE36R(L) . . . . 5' to 1°5'
    All others . . . . 30' to 1°30'
Caster
    KE30R(L) and KE35R(L). . . . . 1°30' to 2°10'
    KE36R(L) . . . . 45' to 1°25'
    All others . . . . 1°20' to 2°20'
Steering axis inclination
    KE30R(L) and KE35R(L). . . . . 7°25' to 8°25'
    KE36R(L) . . . . 7°40' to 8°40'
    KE30L-A and KE35L-A . . . . 7°15' to 8°15'
    All others . . . . 7°20' to 8°20'

3 Routine maintenance

In addition to the checks and service procedures outlined at the front of this manual, the following items must be added, at the intervals specified, for 1979 models:

After first 1000 miles (1600 Km) - (new vehicle)
Check the brake fluid level in the master cylinder

Every 6000 miles (9600 Km)
Check the brake fluid level in the master cylinder
Check the balljoints for wear and make sure the dust cover is not torn

Every 12 000 miles (19 000 Km)
Inspect all vacuum hoses, fittings and connections for leaks
Check the ignition wires for cracks and deterioration
Inspect the distributor cap and rotor (look for cracks, carbon tracks, corroded or burnt terminals, etc.)
Check the ignition timing (initial and advance)
Check all wiring connections for security and corrosion

4 Engine

Camshaft and bearings — examination and renovation
1 Use the procedure in Chapter 1, but note that the cam lobe height has been changed for 1979 models. When checking the cam lobe height to determine the extent of camshaft wear, be sure to refer to the measurements in the Chapter 13 *specifications*.

Valves and valve seats — examination and renovation
2 The procedure outlined in Chapter 1 should be followed, but note that the valves and seats are ground with an interference angle (paragraph 7). Refer to the Chapter 13 *specifications* for the correct valve face angle.

Pistons / connecting rods — reassembly and refitting
3 Use the procedure outlined in Chapter 1, but note the new piston pin installation temperature listed in the Chapter 13 *specifications*.

5 Cooling system

Cooling system — filling
1 Note that the cooling system capacity for 1979 models with the 3K-C engine has been changed.

Thermostat — removal, testing and refitting
2 Follow the procedure in Chapter 2, but note that the opening and fully open temperatures are different for 1979 models. Refer to the Chapter 13 *specifications* for the correct temperatures.

Water pump — overhaul
3 On the 1979 2T-C engine, the impeller-to-water pump body clearance should be 0.040 in (1 mm) (Chapter 2, Section 9).

Fig. 13.1 Check the impeller-to-water pump body clearance when pressing the impeller into place (Sec 5)

Water temperature gauge and sender — testing

4 On 1979 models the sender unit resistances should be as follows:

Coolant temperature	Resistance
140°F (60°C)	104.1 ohms
176°F (80°C)	51.9 ohms
230°F (110°C)	21.1 ohms
266°F (130°C)	12.4 ohms

6 Carburetion, fuel and emissions control systems

Idle speed (3K-C engine) — adjustment

1 Before beginning the idle speed adjustment procedure, visually inspect the carburetor. Look for loose screws and loose mounting bolts. Check for wear in the linkage, missing snap-rings and excessive looseness in the throttle shaft.

2 When the idle speed is adjusted, the air cleaner must be in place, the coolant must be at normal operating temperature and the choke valve must be fully open. Make sure that all electrical accessories are off and leave all vacuum lines connected. The ignition timing must be set to specifications and the transmission should be in Neutral.

3 Pinch shut the vacuum hose between the carburetor heat insulator and the 4-way connector and the hose between the check valve and the carburetor (small C-clamps can be used for this purpose).

4 Using a pliers, break the limiter cap off the *idle mixture adjusting screw*. **Note:** *Do not break the cap off the throttle valve setting screw.*

5 Turn the *idle mixture adjusting screw*, as required, until the maximum engine speed is obtained.

6 Turn the *idle speed adjusting screw*, as required, until the engine idles at 830 rpm. Readjust the *idle mixture adjusting screw* until the maximum engine speed is obtained. Continue the adjustments, alternating between the *idle speed* and *idle mixture adjusting screws*, until maximum engine speed will not increase when the *idle mixture*

adjusting screw is turned.

7 Finally, set the idle speed to 750 rpm by turning the *idle mixture adjusting screw* clockwise.

8 Release the hoses that were pinched shut at the beginning of the procedure.

Idle speed (2T-C engine) — adjustment

9 The procedure for the 2T-C engine is identical to the procedure for the 3K-C engine. Note that no vacuum hoses should be pinched off when adjusting the idle speed on this engine and be sure to use the correct specifications (in this Chapter), for idle speed and idle mixture speed. Also, before beginning the procedure, check the fuel level in the carburetor float bowl. It should be even with the dot in the sight glass.

Throttle positioner — description and adjustment

10 When adjusting the throttle positioner on 1979 models, refer to the Chapter 13 *specifications* for the correct engine speeds.

Carburetor (3K-C engine) — adjustment during reassembly

11 The procedure for adjusting the float level is identical to the procedure outlined in Chapter 3, with one exception. The distance between the fuel inlet needle and the float tang (paragraph 3 in Section 22) should be 0.020 in (0.6mm) for 1979 model carburetors.

12 The remaining adjustments are identical to those in Chapter 3.

Carburetor (2T-C engine) — adjustment during reassembly

Float level

13 The procedure for adjusting the float level is identical to the procedure outlined in Chapter 3, with one exception. With the air horn inverted, the distance between the float and air horn (no gasket) should be 0.160 in (4.0 mm).

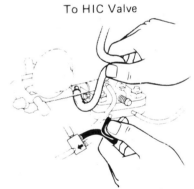

To HIC Valve

Fig. 13.2 Pinching off the vacuum hoses prior to performing the idle speed adjustment (3K-C engine) (Sec 6)

Idle Mixture Adjusting Screw

Fig. 13.3 Idle mixture adjusting screw location (3K-C engine) (Sec 6)

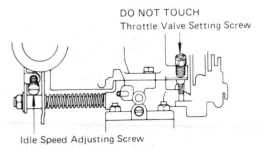

DO NOT TOUCH
Throttle Valve Setting Screw

Idle Speed Adjusting Screw

Fig. 13.4 Idle speed adjusting screw location (3K-C engine) (Sec 6)

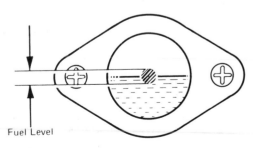

Fuel Level

Fig. 13.5 Checking fuel level in carburetor float bowl sight glass (2T-C engine) (Sec 6)

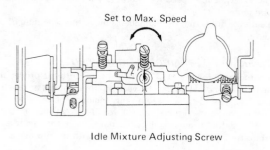

Fig. 13.6 Idle mixture adjusting screw location (2T-C engine) (Sec 6)

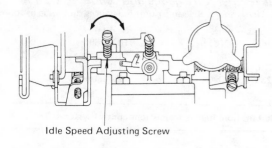

Fig. 13.7 Idle speed adjusting screw location (2T-C engine) (Sec 6)

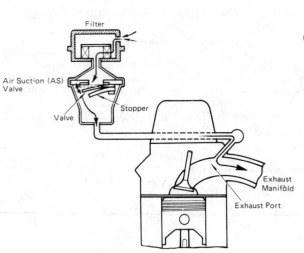

Fig. 13.8 Air Suction (AS) system diagram for 3K-C engine (Sec 6)

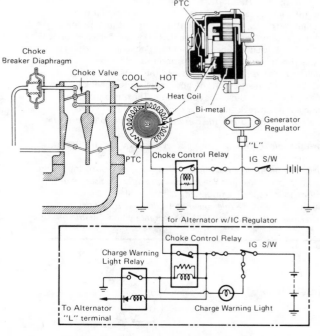

Fig. 13.9 Automatic choke system diagram (2T-C engine) (Sec 6)

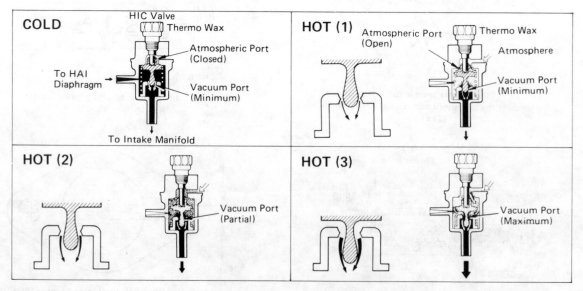

Fig. 13.10 Hot idle compensation (HIC) system diagram (Sec 6)

Fast idle setting

14 The procedure for adjusting the fast idle is unchanged from the procedure in Chapter 3, although the specifications are different. The clearance between the throttle valve and bore (paragraph 5 of Section 23) should be 0.032 in (0.81 mm) for automatic chokes and 0.040 in (1.01 mm) for manual chokes.

Emissions control — general description

15 The emission control systems used on 1979 models are basically the same as those listed in Section 25 of Chapter 3. It should be noted that 1979 vehicles were also equipped, depending on model type, with an *Air Suction (AS) system,* an *Automatic Choke system* (2T-C engines), a *Hot Idle Compensation (HIC) system* and an *Anti-dieseling system* (3K-C engines).

16 The *Air Suction system* is very similar to the air injection system used on some models. The only difference is that negative pressure pulses in the exhaust manifold (rather than a pump) are used to draw fresh air into the manifold to complete the combustion of unburned gases.

17 The *Automatic Choke system* utilizes a temperature-sensitive bi-metal coil to close the choke when the engine is cold. An electrically powered heating coil opens the choke valve at a pre-determined rate as the engine warms up.

18 The *Hot Idle Compensation system* allows small amounts of outside air to be drawn into the intake manifold. This action maintains the proper fuel/air mixture when high temperatures are reached at idle speed.

19 The *Anti-dieseling system* closes the throttle valve completely (cutting off the fuel/air mixture) to prevent dieseling when the ignition switch is turned off.

7 Ignition system

General description

1 All models sold in tbe USA are equipped with a transistorized electronic ignition system. This system has no breaker points and is virtually maintenance free.

Distributor — overhaul

2 The distributor overhaul procedure is nearly the same as for the breaker point type distributor covered in Chapter 4. Refer to the exploded view of the distributor (Fig. 13.12 or Fig. 13.13) during the disassembly and reassembly of the distributor components.

3 Refer to Fig. 13.14 and adjust the air gap before installing the distributor in the vehicle (loosen the screws and move the pickup coil as required).

Distributor (3K-C engine) — installation

4 Follow steps 1 through 3 in Section 9 of Chapter 4.

5 Position the rotor as shown in Fig. 13.15, then slip the distributor into place. As the distributor is installed, the rotor will turn in a clockwise direction until it is pointed at the center of the number 2 spark plug (with the distributor seated completely) (Fig. 13.16).

6 Turn the distributor body until the signal rotor and pickup coil are properly aligned (Fig. 13.17), then tighten the distributor clamp bolt.

7 Check the ignition timing with a strobe light and readjust it if necessary.

Distributor (2T-C engine) — installation

8 Turn the crankshaft until the timing mark on the pulley is aligned

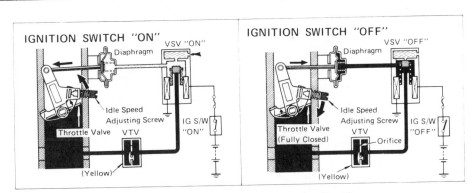

Fig. 13.11 Anti-dieseling system diagram (Sec 6)

Fig. 13.14 Adjusting the distributor air gap (Sec 7)

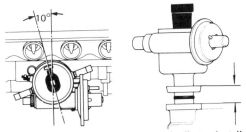

Fig. 13.15 Aligning the rotor prior to distributor installation (3K-C engine) (Sec 7)

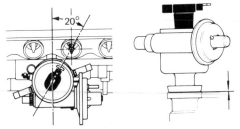

Fig. 13.16 Distributor properly installed (3K-C engine) (Sec 7)

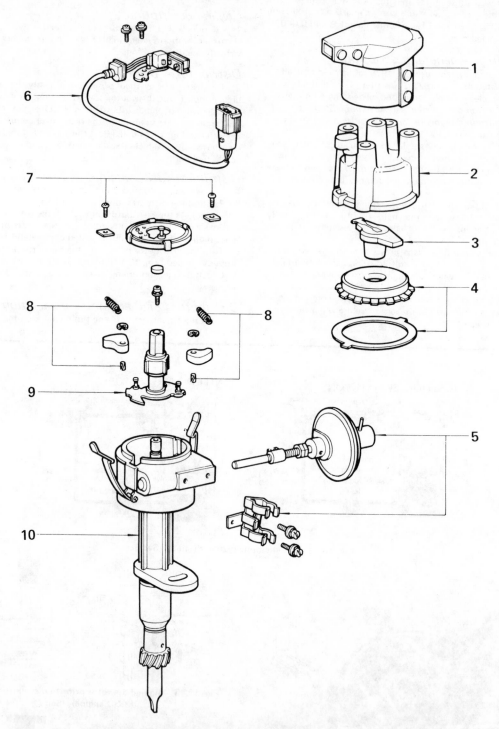

Fig. 13.12 Exploded view of distributor for 2T-C engine (Sec 7)

1	Dust cover	6	Signal generator
2	Cap	7	Breaker plate
3	Rotor	8	E-ring, governor spring & governor weight
4	Dustproof cover & gasket	9	Cam
5	Vacuum advancer	10	Housing

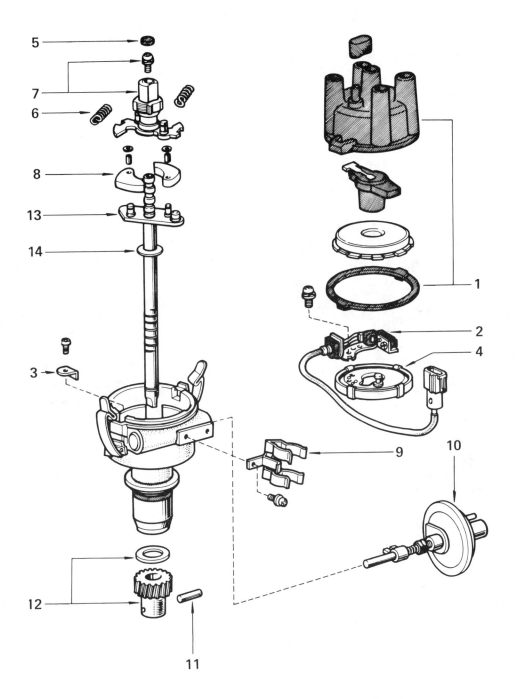

Fig. 13.13 Exploded view of distributor for 3K-C engine (Sec 7)

1	Cap, rotor, cover & packing	8	Governor weight
2	Signal generator	9	Cord clamp
3	Steel plate washer	10	Vacuum advancer
4	Breaker plate	11	Pin
5	Grease stopper	12	Spiral gear & washer
6	Governor spring	13	Governor shaft
7	Signal rotor	14	Steel washer

with the 10° BTDC line with the number 1 cylinder on the compression stroke. To determine when the number 1 cylinder is on the compression stroke, remove the spark plug and place your thumb over the spark plug hole. Turn the crankshaft in a clockwise direction (looking at it from the front) until you can feel the compression pressure building up in the cylinder. Continue turning the crankshaft until the marks line up as mentioned above.

9   Align the oil pump shaft slot as shown in Fig. 13.18. Position the distributor with the rotor pointing directly at the side of the engine (Fig. 13.19).

10 Push down on the distributor to seat it, then check to make sure that the signal rotor points directly at the pickup coil (Fig. 13.17). Tighten the distributor clamp bolt securely.

11 Check the ignition timing with a strobe light and readjust it if necessary.

Ignition timing

12 Use the procedure outlined in Chapter 4 when checking the ignition timing, but refer to the Chapter 13 specifications. Note that the 1979 models do not have an octane selector (paragraph 7) on the distributor.

2T-C engine

13 Note that vehicles with the optional HAC (High Altitude Compensation) system must have the initial ignition timing checked with the vacuum hose to the sub-diaphragm side of the vacuum advance unit disconnected and plugged (Fig. 13.20). Reconnect the hose and check to see if the timing advances to about 20° BTDC. If it does not, pinch the vacuum hose between the HAC valve and the 3-way connector (Fig. 13.21), then recheck the timing (it should now be 20° BTDC).

3K-C engines

14 If the vehicle is equipped with the optional HAC (High Altitude Compensation) system, disconnect the HAC valve-to-BVSV hose on the HAC valve side (Fig. 13.22). Pinch shut the evap line and the HIC hose (Fig. 13.23), then check the initial ignition timing.

15 Pinch shut the hose between the BVSV and the carburetor (Fig.

Fig. 13.17 Proper alignment of signal rotor and pickup coil (Sec 7)

Fig. 13.18 Aligning the oil pump shaft slot prior to distributor installation (2T-C engine) (Sec 7)

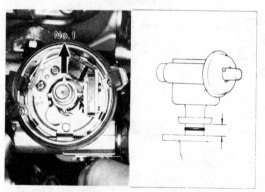

Fig. 13.19 Aligning the rotor prior to distributor installation (2T-C engine) (Sec 7)

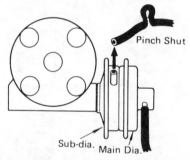

Fig. 13.20 Disconnecting the sub-diaphragm hose (2T-C engine) (Sec 7)

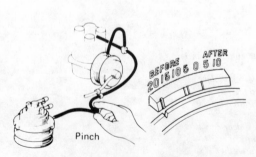

Fig 13.21 Pinching the hose between the HAC valve and the 3-way connector (2T-C engine) (Sec 7)

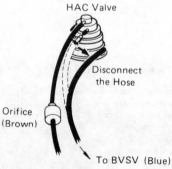

Fig. 13.22 Disconnecting the HAC valve to BVSV hose (3K-C engine) (Sec 7)

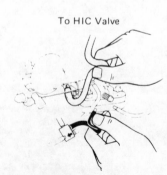

Fig. 13.23 Pinching shut the evap line and the HIC hose (3K-C engine) (Sec 7)

13.24), then check to see if the timing advances to about 18° BTDC.
16 On vehicles equipped with the HAC system, reconnect the hose to the HAC valve and recheck the timing. It should advance to about 18° BTDC. If the timing does not change, pinch the hose shut (Fig. 13.25) and recheck it again (it should now be about 18° BTDC).

Coil polarity and testing
17 The coil primary resistance mentioned in paragraph 4 should be 1.3 to 1.7 ohms (3K-C engine) and 1.3 to 1.5 ohms (2T-C engine) for 1979 models.
18 The coil secondary resistance (paragraph 5) should be 12 000 to 16 000 ohms.

Spark plugs and HT leads
19 The spark plugs recommended for use in 1979 models are listed in the Chapter 13 *specifications*.

8 Clutch and actuating mechanism

Clutch adjustment (cable actuation)
1 The procedure is covered in detail in Section 2 of Chapter 5, but be sure to use the *specifications* (paragraphs 1 and 5) listed in Chapter 13.

Clutch adjustment (hydraulic actuation)
2 Follow the procedure in Section 3 of Chapter 5, but use the *specifications* (paragraphs 1 and 4) listed in Chapter 13.
3 Note that no adjustment of the slave cylinder (paragraph 3) is required on 1979 models.

9 Propeller shaft and universal joints

Driveshaft (2-piece) — removal and installation
1 Removal of the 2-piece driveshaft is the same as for the 1-piece driveshaft, but note that the 2 center bearing mount bolts must be removed before the driveshaft can be slid to the rear. Do not lose the spacer that is installed between the body and the bracket.
2 When installing the 2-piece driveshaft, be sure to reinstall the spacer between the body and the bracket. Also, check to make sure that the bearing bracket is at a 90° angle to the driveshaft. Under a no-load condition, the bearing must be shifted 0.040 in (1 mm) towards the rear of the vehicle (Fig. 13.26).

Center bearing — disassembly, inspection & reassembly
3 Mark the flange and flange yoke to facilitate reassembly, then remove the 4 bolts and nuts to separate the 2 parts of the driveshaft.
4 Mark the flange and the intermediate shaft, then push up the staked portion of the nut with a cape chisel.
5 Hold the flange to keep it from turning, then remove the nut from the end of the intermediate shaft. It is a good idea to support the driveshaft as the nut is removed.
6 With the flange held in a vise, carefully tap the shaft out of the flange (do not let the shaft fall).
7 Check the center support bearing for wear or damage (Fig. 13.28). Replace any worn or damaged parts with new ones.
8 Slide the intermediate shaft into the center bearing, then coat the shaft splines with molybdenum disulfide grease.
9 Line up the marks made before disassembly, then slip the flange onto the shaft and install a *new* nut.

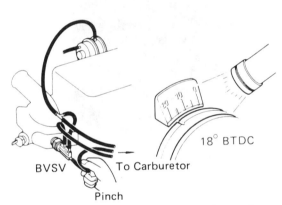

Fig. 13.24 Pinching shut the BVSV-to-carburetor hose (3K-C engine) (Sec 7)

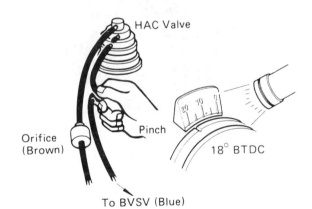

Fig. 13.25 Pinching shut the HAC valve-to-BVSV hose (3K-C engine) (Sec 7)

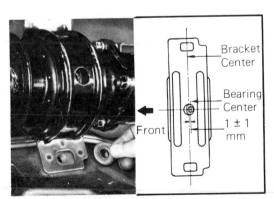

Fig. 13.26 Driveshaft center bearing installation diagram (Sec 9)

Fig. 13.27 Separating the 2-piece driveshaft (note the alignment marks) (Sec 9)

10 Hold the flange to keep it from turning, then tighten the nut to 123 to 144.7 ft-lb. Loosen the nut, then retighten it to 18.1 to 25.3 ft-lb.
11 Stake the flange nut into the groove in the shaft, then reassemble the two parts of the driveshaft. Be sure to align the marks on the flange and flange yoke before installing the bolts.

10 Rear axle

Pinion oil seal — renewal

1   Follow the procedure outlined in Chapter 8, but note that the new seal must be driven below the surface of the housing (paragraph 8). The actual amount varies according to the differential size so be sure to refer to the Chapter 13 *specifications*.
2   When installing the companion flange (paragraph 9), use a *new* nut and be sure to lubricate the threads and the backside of the nut before threading it into place on the shaft.
3   Tighten the pinion nut (paragraph 10) to the specified torque listed in the Chapter 13 *specifications*.

Differential carrier — removal and refitting

4   Note that the 6.7 in size differential requires 1.3 US quarts of lubricant when refilling it.

11 Braking system

Hydraulic system — bleeding

1   Follow the procedure in Chapter 9, but note that DOT 3 brake fluid (or equivalent) must be used when additional fluid is required (paragraph 1).

Brake pedal — adjustment, removal and refitting

2   The procedure is described in Sections 16 (1200 models) and 17 (1600 models) of Chapter 9, but note that brake pedal reserve travel (Fig. 13.31) must also be checked on 1979 models. Refer to the Chapter 13 *specifications* for the required reserve travel measurements.

12 Electrical system

Starter motor — servicing and testing

3K-C engine
1   The starter motor used on the 3K-C engine is basically the same as the motor used on earlier models. For removal and repair procedures, refer to Chapter 10. An exploded view drawing of the 1979 starter

Fig. 13.28 Checking the center bearing for wear (Sec 9)

Fig. 13.29 Line up the marks (arrow) before sliding the flange onto the intermediate shaft (Sec 9)

Fig. 13.30 Support the flange in a vise when tightening and loosening the nut (Sec 9)

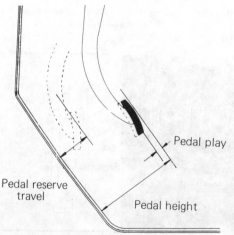

Pedal play

Pedal reserve travel

Pedal height

Fig. 13.31 Brake pedal reserve travel measurement (Sec 11)

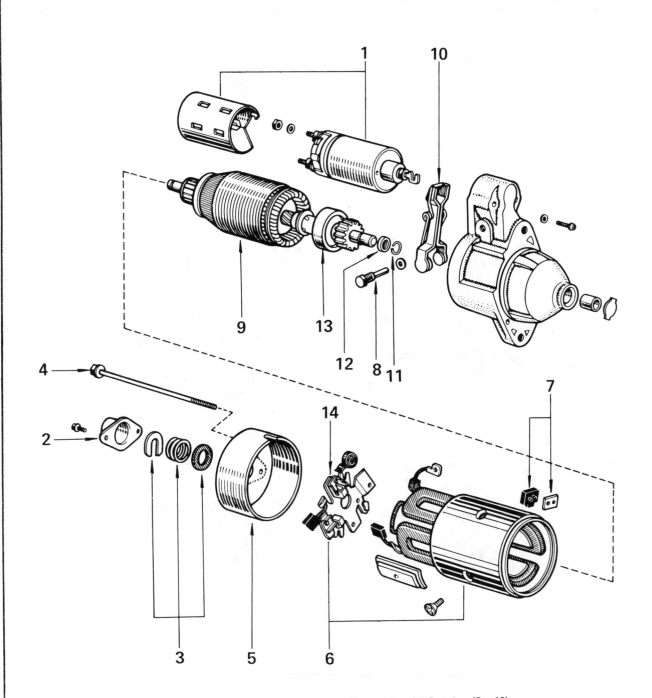

Fig. 13.32 Exploded view of starter motor used on 3K-C engine (Sec 12)

1	Magnetic switch	8	Drive lever bolt
2	Bearing cover	9	Armature
3	Lock plate, spring & rubber	10	Drive lever
4	Bolt	11	Snap-ring
5	Commutator end frame	12	Stop collar
6	Yoke with brush holder	13	Clutch with pinion gear
7	Plate & rubber	14	Brush holder

motor (Fig. 13.32) is included here to illustrate the minor differences and to act as a guide during disassembly and reassembly of the motor.

2   In addition to the procedures in Chapter 10, be sure to check the commutator for excessive wear and runout. Refer to the Chapter 13 *specifications* for the recommended limits.

3   Check the pinion gear and starter clutch for proper operation as shown in Fig. 13.35, and measure the distance from the end of the solenoid body to the end of the plunger (Fig. 13.36).

4   When installing the brush holder (paragraph 5 of Section 15, Chapter 10), position it as shown in Fig. 13.37.

2T-C engine

5   The 2T-C engine is equipped with a reduction-gear starter motor which may be one of two types: a 0.9 kW motor or a 1.4 kW motor. The two types are very similar in construction and disassembly and

repair procedures are virtually identical.

6   Refer to the direct drive starter motor disassembly, servicing, testing and reassembly procedures outlined in Chapter 10 and the exploded view drawings of the reduction-gear starter motors (Fig. 13.38 and Fig. 13.39) for the disassembly and repair of this type motor. Be sure to use the *specifications* in Chapter 13.

7   Note that the starter drive clutch has a steel ball in its bore that must be removed with a magnet.

8   Be sure to inspect the reduction drive gears for wear and damage and make sure the armature ball bearings turn smoothly without excessive play.

9   When reassembling the motor, note the following points:
    a)   The brush holder must be positioned so that the tab fits into the notch in the field frame (Fig. 13.42).
    b)   The 1.4 kW motor has an O-ring that must be installed around the brush holder (Fig. 13.43).

Fig. 13.33 Checking starter motor commutator for excessive runout with a dial indicator setup (Sec 12)

Fig. 13.34 Measuring the diameter of the starter motor commutator (Sec 12)

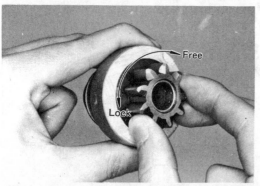

Fig. 13.35 Checking the starter clutch for proper operation (Sec 12)

Fig. 13.36 Measuring the installed length of the solenoid plunger (Sec 12)

Fig. 13.37 Proper alignment of brush holder with motor housing (3K-C engine) (Sec 12)

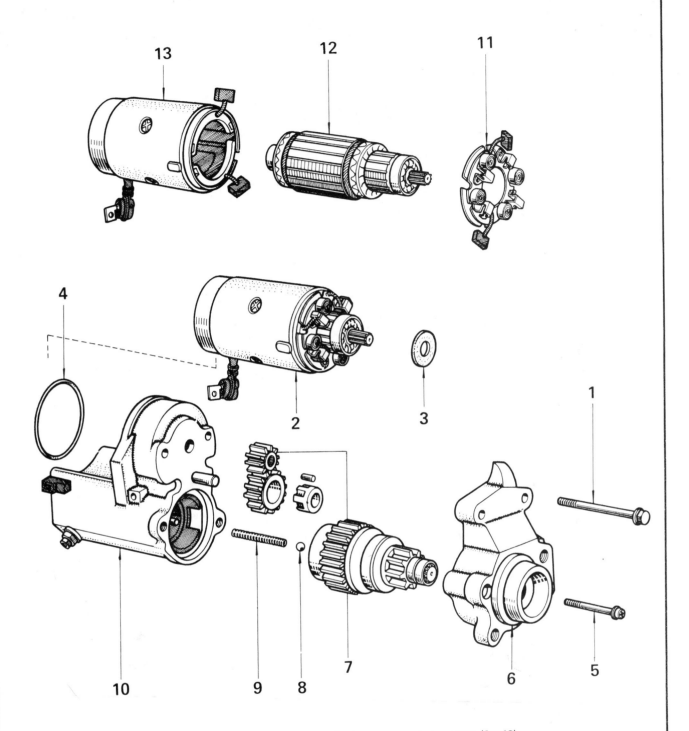

Fig. 13.38 Exploded view of 1.4 kW reduction-gear type starter motor (Sec 12)

1	Bolt	5	Bolt	10	Magnetic switch
2	Armature & field frame	6	Starter housing	11	Brush holder
3	Felt seal	7	Clutch, idler gear & pinion gear	12	Armature
4	O-ring	8	Steel ball	13	Field frame
		9	Plunger return spring		

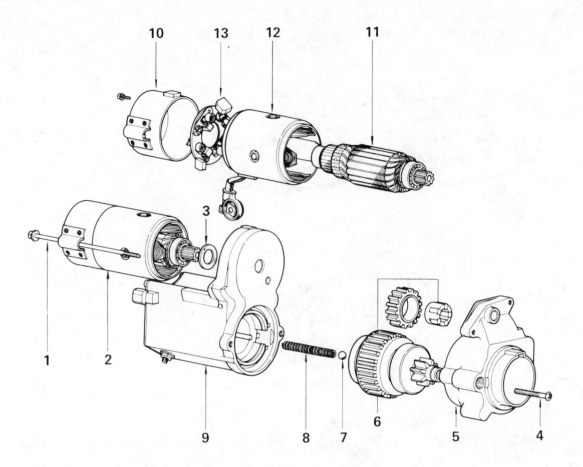

Fig. 13.39 Exploded view of 0.9 kW reduction-gear type starter motor (Sec 12)

1	Through-bolt	5	Starter housing	10	End cover
2	Field frame	6	Clutch & idler gear	11	Armature
3	Felt seal	7	Steel ball	12	Field frame
4	Bolt	8	Plunger return spring	13	Brush holder
		9	Magnetic switch		

Fig. 13.40 Removing the steel ball from the starter clutch bore (Sec 12)

Fig 13.41 Check the reduction drive gears for wear and damage (Sec 12)

c) Refer to Fig. 13.44 (1.4 kW motor) or Fig. 13.45 (0.9 kW motor) when joining the armature/field frame assembly to the starter housing, as the alignment is critical.
d) Apply grease to the steel ball and insert it into the starter clutch bore (Fig. 13.46).
e) Refer to Fig. 13.47 when installing the idler gear roller bearing.

13 Suspension and steering

Steering angles and front wheel alignment

1 Note that the toe-in, caster, camber and steering axis angles have been changed for the 1979 models. See Chapter 13 *specifications*.

Fig. 13.42 Aligning the brush holder with the motor housing with the motor housing (reduction-gear type motor) (Sec 12)

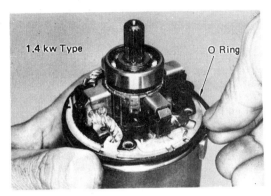

Fig. 13.43 Installing the brush holder O-ring (1.4 kW motor) (Sec 12)

Fig. 13.44 Aligning the armature/field frame assembly with the housing (1.4 kW motor (Sec 12)

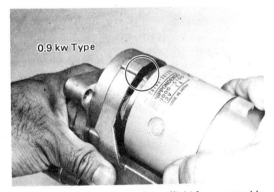

Fig. 13.45 Aligning the armature/field frame assembly with the housing (0.9 kW motor) (Sec 12)

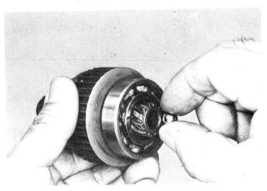

Fig. 13.46 Installing the steel ball in the starter clutch bore (Sec 12)

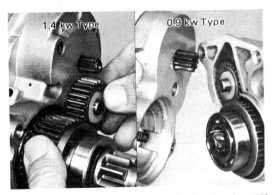

Fig. 13.47 Installing the idler gear roller bearing (Sec 12)

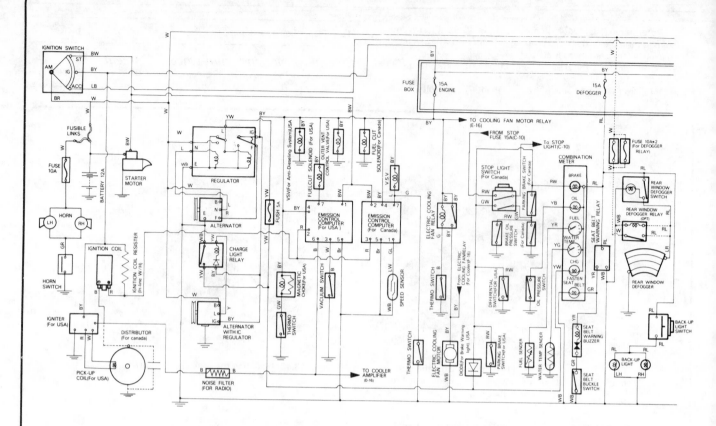

Fig. 13.48 Wiring diagram for vehicles equipped with 3K-C engine

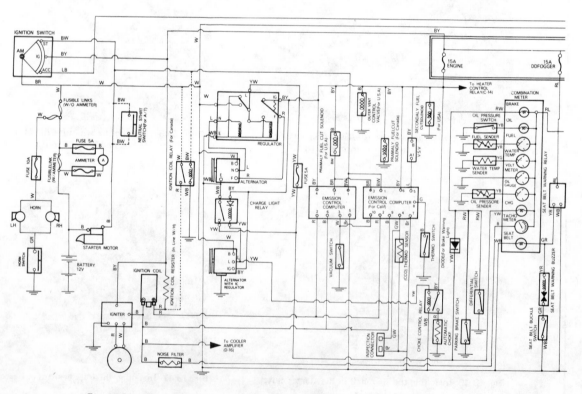

Fig. 13.50 Wiring diagram for vehicles equipped with 2T-C engine

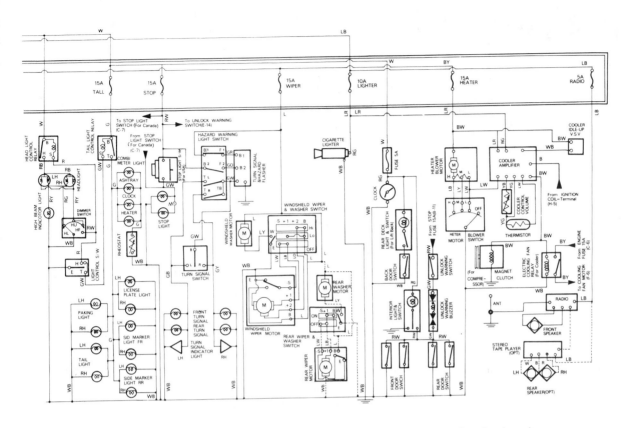

Fig. 13.49 Wiring diagram for vehicles equipped with 3K-C engine (cont.)

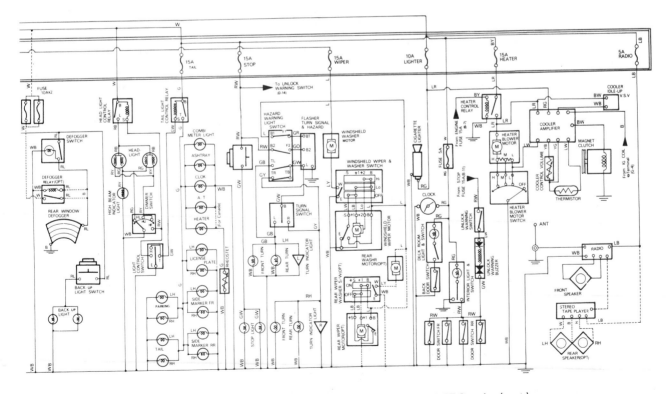

Fig. 13.51 Wiring diagram for vehicles equipped with 2T-C engine (cont.)

Safety first!

Professional motor mechanics are trained in safe working procedures. However enthusiastic you may be about getting on with the job in hand, do take the time to ensure that your safety is not put at risk. A moment's lack of attention can result in an accident, as can failure to observe certain elementary precautions.

There will always be new ways of having accidents, and the following points do not pretend to be a comprehensive list of all dangers; they are intended rather to make you aware of the risks and to encourage a safety-conscious approach to all work you carry out on your vehicle.

Essential DOs and DON'Ts

DON'T rely on a single jack when working underneath the vehicle. Always use reliable additional means of support, such as axle stands, securely placed under a part of the vehicle that you know will not give way.

DON'T attempt to loosen or tighten high-torque nuts (e.g. wheel hub nuts) while the vehicle is on a jack; it may be pulled off.

DON'T start the engine without first ascertaining that the transmission is in neutral (or 'Park' where applicable) and the parking brake applied.

DON'T suddenly remove the filler cap from a hot cooling system – cover it with a cloth and release the pressure gradually first, or you may get scalded by escaping coolant.

DON'T attempt to drain oil until you are sure it has cooled sufficiently to avoid scalding you.

DON'T grasp any part of the engine, exhaust or catalytic converter without first ascertaining that it is sufficiently cool to avoid burning you.

DON'T allow brake fluid or antifreeze to contact vehicle paintwork.

DON'T syphon toxic liquids such as fuel, brake fluid or antifreeze by mouth, or allow them to remain on your skin.

DON'T inhale dust – it may be injurious to health (see Asbestos below).

DON'T allow any spilt oil or grease to remain on the floor – wipe it up straight away, before someone slips on it.

DON'T use ill-fitting spanners or other tools which may slip and cause injury.

DON'T attempt to lift a heavy component which may be beyond your capability – get assistance.

DON'T rush to finish a job, or take unverified short cuts.

DON'T allow children or animals in or around an unattended vehicle.

DO wear eye protection when using power tools such as drill, sander, bench grinder etc, and when working under the vehicle.

DO use a barrier cream on your hands prior to undertaking dirty jobs – it will protect your skin from infection as well as making the dirt easier to remove afterwards; but make sure your hands aren't left slippery.

DO keep loose clothing (cuffs, tie etc) and long hair well out of the way of moving mechanical parts.

DO remove rings, wristwatch etc, before working on the vehicle – especially the electrical system.

DO ensure that any lifting tackle used has a safe working load rating adequate for the job.

DO keep your work area tidy – it is only too easy to fall over articles left lying around.

DO get someone to check periodically that all is well, when working alone on the vehicle.

DO carry out work in a logical sequence and check that everything is correctly assembled and tightened afterwards.

DO remember that your vehicle's safety affects that of yourself and others. If in doubt on any point, get specialist advice.

IF, in spite of following these precautions, you are unfortunate enough to injure yourself, seek medical attention as soon as possible.

Asbestos

Certain friction, insulating, sealing, and other products – such as brake linings, brake bands, clutch linings, torque converters, gaskets, etc – contain asbestos. Extreme care must be taken to avoid inhalation of dust from such products since it is hazardous to health. If in doubt, assume that they do contain asbestos.

Fire

Remember at all times that petrol (gasoline) is highly flammable. Never smoke, or have any kind of naked flame around, when working on the vehicle. But the risk does not end there – a spark caused by an electrical short-circuit, by two metal surfaces contacting each other, by careless use of tools, or even by static electricity built up in your body under certain conditions, can ignite petrol vapour, which in a confined space is highly explosive.

Always disconnect the battery earth (ground) terminal before working on any part of the fuel or electrical system, and never risk spilling fuel on to a hot engine or exhaust.

It is recommended that a fire extinguisher of a type suitable for fuel and electrical fires is kept handy in the garage or workplace at all times. Never try to extinguish a fuel or electrical fire with water.

Fumes

Certain fumes are highly toxic and can quickly cause unconsciousness and even death if inhaled to any extent. Petrol (gasoline) vapour comes into this category, as do the vapours from certain solvents such as trichloroethylene. Any draining or pouring of such volatile fluids should be done in a well ventilated area.

When using cleaning fluids and solvents, read the instructions carefully. Never use materials from unmarked containers – they may give off poisonous vapours.

Never run the engine of a motor vehicle in an enclosed space such as a garage. Exhaust fumes contain carbon monoxide which is extremely poisonous; if you need to run the engine, always do so in the open air or at least have the rear of the vehicle outside the workplace.

If you are fortunate enough to have the use of an inspection pit, never drain or pour petrol, and never run the engine, while the vehicle is standing over it; the fumes, being heavier than air, will concentrate in the pit with possibly lethal results.

The battery

Never cause a spark, or allow a naked light, near the vehicle's battery. It will normally be giving off a certain amount of hydrogen gas, which is highly explosive.

Always disconnect the battery earth (ground) terminal before working on the fuel or electrical systems.

If possible, loosen the filler plugs or cover when charging the battery from an external source. Do not charge at an excessive rate or the battery may burst.

Take care when topping up and when carrying the battery. The acid electrolyte, even when diluted, is very corrosive and should not be allowed to contact the eyes or skin.

If you ever need to prepare electrolyte yourself, always add the acid slowly to the water, and never the other way round. Protect against splashes by wearing rubber gloves and goggles.

When jump starting a car using a booster battery, for negative earth (ground) vehicles, connect the jump leads in the following sequence: First connect one jump lead between the positive (+) terminals of the two batteries. Then connect the other jump lead first to the negative (–) terminal of the booster battery, and then to a good earthing (ground) point on the vehicle to be started, at least 18 in (45 cm) from the battery if possible. Ensure that hands and jump leads are clear of any moving parts, and that the two vehicles do not touch. Disconnect the leads in the reverse order.

Mains electricity

When using an electric power tool, inspection light etc, which works from the mains, always ensure that the appliance is correctly connected to its plug and that, where necessary, it is properly earthed (grounded). Do not use such appliances in damp conditions and, again, beware of creating a spark or applying excessive heat in the vicinity of fuel or fuel vapour.

Ignition HT voltage

A severe electric shock can result from touching certain parts of the ignition system, such as the HT leads, when the engine is running or being cranked, particularly if components are damp or the insulation is defective. Where an electronic ignition system is fitted, the HT voltage is much higher and could prove fatal.

General repair procedures

Whenever servicing, repair or overhaul work is carried out on the car or its components, it is necessary to observe the following procedures and instructions. This will assist in carrying out the operation efficiently and to a professional standard of workmanship.

Joint mating faces and gaskets

Where a gasket is used between the mating faces of two components, ensure that it is renewed on reassembly, and fit it dry unless otherwise stated in the repair procedure. Make sure that the mating faces are clean and dry with all traces of old gasket removed. When cleaning a joint face, use a tool which is not likely to score or damage the face, and remove any burrs or nicks with an oilstone or fine file.

Make sure that tapped holes are cleaned with a pipe cleaner, and keep them free of jointing compound if this is being used unless specifically instructed otherwise.

Ensure that all orifices, channels or pipes are clear and blow through them, preferably using compressed air.

Oil seals

Whenever an oil seal is removed from its working location, either individually or as part of an assembly, it should be renewed.

The very fine sealing lip of the seal is easily damaged and will not seal if the surface it contacts is not completely clean and free from scratches, nicks or grooves. If the original sealing surface of the component cannot be restored, the component should be renewed.

Protect the lips of the seal from any surface which may damage them in the course of fitting. Use tape or a conical sleeve where possible. Lubricate the seal lips with oil before fitting and, on dual lipped seals, fill the space between the lips with grease.

Unless otherwise stated, oil seals must be fitted with their sealing lips toward the lubricant to be sealed.

Use a tubular drift or block of wood of the appropriate size to install the seal and, if the seal housing is shouldered, drive the seal down to the shoulder. If the seal housing is unshouldered, the seal should be fitted with its face flush with the housing top face.

Screw threads and fastenings

Always ensure that a blind tapped hole is completely free from oil, grease, water or other fluid before installing the bolt or stud. Failure to do this could cause the housing to crack due to the hydraulic action of the bolt or stud as it is screwed in.

When tightening a castellated nut to accept a split pin, tighten the nut to the specified torque, where applicable, and then tighten further to the next split pin hole. Never slacken the nut to align a split pin hole unless stated in the repair procedure.

When checking or retightening a nut or bolt to a specified torque setting, slacken the nut or bolt by a quarter of a turn, and then retighten to the specified setting.

Locknuts, locktabs and washers

Any fastening which will rotate against a component or housing in the course of tightening should always have a washer between it and the relevant component or housing.

Spring or split washers should always be renewed when they are used to lock a critical component such as a big-end bearing retaining nut or bolt.

Locktabs which are folded over to retain a nut or bolt should always be renewed.

Self-locking nuts can be reused in non-critical areas, providing resistance can be felt when the locking portion passes over the bolt or stud thread.

Split pins must always be replaced with new ones of the correct size for the hole.

Special tools

Some repair procedures in this manual entail the use of special tools such as a press, two or three-legged pullers, spring compressors etc. Wherever possible, suitable readily available alternatives to the manufacturer's special tools are described, and are shown in use. In some instances, where no alternative is possible, it has been necessary to resort to the use of a manufacturer's tool and this has been done for reasons of safety as well as the efficient completion of the repair operation. Unless you are highly skilled and have a thorough understanding of the procedure described, never attempt to bypass the use of any special tool when the procedure described specifies its use. Not only is there a very great risk of personal injury, but expensive damage could be caused to the components involved.

Conversion factors

Length (distance)

Inches (in)	X	25.4	= Millimetres (mm)	X 0.039	= Inches (in)
Feet (ft)	X	0.305	= Metres (m)	X 3.281	= Feet (ft)
Miles	X	1.609	= Kilometres (km)	X 0.621	= Miles

Volume (capacity)

Cubic inches (cu in; in^3)	X	16.387	= Cubic centimetres (cc; cm^3)	X 0.061	= Cubic inches (cu in; in^3)
Imperial pints (Imp pt)	X	0.568	= Litres (l)	X 1.76	= Imperial pints (Imp pt)
Imperial quarts (Imp qt)	X	1.137	= Litres (l)	X 0.88	= Imperial quarts (Imp qt)
Imperial quarts (Imp qt)	X	1.201	= US quarts (US qt)	X 0.833	= Imperial quarts (Imp qt)
US quarts (US qt)	X	0.946	= Litres (l)	X 1.057	= US quarts (US qt)
Imperial gallons (Imp gal)	X	4.546	= Litres (l)	X 0.22	= Imperial gallons (Imp gal)
Imperial gallons (Imp gal)	X	1.201	= US gallons (US gal)	X 0.833	= Imperial gallons (Imp gal)
US gallons (US gal)	X	3.785	= Litres (l)	X 0.264	= US gallons (US gal)

Mass (weight)

Ounces (oz)	X	28.35	= Grams (g)	X 0.035	= Ounces (oz)
Pounds (lb)	X	0.454	= Kilograms (kg)	X 2.205	= Pounds (lb)

Force

Ounces-force (ozf; oz)	X	0.278	= Newtons (N)	X 3.6	= Ounces-force (ozf; oz)
Pounds-force (lbf; lb)	X	4.448	= Newtons (N)	X 0.225	= Pounds-force (lbf; lb)
Newtons (N)	X	0.1	= Kilograms-force (kgf; kg)	X 9.81	= Newtons (N)

Pressure

Pounds-force per square inch (psi; lbf/in^2; lb/in^2)	X	0.070	= Kilograms-force per square centimetre (kgf/cm^2; kg/cm^2)	X 14.223	= Pounds-force per square inch (psi; lbf/in^2; lb/in^2)
Pounds-force per square inch (psi; lbf/in^2; lb/in^2)	X	0.068	= Atmospheres (atm)	X 14.696	= Pounds-force per square inch (psi; lbf/in^2; lb/in^2)
Pounds-force per square inch (psi; lbf/in^2; lb/in^2)	X	0.069	= Bars	X 14.5	= Pounds-force per square inch (psi; lbf/in^2; lb/in^2)
Pounds-force per square inch (psi; lbf/in^2; lb/in^2)	X	6.895	= Kilopascals (kPa)	X 0.145	= Pounds-force per square inch (psi; lbf/in^2; lb/in^2)
Kilopascals (kPa)	X	0.01	= Kilograms-force per square centimetre (kgf/cm^2; kg/cm^2)	X 98.1	= Kilopascals (kPa)

Torque (moment of force)

Pounds-force inches (lbf in; lb in)	X	1.152	= Kilograms-force centimetre (kgf cm; kg cm)	X 0.868	= Pounds-force inches (lbf in; lb in)
Pounds-force inches (lbf in; lb in)	X	0.113	= Newton metres (Nm)	X 8.85	= Pounds-force inches (lbf in; lb in)
Pounds-force inches (lbf in; lb in)	X	0.083	= Pounds-force feet (lbf ft; lb ft)	X 12	= Pounds-force inches (lbf in; lb in)
Pounds-force feet (lbf ft; lb ft)	X	0.138	= Kilograms-force metres (kgf m; kg m)	X 7.233	= Pounds-force feet (lbf ft; lb ft)
Pounds-force feet (lbf ft; lb ft)	X	1.356	= Newton metres (Nm)	X 0.738	= Pounds-force feet (lbf ft; lb ft)
Newton metres (Nm)	X	0.102	= Kilograms-force metres (kgf m; kg m)	X 9.804	= Newton metres (Nm)

Power

Horsepower (hp)	X	745.7	= Watts (W)	X 0.0013	= Horsepower (hp)

Velocity (speed)

Miles per hour (miles/hr; mph)	X	1.609	= Kilometres per hour (km/hr; kph)	X 0.621	= Miles per hour (miles/hr; mph)

Fuel consumption*

Miles per gallon, Imperial (mpg)	X	0.354	= Kilometres per litre (km/l)	X 2.825	= Miles per gallon, Imperial (mpg)
Miles per gallon, US (mpg)	X	0.425	= Kilometres per litre (km/l)	X 2.352	= Miles per gallon, US (mpg)

Temperature

Degrees Fahrenheit (°F) $= (°C \times \frac{9}{5}) + 32$

Degrees Celsius (Degrees Centigrade; °C) $= (°F - 32) \times \frac{5}{9}$

*It is common practice to convert from miles per gallon (mpg) to litres/100 kilometres (l/100km), where mpg (Imperial) x l/100 km = 282 and mpg (US) x l/100 km = 235

Index

Printed by
J H Haynes & Co Ltd
Sparkford Nr Yeovil
Somerset BA22 7JJ England